Behaviour Analysis in Educational Psychology

BEHAVIOUR ANALYSIS IN EDUCATIONAL PSYCHOLOGY

Edited by KEVIN WHELDALL, FRANK MERRETT and TED GLYNN

Published by
CROOM HELM
London • Sydney • Wolfeboro, New Hampshire
in association with POSITIVE PRODUCTS.

Croom Helm Ltd, Provident House, Burrell Row,
Beckenham, Kent BR3 1AT

Croom Helm Australia Pty Ltd, Suite 4, 6th Floor,
64-76 Kippax Street, Surry Hills, NSW 2010, Australia

British Library Cataloguing in Publication Data

Behaviour analysis in educational psychology.
1. Educational psychology 2. Behavioral assessment
I. Wheldall, Kevin II. Merrett, Frank
III. Glynn, Ted
370.15'3 LB 1051

ISBN 0-7099-3689-3

Croom Helm, 27 South Main Street,
Wolfeboro, New Hampshire 03894-2069, USA

Library of Congress Cataloging in Publication Data applied for

Printed and bound in Great Britain by Mackays of Chatham Ltd, Kent

Contents

ABOUT THE EDITORS ...

Dr Kevin Wheldall is Director of the Centre for Child Study in the Department of Educational Psychology at the University of Birmingham where **Dr Frank Merrett** is Honorary Research Fellow. **Professor Ted Glynn** is Head of the Department of Education at Otago University, Dunedin, New Zealand. All three have been actively involved in behavioural research in education for a number of years and have published numerous articles and books in this area. Half of the papers in this collection report work carried out by the editors in collaboration with their students and colleagues.

OTHER CONTRIBUTORS INCLUDE ...

Mary Baker, Department of Education, Auckland University, New Zealand.
Keith Ballard, Department of Education, University of Otago, Dunedin, New Zealand.
Diane Berryman, School of Education, Macquarie University, Australia.
Dorothy Blundell, Sandwell Education Authority.
Helen Charles, New Zealand Psychological Service.
Bryce Cooper, School of Education, Macquarie University, Australia.
Mary Foley, Department of Education, Auckland University, New Zealand.
Yin Yuk Lam (nee Ng), Cumbria.
Elizabeth Limbrick, Department of Education, Auckland University, New Zealand.
Sue McCullough, University of Oregon.
Eddie McNamara, Lancashire Schools Psychological Service.
Stuart McNaughton, Department of Education, Auckland University, New Zealand.
Reg Marsh, Department of Education, Victoria University of Wellington, New Zealand.
Paul Mettem, Wolverhampton Education Authority.
Michael Miller, Department of Special Education, Ball State University, U.S.A.
Dennis Moore, Department of Education, Auckland University, New Zealand.
Marion Morris, Birmingham Education Authority.
Walt Musgrove (deceased).
Brian Pickthorne, Bromsgrove College of Higher Education.
Ingrid Rumsey, New Zealand Psychological Service.
Josh Schweiso, Bulmershe College of Higher Education, Reading.
Jeanette Scott, Department of Education, University of Otago, Dunedin, New Zealand.
Jerome Ulman, Department of Special Education, Ball State University, U.S.A.
Pamela Vaughan, Solihull Education Authority.
Sam Winter, Department of Education, University of Hong Kong.

Introductory Preface

Over the first five years of its existence, the journal *Educational Psychology* has been proud to publish many articles on behaviour analysis in education. There is, indeed, evidence to support the claim that *Educational Psychology* is becoming a major forum for publications in this area and is thereby achieving one of its founding aims.

As members of the editorial board of the journal (with particular interests in the behavioural research papers) we thought that many of these papers deserved a wider audience, not least among educational psychology students both undergraduate and post-graduate. Indeed many lecturers already refer their students to the journal regularly as a major source of relevant research. Consequently, with the agreement of the journal's publishers, Carfax Publishing Company, we have edited this book of selected behavioural papers from *Educational Psychology.*

This edited collection of twenty papers is structured in five sections. In some respects this is almost arbitrary since many of the papers could equally well be included under more than one section heading. But we chose this structure deliberately, and the consequent distribution of papers, in order to create the emphases we intended.

First, since we wanted this book to be accessible to students, teachers, educational psychology practitioners and other educationalists, as well as to behavioural researchers, we have included a preliminary preparatory section on the methodology of behaviour analysis. In its short history, *Educational Psychology* has, from time to time, published articles highlighting basic behavioural methodology. This has been deliberate policy with the aim of encouraging educational researchers to consider employing behaviour analysis methodology in future investigations. The papers included review basic considerations, introduce the essential procedures, provide an example of a behavioural observation schedule and show how traditional statistical analyses may be incorporated into behaviour analysis.

Another important consideration in selecting papers for this book was the need to stress antecedent control of behaviour. In order to do justice to our conviction that the manipulation of setting events and other antecedent stimuli has been relatively neglected in behaviour analysis in education, we have included a section specifically on this topic. Following a review paper spelling out the importance of antecedent control, several illustrative studies are presented.

The following section, on the control of social behaviour by its consequences, is more traditional in that this type of research is most commonly associated with a behavioural approach. Examples are provided of the effective use of consequence management strategies to control various classroom social behaviours. The two papers featuring studies in secondary school classrooms are particularly important given the relative dearth of such studies with older pupils.

The fourth section again stresses a commonly neglected area, control of academic behaviour. It is now generally accepted that the behavioural approach has something to offer classroom management, but the contribution behaviour analysis can make to academic instruction is frequently not appreciated. Language, reading, writing and even tertiary level physics are included as examples of academic areas in which the behavioural approach has been shown to be effective.

Finally, we conclude with two papers on training teachers and parents to use behavioural methods. The behavioural approach is too important, too powerful and too useful for its use to be restricted to behaviour analysts. Real change can come about only by passing on behavioural skills and methods to those in most frequent contact with the various client groups within education.

We have selected papers to fit the structure we have set for ourselves and to meet best the needs of our prospective readers. This policy has sometimes meant the exclusion of otherwise excellent papers on behavioural topics and their non-inclusion here should certainly not be taken as any slight on their quality.

A further editorial policy has been to include as many papers as possible featuring the research of education students (almost always conducted and written up jointly with their supervisors) to serve as encouragement and to show that effective, relevant behavioural research is well within their capabilities. Many of these studies were carried out from three centres of behavioural research in education: the Centre for Child Study in the Department of Educational Psychology, University of Birmingham, England; the Department of Education, University of Auckland, New Zealand; and the Department of Education, University of Otago, Dunedin, New Zealand. Many of these papers also reflect the cross-fertilization of ideas (through correspondence and exchange of visits) between these centres which we, the editors, have enjoyed over the last six years.

It remains only to express our sincere thanks to the editorial board and panel of referees of *Educational Psychology* for all their work on the papers collected here and to Roger Osborn-King of Carfax Publishing Company for his generous help and encouragement. Readers who enjoy reading this collection of articles would be well advised to consider subscribing to *Educational Psychology* in order to keep up to date with current developments in behaviour analysis in education in the future.

Kevin Wheldall, Frank Merrett and Ted Glynn, 1986.

Section A.

Methodology of Behaviour Analysis

Why Measure Behaviour?

SAM WINTER

ABSTRACT *The upsurge in the use of behavioural* change *techniques with children in education and residential settings has not always involved an equally strong commitment to behavioural* measurement *(by which is meant quantitative data collection relating to latency, duration or, most often, frequency of the target behaviour in question). This paper outlines several advantages, other than effectiveness evaluation, which accrue from behavioural measurement; in relation to (a) deciding whether to change behaviour, (b) deciding the type of intervention required, (c) assessment of caregiver skills and commitment, (d) therapeutic effects, (e) reinforcement, (f) analysis of critical variables and (g) analysis of caregiver attitudes and behaviour. Case examples are included throughout.*

The social learning approach to children with adjustment problems will be familiar to most readers. There is a growing appreciation that behavioural techniques, wisely used, are both effective and efficient ways of helping children with various problems of learning. The recent formation of the Association for Behavioural Approaches with Children testifies to this development in Great Britain.

Writers such as Bandura (1969), Gelfand & Hartmann (1975) and Sulzer-Azaroff & Mayer (1977) have all emphasised the important role played by behavioural measurement (quantitative data collection) in the process of applied behaviour analysis. They argue that measurements should be made of the frequency of the target behaviour (or occasionally its duration or latency) before, during and after the intervention programme in question. They maintain: (1) that adults should focus their attempts at change upon patterns of overt behaviour between children and those around them, but (2) that adults are often very poor observers of their own and children's behaviour, and (3) that they consequently fail to obtain the reliable and objective information they need as change agents. Despite this generally agreed good practice, however, none of us need look far for cases in which teachers, care staff, social workers and psychologists profess to use a behavioural approach and yet fail to measure target behaviours to which change techniques are being applied.

Much of this work remains 'invisible'; for obvious reasons it does not find its way into the journals. Instead we have to look around us at the work of our colleagues. In the north-east of England we know of a special school and special unit which both actually enjoy a local reputation for employing a behavioural approach, and yet do not commonly engage in behavioural measurement. How many individual teachers in special and mainstream education, and how many social workers, profess the use of 'behaviour modification' techniques, and yet neglect measurement? We suspect the number is very large indeed. One reason may be that psychologists, advisers and trainers advocating the behavioural approach have themselves minimised the importance of measurement, despite the undeniable fact that it underpins the empirical method which has traditionally characterised the approach.

The importance of behavioural measurement in single case therapy effectiveness evaluation (especially in the absence of independent advocacy groups visiting schools, psychological services and social services departments on a daily basis) is widely accepted in the literature. It provides the child with protection against the possibility of being subjected to prolonged but ineffective change programmes. Texts such as Sulzer-Azaroff & Mayer (1977) investigate the question of accountability in some depth, and hence it will not be dwelt on in any greater detail here. Instead, in this article we will attempt to list a few other benefits of behavioural measurement, some of which are paid little attention in the existing literature. The order of presentation is as follows—

Benefits of Pre-intervention Measurement

(1) Information on the need for behaviour change, and, where there is a need, which behaviour.
(2) Information on the type of intervention required.
(3) Information on caregiver skills and commitment, and existing environmental demands.
(4) The therapeutic effect of baselining.

Benefits of Within-intervention Measurement

(1) Reinforcement value.
(2) Information on critical variables.
(3) Information on caregiver attitudes and behaviour.

Attention throughout this paper will be focused upon the measurement of target behaviour *frequency* (rather than latency or duration) *by caregivers themselves* (rather than consultants or the child himself); this is because of the substantial predominance of this type of data collection in clinical work. Other important issues relating to measurement reliability, validity and obtrusiveness lie beyond the scope of this paper. For a fuller discussion see texts such as Sulzer-Azaroff & Mayer (1977) and Gelfand & Hartmann (1975). But 'caregivers' is meant those in direct daily contact with the child. Here the term is synonymous with 'caregivers' (Gelfand & Hartmann, 1975), 'mediators' (Tharp & Wetzel, 1969), 'contingency managers' (Sulzer-Azaroff & Mayer, 1977), 'change agents' (Bandura, 1969) and 'direct contact personnel' (Westmacott & Cameron, 1981). Parents, residential care workers, teachers and school auxiliaries are all caregivers.

By distinction, the term 'consultant' will be used to denote any person called in to give advice on child management and training. It is synonymous with 'behaviour analyst' (Sulzer-Azaroff & Mayer, 1977; Tharp & Wetzel, 1969) or 'therapist' (as used by McAuley & McAuley, 1977).

Psychologists and social workers act as consultants, although caregivers may occasionally adopt the role of consultant for others.

(a) Pre-intervention Measurement (Baselining)

In most cases caregivers will co-operate in collecting data (at least for a week or two), *after* the target behaviour has been identified and *before* any discussion regarding change techniques. The major exceptions are cases in which the target behaviour: (a) constitutes a danger to the child or those who surround him or, (b) shows a frequency which all caregivers concerned agree upon (e.g. 'We are both absolutely sure he wets the bed each night. We change the sheets each morning'). Caregivers who are reluctant to baseline may be persuaded by the effectiveness evaluation argument or by reference to some of the other benefits listed below.

(1) *Information on the Need for Behaviour Change and, Where There is a Need, Which Behaviour*

The decision to institute behavioural change necessarily depends upon a large number of factors (including the age and developmental level of the child, the effects which the target behaviour has upon his life quality, and that of his peers and caregivers, etc.) and often demands careful consideration. Decision-making is rendered even more difficult where reliable frequency information is absent, as in cases where: (a) caregivers give poor or conflicting verbal reports, or (b) the frequency apparently fluctuates. In each case measurements can provide a basis for more informed choice when combined with other types of assessment data.

Similarly, in situations in which caregivers are concerned about a wide variety of problem behaviours, only one of which can realistically be dealt with at a time, behavioural measurement can once again provide a basis for informed joint decision-making, regarding the specific behaviour to be changed.

(2) *Information on the Type of Intervention Required*

Objective frequency data are often helpful in making decisions regarding the type of change techniques required.

> Derek was a 4-year-old in a reception class. His aggressive behaviour caused concern to peers and adults alike. We decided to use DRO procedures as a component in an intervention package which also included modelling, time-out and self-control training. DRO (Differential Reinforcement of Other Behaviour) involved positive reinforcement at the end of each time interval during which problem behaviour (in this case, aggression) was absent. (For a fuller discussion of the technique see Sulzer-Azaroff & Mayer, 1977, Repp & Dietz, 1974 and Gelfand & Hartmann, 1975.)
>
> Wherever this type of technique is used it is essential to select a time period which will ensure high levels of positive reinforcement for the child throughout the day. Baseline data collected by Derek's teacher over a period of one week revealed that violently aggressive behaviour (appropriately defined) ran at a daily frequency of 6.2 (with a range from 4 to 9). The clear implication was that on 'bad days' Derek was refraining from aggressive behaviour for periods averaging only 30 to 35 minutes. On the basis of this information, and allowing for random fluctuations within a day, a DRO interval of 10 minutes was chosen; that is, from the outset of the change programme Derek's teacher and peers praised him whenever he succeeded in refraining from aggressive behaviour for

the whole of a 10 minute period. For further details of this intervention see Winter (1980).

Baseline data can be used in a similar way where DRH and DRL techniques (Differential Reinforcement of High or Low frequency behaviour) are under consideration.

A rather different example concerns those cases in which the target behaviour apparently fluctuates with time. Behavioural measurement may reveal that the fluctuations are related to (for example) the teachers or tasks involved at school or the father's working hours at home. Information such as this may prove invaluable in decisions regarding intervention techniques themselves, as well as the caregivers by whom, and the settings within which, they should be implemented.

(3) *Information on Caregivers Skills and Commitment, and Existing Environmental Demands*

Failure of a caregiver to collect data as agreed may be an indication of the absence of skills or of the commitment necessary for later implementation of change techniques. Further discussion may reveal the precise cause of failure. Alternatively, it may be due to genuine forgetfulness in which case some signalling device such as a kitchen timer or pre-recorded tape may be used as a reminder during the period of baseline, and during intervention itself.

> Stephen was 4-years old and had been described as 'hyperactive'. Of all the problem behaviours he engaged in the most worrying to his teacher was that of non-attending behaviour during group sessions such as storytime, newstime, etc. The teacher was asked to collect baseline data for a week.
>
> As specific moments during these sessions she was to observe Stephen's behaviour and write a tick on her hand if he was standing up, shuffling, walking around, interfering or talking with other children, staring elsewhere or making disruptive noises (all of which were considered to indicate non-attending behaviour). She was to write a cross if he was refraining from these behaviours (and thereby possibly attending to what was going on).
>
> An immediate problem presented itself. The teacher found that she was too concerned with the content of these group sessions to remember to observe Stephen's behaviour using the 'interval' method described above. The solution was to provide a pre-recorded tape which played signals at one minute intervals. The teacher switched on the tape before each group session began and observed and recorded Stephen's behaviour quite successfully each time the taped signal reminded her to do so. Throughout the actual intervention, which involved DRO (as well as training and modelling sessions and extinction), it was necessary to continue to use the pre-recorded tape as a way of reminding the teacher to reinforce intervals of attentive behaviour.

Several possibilities exist where failure to collect baseline data seems to be due to a lack of commitment. The target behaviour which has been chosen may be low priority for the caregiver, despite the care previously taken when defining the problem behaviour. The solution to this particular situation is obvious.

More commonly the lack of commitment may stem from reservations about a 'symptom' approach (best dealt with through further discussion) from general pessimism about the possibilities for change (dealt with by further discussion and in increased consultant reinforcement of caregiver behaviour once intervention begins) or from a desire (expressed or otherwise) to have the child removed rather than engage in *in situ* intervention. This last possibility (perhaps encountered more often in schools and largely the result of an abundance of special schools and units) may be the most difficult to deal with. Three possible solutions involve: (a) the enlistment of support from colleagues within the school, (b) the use of measurement and change techniques involving minimal caregiver effort (extreme forms of which are strategies which involve the child in self-reinforcement or involve reinforcement by other caregivers) and (c) choosing and training target behaviours which will result in the child quickly becoming more reinforcing to the caregiver (Hutchings & Jones, 1979).

(4) *The Therapeutic Effect of Baselining*

A certain proportion of target behaviours appear to improve under baseline. Lindsley (in Duncan, 1969) reports a figure of 5% in his review of 2000 cases, whilst Tharp & Wetzel (1969) report 7% in a rather smaller sample of 83. A review of 36 of our own cases yielded a rather higher 14% (unpublished).

Sometimes this baseline effect is a result of the discussions which precede it. In particular the consultant will typically 'prepare' the caregivers for targeting and then baselining a behaviour by telling them that the child's behaviour is a problem of learning, the solution to which lies in a teaching approach which they themselves will be required to adopt as the major participants of therapy. In certain cases all this is bound to change long-held attitudes and result in changes in caregiver behaviour *via-à-vis* the child.

Alternatively the acts of targeting (i.e. defining the child's 'problem' in observable behavioural terms) may make possible (and indeed result in) more consistent management by caregivers than has been possible hitherto. This in turn may lead to improvements under baselining. Finally, there are cases in which the child observes or is told that the consultant is visiting the home or school in connection with his or her problems. This may lead to behavioural improvement by way of a sort of 'bogeyman' effect. Strictly, speaking, however, these are examples in which behavioural improvements are made visible by, rather than actually resulting from, baselining. It is this second phenomenon to which we now turn.

Where the child is told or observes that his or her behaviour is under scrutiny he/she may exert a self-control that has hitherto been absent, with a consequent improvement in target behaviour. Unfortunately, the former pattern of behaviour may reappear when baselining stops. One solution involves asking the caregivers to withdraw the offending record card or graph paper on one in every 5 days, then in every 4 and so on, until the baselining has eventually been phased out, hopefully with no return of problem behaviour. Another solution may lie in transferring record keeping to the child itself.

(b) Within Intervention Measurement

The benefits which accrue from collecting quantitative data throughout the duration of an intervention programme are numerous.

(1) *Reinforcement Value*

Behavioural measurements provide a powerful source of reinforcement for the child, for caregivers and for the consultant especially when improvements in target behaviour are shown visually (Gelfand & Hartmann, 1975). This is particularly important in two special cases.

(a) Where behavioural change is expected to be (or actually turns out to be) gradual. Indeed changes of this sort may pass unnoticed altogether if measurements are not kept. In this connection it may be worth listing some of the conditions under which behavioural change may be expected to proceed gradually, if at all:
   (i) Where one or more caregivers deviate from the agreed techniques, either through 'behavioural inertia' or 'sabotage'. All these possibilities are more likely to occur not only where a large number of caregivers are involved in the task of behavioural change (as in a residential school or a comprehensive) but also where important caregivers have not been co-opted into the programme (as where a grandmother has been left uninvolved in a programme which involves the use of pocket money as a reward).
   (ii) Where the target behaviour is difficult to distinguish from non-target behaviour; has been poorly defined (i.e. 'naughty' or 'difficult' behaviour) or (as in Stephen's case earlier) itself consists of a particularly wide variety of constituent targets. All these are likely to reduce the consistency with which caregivers apply the programme.
   (iii) Where the problem behaviour has been established for a particularly long time.
   (iv) Where the intervention is planned for a limited setting (for example where withdrawn behaviour in home and school is being modified at school only).

(b) Where caregivers perceive that response cost is high. By this is meant that they ask themselves 'Is what we are being asked to do worth it?', and conclude that it is not.

In answering the second question caregivers will weigh the physical effort and time involved or anticipated (in attending review meetings with the consultants as well as in implementing the behavioural techniques themselves) against the reinforcement received or expected (for themselves, their colleagues and superiors, the consultants and the child himself). Sometimes the physical effort and time expended in the early stages of intervention is very high indeed. For example an intervention package involving DRO, modelling, time-out and self-control training obviously involves quite a lot of effort during class hours as well as several hours discussion outside (Winter, 1980). Similarly reinforcement available to caregivers may be quite limited. They may fail to reinforce their own adherence to the programme because they feel uncomfortable using the techniques, are sceptical about their effectiveness or feel they are acting under duress. Superiors and colleagues may show scepticism about and even ridicule the techniques the caregivers are being asked to use. Most importantly the child himself may, through his or her continuing aversive presence in a classroom, punish a teacher for adhering to techniques which at best, 'only put off the day that the child goes to the unit'.

In a minority of cases the perceived response cost may be so high as to prevent behavioural techniques being used at all. For example, in a review of 36 of our own cases, 14% of the interventions terminated after unsuccessful attempts to negotiate a set of behavioural techniques acceptable to the caregiver(s). However, there are many methods by which apparently high response cost can be reduced. For example, the consultant might ask them to consider less effortful and time-consuming behavioural techniques. He might arrange for discussions to take place within school hours or probe other adults who might reinforce programme implementation and, perhaps, encourage participation by caregivers in the whole business of designing a behavioural intervention—indeed, this is essentially what is meant by programme *negotiation.* Most importantly, behavioural measurements may be used as a source of reinforcement to the caregivers. Indeed, they may constitute the simplest method by which response-cost is reduced.

(2) *Information on Critical Variables*

Throughout the duration of a programme a number of incidents take place, some of which may have an effect upon the target behaviour and may therefore be termed 'critical'. Their effect may pass unnoticed but for detailed behavioural measurements. Three examples may illustrate the point.

David was 5 years old and was the eldest son of an affluent working-class family. Despite being presented with well-prepared and wholesome food of all types he vomited in about four out of every 10 mealtimes at home, whatever the time of day. He had engaged in this behaviour for 2½ years despite being declared medically fit and, interestingly enough, ate perfectly normally at school. To relate the history of this case would be to digress; suffice it to say that the vomiting behaviour seemed to be maintained by attention, and by the individualised menu (consisting largely of puddings, sweets and crisps) in which it resulted. The chosen intervention, consisting of: (a) parental praise for problem-free eating, (b) time-out for baulking or vomiting behaviour and (c) an orthodox menu, resulted in a gradual and almost total elimination of vomiting behaviour after 120 days. It was then that a critical incident occurred. For some reason David began to vomit occasionally and the father, after very little consultation with his wife, decided to send David to bed after any instance of vomiting behaviour during the evening meal. After 11 days the data were inspected. It was quite clear that the sole outcome of the new strategy had been that David's vomiting behaviour had increased further and, even more striking, had increased only during the evening meal.

Indeed, evening vomiting had increased by a factor of six as compared with the 11 day period prior to this departure from the programme. Faced with such clear data the father had no choice but to stop sending his son to bed, and return to the agreed procedures, the result of which was the prompt reduction of evening vomiting back to initial frequency.

Peter was 4½ years old and had frequently soiled in his home over an 18 month period. Baselining yielded a rate of at least once every 2 days. The problem seemed to be maintained by the various forms of attention in which it resulted. Intervention consisted of positive reinforcement (involving praise, stickers, a chart and back-up activity rewards), over-correction (involving a requirement to wash out his own and other people's clothes for about half an hour in the bathroom) and prompting (involving a once nightly reminder to use the toilet). Soiling was immediately eliminated for 13 days only to return on days 14 and 15. There appeared to be several possible reasons for the return of the target behaviour. The most pertinent critical incidents seemed to be:

(i) Parents had stopped prompting him to use the toilet.

(ii) The father had moved south in search of work whilst the steel strike was on.
(iii) Parents had told Peter that his good behaviour meant that the psychologist would no longer need to visit the home.

Over the next few weeks each factor was manipulated, and daily records were kept throughout. In this way it was discovered that the third item in the list of critical incidents was the controlling variable. The implications for the entire intervention programme were considerable and changes were made accordingly.

Behavioural measurement facilitates investigation of a number of other programme variables, such as the comparison of differences between different caregivers, settings and reinforcers or the evaluation of any of these three components over time. For example data may suggest (or confirm a suspicion) that behavioural change is taking place in only one class, at home rather than school, or for one parent only. Alternatively, it may show that what was once a reinforcer is no longer reinforcing.

In an effort to increase academic output and decrease disruptive behaviours in his class of 9–10-year-olds, a class teacher began to use a variant of the 'Good Behaviour Game', originally developed by Barrish, Saunders & Wolf (1969) in the USA and used in this country by, amongst others, Merrett & Wheldall (1978). The game involved dividing a class into teams, establishing clear criteria for behaviour, and a points system backed up by a menu of reinforcers. After an initial improvement in on-task behaviour a decline set in. One possible cause was that the teacher was no longer observing the teams frequently enough, with the consequence that he was awarding points on a poor ratio schedule that was extinguishing the newly established behaviour. Daily records confirmed this, and the teacher took steps to resolve the problem. However, the decline continued over the next fortnight. A possible remaining factor was that the reinforcer variety was not high, and that each reinforcer was losing its attractiveness. Final confirmation that this was happening came from close inspection of the records for one particular day on which four reinforcers were available to the children: (1) being allowed out first to lunch, (2) reading comics, (3) playing board games and (4) orange juice. The first three had been used on previous days. Orange juice was being used for the first time. The day began in heavy rain, and turned to brilliant sunshine at lunchtime. The points earnings of the class began at a very low level and suddenly rose in the afternoon.

Looking at the data, one gained a clear impression that the children were satiated upon three reinforcers, and orange juice only acquired incentive value with the improvement in the weather. Accordingly, the teacher increased the range and variability of reinforcers available daily. The result was a substantial and long-lasting improvement in target behaviours.

Even more startling investigations are possible. At one point inspection of the daily records shows that David's vomiting behaviour (earlier example) followed a cyclical pattern that was related to his mother's abnormally painful menstruation (see Fig. 1). It transpired that mother experienced great difficulty in reacting calmly to David's baulking behaviour at these points in her menstrual cycle. Consequently the parents and writer discussed ways in which this problem could be eliminated, for example through medication for the mother or alternatively through the father assuming responsibility for programme implementation during her menstrual period.

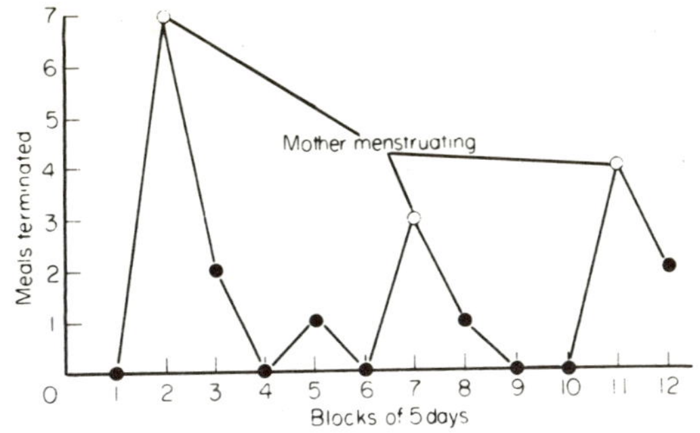

FIG. 1. The relationship between child's behaviour and mother's menstrual cycle.

(3) *Information on Caregiver Attitudes and Behaviour*

Measurements occasionally conflict with opinions about the effectiveness of the behavioural programme which are expressed by caregivers. Contradictory evidence of this sort gives rise to a number of questions less likely to be posed when the consultant is dependent only upon the caregiver's subjective judgments. Clearly there are two possibilities, the first being that in which the caregivers judge the intervention a failure despite data which they themselves have collected which shows it to be a success. Amongst possible explanations for such a state of affairs are:

(a) The target behaviour is not one considered by the caregivers to be of high priority. Although it has been successfully modified, they feel that the child is as serious a problem as before and consequently conclude that intervention has been a failure. The solution is straightforward; select another target behaviour.

(b) The target behaviour has been poorly recorded. For example undesirable behaviour appears to have been eliminated simply because, although observed, it has been left unrecorded. This problem is essentially the same as that described earlier in the section entitled 'caregiver skills and commitment'. A number of solutions described there apply here also.

Lee A was 8 years old and engaged in a number of difficult behaviours when with his father (elderly and speech defective), who oscillated between over-indulgent and physically negative management methods. Two target behaviours were selected; demanding behaviour (e.g. 'I want money', 'I want to have those sweets') and refusal to comply with simple requests (e.g. 'No, I won't come in for my tea', 'No I won't sleep in my bed' etc.). Intervention consisted of DRO (1 hour periods—see example 1 earlier in this paper) using praise and home movie film parties as rewards, and time-out. Over several months the behavioural measurements which Mr A collected showed a dramatic reduction (by a factor of 6) in the two target behaviours.

Despite these results, Mr A maintained that Lee was only a little better behaved. It was only after a number of lengthy discussions, some rather heated, that Mr A admitted failing to record a substantial number of refusals and demands made be his son.

Significantly, he had failed to impose the time-out contingency for such

> unrecorded misdemeanours, choosing instead to 'tell the boy off' threaten him with care (albeit quite emptily) and smack him. As a result we had every reason to believe that the frequency of the target behaviours were, and would remain, as high as at baseline. Fortunately, Mr A finally chose to adhere to the recommended programme, after which point the reverse situation occurred; the data showed a temporary increase in target behaviour, despite verbal reports from Mr A that the boy's behaviour was slowly improving.

The second of the two possibilities is that in which the caregivers judge intervention to be a success despite their own data which suggest that it has failed up to that point. The most acceptable explanation seems to be that their criteria for what constitutes an instance of the target behaviour has changed as the programme has proceeded. By way of example, consider the case of a teacher who is attempting to increase interaction behaviour in a withdrawn child through the use of social reinforcement. It is possible that the teacher's judgment of what constitutes interactive behaviour will become more stringent as the behaviour itself becomes well-established in the child's repertoire. If this happens the result may be a behavioural record which shows precious little improvement, set against subjective judgments that gains have occurred.

An unfortunate consequence of this state of affairs is that the teacher may lapse into non-reinforcement of target behaviour at a time when it is still quite essential, the result being that any further improvements are discouraged. The simplest method of dealing with this problem may be to define the target behaviour more carefully, thereby reducing the need for interpretation.

Conclusion

Those whose use behavioural change techniques without concurrent measurement do a disservice to themselves, their clients and the approach itself. It is a criticism of many therapies developed over recent years (for example counselling, play therapy, psychoanalytic approaches and drug therapy) that such scant regard has been paid to reliable and objective data collection. As a result large numbers of children and their caregivers have been drawn into interventions provided by expensive services and only later found wanting. Gelfand & Hartmann (1975) argue that the firm data base provided by the behavioural approach should reduce the faddism that has hitherto prevailed and may prove to be its most important and perhaps most enduring contribution to the helping professions. The implication for the responsibility of caregivers and consultants purportedly employing the behavioural approach is clear.

REFERENCES

BANDURA, A. (1969) *Principles of Behaviour Modification* (New York, Holt, Rinehart & Winston).

BARRISH, H., SAUNDERS, M. & WOLF, M. (1969) The good behaviour game—effects of individual contingencies for group consequences on disruptive behaviour in the classroom, *Journal of Applied Behaviour Analysis*, 2, pp. 119–124.

DUNCAN, A.D. (1969) Self-application of behaviour modification techniques by teenagers, *Adolescence*, 4, pp. 541–556.

GELFAND, D.M. & HARTMANN, D.P. (1975) *Child Behaviour Analysis and Therapy* (New York, Pergamon Press).

HUTCHINGS, J. & JONES, D. (1979) Child abuse and parenting skills, in 'Prevention in Mental Health'; *Proceedings of the 1979 MIND annual conference* (London, MIND).

MCAULEY, R. & MCAULEY, P. (1977) *Child Behaviour Problems: an Empirical Approach to Management* (London, MacMillan).

MERRETT, F. & WHELDALL, K. (1978) Playing the game: a behavioural approach to classroom management in the junior school, *Educational Review*, 30, pp. 41–50.

REPP, A.C. & DIETZ, S.M. (1974) Reducing aggressive and self-injurious behaviour of institutionalised retarded children through reinforcement of other behaviours, *Journal of Applied Behaviour Analysis*, 7, pp. 313–325.

SULZER-AZAROFF, B. & MAYER, G.R. (1977) *Applying Behaviour Analysis Procedures with Children and Youth* (New York, Holt, Rinehart & Winston).

THARP, R.G. & WETZEL, R.J. (1969) *Behaviour Modification in the Natural Environment* (New York, Academic Press).

WESTMACOTT, E. & CAMERON, R. (1981) *Behaviour can Change* (Basingstoke, Globe Education).

WINTER, S.J. (1980) Treatment of aggression in a 4-year old: a close replication of a study reported in an earlier newsletter, *Behaviour Modification with Children*, Vol. 4, No. 2, pp. 5–10.

Baselines and Basics: some issues in the assessment of behavioural interventions in education

JOSHUA SCHWIESO

ABSTRACT *Teachers are increasingly making use of behavioural techniques in their everyday classroom practice. The need for empirical demonstration of effectiveness is integral to the behavioural approach and calls for the use of some sort of experimental design, both to show a relationship between the teacher's actions and change in the child's behaviour, and to discount alternative explanations of such change. The baseline, a measure of the behaviour to be changed, is seen as performing a key function in any such design. The advantages and disadvantages for applied research of group and single case experimental designs are examined. It is argued that the latter provide a particularly appropriate means for practising teachers to evaluate their own work. Five well-established forms of single case design are discussed in detail and an actual example of each in use is given.*

Introduction

Interventions based on behavioural principles are of growing importance in the work of educationalists. Behaviour modification (1) has been used to control social behaviour in the primary and secondary classroom and in special schools. Structured behavioural curricula have been applied to the education of pre-school children, backward learners, the mentally handicapped and undergraduates. In the first flush of excitement following the discovery that there are scientifically grounded procedures which can be applied to conduct disorders, emotional problems and learning difficulties, it may seem obvious to the teacher that the changes they see in pupils are the direct result of their work. However the accumulated wisdom of the experimental social sciences suggests that matters may not be quite so simple. Leaving aside the possibility that change may be in the eye of the beholder rather than in the behaviour of the child there are numerous ways in which genuine improvements in the child's skills or behaviour may occur which are not the direct outcome of the teacher's actions. Real improvements may be wrought by non-specific features of the intervention (such as the attention paid to the child) rather than by the carefully structured change programme. Other features of the child's environment, whether social or physical, may alter and hence lead to beneficial outcomes. Finally physiological maturation, contiguous with ageing, may lead to the child's 'growing out' of a problem.

Since the experimental social sciences have also faced these problems in their search for knowledge, we might suppose that the diligent teacher could simply borrow their procedural tools to help him rule out alternative explanations of educational success. The researcher's purposes, however, differ from those of the practitioner. The former is in the (relatively leisurely) business of testing theoretical models and of building up a corpus of knowledge in a particular discipline. Knowing *why* is a first order priority. The latter, on the other hand, often working against the clock with large groups, is mainly interested in producing appropriate changes in or for pupils. *What* happens is more important than *why* and there may be a supposition that so long as appropriate change is seen to have occurred by school staff, parents, and other interested parties then the matter can rest there.

One of the virtues of the behavioural tradition has been its insistence that its own effectiveness should be judged using rigorous scientific criteria, whether in applied, or experimental, settings. Proof of success is a basic requirement rather than an optional extra (see Winter, 1982). It requires two things; first that an appropriate change should be objectively demonstrable and, second, that the change should be shown to be the logical outcome of the teacher's or educationalist's activities. There is a vast literature on the issue of measurement and on the setting of appropriate learning objectives. This article is a review of some of the ways in which workers using behavioural techniques have tried to meet the second of these two requirements. We shall see that the differences in purpose between 'pure' and 'applied' research have led practitioners of the latter to the use and development of 'research designs' different from those commonly used in mainstream social science. It will be suggested that these 'Single Case Designs' are, or should be, of great importance to practitioners and researchers in education.

Demonstrating causal relationships (2)

There seem to be two possible frameworks within which one can analyse the effects of factors upon one another. Either one shows that a particular factor was, beyond reasonable doubt, the cause of an observed change or one demonstrates that had a particular event not occurred then matters would have gone on as before. In the first case the emphasis is upon the relationship between intervention and change; in the second case the emphasis is upon the lack of convincing alternatives. In practice these frameworks are rarely distinguished in scientific reasoning but the distinction between them is emphasised here because it is helpful in conceptualising, within a unitary framework, different approaches to demonstrating the effectiveness of an educational intervention.

To do this we also need to involve that tried and tested behavioural tool the baseline or reference phase. (White (1971) has argued that, properly speaking, the term baseline describes only a measure of the stability of behaviour over a period of time and that the pre-intervention measurement commonly labelled as the baseline should be termed the reference phase. This article bows to common usage and sticks to baseline.) The baseline is an index of the behaviour to be changed, based upon repeated measurements taken before intervention. It also serves in various ways as an indication of what the behaviour would have been had the intervention not occurred; in other words as a measure of the likelihood of factors external to the intervention having caused the observed changes. (This argument is developed in greater depth below.)

What is needed, therefore, is a measure of how a learner's behaviour changes when the teacher applies some intervention together with a measure of how it would have continued unchanged had the intervention not been applied. This sounds a bit like eating one's cake and having it, and, lacking the parallel universes beloved of science fiction writers, researchers have evolved two distinct approaches to achieving it. These are:

(a) group designs (across subjects or extensive designs);
(b) single case/subject designs (within subject or intensive designs).

We shall examine them in more detail later but the differences are, briefly, these. In Group Designs the measured changes in the behaviour of a number of individuals who have undergone the behavioural intervention are pooled statistically and compared with the similarly treated results from a number of comparable individuals who have not been affected by the intervention. This second, or control group provides the material for an external baseline which (it is hoped) shows what the state of the experimental or treatment subjects would have been had they not been the subjects of the intervention. (Note that "groups" are groups of results; the people involved need not meet or be dealt with collectively). In most Single Case Designs the individual is used as his own control, e.g. by showing that when the intervention is withdrawn, his behaviour reverts to what it was during the baseline phase.

These two models originate in the experimental situation, an experiment being a simplified or even artificial setting created in order that the effects of one or a very few factors upon a subject of interest might be unambiguously identified. Experiments are widely used in research work but it is often difficult to transpose experimental findings to the classroom settings where the work of educationalists occurs. To what degree can these powerful tools for demonstrating causation be applied to the study of teacher's classroom activities? Applied educational research has followed mainstream psychology in using Group Designs to investigate issues such as the effect of teacher's expectations for pupils (e.g. Rosenthal & Jacobson, 1968). For the classroom teacher, however, such work is not always very helpful. The users of behavioural methods, in particular, have favoured Single Case Designs. Later, suggestions are made as to why this has been so and some of the commoner forms of Single Case design that have been developed over the last two decades are reviewed.

Group Designs: some advantages

First, however, it is necessary to consider what, until very recently, has passed as the acme of scientific practice in much social science and research; the Group Design. It offers the researcher or practitioner a number of advantages in his search for causal relationships.

(1) The control group, if randomly assigned from the same population (i.e. having the same characteristics) as the experimental group, permits the establishment of a baseline external to the intervention in order to show the impact upon this group of changes in social, environmental or maturational factors which would also be expected to affect the experimental group.

(2) The use of grouped outcomes can be said to represent typical behaviour and to minimise the impact of extreme or idiosyncratic individuals upon the study.

(3) The effect of subjects being lost to the study, for whatever reason, should be minimised by the use of adequately sized groups.

(4) By grouping results, and randomly allocating his subjects to groups, the investigator can employ the tools of inferential statistics to give precise estimates of the degree to which observed outcomes can be generalised to the whole class of persons from whom the experimental groups are drawn.

(5) The established position of Group Designs in the natural sciences allows social science and research, by borrowing such respectable techniques, both to gain kudos and, also, to join in the search for general laws which has often been seen as the goal of scientific endeavour.

When we recall the function of the baseline in providing measures of experimental impact or of the lack of competing explanations for a change, we can easily grasp the appeal of Group Designs. The experimental group provides a measure of the impact of the intervention whilst the control group furnishes an external baseline from which to estimate the impact of contextual factors affecting both groups such as history or maturation. Both approaches to the demonstration of causality are available in one design. (It is necessary to add that in circumstances where testing the experimental group before the intervention might affect the to-be-manipulated behaviour, the pre-intervention state of the experimental group may be deduced from measurements derived from a control group. There are varieties of group design, not all of which are as conceptually neat as the model outlined here.)

Group Designs: some problems

Group Designs have proved of great utility in 'pure' research where the demonstration of causal, or at least correlational, relationships between events is a prime concern. They are particularly convenient for the demonstration of general effects (e.g. the impact of alcohol on the average person's car driving skills) or trends (e.g. the relationship between children's age and their verbal performance). However, the interests of educational researchers and teachers do not always coincide. Hersen & Barlow (1976) have suggested that some of the advantages derived by the scientist from these designs may be seen as disadvantages from the point of view of the practitioner.

(a) The use of a control group has two drawbacks. First, the denial, to members of this group, of the 'treatment' may be seen as incompatible with the goals of the teaching professions. Secondly, it may be impracticable to gather sufficient examples of a rare case or to find enough clearly comparable individuals to assemble groups large enough to satisfy the conditions for a statistical analysis.

(b) The averaging of results across subjects may conceal important individual changes. Imagine a new reading scheme which results in half of the children taught by it gaining a year on their expected reading age and the other half ending up a year behind expectations. On average the group will have done no better, and no worse, than normal but the intervention will clearly have had considerable individual impact.

(c) The teacher deals, not with an abstract, normative individual, but with real, particular ones. The synthetic results of group studies may give the practitioner no practical guide as to how to help particular pupils.

(d) Statistically weak effects may be important to the individual whilst statistically striking outcomes may still be insufficient to achieve a solution to one child's problem.

(e) The preference for Group Designs shows a disregard for the advances that have already occurred, especially in the Behavioural Tradition, through the use of single case studies. Most of Skinner's & Pavlov's work was of this nature!

(f) Group designs often require no more than a single measurement before, and after, intervention and are therefore unlikely to reveal trends in the behaviour of interest. Hence they may conceal a relapse, or a slow but progressive improvement, in this behaviour [3].

The teacher will see all too clearly the problems of attempting to evaluate school-based interventions through group designs. Finding two comparable groups or classes is hard enough. Applying different treatments consistently would also be difficult. Moreover, any long term differences in the treatment of children might provoke all sorts of ethical questions.

Single Case Designs: some advantages

When we turn to Single Case designs the immediate advantages for the educator are clear. His interventions usually have, as their final goal, the changing of an individual's behaviour. Even when his immediate contact is with the group, as in much classroom work, the final criterion of success is measured in terms of individual achievement. Hence an approach based upon single subjects is inherently attractive and clearly practical in the classroom situation. Indeed such models have been developed over the last 20 years mainly within, and for, such applied contexts (The classic source here is Campbell & Stanley, 1966).

Another benefit of the Single Case approach lies in its use of repeated measurements of the behaviour(s) of interest. In group designs the variable (behaviour) of interest is typically measured only twice, once before and once after the intervention or experimental manipulation. The reliability of the information as a measure of the behaviour in question lies in its being a pooled measure derived from a range of subjects. In single case studies, on the other hand, the behaviour of interest is measured a number of times under everyday conditions before the intervention begins. The aim of this baseline or reference phase is to ensure that a realistic estimate of the stability (or lack of it) of these behaviours is obtained—in other words to avoid being misled by a single, and potentially abnormal, measure. Similarly a set of measurements are taken during and, or, after the intervention in order to check upon the stability of any change. Because of this richness of information which can usefully be represented in two dimensions (time of measurement and behaviour variation) Single Case studies usually present their results visually in the form of graphs which allow an immediate estimate of whether an intervention has been successful without the use of inferential statistics. This must be seen as advantageous to those not familiar with the use of such techniques. There are formulae available which allow probabilistic estimates concerning the impact of interventions in Single Case designs (e.g. Marsh, 1982). Currently, however, there is no clear agreement that these offer any gain over simple visual inspection ('eyeballing') of graphically presented results. This issue is discussed by Kazdin in Hersen & Barlow (1976) and by Berryman & Cooper (1982).

Single Case Designs: some problems

There are, however, three drawbacks to the Single Case approach. The first, relatively minor, is that sheer numbers are, subjectively, convincing. A small average gain of social skill across a group of 15 seems more impressive than clear and striking advances achieved with one or two children. General acceptability here must be gained by the systematic replication of successful studies with a variety of pupils. The teacher will surely not lack plenty of opportunities for such replications! The second problem is that certain behaviours do not lend themselves to the repeated measurement that is normal in order to provide data from which the single case baseline is constructed. Getting the same sums right time and time again will hardly demonstrate an improvement. Here, the devising of tests of equivalent difficulty is called for. The third problem is less tractable; how can one convincingly use a single subject both as a measure of continuity (to exclude alternative explanations of change) and of change co-related to intervention? In the discussion that follows I shall call upon our previous discussion of the baseline but it is first necessary to review briefly the nature of the changes which the practitioner attempts to produce.

Broadly speaking we can distinguish three reasons why a specific action is not performed; lack of motivation, lack of skill or due to the impact of a powerful setting event (such as illness). Motivation is an entity that can, and does, fluctuate according to a variety of factors. The acquisition of skill, however, represents a relatively permanent change in the total organism (see Bandura, 1969, chapter 4 for a thorough discussion of this matter). Any setting event which is currently operating (e.g. a headache, excessive room temperature, inappropriate seating arrangements) may impede learning or disrupt performance. Now as we shall see, some very commonly used single case experimental designs try to demonstrate the specific impact of the intervention by showing the teacher's ability to restore the pre-intervention level of performance (i.e. baseline). This is likely to be easy when setting events are manipulated, impossible when actual skills or knowledge have been learned and sometimes possible when motivation has been manipulated. These considerations need to be kept in mind in the following discussion of the advantages and disadvantages of particular experimental designs.

Single Case Designs: some examples

Single Case designs are a growth industry (see Berryman & Cooper (1982) for an excellent overview). I propose to review just five well established models: Withdrawal, Reversal, Changing Criterion, Multiple Schedule and Multiple Baseline Designs (for description of others and a catalogue of the numerous alternative terms used in this field see Berryman & Cooper, 1982).

Withdrawal Designs (A-B-A)

These are amongst the most useful of Single Case designs due to their inherent simplicity, convenience and experimental strength. In them, the teacher, having achieved the predicted improvements in the child's activities withdraws (i.e. stops) the intervention. (They may simply remove the 'active' ingredient of the intervention or may, in effect, allow pre-intervention forces to resume control of the target behaviour. If the latter were known to be so we should have a reversal design (see below). In other words some withdrawal designs may actually be reversal designs).

If the behaviour relapses to its pre-intervention baseline levels, it is assumed that the cancelled intervention was responsible for the improvement. Systematic changes in the independent or manipulated variable—the behaviour of the teacher, seating arrangement or whatever—have correlated with changes in the dependent variable—the target behaviour. This model offers both a measure of the impact of the intervention and some measure of the probable absence of alternative explanations in the return to baseline.

Withdrawal Designs have two limitations. First they are mainly appropriate to situations where motivation (or rather an insufficiency of it!) is the key to the problem; it is not clear how one could reliably hope to withdraw learned skills. Secondly the practitioner may be hesitant to undo, by the use of such a design, his or her good work either on ethical or practical grounds. The addition of a second period of intervention (A-B-A-B) can only partially ameliorate these limitations.

Madsen, Madsen & Thompson (1974) used a withdrawal design to assess the effectiveness of verbal and edible reinforcements in increasing the consumption of nutritional breakfasts by disadvantaged children attending a 'Headstart' summer school. The childrens 'spontaneous' eating was assessed through a momentary time sampling schedule. Verbal approval and sugar coated cereal treats were then delivered contingent upon the child being caught eating by patrolling teachers. The overall index of eating behaviour rose. When the reinforcement phase was withdrawn eating activity dropped, showing the impact of the intervention.

Reversal Designs

These are similar to the above except that instead of simply withdrawing the intervention (e.g. by discontinuing the reinforcing of a behaviour) the practitioner actively reverses the intervention (e.g. by reinstating previous seating arrangements). Such designs are harder to construct since the teacher needs both to be able to identify the conditions that maintained the pre-intervention behaviour and also to have the nerve and capability to reinstate them. Compared to the passive strategy of withdrawal this is an active restoration strategy. Its use is particularly likely when the pre-intervention situation was not seriously undesirable and when the controlling variables are thought to be powerful setting events such as room arrangements which can be changed around relatively easily.

These two designs are very similar and, as suggested above, it may not always be clear whether some withdrawal designs are not, in effect, reversal designs. This has led to a looseness of terminology. Hence Musgrove (1981) refers to a one day *reversal* period when the phase in question seems only to involve *withdrawal* of the intervention conditions. A clear example of a true reversal is provided by Lew & Bryant (1984). They predicted that learning in a cooperative group would enhance pupils' spelling performance over that obtained under normal learning conditions. Reinstatement of individual conditions led to a clear drop in performance for a number of pupils whilst restoration of group conditions reinstated improved levels of achievement. Reversal designs suffer the same problems as do withdrawal designs (see above).

Changing Criterion Designs

Here systematic and predictable changes in the target behaviour (without any attempt to restore the baseline) are used as evidence of the efficacy of the intervention. The teacher systematically raises the standard of performance required and adjusts the criteria for a reinforced response, or whatever, accordingly. The correlation of these changes in the intervention with changes in measured target behaviour are held to demonstrate the relationship between the two. Such a design is particularly suited to any situation where cumulative learning may occur. Individual judgement enters into the decision as to how many correlated intervention/target behaviour changes are required before the causal link between the two is accepted.

Glynn (1981) reports the use of changing criterion design to improve an 11 year old boy's spelling. Arvidson's Alphabetical Spelling Test, which is arranged in grades of progressive difficulty, was used to set criteria for assessing the effects of home and school educational programmes to improve spelling. The child's performance was sequentially raised level by level three times; performance on a fourth, untaught, level actually deteriorated, showing the specific effects of the intervention.

Multiple Schedule Designs

In the Multiple Schedule Design a variety of differing treatment conditions are applied in sequence and their effects compared with one another. Often treatments are repeated so as to confirm their different impacts. Once again the manipulation of levels of the target behaviour is taken to demonstrate the impact of the intervention. Such designs offer an alternative to Reversal Designs for motivational problems since they overcome, to some degree, the ethical problems of simple reversal or withdrawal of a treatment.

Charles, Glynn & McNaughton (1984) provide a good example of a multiple schedule design. Here a variety of methods for training staff working in a day care centre for children were evaluated. Two different approaches to developing children's language—Talking Up and Incidental Teaching—were taught by two methods—standard training and self-management. To begin with staff use of both approaches was baselined. In the Second Phase both teaching approaches were taught using standard training procedures. In Phase Three the Incidental Teaching approach was taught to the staff using the self management method whilst the Talking Up approach continued to be taught using standard training. In the final Phase (Four) the Incidental Teaching approach was returned to the standard training method whilst the Talking Up approach was now taught using the self-management method. Hence both the effectiveness of two methods for training staff (standard training versus self-management) as well as any possible interaction between method and skill being taught (Incidental Teaching or Talking Up) was assessed.

Multiple Baseline Designs

Here the effects of other factors are controlled for by the provision of a second baseline as in Group Designs. In Multiple-Baseline-Across-Situation Designs the teacher uses the individual's own behaviour, in situations other than the teaching one, to provide the second (control) baseline. The generalisation of behaviourally taught skills is bedevilled by the situational specificity of many behaviours. This 'nuisance factor' is turned to advantage in this design: if the target behaviour changes only in the teaching situation but not outside it, then it seems reasonable to conclude that it is the intervention rather than any other factor which has produced the change. Therefore, the rate of occurrence of the target behaviour is recorded in more than one setting. The intervention is then applied in one setting at a time. Failure of the improvement to generalise without specific training is taken to show the specific impact of the teachers actions.

Getliffe (1982) used this design to demonstrate the role of a verbal stimulus in controlling, and assisting the generalisation of self-help behaviours in young adults with severe learning difficulties. In one study a student was taught to tie his own shoelaces in a day training situation. The skill was initiated by the command "X, tie your shoelaces". During tuition shoelace tying was baselined in the student's residential quarters also. No generalisation occurred to the residential situation until the precise verbal discriminative stimulus was employed.

Incidentally we can recognise, in discussing this design, that research and practice may not always be good neighbours. Behaviour modification, like all successful teaching approaches, has found its greatest challenge in the difficulty of getting beneficial results to generalise from the teaching situation to other appropriate classroom situations. With a Multiple-Baseline-Across-Situations Design spontaneous generalisation early in the programme, an event highly desirable for both teacher and pupil, would obfuscate the degree to which the intervention had been the cause of the changes!

In Multiple-Baseline-Across-Behaviours a similar model is used, though there it is the failure of the intervention to generalise to other problem behaviours without deliberate programming that constitutes evidence of behavioural control. In both these designs 'intuitive' judgements dictate how many situational or behavioural settings are taken to be necessary. Komaki & Barnett (1977) report the use of this design to evaluate the effects of coaching five boys in three of the highly elaborate 'play' manoeuvres used in American football. Each play was baselined. Coaching was introduced sequentially for each manoeuvre. Improvements in the execution of specific plays occurred only when the specific play was being coached.

In Multiple-Baseline-Across-Persons the educator identifies one person 'control groups', being comparable individuals with similar behavioural problems. This is regarded as a weak design, having many of the drawbacks of Group Designs with none of their statistical power. Nevertheless it is a convenient, and widely used design. Scott & Ballard (1983) provide an example of such a design in operation. They used it to evaluate the impact of coaching by teachers and mothers, trained in specific tutoring skills, upon the reading performance of children who had learning difficulties. After baselining current reading levels, the new skills were introduced, tutor by tutor. As each intervention occurred the performance of the specific target child of the tutor also improved. The specific impact of the intervention was demonstrated by the fact that children whose tutors had not yet been trained did not improve. Since these children were receiving the attention of frequent testing a 'Hawthorne' effect seems unlikely to have occurred (i.e. the improvement being a result of the child receiving more attention rather than of the special teaching).

Mixed Models

It would be misleading, in a review such as this, to conclude without warning the reader against the attaching of undue importance to the precise form of the above designs. In any Journal where single case studies predominate the neat categories outlined (but not originated) here break down. Some authors use reversal designs with groups (e.g. Wheldall, Morris, Vaughan & Ng (1981). Others incorporate elements from a variety of models (e.g. Moore & Glynn, 1984). In the study cited above, by Komaki & Barnett (1977) a group was the 'single subject'. The important matter, to misquote St Paul, is to maintain the spirit of single case methodology, rather than to adhere mechanically to the letter of named designs. The descriptive categories used are conventions which do not necessarily describe totally discrete phenomena; they are labels for the approaches that have been taken by different applied researchers in order to demonstrate the impact of their actions and, or, exclude the possibility of other factors having intervened in the teaching situation.

Conclusion

It has been argued that teachers coming to use behaviour modification for the first time may too readily assume that the changes they see in their pupils are the direct result of their newly adopted practices. This cannot be taken for granted; the connection needs to be demonstrated in some way. The experimental social sciences have considerable experience of the problems involved in such demonstrations. It is suggested that teachers should be willing to learn from this experience, although it is emphasised that care needs to be exercised in transposing techniques from pure research to everyday classroom practice since the purposes of the two activities are not necessarily identical.

If the scientific framework is accepted as providing an appropriate model for applied research, then it offers two ways of demonstrating the effectiveness of (behavioural) work with children. The first requires the showing of strong correlations between the educationalist's intervention and change in the student's behaviour ('proof' of an effect). The second calls for an attempt to discount alternative explanations for such change (elimination of competing hypotheses). Group Designs attempt to meet both these requirements by showing a 'before-after' effect of the intervention upon the measured behaviour of members of an experimental group, there being no corresponding change in similar data derived from a comparable control group. These two sets of measurements can be seen as providing simple internal and external baselines, the former providing an index of effectiveness, the latter a measure of the impact of external factors. In Single Case Designs an individual's own behaviour, or behaviours, are used in various ingenious ways to supply the two baselines. Sometimes measurements of the same behaviour serve both functions at different points in the intervention. Sometimes other parts of a person's behavioural repertoire, or the same behaviour in other settings, are used for this end. Group Designs, giving independent estimates of the impact of the intervention and of external factors, are experimentally 'strong'; hence they permit the use of powerful statistics but are insensitive to the exact relationship between intervention and behaviour change. Single Case designs offer greater sensitivity in this respect but are experimentally weaker, hence are less able to call upon statistical support. Such designs, despite these drawbacks, are arguably more practicable within, and more appropriate to, the ethos of the teaching situation.

Five commonly employed Single Case Designs were reviewed in detail: Withdrawal Designs, Reversal Designs, Changing Criterion Designs, Multiple Schedule Designs and Multiple Baseline Designs. It was suggested that the precise form of a Single Case Design was less important than whether it fulfilled the need to provide the two types of baseline data previously identified as crucial to any experimental design.

The demonstration of the effectiveness of an intervention is an integral part of the behavioural approach rather than an optional extra. The developing field of Single Case Designs offers those professionally concerned with education an increasing variety of tools by which to publicly demonstrate the beneficial impact of their work.

NOTES

[1] The term 'Behaviour Modification' is used throughout this paper. I understand it to be a more general, and more widely understood, phrase than similar ones such as Applied Behaviour Analysis. It seems doubtful whether any clear distinction now exists between the various labels used to describe this area.

[2] 'Causal' is used here in its everday sense to mean only that one factor affects another in some way. No mechanistic cause and effect link is necessarily implied.

[3] I owe this point to Barbara Wilson of the Rivermead Rehabilitation Centre, Oxford.

REFERENCES

BANDURA, A. (1969) *Principles of Behavior Modification* (New York, Holt, Rinehart & Winston).

BERRYMAN, D. & COOPER, D. (1982) The use of single subject research methodology in special education, *Educational Psychology*, 2, pp. 197–213.

CAMPBELL, D.T. & STANLEY, J.C. (1966) *Experimental and Quasi Experimental Designs for Research* (Chicago, Rand McNally).

CHARLES, H., GLYNN, T. & MCNAUGHTON, S. (1984) Childcare workers' use of talking up and incidental teaching procedures under standard and self management staff training packages, *Educational Psychology*, 4, pp. 199–212.

GETLIFFE, C. (1984) The generalisation of self-help skills in mentally handicapped adults from day to residential provision. *Unpublished thesis* submitted as partial satisfaction of the requirements for the award of Diploma in Special Needs, Bulmershe College of Higher Education, Reading.

GLYNN, T. (1981) Behavioural research in remedial education: more power to the parents, in: K. Wheldall (Ed.) *The Behaviourist in the Classroom: aspects of applied behavioural analysis in British educational contexts* (Birmingham, Educational Review Publications).

HERSEN, M. & BARLOW, P. (1976) *Single Case Experimental Designs* (Oxford, Pergamon).

KAZDIN, A.E. (1976) Statistical analyses for single-case experimental designs, in: M. Hersen & P. Barlow, *Single Case Experimental Designs* (Oxford, Pergamon).

KOMAKI, J. & BARNETT, F.T. (1977) A behavioural approach to coaching football: improving the play execution of the offensive backfield of a youth football team, *Journal of Applied Behavior Analysis*, 10, pp. 657–664.

LEW, M. & BRYANT, R. (1984) The effects of cooperative groups on regular class spelling achievement of special needs learners, *Educational Psychology*, 4, pp. 275–283.

MADSEN, C.H., MADSEN, C.K. & THOMPSON, F. (1974) Increasing rural head start children's consumption of middle class meals, *Journals of Applied Behavior Analysis*, 7, pp. 257–62.

MARSH, R.W. (1982) The use of serial correlation in the analysis of data from interrupted time series trials with single subjects in educational research, *Educational Psychology*, 2, pp. 317–20.

MOORE, D.W. & GLYNN, T. (1984) Variation in question rate as a function of position in the classroom, *Educational Psychology*, 4, pp. 233–248.

MUSGROVE, W.J. (1981) The establishment and decline of a token reinforcement program with three emotionally disturbed pre-school children, *Educational Psychology*, 1, pp. 81–85.

ROSENTHAL, R. & JACOBSON, L. (1968) *Pygmalion in the Classroom* (New York, Holt, Rinehart & Winston).

SCOTT, J.M. & BALLARD, K.D. (1983) Training parents and teachers in remedial reading procedures for children with learning difficulties, *Educational Psychology*, 3, pp. 15–30.

WHELDALL, K., MORRIS, M., VAUGHAN, P. & NG, Y.Y. (1981) Rows versus tables: an example of the use of behavioural ecology in two classes of eleven-year-old children, *Educational Psychology*, 1, pp. 171–184.

WHITE, O.R. (1971) *A Glossary of Behaviour Modification* (Champaign, Research Press).

WINTER, S. (1982) Why measure behaviour? *Educational Psychology*, 2, pp. 185–196.

The Use of Single-subject Research Methodology in Special Education

DIANE BERRYMAN & BRYCE COOPER

ABSTRACT *This paper discusses the importance and use of single-subject experimental analysis for special education practitioners. Brief descriptions are presented for the basic* N = *1 research designs available to evaluate instructional and treatment strategies. The ability of these designs to control threats to internal validity is examined and the present state of measuring and interpreting single-subject data is described. Replication of studies is discussed as the ultimate test of the effectiveness of an intervention. The need for documentation of procedures and results is seen as a primary means for allowing practitioners to incorporate research and methodology into their own practices and as part of the process of developing an effective instructional technology for people with special education needs.*

Within the field of special education, there is an increasing demand from both consumers and professionals for practitioners to be accountable for the outcomes of the instructional practices that they employ in the delivery of service to clients with special education needs. This is a healthy demand as it reflects an optimism by concerned members of the community that socially valued outcomes of special education procedures can exist. Such an optimism is well justified. Research findings over the past decade have indicated empirically that the use of systematic instruction based on behavioural principles can result in clients acquiring a diverse array of social and academic classroom behaviours, vocational skills, daily living skills and other social skills that are critical for age-appropriate community functioning (for example, Bellamy, 1976; Bellamy, Horner & Inman, 1977; Horner & Bellamy, 1980; O'Leary & O'Leary, 1972, 1977; *The Journal of Applied Behavior Analysis* (*JABA*), 1968–1982; *The Journal of Special Education*, 1967–1982).

However such an optimism cannot be said to be reflected in the actual day-to-day practice in special education classrooms. The lack of transfer from the arena of applied educational research to these classrooms is depressing. Much of what teachers teach and how they teach it continues to be based on "conjecture and anecdotal evidence" (Murphy & Bryan, 1980, p. 325) or at best "theory which has logical or personal appeal and traditional usage which produces time-honoured, if not empirically supported practices" (Fields, 1980, p. 3). For the products of applied research to become part of the powerful instructional technology long awaited by the community, such products must be integrated with field application. For this to become a reality, research findings must be presented to teachers, preferably in their initial training, in such a manner that they can and will use them in their own teaching (Baer, Wolf & Risley, 1968; Birnbrauer, 1981; Brigham & Catania, 1978; Kazdin, 1981). In addition, teachers must acquire specific skills in research methodology so that they can critically examine current research literature and actively fulfil their own role in the development of such a technology by validating and integrating research findings in their own classrooms.

At present, special education practitioners, along with practitioners in related fields (Hayes & Nelson, 1981), tend to emerge from their training with the belief that educational research is far removed from their own practical professional needs and with little realisation that they can have an active role in contributing to the advancement of an empirically based instructional technology. An examination of the course handbooks of schools of education in Australian universities and teacher-training establishments reveals one possibility for such beliefs continuing to be held: the only courses in research methodology available to either undergraduate or postgraduate students in education appear to be in group-comparison research procedures with specific courses in single-subject experimental analysis conspicuous by their absence.

Although much valuable knowledge in education has obviously been gained through group-comparison research, such procedures do present fundamental difficulties when working with human subjects in applied settings. This is especially so for the practitioner working with low-instance populations as are usual in special education. The main limitation is that basic practices of the group-comparison approach rely on statistical inferences from averaged group data. Responses of individuals within the group, which may vary widely, are therefore not assessed, hence it is difficult to make reliable educational decisions concerning effective intervention strategies for particular clients. Other limitations include:

(1) the ethical problem of withholding treatment from a no-treatment control group;
(2) the practicalities of finding large homogeneous groups of subjects with a particular behaviour disorder, and then randomly assigning them;
(3) the costs in terms of funding and time required to acquire such groups, as well as collect and analyse data; and
(4) the educational reliance on statistically significant findings as distinct from the educationally significant outcomes required for applied research (Hersen & Barlow, 1976; Wells *et al.*, 1981).

Due to the recognition of these difficulties, it is frequently suggested that the single-subject experimental approach offers a viable alternative when working in field settings (Hersen & Barlow, 1976). An examination of the wealth of experimental research conducted by applied behaviour analysts with special education clients over the past seventeen years certainly adds weight to this viewpoint. However, without specific training in such experimental procedures, it appears unlikely that educational practitioners would have the competence to evaluate the work of applied behaviour analysts critically, much less integrate and evaluate such research findings in their own instructional practices.

The purpose of this paper is therefore to review the current literature pertaining to single-subject experimental research methodology in the context of its relevance for special education practitioners. As alluded to above, it is the opinion of the present authors that for the detailed coverage of this topic to be of functional value to special education practitioners, a full course at the teacher training level is required, and thus well beyond the scope of a single paper. Hence, the objective of this paper is limited to providing a brief overview of the main strategies and issues related to single-subject research procedures, with selected references included for further reading.

Single-subject Research Methodology

The primary objective of single-subject research methodology is to investigate functional relationships between treatment or instructional procedures and the behaviour change within the subject. The second main objective is to document these procedures in such a manner that findings can be used by other researchers or practitioners when working with clients who exhibit similar behaviour deficits or excesses under similar environmental conditions.

The Investigation of a Functional Relationship Between Treatment and Behaviour Change (Internal Validity)

There are three basic types of research design used in within-subject studies to examine the functional relationship between treatment/instructional procedures (the independent variable(s)) and the change in the client's specified behaviour (the dependent variable). These are the withdrawal/reversal type design, the multiple baseline type design, and the alternating treatments type design. All of these designs have two common characteristics: the repeated measurement of the dependent variable, and a baseline before the commencement of treatment/instructional procedures.

As each subject acts as his own control, the effects of *statistical regression* and *selection* (Campbell & Stanley, 1966, p. 5) cannot present rivalling hypotheses for the changes in behaviours in these within-subject designs. *Mortality* (in the connotations of the group design) (Campbell & Stanley, 1966, p. 5) is not a problem in itself as a study is terminated by the loss of the subject. However, the implications of this loss on the effectiveness of the treatment are also lost because such an event is rarely reported, thus valuable knowledge, perhaps about what not to do, is regrettably concealed. The effects of specific events other than the experimental variables that occur during the experimental period (*history*—Campbell & Stanley, 1966, p. 5), and the effects of processes within the organism that occur as a function of time (*maturation*—Campbell & Stanley, 1966, p. 5) are discussed here within each experimental design. The effects of repeated assessment during the experimental period (*testing*—Campbell & Stanley, 1966, p. 5) and the effects of changes in the measuring procedures (*instrumentation*—Campbell & Stanley, 1966, p. 5) are addressed within discussion of the measurement techniques.

The Baseline

With the exception of the BAB design (see below), a variation of the reversal design, all experimental within-subject designs employ an initial period of observation where repeated measurement of the natural frequency of the target behaviour is taken. This initial period of measurement is termed the baseline and is usually known as the A-phase of the study (Kazdin & Bootzin, 1972). In Campbell and Stanley terms, this phase is labelled $0_1 0_2 0_3 \ldots 0_n$, where these refer to data points in the baseline.

Basic Within-subject Research Designs

The Reversal or Withdrawal Type Design. This design, which is illustrated in Fig. 1, is the most frequently used within-subject design and provides the most graphic demonstration that changes in the client's behaviour are attributable to the treatment procedures (Leitenberg, 1973). The characteristic form of this design is an ABAB format, where A represents baseline or pre-treatment conditions, and B represents treatment phases. Variations of this design are ABA, BAB, ABABA type formats. When a second treatment is also evaluated, it is termed the C phase, yielding a format such as ABACABC, and so forth.

The main advantage of using this design is that a functional relationship between the dependent variable and the treatment strategy can be assessed when treatment procedures are withdrawn and then reinstated. In addition, the design can demonstrate the effectiveness of the treatment strategy to the client's caretakers (Sulzer-Azaroff & Mayer, 1977). The effects of the rivalling hypotheses of *history* and *maturation* are controlled for by the use of the reversal strategy in this design. If other events external or internal to the client and not associated with the independent variable were responsible for the behavioural change, the behaviour would not be expected to revert to baseline levels during the second A-phase. However, as pointed out by Huck, Cormier & Bounds (1974), each study must be evaluated on the evidence presented.

This design is unsuitable when ethical considerations do not permit a lengthy baseline period (which does not actually contribute to the behavioural change) since a stable baseline is required before treatment procedures can begin. For example, if a client exhibits life-threatening behaviours, one cannot justify the collection of stable baseline data simply to demonstrate experimental control. Similarly, withdrawing successful treatment even for a brief period may appear irresponsible to caretakers. This design is also inappropriate when behaviours are not reversible, such as when the treatment strategy is a method of teaching maths or reading skills.

The Multiple Baseline Type Design. The multiple baseline design (see Fig. 2) may offer a viable alternative when the reversal design is inappropriate. There are several variations of this design: across behaviours, across individuals, and across situations. In the multiple baseline design across behaviours, a number of the subject's responses are defined and measured to provide separate baselines, against which the effects of the independent variable can be measured. The treatment/instructional procedure is then introduced for one behaviour, and changes measured and compared, with (one hopes) little or no change in the other measured behaviours. The treatment is then applied to the next behaviour whilst measures are continued for all other targeted behaviours, until baselines are exhausted. In this way the experimen-

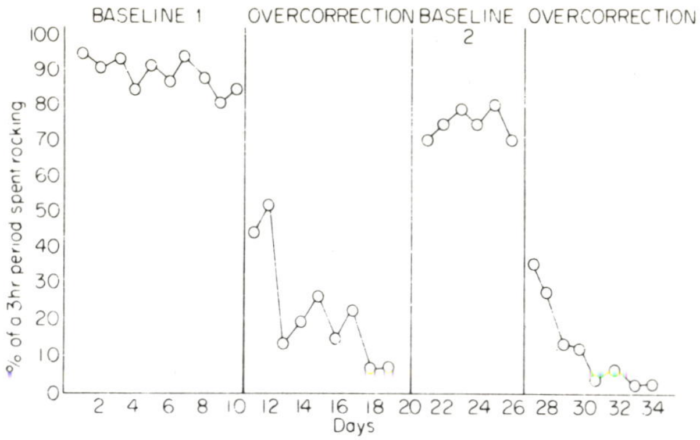

FIG. 1. The effects of the use of an over-correction procedure on a 15-year-old severely intellectually handicapped girl's rocking behaviour (hypothetical data).

ter demonstrates the cause and effect relationship between the dependent and independent variables, as each behaviour changes only when the experimental procedure is applied to it (Baer *et al.*, 1968).

A similar experimental procedure can be conducted across individuals, when baselines are established for several clients exhibiting similar behaviours (for example, Kolko, Dorsett & Milan, 1981). The third variation consists of a multiple baseline across situations (for example, Piersal & Kratochwill, 1981).

When using this design to demonstrate experimental control it is important to be reasonably sure beforehand that the target behaviours are independent and are not likely to convary, otherwise generalisation could occur across behaviours or situations. When immediate action is required this design is not appropriate as lengthy baselines are essential for all but the initial behaviour, subject, or situation. The multiple baseline across subjects design is possibly the weakest of these designs, as inter-subject differences may introduce threats related to *selection*, *mortality* and *maturation* not normally present in within-subject designs.

The advantage of this design is that interventions do not have to be interrupted or withdrawn to show effects, as with withdrawal designs, so that caretakers are much more likely to co-operate (Murphy & Bryan, 1980). Essentially, this design consists of a series of staggered AB designs where the effects of *history* and *maturation* are controlled for by the extended baselines in the second and subsequent behaviours, clients or situations.

A further advantage of this basic design is its flexibility, which is reflected in designs that have developed as extensions of this concept. For instance, the multi-baseline component analysis (Dericco, Brigham & Garlington, 1977) is a slight refinement of the multiple baseline across settings and individuals. Another refinement, known as the multiple-probe design (Horner & Baer, 1978; Murphy & Bryan, 1980), employs intermittent probes of short duration to measure the application of experimental treatments, as an alternative to continual baseline measurements. This adaptation is especially economical in terms of resources available when behaviour cannot occur unless treatment procedures are introduced as, for example, in the case of developing decoding skills.

The changing-criterion design (Guralnick, 1978; Hartmann & Hall, 1976; Sulzer-Azaroff & Mayer, 1977), which is conceptually related to the process of shaping, can also be seen as a variation of a staggered AB type design, as each step acts as an 'A' phase for the next treatment condition. It allows for behaviour change to be adjusted in a step-wise fashion, with each adjustment representing a potential replication of the effectiveness of the experimental treatment with full experimental control. The limitation of this design is related to the degree to which each adjustment can be predicted to replicate the treatment effect. Even so, it is particularly useful for assessing shaping of low level behaviours.

Combinations of designs have also provided tools for complex analyses of independent variables, improving the experimental control of studies and in-depth examination of treatments (Wong & Liberman, 1981). These have included designs that incorporate two or more multiple baseline designs such as across behaviours within subjects and across subjects (Kolko *et al.*, 1981) and multiple baselines with reversal or alternating treatment designs.

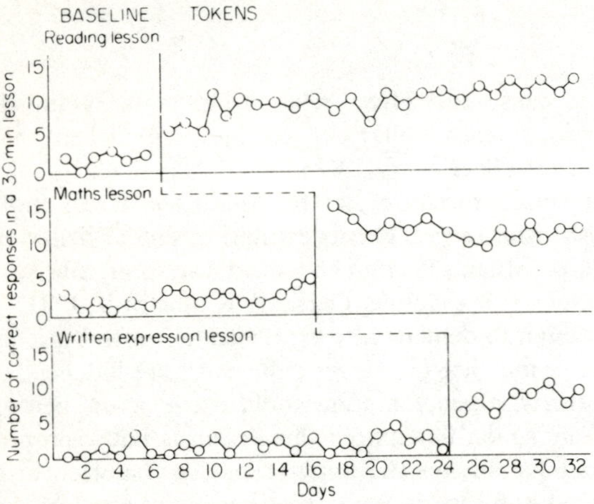

FIG. 2. A multiple baseline analysis of the effects of token reinforcement on the number of correct responses made during reading, mathematics and written expression lessons by a 10-year-old emotionally disturbed boy (hypothetical data).

The Alternating Treatments Type Design. This design is an infrequently used procedure which is capable of comparing two treatments within a single subject (Barlow & Hayes, 1979). It is also known as a multiple-schedule design (Barlow & Hersen, 1973; Hersen & Barlow, 1976; Leitenberg, 1973), a randomised design (Edgington, 1967, 1980), a multielement design (Sidman, 1960; Sulzer-Azaroff & Mayer, 1977) and a simultaneous-treatment design (Kazdin & Hartmann, 1978). Essentially the subject is exposed to baseline and alternating independent variables (see Fig. 3) throughout the research period, where each phase is usually of short duration. An advantage of this design is that only a short baseline is required. Furthermore, it is particularly useful in analysing complex behaviours such as maths performance (Harris & Sherman, 1973) and the use of study questions on mastery (Semb,

Hopkins & Hursh, 1973). It is also useful when there is a likelihood that differential effects will emerge relatively quickly, thus maximising the use of experimental time.

These designs are very useful in controlling for the effects of *history* and *maturation*, due to the rapid changes in experimental conditions. However, the effects of multiple-treatment interaction (Campbell & Stanley, 1966) or condition change interaction (Ulman & Sulzer-Azaroff, 1975) may present serious confounding variables leading to questionable external validity (Barlow & Hayes, 1979). These are serious limitations, thus their effects must be judged in each study.

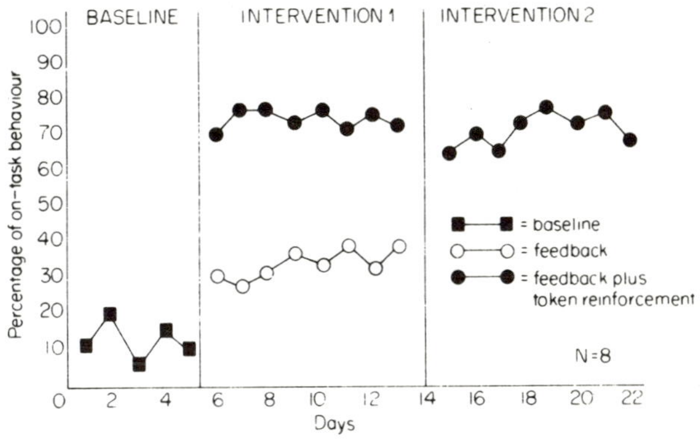

FIG. 3. The effects of feedback and feedback plus token reinforcement on the 'on-task' behaviour of learning disabled children in a resource room (hypothetical data).

Generalisation Designs. In recent years new designs have begun to be developed to address generalisation across time (maintenance), settings (stimulus generalisation) and behaviours (response generalisation) of treatment effects. Primarily these are extensions of basic designs mentioned above. They include the use of partial-withdrawal (Russo & Koegel, 1977; Vogelsburg & Rusch, 1979) where experimental components are sequentially withdrawn after fluency in the targeted behaviour is reached. Generalisation probes throughout the study have also been conducted (Nutter & Reid, 1978; Schreibman & Carr, 1978). Page, Iwata & Neef (1976) used a multiple baseline across behaviours to assess generalisation, in combination with a multiple baseline across individuals to demonstrate experimental control. Other studies have reported follow-up data without experimental control (O'Connor, Stuck & Wyne, 1979; Walker & Buckley, 1972).

Repeated Measurement Techniques

The use of repeated measurement of the dependent variable is one of the most important strategies of single-subject research. Essentially, data are collected over the entire research period to allow for the systematic monitoring of day-to-day variability in the individual's behaviour. Data can be collected directly, as in the case of an investigation into the relationship between food quantity and ruminating behaviour conducted by Rast *et al.* (1981). In this study each client was observed by human observers for a 60 minute period following meals, over 200 successive calendar days which covered six experimental phases. Similarly, indirect measurement techniques, such as examining test results on a child's daily maths or reading worksheets, can also be used.

Although this procedure allows for the fine, in-depth analysis of behavioural change under different experimental conditions which is characteristic of within-subject research, it also presents the most problems associated with attributing the changes to the intervention (internal validity). The rivalling hypotheses of *testing* and *instrumentation* must be carefully attended to and reported if such confounding variables are to be ruled out.

When direct measurement of human behaviour is used, as was the case in 76% of the 293 research papers published in *The Journal of Applied Behavior Analysis (JABA)* from 1968 through to 1975 (Kelly, 1977), the effects of observer drift, experimenter bias and observer bias can contribute to the effects of changes in the measuring procedures presenting confounding effects (*instrumentation*). In order to control for these variables, interobserver/rater/assessor reliability checks are usually conducted at least once in each experimental phase (Kelly, 1977). These reliability assessments are typically reported as percentage agreements between the independent scores. Attempts are also often made to use experimentally naive trained observers instead of experimenters. A reasonable number of observers used at random during the research period is also an advantage. The importance of this aspect, and the need to consider such confounding effects, particularly methods of assessing inter-observer reliability, is evident from the continuing discussion related to this topic in the applied behaviour analysis literature (Baer, 1977; Berkimer & Brown, 1979; Cone, 1979; Hartmann, 1977; Hawkins, 1979; Hopkins & Hermann, 1977; Kazdin, 1977, 1979; Kelly, 1977; Kent *et al.*, 1979; Kratochwill & Wetzel, 1977; Lewin & Wakefield, 1979; Nelson & Hayes, 1979; Yelton, Wildman & Erickson, 1977).

The effects of assessment before and during the treatment period on the client's behaviour (*testing*) may also present a behavioural change not associated with the treatment procedures. This is controlled for by ensuring a stable baseline before intervention. Frequently, observations are conducted during an informal observation period prior to the recording of the formal baseline to ensure that clients are accustomed to observers being present in the experimental setting. One-way mirrors and video equipment can also be used (Kazdin, 1979; Kent *et al.*, 1979).

Interpretation of Single-Subject Data

Interpretation of single-subject data is becoming a controversial issue in the literature, dichotomised by preferences for analysis using either visual judgments (Furlong & Wampold, 1981; Parsonson & Baer, 1978) or statistical procedures (Edgington, 1967; Gentile, Roden & Klein, 1972; Glass, Willson & Gottman, 1973; Gottman, 1973; Hartmann *et al.*, 1980; Jones, Weinrott & Vaight, 1978; Murphy & Bryan, 1980). Some writers suggest using both, stating typically that statistics are useful to supplement or confirm visual analysis (for example, Jones, Vaught & Weinrott, 1977).

In applied settings, experimenters seek an unambiguous and dramatic change in behaviour, so that visual analysis of data can be compatible with informed but nevertheless subjective evaluations by involved personnel (see, for example, Fig. 1).

Interpretable plotted data depend on a stable baseline, with an absence of slope or drift, and with immediately obvious changes in level when an intervention is initiated (Hersen & Barlow, 1976). However, a disadvantage that is becoming increasingly recognised by researchers is that visual interpetation may differ according to who analyses the data. A detached visual analysis by an uninvolved person may result in a different conclusion from that reached by the experimenter, who is likely to be biased towards recognising significant effects which may otherwise be considered to be too subtle or too variable. Experience appears to be no guarantee against different interpretations, and inter-evaluator reliability has been found to be low (DeProspero & Cohen, 1979; Jones *et al.*, 1978). In addition, applied research is often concerned with low rate behaviours which may cause considerable educational concern, but are unstable and therefore not always easy to evaluate visually from plotted data (Barlow & Hayes, 1979). When the baseline does not stabilise, perhaps exhibiting a clear trend, or extremes of variability (Kazdin, 1976), visual interpretation of data is open to accusations of confounding effects, and unknown internal validity.

A solution for this problem is to employ a statistical analysis of the data collected. Statistical procedures have also been proposed for both particular time-series designs, and specific methodological techniques (Kratochwill, 1978). Selecting the correct statistical model, however, creates a new set of problems (Elashoff & Thoresen, 1978), particularly for the experimenter who may be familiar with widely-known statistical techniques for group-comparison research, but is unfamiliar with the entirely different set of assumptions underlying data collected from single-subject time-series research.

A common property of single-subject research and multiple baseline time-series research is *serial dependency,* where an observation or score will often predict or be related to subsequent observations (Jones *et al.*, 1978; Kazdin, 1976). This is measured by *autocorrelation*, a correlational value computed by analysing differences between regularly nominated successive data points. Conventional statistics are thus usually unsuitable because they are based on assumptions of independent responses or scores, and random sampling of subjects. Serial dependency biases estimates of the error variance, and distorts conventional statistics (Hartmann *et al.*, 1980). Orthodox assumptions of independent observations are rarely established in time-series research (Keselman & Leventhal, 1974; Kratochwill *et al.*, 1974). In many applied behavioural settings, serial dependency is a necessarily inherent prerequisite to effective treatment; for example, shaping of behaviours, and the whole predictive mode of therapy (Jones *et al.*, 1978, Kratochwill *et al.*, 1974). In time series methodology, visual and statistical analyses will differ most when a high degree of serial dependency is indicated by autocorrelation (Jones *et al.*, 1978), although Hartmann *et al.* (1980) suggest that it is not yet known whether the effects of serial dependency on visual analysis parallel the effects of serial dependency on conventional statistics.

Statistical techniques have been adapted to analyse such data, although not always appropriately. Variations on the *t*-test and ANOVA (for example, Gentile *et al.*, 1972; Shine & Bower, 1971) have been strongly criticised for ignoring the effects of serial dependency, or for adapting the procedures inadequately. (For intensive discussion of this see the winter issue of *JABA*, 1974). Other statistical procedures suggested include time-series analysis, which takes serial dependency into account, but requires a long baseline phase of at least 50 data points (which are normally impractical), and a computer program to analyse the data (Box & Tiao, 1965; Glass,

Willson & Gottman, 1975; Gottman, 1973; Jones, Vaught & Reid, 1975); Markov chain analysis (Gottman & Notarius, 1978); the R_n statistic (Kazdin, 1976; Revusky, 1967); and randomisation tests (Edgington, 1967, 1975, 1980; Kazdin, 1976).

The difficulties of using statistical procedures for analysis, even by specialist statisticians, have been reflected in criticisms of inappropriate use and misleading assumptions. Visual presentations of data have the advantages of being simple to plot after each measurement session, require simple recording procedures, and can be explained to other people relatively easily, with the added benefit that the original raw data are immediately available (Parsonson & Baer, 1978).

It must be realised however, that experimenters do use statistical concepts to analyse data visually in terms of stability, variability, and numbers of scores or responses (Kratochwill, 1978). The main differences therefore exist in the conclusions drawn from group research (through which have evolved conventional parametric statistics), and those drawn from single-subject time-series research. While group studies have a reasonable likelihood of making a Type 1 error (concluding a difference exists when it does not) and a lesser chance of making a Type 2 error (failing to recognise a difference), the opposite is the case in single-subject research (Baer, 1977). If suitable statistics can be used, the experimenter has to have a very clear idea of the difference that is likely to occur between statistical significance and educational significance. An interesting aspect is that statistical procedures place an emphasis on statistical as opposed to experimental control (Michael, 1974). This can encourage inflexibility regarding the experimenter's reactions to variations within the subject's responses, and inhibit desirable procedural changes during the experiment. The method of interpretation should therefore be selected with these features in mind, because of the practical implications of incorrect conclusions.

Methods of interpreting single-subject data are not yet as clear-cut as those used to draw conclusions from group data. The empirically based decision rules of precision teaching (White & Haring, 1980; Haring, Liberty & White, 1980) provide a solution to this problem in some circumstances, with decisions made from plotted data which have been scrutinised using specified mathematical and descriptive procedures. Michael's (1974) sound arguments against using statistical procedures to control internal validity are only one part of the problem, and do not acknowledge that simple statistical procedures may one day help in drawing useful conclusions from the data. Further inspiration is needed to devise reliable and simple formal procedures for confirming visual analysis of data in single-subject research methodology, so that realistic educational decisions can be made.

The Generalisability of Single-subject Research Findings (External Validity)

The term 'external validity' refers to the extent to which the findings of a study can be generalised to other clients and other environmental conditions, such as across investigators and settings (Bracht & Glass, 1968; Birnbrauer, 1981; Campbell & Stanley, 1966; Hersen & Barlow, 1976; Huck *et al.*, 1974, Kazdin, 1981; Sidman, 1960).

Whereas possible threats to internal validity can be controlled for as a function of the experimental design used in both between-group and within-subject studies, the same cannot be said for threats to external validity for either paradigm. In the group-comparison approach, generalisability of findings across individuals depends upon the degree to which any study meets the fundamental assumption that the subjects within the sample are representative of a given population. In theory at least, this is controlled for by the random selection of a sizeable sample and random assignment of subjects to experimental groups. However, as stated above, random selection and assignment of large homogeneous groups for research purposes are rarely feasible in natural settings. In addition, predicting generalisability of findings from group studies also assumes that the particular client or clients to whom findings are to be generalised will respond in the same manner as did the majority of the sample, rather than as those for whom the intervention was unsuccessful. Thus successful predictions and replications of group-comparison research findings remain elusive (Birnbrauer, 1981; Epstein, 1980).

External validity of single-subject research studies is addressed according to a different frame of reference: findings gain generalisability across individuals by *direct replication* (Birnbrauer, 1981; Hersen & Barlow, 1976; Kazdin, 1981; Sidman, 1960). This is usually achieved by an investigator replicating a study with several different clients under similar conditions. The considerable advantage of this approach is that variability between individuals and the interaction between different subject characteristics and the intervention procedure can be examined closely due to the direct and continuous measurement of dependent variables (Hersen & Barlow, 1976; Leitenberg, 1973). Hence systematic adjustments in the procedure can be made and examined under experimental control, which further adds to the cumulative knowledge of the limitations and generality of an intervention strategy.

However, the ultimate test of the external validity of any research finding is whether consumers (other investigators or practitioners), can implement the intervention procedure under other situational conditions with other clients, and achieve similar outcomes. That is, a study gains external validity by *systematic replication* (Sidman, 1960). Such replications, and therefore generalisability of findings, rely heavily on the documentation of the study and dissemination of findings to colleagues. Thus, operational definitions of dependent variables, precise and detailed descriptions of independent variables, and of measurement procedures (including reliability), are typically reported. In addition, subject, setting, teacher and observer characteristics are becoming increasingly well documented.

Birnbrauer (1981) argues that detailed documentation of pre-experimental (baseline) conditions is central to the predictions about the effectiveness of an intervention so that consumers can evaluate whether a functional similarity exists between the pre-experimental behaviours and conditions of their client and the subject(s) previously studied. He also cautions consumers to conduct careful, systematic baselines themselves in order to ascertain which treatment for which client and under what conditions.

Single-subject Research Methodology and the Special Education Practitioner

For the practitioner in special education settings, within-subject research procedures provide a basic methodology for the scientific field validation of the findings of applied researchers. Furthermore, this methodology provides tools for the effective evaluation and manipulation of important instructional variables in classrooms. An advantage, especially for the classroom teacher, is that such evaluations can usually be conducted within the classroom with a minimum of disruption to classroom schedules and with few extra resources.

The reversal type design is particularly useful in conducting a fine-grained analysis of the effectiveness of various intervention strategies in increasing low-level socially valued classroom behaviours (see O'Leary & O'Leary, 1972, 1977). In addition such data could possibly be shown to parents and help given to them to improve social behaviours beyond the classroom (see Sulzer-Azaroff & Meyer, 1977). When examining the effect of an instructional technique reported to be effective in developing, for instance, reading, writing or maths skills, a multiple baseline across subjects or behaviours is generally suitable. The use of the multiple-probe technique is especially cost-effective in a classroom setting. Given a realisation of the limitations of the alternating treatments type design discussed above, such designs can also be utilised within a classroom setting.

Due to the logic underlying single-subject research, where the consumer is an active participant in developing generalisability of findings by replicating studies, precise and detailed descriptions of variables, measurement techniques and outcomes are typically reported. This is of considerable value to practitioners when attempting to treat similar clients under similar conditions. However, it requires these consumers to keep informed on current developments related to their planned intervention procedures. This also involves conducting planned and sytematic preliminary formal and informal baselines, selecting an appropriate design, collecting data systematically, and, ideally, disseminating findings to colleagues. In this way the development of a powerful instructional technology, field tested under natural conditions, and thus suitable for use by teachers, will become a reality.

Systematic and accurate collection and plotting of data are central to single-subject research. This requires the consumer to examine recording procedures, especially where direct observation of overt behaviours is used, as it appears that such procedures are open to the confounding effects of experimenter and observer bias and drift. When collecting data themselves, practitioners should keep in mind such problems and attempt to use independent observers (perhaps a teacher's aide, a school secretary or a fellow teacher) at regular intervals. Conversely, audiovisual equipment, and in some cases computer terminals, can be used to record data as a permanent product.

When analysing data, much controversy surrounds the usual practice of visual analysis compared with statistical analysis or the combination of both procedures. To date, it appears that suitable statistical procedures for single-subject research designs require further refinement. For the teacher, the use of visual analysis provides a very real advantage, as skill in statistical procedures, access to computers and sufficient time to analyse data are not usually available.

For both practitioners and researchers the power of data which can be analysed visually should never be underestimated in bringing about social change. It has been the experience of the present writers that administrators in the fields of education, health and social welfare are very ready to initiate social change when presented with easily interpretable, graphed 'proof' of successful intervention strategies conducted with specific children or adults in their care. For example, Berryman, O'Brien & Cummins [1] found that social welfare staff, and teachers in several local neighbourhood schools, were prepared to agree to the mainstreaming of subjects whose classroom behaviours were shown to be stable at an 'appropriate' level after a systematic behavioural change in an institution special school. Maintenance of behavioural gains made in this study were presented according to the partial sequential withdrawal design. Furthermore, when follow-up generalisation data were presented to district educational administrators, added support was given to the special school programme. Similarly, when Berryman & Renshaw [2] where able to present plotted multiple baseline data showing the effectiveness of satiation and DRO in reducing ruminating behaviour and increasing manipulative skills with one man in a ward for profoundly intellectually handicapped men, co-operation was given in introducing an educational programme for other residents in the ward.

Summary

The purpose of this paper has been to provide an overview of single-subject experimental analysis and its relevance to the field evaluation of instructional variables together with effective decision-making by special education practitioners. The specific methodological procedures discussed have been the basic single-subject designs and the strategies they employ to control internal validity, the measurement and interpretation of data, and the issue of the generalisability of research findings.

A powerful instructional technology is desperately needed to ensure that clients with special education needs emerge from the educational system with those skills necessary for dignified community functioning. It has been argued that for such a technology to be developed, teacher competence in single-subject procedures is critical. The opinion expressed has been that it is possible, and indeed essential, for teachers to view themselves as empiricists by systematically evaluating the relationship between instructional procedures and pupil achievement and thus being accountable for the outcomes of the instruction they provide.

As practitioners ourselves it has been our experience that conducting research using the fine-grained analytical $N=1$ procedures with our own clients can be intellectually stimulating, contributing to our own personal growth as well as our professional competence.

NOTES

Berryman, D., O'Brien, P. & Cummins, R. (1982) Preparing children with behavioural problems and learning difficulties for the neighbourhood school: the development of fluency, stimulus generalisation and response maintenance validated against normative peer data, *unpublished manuscript*, Institute of Special Education, Victoria College, Melbourne.

Berryman, D. & Renshaw, H. (1981) The use of satiation and over-correction oral hygiene to facilitate the introduction of an educational program for a ruminating institutionalised, profoundly handicapped adult, *unpublished manuscript*, Macquarie University, New South Wales.

REFERENCES

Baer, D.M. (1977) Perhaps it would be better not to know everything, *Journal of Applied Behavior Analysis*, 10, pp. 167–172.

Baer, D.M., Wolf, M.M. & Risley, T.R. (1968) Some current dimensions of applied behavior analysis, *Journal of Applied Behavior Analysis*, 1, pp. 91–97.

Barlow, D.H. & Hayes, S.C. (1979) Alternating treatments design: one strategy for comparing the effects of two treatments in a single subject, *Journal of Applied Behavior Analysis*, 12, pp. 199–210.

Barlow, D.H. & Hersen, M. (1973) Single case experimental designs: use in applied clinical research, *Archives of General Psychiatry*, 29, pp. 319–325.

Bellamy, C.T. (Ed.) (1976) *Habilitation of severely and profoundly retarded adults,* Specialized Training Program, Monograph Number 1, College of Education, University of Oregon, Eugene, Oregon.

Bellamy, G.T., Horner, R.H. & Inman, D.P. (Eds) (1977) *Habilitation of severely and profoundly retarded adults,* Vol. 2, Specialized Training Program, Monograph Number 3, College of Education, University of Oregon, Eugene, Oregon.

Berkimer, J.C. & Brown, J.H. (1979) A graphical judgmental aid which summarizes obtained and chance reliability data and helps assess the believability of experimental effects, *Journal of Applied Behavior Analysis,* 12, pp. 523–533.

Birnbrauer, J.S. (1981) External validity and experimental investigation of individual behavior, *Analysis and Intervention in Developmental Disabilities,* 1, pp. 117–132.

Box, G.E.P. & Tiao, G.C. (1965) A change in level of non-stationary time series, *Biometrika,* 52, pp. 181–192.

Bracht, G.H. & Glass, G.U. (1968) The external validity of experiments, *American Educational Research Journal,* 5, pp. 437–474.

Brigham, T.A. & Catania, A.C. (1976) The behavior analysis technology, in: Catania, A.C. & Brigham, T.A. (Eds) *Handbook of Applied Behavior Analysis: Social and Instructional Processes* (New York, Worthington).

Campbell, D.T. & Stanley, J.C. (1966) *Experimental and Quasi-experimental Designs for Research* (Chicago, Rand McNally).

Cone, J.D. (1979) Why the "I've got a better agreement measure" literature continues to grow: a commentary on two articles by Birkimer and Brown, *Journal of Applied Behavior Analysis,* 12, p. 571.

DeProspero, A. & Cohen, S. (1979) Inconsistent visual analyses of intrasubject data, *Journal of Applied Behavior Analysis,* 12, pp. 573–579.

Dericco, D.A., Brigham, T.A. & Garlington, W.K. (1977) Development and evaluation of treatment paradigms for the suppression of smoking behavior, *Journal of Applied Behavior Analysis,* 10, pp. 173–181.

Edgington, E.S. (1967) Statistical inference from $N=1$ experiments, *Journal of Psychology,* 65, pp. 195–199.

Edgington, E.S. (1975) Randomization tests for one-subject operant experiments, *Journal of Psychology,* 90, pp. 57–68.

Edgington, E.S. (1980) Validity of randomization tests for one-subject experiments, *Journal of Educational Statistics,* 5, pp. 235–251.

Elashoff, J.D. & Thoresen, C.E. (1978) Choosing a statistical method for analysis of an intensive experiment, in: Kratochwill, T.R. (Ed.) *Single Subject Research Strategies for Evaluating Change* (New York, Academic Press).

Epstein, S. (1980) The stability of behavior II. Implications for psychological research, *American Psychologist,* 35, pp. 790–806.

Fields, B. (1980) Guest editorial, *Australian Journal of Special Education,* 4, p. 3.

Furlong, M.J. & Wampold, B.E. (1981) Visual analysis of single-subject studies by school psychologists, *Psychology in the Schools,* 18, pp. 80–86.

Gentile, J.R., Roden, A.H. & Klein, R.D. (1972) An analysis of variance model for the intrasubject replication design, *Journal of Applied Behavior Analysis,* 5, pp. 193–198.

Glass, G.V., Willson, V.C. & Gottman, J.M. (1973) *Time Series Analysis in the Behavioural Sciences* (Boulder, Laboratory of Educational Research, University of Colorado).

Glass, G.V., Willson, V.C. & Gottman, J.M. (1975) *Design and Analysis of Time Series Experiments* (Boulder, University of Colorado).

Gottman, J.M. (1973) *N*-of-one and *N*-of-two research in psychotherapy, *Psychological Bulletin,* 80, pp. 93–105.

Gottman, J.M. & Notarius, C. (1978) Sequential analysis of observational data using Markov chains, in: Kratochwill T.R. (Ed.) *Single Subject Research Strategies for Evaluating Change* (New York, Academic Press).

Guralnick, M.J. (1978) The application of single-subject research designs to the field of learning disabilities, *Journal of Learning Disabilities,* 11, pp. 415–421.

HARING, N.G., LIBERTY, K.A. & WHITE, O.R.(1980) Rules for data-based strategy decisions in instructional programs: Current research and instructional implications, in: SAILOR, W., WILCOX, B. & BROWN, L. (Eds) *Methods of Instruction for Severely Handicapped Students* (Baltimore, Paul Brookes).

HARRIS, V.W. & SHERMAN, J.A. (1973) Use and analysis of the "Good Behavior Game" to reduce disruptive classroom behavior, *Journal of Applied Behavior Analysis*, 6, pp. 405–417.

HARTMANN, D.P. (1977) Considerations in the choice of interobserver reliability estimates, *Journal of Applied Behavior Analysis*, 10, pp. 103–116.

HARTMANN, D.P., GOTTMAN, J.M., JONES, R.R., GARDNER, W., KAZDIN, A.E. & VAUGHT, R. (1980) Interrupted time-series analysis and its application to behavioral data, *Journal of Applied Behavior Analysis*, 13, pp. 543–560.

HARTMANN, D.P. & HALL, R.V.A. (1976) A discussion of the changing criterion design, *Journal of Applied Behavior Analysis*, 9, pp. 527–532.

HAWKINS, R.P. (1979) The functions of assessment: Implications for selection and development of devices for assessing repertoires in clinical, educational, and other settings, *Journal of Applied Behavior Analysis*, 12, pp. 501–516.

HAYES, S.C. & NELSON, R.O. (1981) Clinically relevant research: requirements, problems, and solutions, *Behavioral Assessment*, 3, pp. 209–213.

HERSEN, M. & BARLOW, D.H. (1976) *Single-Case Experimental Designs: Strategies for Studying Behaviour Change* (Oxford, Pergamon Press).

HOPKINS, B.L. & HERMANN, J.A. (1977) Evaluating interobserver reliability of interval data, *Journal of Applied Behavior Analysis*, 10, pp. 121–126.

HORNER, R.D. & BAER, D.M. (1978) Multiple-probe technique: a variation of the multiple baseline, *Journal of Applied Behavior Analysis*, 11, pp. 189–196.

HORNER, R.H. & BELLAMY, G.T. (Eds) (1980) *Habilitation of severely and profoundly retarded adults*, Vol. 3, Specialized Training Program, Monograph Number 2, College of Education, University of Oregon, Eugene, Oregon.

HUCK, S.W., CORMIER, W.H. & BOUNDS, W.G. (1974) *Reading Statistics and Research* (New York, Harper & Row).

JONES, R.R., VAUGHT, R.S. & REID, J.B. (1975) Time-series analysis as a substitute for single-subject analysis of variance designs, in: PATTERSON, G.R., MARKS, I.M., MATARAZZO, J.D., MYERS, R.A., SCHWARTZ, G.E. & STRUPP, H.H. (Eds) *Behavior Change* (Chicago, Aldine).

JONES, R.R., VAUGHT, R.S. & WEINROTT, M. (1977) Time series analysis in operant research, *Journal of Applied Behavior Analysis*, 10, pp. 151–166.

JONES, R.R., WEINROTT, M.R. & VAUGHT, R.S. (1978) Effects of serial dependency on the agreement between visual and statistical inference, *Journal of Applied Behavior Analysis*, 11, pp. 277–283.

KAZDIN, A.E. (1976) Statistical analyses for single-case experimental designs, in: HERSEN, M. & BARLOW, D.H. (Eds) *Single-Case Experimental Designs: Strategies for Studying Behaviour Change* (Oxford, Pergamon Press).

KAZDIN, A.E. (1977) Artifact, bias and complexity of assessment: The ABC's of reliability, *Journal of Applied Behavior Analysis*, 10, pp. 141–150.

KAZDIN, A.E. (1979) Unobtrusive measures in behavioural assessment, *Journal of Applied Behavior Analysis*, 12, pp. 713–724.

KAZDIN, A.E. (1981) External validity and single-case experimentation: Issues and limitations (A response to J.S. Birnbrauer), *Analysis and Intervention in Developmental Disabilities*, 1, pp. 133–143.

KAZDIN, A.E. & BOOTZIN, R. (1972) The token economy: an evaluative review, *Journal of Applied Behavior Analysis*, 5, pp. 343–372.

KAZDIN, A.E. & HARTMANN, D.P. (1978) The simultaneous-treatment design, *Behavior Therapy*, 9, pp. 912–922.

KELLY, M.B. (1977) A review of the observational data-collection and reliability procedures reported in *The Journal of Applied Behavior Analysis*, 1977, *Journal of Applied Behavior Analysis*, 10, pp. 97–102.

KENT, R.N., O'LEARY, K.D., DIETZ, A. & DIAMENT, C. (1979) Comparison of observational recordings in vivo, via mirror, and via television, *Journal of Applied Behavior Analysis*, 12, pp. 517–522.

KESELMAN, H.J. & LEVENTHAL, L. (1974) Concerning the statistical procedures enumerated by Gentile *et al.*: another perspective, *Journal of Applied Behavior Analysis*, 7, pp. 643–645.

KOLKO, D.J., DORSETT, P.G. & MILAN, M.A. (1981) A total-assessment approach to the evaluation of social skills training: the effectiveness of an anger control program for adolescent psychiatric patients, *Behavioral Assessment*, 3, pp. 383–402.

KRATOCHWILL, T.R. (1978) Foundations of time-series research, in: KRATOCHWILL, T.R. (Ed.) *Single Subject Research Strategies for Evaluating Change* (New York, Academic Press).

KRATOCHWILL, T.R., ALDEN, K., DEMUTH, D. DAWSON, D., PANICUCCI, C., ARNTSON, P., MCMURRAY, N., HEMPSTEAD, J. & LEVIN, J. (1974) A further consideration in the application of an analysis of variance model for the intrasubject replication design, *Journal of Applied Behavior Analysis*, 7, pp. 629–633.

KRATOCHWILL, T.R. & WETZEL, R.J. (1977) Observer agreement, credibility, and judgment: some considerations in presenting observer agreement data, *Journal of Applied Behavior Analysis*, 10, pp. 133–145.

LEITENBERG, H. (1973) The use of single-case methodology in psychotherapy research, *Journal of Abnormal Psychology*, 82, pp. 87–101.

LEWIN, L.M. & WAKEFIELD, J.A. (1979) Percentage agreement and phi: a conversion table, *Journal of Applied Behavior Analysis*, 12, pp. 299–301.

MICHAEL, J. (1974) Statistical inference for individual organism research: mixed blessing or curse?, *Journal of Applied Behavior Analysis*, 7, pp. 647–653.

MURPHY, R.J. & BRYAN, A.J. (1980) Multiple-baseline and multiple-probe designs: practical alternatives for special education assessment and evaluation, *Journal of Special Education*, 14, pp. 325–335.

NELSON, R.D. & HAYES, S.C. (1979) The nature of behavior assessment: a commentary, *Journal of Applied Behavior Analysis*, 12, pp. 491–500.

NUTTER, D. & REID, D. (1978) Teaching retarded women a clothing selection skill using community norms, *Journal of Applied Behavior Analysis*, 11, pp. 475–488.

O'CONNOR, P., STUCK, G. & WYNE, M. (1979) Effects of a short-term resource room program on test orientation and achievement, *Journal of Special Education*, 13, pp. 375–385.

O'LEARY, K.D. & O'LEARY, S.G. (1972) & (1977) *Classroom Management: the Successful Use of Behavior Modification* (New York, Pergamon Press).

PAGE, T.J., IWATA, B.A. & NEEF, N.A. (1976) Teaching pedestrian skills to retarded persons: Generalization from the classroom to the natural environment, *Journal of Applied Behavior Analysis*, 9, pp. 433–444.

PARSONSON, B.S. & BAER, D.M. (1978) The analysis and presentation of graphic data, in: KRATOCHWILL, T.R. (Ed.) *Single Subject Research Strategies for Evaluating Change* (New York, Academic Press).

PIERSAL, W.C. & KRATOCHWILL, T.R. (1981) A teacher-implemented contingency management package to assess and treat selective mutism, *Behavioral Assessment*, 3, pp. 371–382.

RAST, J., JOHNSTON, J.M., DRUM, C. & CONRIN, J. (1981) The relation of food quantity to ruminating behavior, *Journal of Applied Behavior Analysis*, 14, pp. 121–130.

REVUSKY, S.H. (1967) Some statistical treatments compatible with individual organism methodology, *Journal of the Experimental Analysis of Behavior*, 10, pp. 319–330.

RUSSO, D.C. & KOEGEL, R.L. (1977) A method for integrating an autistic child into a normal public school classroom, *Journal of Applied Behavior Analysis*, 10, pp. 579–590.

SCHREIBMAN, L. & CARR, E. (1978) Elimination of echolalic responding to questions through the training of generalized verbal response, *Journal of Applied Behavior Analysis*, 11, pp. 453–464.

SEMB, G., HOPKINS, B.L. & HURSH, D.E. (1973) The effects of study questions and grades on student test performance in a college course, *Journal of Applied Behavior Analysis*, 6, pp. 631–642.

SHINE, L.C. & BOWER, S.M. (1971) A one-way analysis of variance for single-subject designs, *Educational and Psychological Measurement*, 31, pp. 105–113.

SIDMAN, M. (1960) *Tactics of Scientific Research: Evaluating Experimental Data in Psychology* (New York, Basic Books).

SULZER-AZAROFF, B. & MAYER, G.R. (1977) *Applying Behavior Analysis Procedures with Children and Youth* (New York, Holt, Rinehardt & Winston).

ULMAN, J.D. & SULZER-AZAROFF, B. (1975) Multi-element baseline design in educational research, in: RAMP, E. & SEMB, G. (Eds) *Behavior Analysis: Areas of Research and Application* (Englewood Cliffs, New Jersey, Prentice Hall).

VOGELSBERG, T. & RUSCH, F.R. (1979) Training three severely handicapped young adults to walk, look and cross uncontrolled intersections, *AAESPH Review*, 4, pp. 264–273.

WALKER, H. & BUCKLEY, W. (1972) Programming generalization and maintenance of treatment effects across time and across settings, *Journal of Applied Behavior Analysis*, 5, pp. 209–224.

WELLS, K.C., CONNERS, C.K., IMBER, L. & DELAMATER, A. (1981) Use of single-subject methodology in clinical decision-making with a hyperactive child on the psychiatric inpatient unit, *Behavioral Assessment*, 3, pp. 359–369.

WHITE, O.R. & HARING, N.G. (1980) *Exceptional Teaching* (Ohio, Charles Merrill).

WONG, S.E. & LIBERMAN, R.P. (1981) Mixed single-subject designs in clinical research: variations of the multiple-baseline, *Behavioral Assessment*, 3, pp. 297–306.

YELTON, A.R., WILDMAN, B.G. & ERICKSON, M.T. (1977) A probability-based formula for calculating interobserver agreement, *Journal of Applied Behavior Analysis*, 10, pp. 127–132.

An Observation Procedure for Assessing Children's Social Behaviours in Free Play Settings

KEITH D. BALLARD

ABSTRACT *An observation system yielding information on children's social behaviours in free play settings together with procedures for training observers to achieve reliable data is described. Assessment of social involvement in play activities using the Parten Scale is combined with frequency and topographic information on social interactions to describe individual child behaviour while simultaneous observation of three children gives comparison data against which to evaluate behaviours of a target child. Results from observations of three children in each of three kindergartens over twelve sessions showed high interobserver reliability with validity indicated by data discriminating teacher identified low socially involved children from randomly selected comparison children. Sensitivity to the effects of intervention was also shown and examples given of the use of the procedures in clinical assessment. Data from an evaluation of the effects of priority coding versus recording of all codes in each interval showed priority coding to give conservative data on social involvement in play, and this must be set against additional observer training necessitated by the more complex procedures when using the system.*

Introduction

The observation of children in natural settings is a valuable source of data on child behaviour (Bijou *et al.*, 1969; Wright, 1960), and the activities of young children in preschools have in particular attracted the interest of child psychologists over a long period of time (e.g. Parten, 1932; Green, 1933; Wahler, 1967; Leiter, 1977).

Various approaches to observational assessment such as the life history record of the diary description (Wright, 1960) and the molecular analysis of the ethologist (Smith & Connolly, 1972) have contributed to a descriptive account of child social behaviour and development. While each procedure has advantages and disadvantages as regards the validity and reliability of the material generated (Strain, Cooke & Apolloni, 1976; Wright, 1960), behavioural observation procedures have been used increasingly in descriptive (e.g. Cunningham & Barkley, 1979; Reuter & Yunik, 1973) and experimental studies (Essa, 1978; Thomson, Holmberg & Baer,

1978) and have been subjected to empirical methodological scrutiny (Johnson & Bolstad, 1973; Kent & Foster, 1977; O'Leary & Kent, 1977).

The assessment procedures presented in this paper deriving from the approach of applied behaviour analysis (Baer, Wolf & Risley, 1968; Bijou, 1979), emphasise the collection of behavioural data in natural settings (Johnson & Bolstad, 1973) and attention to precision and reliability in observation procedures. Essa (1978) and Moore (1978) have recently suggested the value of behavioural observation and analysis for studying child activities and for evaluating teaching strategies and teacher training programmes in the preschool. As Gewirtz (1978) has argued, however, this is not to suggest that this level of analysis or conceptual complexity is necessarily more appropriate than another across all problem areas. Rather, it is argued here that behavioural procedures have two particularly valuable features. First, in providing objective, quantifiable data; and secondly, in allowing the same procedures to be used for both descriptive and experimental field studies, so that data and empirical terms used in these two areas are directly comparable and interchangeable (Bijou, Peterson & Ault, 1968).

The observation procedures described in this paper were developed as a result of an interest in studying young children's social behaviour during free play in natural settings. A related concern was to evaluate intervention strategies designed for children who showed low levels of social involvement with peers. Research evaluating such interventions has typically used a variety of dependent measures creating difficulties in relating studies one to another (Thelen *et al.*, 1979). Of greater concern, however, has been Gottman's criticism of measurement in this area where he notes a lack of detail in coding systems, a failure to control observer bias, drift and decay, and the use of error prone time sampling procedures (Gottman, 1977). Also, both Gottman and Hohaus & Prior (1980) have criticised the often used frequency measures of peer interaction as inadequate by themselves for describing children's social behaviours.

The procedures presented here were designed in an attempt to resolve some of the problems of observation in free play settings and to meet a need noted by Gottman (1977), among others (Van Hasselt *et al.*, 1979), for more detailed and discriminating observation systems to assess social behaviours in the natural environment. A free play setting is defined here as an environment in which a group of children has access to a variety of materials and may spend as much or as little time as they choose at available activities. While adults are present and may join in discussion, play with the children or replenish materials, they do not organise or direct activities.

Observation Definitions and Procedures

Two areas of potential data on social behaviour that behaviour observation procedures have focused on have been children's social interactions (e.g. O'Connor, 1969; Strain, Shores & Kerr, 1976) and ratings of social involvement in play activities (Wintre & Webster, 1974). The procedures to be described here combine these two approaches. While reciprocal interactions provide important data on social behaviour an evaluation of qualitative aspects of children's play provides additional information on children's engagement with their social environment.

The observation procedures were designed to provide both a measure of frequency of interaction for each child over the observation period and to provide topographic details of interactions. The advantages of a frequency measure have been noted by

Kazdin (1978) and include a ready reflection of changes in behaviour over time (see also Bijou *et al.*, 1969; Reuter & Yunik, 1973) and sensitivity to alterations in environmental contingencies.

(1) *Assessment of Social Interaction*

Social interaction is here defined in terms of a dyadic interchange between two individuals emphasising a reciprocal conceptualisation of social behaviour (Strain *et al.*, 1976, p. 87; Strain & Shores, 1977). The interaction definitions used here combine those used by Walker & Hops (1976), Hops, Walker & Greenwood (1977) and Strain *et al.* (1976), with additional codes to indicate sharing and interactions involving adults. The interaction codes and definitions are as follows:

An interaction, I, is defined as a reciprocal interchange between two individuals involving; (a) a directed social stimulus (initiation) by one child, and (b) an observable response to that stimulus by another child. When the target child initiates the interaction an arrow is directed away from the code letter and when the target child responds to another person's initiation the observer records the arrow pointing towards the code letter. The first interaction that occurs in an observation interval is coded so that the code shows either an interaction from or to the target child. When the interaction involves speech the letter V, for verbal, is included. A positive verbal interaction is defined as talking or whispering to another child, or listening to another child, and a plus sign is recorded. A negative verbal interaction is defined as talking with angry facial features or gestures and shouting, and involves a minus sign recorded next to V. Whenever speech occurs a verbal interaction is coded. Where speech does not occur there are two non-verbal interaction codes, G and MG.

When the target child gives someone something or receives something from someone; or pours something into a child's hands or into a container s/he is holding, or receives water or sand poured in this way; and neither child says anything, the code G is used. This code defines sharing and as sharing is always a positive interaction no positive or negative sign is needed. The other non-verbal interaction code is MG, for motor-gestural movements. MG positive is defined as affectionate physical contact (hug, hold hands) wave or other communicative gesture which is responded to by another. MG negative is defined as hitting, kicking, non-playful pushing, grabbing an object from someone, or destroying someone's construction while they are present.

Finally, whenever an adult initiates or receives an interaction, the code A is included.

(2) *Assessment of Social Involvement in Play*

Evaluation of the extent of social involvement in children's play is achieved in the observation procedures using the play categories developed by Parten (1932). The Parten Scale has been shown to yield play activity data with high interrater reliability (Parten, 1932; Wintre & Webster, 1974). Also, as Wintre & Webster (1974) note, the scale is compatible with Piaget's developmental theory (Piaget, 1932), and received endorsement in the child development literature (Ausubel & Sullivan, 1970; Hartup, 1970).

The Parten Scale is used here with slight modification. In the development of the observation procedures presented here it was found that additional specification of presence of play equipment for the second Parten play category, and absence of play equipment for category one and three, plus specification of duration of category three, Onlooker, improved inter-observer agreement with the interval time sampling procedure used. The six categories of the scale are Unoccupied behaviour, Solitary independent play, Onlooker, Parallel activity, Associative play and Cooperative play. Detailed definitions are presented in Table 1.

TABLE I. Code letters and definitions for the Parten play categories

U UNOCCUPIED BEHAVIOUR
This child apparently is not playing, but is occupied with watching anything that happens to be of momentary interest. When there is nothing exciting taking place, s/he plays with her/his own body, gets on and off chairs, just stands around, follows the teacher, or sits in one spot glancing around the room. The child does not have play equipment.

S SOLITARY INDEPENDENT PLAY
The child plays alone and independently with toys that are different from those used by the children within speaking distance and makes no effort to get close to other children. S/he pursues her/his own activity without reference to what others are doing. The child has play equipment.

O ONLOOKER
The child spends most of her/his time watching the other children play. S/he often talks to the children whom s/he is observing, asks questions, or gives suggestions, but does not overtly enter into the play her/himself. This type differs from the unoccupied in that the onlooker is definitely observing particular groups of children rather than anything that happens to be exciting. The child stands or sits within speaking distance of the group so that s/he can see and hear everything that takes place. The child does not have play equipment and to be coded ONLOOKER would behave as defined for the entire 10-second observation interval.

P PARALLEL ACTIVITY
The child plays independently, but the activity s/he chooses naturally brings her/him among other children. S/he plays with toys that are like those which the children around her/him are using but s/he plays with the toy as s/he sees fit and does not try to influence or modify the activity of the children near her/him. S/he plays beside rather than with the other children. There is no attempt to control the coming or going of children in the group.

A ASSOCIATIVE PLAY
The child plays with other children. The conversation concerns the common activity; there is borrowing and loaning of play material; following one another with trains or wagons; mild attempts to control which children may or may not play in the group. All the members engage in similar if not identical activity; there is no divisions of labour, and no organisation of the activity of several individuals around any material goal or product. The children do not subordinate their individual interests to that of the group; instead each child acts as s/he wishes. By her/his conversation with the other children one can tell that her/his interest is primarily in her/his associations, not in her/his activity. Occasionally, two or three children are engaged in no activity of any duration, but are merely doing whatever happens to draw the attention of any of them.

C COOPERATIVE OR ORGANISED SUPPLEMENTARY PLAY
The child plays in a group that is organised for the purpose of making some material product, or of striving to attain some competitive goal, or of dramatising situations of adult and group life, or of playing formal games. There is a marked sense of belonging or of not belonging to the group. The control of the group situation is in the hands of one or two of the members who direct the activity of the others. The goal as well as the method of attaining it necessitates a division of labour, taking of different roles by the various group members and the organisation of activity so that the efforts of one child are supplemented by those of another.

A concise summary of information from the play categories can be achieved by calculating a Play Score for each child for each observation session. The Play Score is calculated by weighting the Parten categories from one, Unoccupied, to six, Cooperative play, multiplying the number of occurrences in each category by its weighting, summing these scores, and dividing by the total number of occurrences.

(3) *Observation Procedures*

Observation in natural settings poses problems affecting both the observer and the setting. The present procedures were designed to sample behaviours across a period of about 30 minutes. This was found to be optimal both in terms of observer fatigue and in terms of the time available for free play in various settings. In New Zealand kindergartens, for example, after such a period of free play some structure is imposed by teachers in the form of story reading, music or other adult-directed activites.

The observation procedures were designed using interval time sampling and recording to achieve reliable data on simultaneously observed behaviours (Doke, 1976; Mann, 1976). A ten second observation interval is followed by a five second interval for recording, an electronic timer attached to one observer's clip-board emitting auditory signals of different pitch for each interval via earpieces for both observers. It was found that in an active free play setting with up to 40 children engaged in both indoor and outdoor play, searching for a different child each 15 seconds was both demanding and time-consuming. This problem was resolved by grouping observations on each child into sets of four so that a change to the next subject occurred after 60 seconds making location of children less onerous over the entire period. This modification still retained sequential time sampling which has been shown to be less open to error than contiguous sampling across a session (Thomson *et al.*, 1978).

The procedures involve observation of three children in each observation session with each child being observed for 36 intervals per session. Because of the overall complexity of observation within an active natural setting the procedures were initially designed with a priority coding system such that when an interaction occurred during an interval this was recorded and when no interaction occurred the child's play activity was rated on the Parten Scale and this recorded. Priority coding is a common procedure when the goal is to record as much as possible of observed behaviour but to do so using a manageable number of behavioural categories (Jones, Reid & Patterson, 1974). There are however, advantages, noted in detail below, in having observers code both interactions when they occur and a play category in every interval so long as training is sufficient to allow observers to code in five seconds from eleven possible alternatives (six play categories and up to five components of interaction). While research reported in this paper is based on the priority coding system, data are also presented below comparing the two procedures.

(4) *Observer Reliability and Accuracy*

In applied behaviour analysis the term observer reliability has been used interchangeably with the term interobserver agreement. Despite the fact that observer agreement does not necessarily imply consistency in measurement in the traditional psychometric sense of reliability (Johnson & Bolstad, 1973) the two terms are commonly used to refer to agreement between observers who independently record responses at the same time in the same setting (Kazdin, 1978) and are so used here.

Interpretation of agreement between two observers may be influenced by a variety of factors and the following tactics have been used with the observation procedures described in this paper, to reduce possibly confounding events. Following training, observers may drift from original response definitions either individually or within pairs (O'Leary & Kent, 1973). One procedure that may help control drift involves pairing each observer with independent observers regularly throughout the study (Lipinski & Nelson, 1974). Also, when observers are directed not to discuss their observation record sheets with each other or with the reliability person (O'Leary & Kent, 1973), are not allowed to tally their own data (Johnson & Bolstad, 1973), and are not provided with feedback on assessment of agreement (Johnson & Bolstad, 1973), there is some assurance that they are independently applying the behaviour definitions and that interobserver agreement scores reflect the assessment of two independent observers.

Observer bias and observer reactivity pose futher possible threats to the validity of observational data. Observer bias occurs when the observer has attitudes or information regarding the subjects under study (Johnson & Bolstad, 1973). To reduce the probability or degree of bias observers should be selected for and further trained in scientific integrity, encouraged to reveal hypotheses they may have regarding the study and should not be provided with information concerning subjects or experimental procedures (Haynes, 1978; Johnson & Bolstad, 1973). Observer reactivity refers to changes in the behaviour of the subject as a result of being observed. Reduction of potentially confounding influences in this area may be achieved by ensuring that observers remain as inconspicuous as possible, controlling observer characteristics such as dress (Johnson & Bolstad, 1973) and training observers not to interact with children or adults in the setting of interest. Also, whenever possible, observers should work in the setting for a period before data collection proper begins to allow children and adults to habituate to observer presence (Johnson & Bolstad, 1973).

Kent & Foster (1977) and Haynes (1978) have stressed the importance of observer training for the accuracy of subsequent behaviour observations. Kent & Foster (1977) recommend that training ensures accuracy in the use of definitions by using criterion protocols and covering the full range of complexities allowed for in the procedures. For the observation procedures described here observers are required to study a training manual containing general instructions and interaction and play category definitions; view a videotape training programme which teaches the observation procedures and the interaction definitions; and to undertake field training in free play settings.

In accord with Kent *et al.'s* (1977) recommendation training focuses on the definition of each behaviour rather than allowing observers to discuss and eventually reach possibly idiosyncratic interpretations of the behaviour category. Each observer is paired with every other observer during field training in an attempt to control for differential drift (Kazdin, 1978) and training continues until greater than 90% agreement is achieved across all pairings. Training is undertaken in free play settings other than those used for data collection.

Results of an Evaluation of the Observation Procedures

(1) *Reliability*

The observation procedures described here were evaluated in a study that involved observing children in each of three kindergartens on four mornings per week for three weeks (Ballard, 1980a). Observations took place during free play and in each setting up to 40 children between 4 years and 4 years 11 months of age, two teachers and two parent helpers were usually present. Children had free movement both to inside and, on fine days, to outside areas and equipment. One child in each kindergarten was identified by the teacher as having low levels of interaction with other children. No discussion is included here on a fourth child identified by his teacher as a possible subject but whose data showed him to have been wrongly selected as displaying low levels of social involvement with others. Two other children in each setting were selected at random from the roll for observation as comparison subjects. The children's ages ranged from 4 years 3 months to 4 years 8 months, mean age 4 years 5 months.

Following a week's training in the use of the observation procedures observers worked in the kindergartens for three days to allow children and staff to become used to their presence. Data collection was then made by three observers with a fourth observer pairing with each in turn to provide reliability checks on 12 occasions. In each observation setting 108 intervals were coded giving a total of 3885 intervals (3 × 108 × 12) coded over the 12 days.

For the 12 sessions in which an observer paired with the reliability observer interobserver agreement for interactions, for play categories and total agreement reliability was calculated using the formula

$$\frac{\text{number of agreements}}{\text{number of agreements and disagreements}} \times \frac{100}{1}.$$

Agreement was reached only when both observers recorded the same category for the Parten scale or coded the same interaction. Where one observer coded an interaction and the other a play category this was counted as a disagreement for interaction. Estimation of reliability thus involved occurrence agreement for both interactions and play category and interval by interval agreement for the overall reliablity calculation.

Agreement for interaction required both observers to have coded the interval with the same direction of interaction (initiated by the target child or that child's response to another's initiation), the same type of interaction, the same quality of interaction (positive or negative) and whether or not an adult was involved. Agreement on interaction therefore required always four and sometimes five identical symbols in one interval.

The mean interobserver agreement for the Parten play categories was 99.45% with a range from 95.93 to 100%. The total number of disagreements and agreements respectively for each play category were as follows; Unoccupied 2/131; Solitary 0/139; Onlooker 1/52; Parallel 0/282; Associative 0/32; Cooperative 2/92.

Interobserver agreement for interaction ranged from 84 to 100% with a mean of 95.30%. Total (interval by interval) agreement ranged from 94 to 100% with a mean of 97.77%.

(2) *Validity*

(a) *Assessment of social interaction and social involvement in play.* Data from the observation procedures may be summarised in several ways. The most concise form involves the total number of interactions for each child per session and the Play Score.

Data from the study referred to above (Ballard, 1980a), is summarised in Table

II. These data show that the observation procedures can discriminate between children identified by teachers as having low levels of social interaction and children randomly selected within the same setting. Also, figures for the target child in each kindergarten show evident changes in responding for post-treatment as against baseline phases, showing the sensitivity of the observation procedures to intervention effects, in this case videotape modelling sequences shown to target children.

Table III presents the interaction components data from the same study. Baseline observations of the target children show them to initiate far fewer interactions than they respond to, whereas the data for the comparison children suggest that a higher proportion of initiated interactions may be the norm. Post-treatment observations show an increase in interactions initiated by target children. It is interesting to note also a marked decrease in adult involvement for S1 following intervention.

TABLE II. Mean number and standard deviation of interactions and mean and standard deviation of Play Scores across observation sessions for one target child and two comparison children in each of three kindergartens

Setting	Child		Interactions		Play Score	
			Mean	SD	Mean	SD
	Target S_1	Baseline	3.0	1.0	1.16	0.07
		Post-treatment	7.66	3.96	2.59	0.53
A	$Comparison_1$		10.42	3.40	3.31	0.72
	$Comparison_2$		18.62	4.27	3.01	0.64
	Target S_2	Baseline	3.0	1.41	2.45	0.92
		Post-treatment	14.0	2.87	3.20	0.91
B	$Comparison_1$		20.5	5.95	3.49	0.46
	$Comparison_2$		17.0	4.18	3.66	0.77
	Target S_3	Baseline	9.1	7.3	2.45	0.50
		Post-treatment	19.0	8.83	2.96	0.81
C	$Comparison_1$		20.16	3.37	3.11	0.40
	$Comparison_2$		11.5	5.04	4.35	0.64

The observation procedures enhance the evaluation of treatment effects obtained by contrasting data from pre- and post-intervention phases by also providing comparison data on randomly selected children observed in the same setting across the same time period. Evaluating the effectiveness of intervention against such normative peer data provides an indication of the social validity of treatment outcomes (Hartman, Roper & Bradford, 1979).

(b) *Evaluation of the effects of priority coding.* As mentioned earlier there is a possible ipsative measurement problem (Jones, 1973; Moore, 1978) when, as occurs in the present recording system, one observation category takes precedence over another. While the validity of the dominant category, in this case interactions, is not in question, measurement of the subordinate category may be affected by the fact that sampling of the subordinate category varies according to the frequency of occurrence of the dominant category. It may not, then, be valid to compare data for the subordinate category across sessions where the frequency of occurrence of the dominant category varies.

Table III. Interaction components as a percentage of total interactions within baseline and post-treatment phases for target children and across all observations for comparison children

	Target								Comparison							
	→				←				→				←			
	V	G	MG	A	V	G	MG	A	V	G	MG	A	V	G	MG	A
S1																
baseline	0	0	0	0	89	0	11	78	C1							
									58	0	1	12	39	0	2	10
									C2							
									51	0	2	10	47	0	0	11
Post-treatment	25	0	0	2	67	7	0	22								
S2																
baseline	33	0	0	0	58	0	8	8	C1							
									49	0	5	4	42	0	4	6
									C2							
									57	0	0	1	43	0	0	4
Post-treatment	54	0	0	2	45	0	1	8								
S3																
baseline	38	0	5	3	54	0	3	5	C1							
									45	0	5	1	45	0	4	1
									C2							
									71	0	2	5	25	0	2	6
Post-treatment	63	0	2	7	34	0	0	5								

Key
→ interaction initiated by S.
← interaction initiated by other child to S.
V verbal interaction.
G sharing interaction.
MG motor-gestural interaction.
A adult interaction.

In both the study referred to earlier and in a later series of observations of 19 children over 26 weeks (Ballard, 1981), the Play Score seemed to reflect accurately the social component of the children's play. For example, a child might have both a low number of interactions (around zero to five) and a low Play Score (around one to two) if mostly unoccupied or alone.

Also observed was a relatively high number of interactions (10 or more) perhaps with one other child, yet a relatively low Play Score as a result of periods of limited social play. Some children will remain at an activity when joined by one other child and will interact with that child but move away to an unoccupied area when more children approach. Another pattern observed is a high Play Score (four and above) resulting from involvement in associative and cooperative activities yet a relatively low frequency of interaction. For active, socially involved children, however, both a high Play Score (four and above) and high frequency of interaction (often 20 and above) can be recorded.

To check on the possibility of the Play Score being variously affected by the number of intervals in which a play category is recorded, a series of observations were undertaken in which trained observers working in pairs recorded a play category in all observation intervals. That is, whenever an interaction occurred this was recorded as usual, but in addition a play category for that interval was also recorded. These data were compared with that which would have been obtained using the established procedure of recording a play category only when no interaction occurred in the observation interval. Observations continued until examples were obtained varying from low to high frequency of interactions. The results, presented in Table IV, are for observations where inter-observer agreement was 100% for both interactions and play categories, that is both observers agreed on all codes in every interval.

It is evident from Table IV that a difference between the Play Score calculated by the priority method and the Play Score calculated by the all intervals method is more likely to occur when interaction frequency is above 17 than when interaction frequency levels are lower. In most instances where a discrepancy occurs the priority method gives a lower Play Score than the all intervals method. It would seem that higher interaction frequencies do not allow an adequate sampling of play activities. For the data in Table IV the correlation of interactions and the priority method Play Score was negligible at 0.01 while the correlation of interactions and the all intervals method Play Score was 0.32, suggesting a modest relationship between these two measures. Using the observation system, then, one must balance problems in observer training and fatigue involved in coding play categories in all intervals against a conservative estimate of the Play Score that arises from the priority coding system.

Obviously it might also be considered that the priority coding system used with the interaction codes could be replaced with coding of all features of each interaction. This, however, would require the observer to considerably increase the judgements made discriminating non-verbal and verbal components of the interaction and require recording of an increased number of codes. The combined effect would undoubtedly challenge inter-observer reliability and the investigator interested in such fine-grained analysis might consider alternative observation strategies such as those of the ethologist (e.g. Smith & Connolly, 1972).

(c) *Use in clinical assessment.* In addition to their use in studies of children in pre-school settings the observation procedures have been found valuable as part of the psychological assessment of five- and six-year-olds. For example data on the

TABLE IV. Social interaction frequencies and their corresponding Play Scores calculated from the priority coding method and the all intervals coding method

Number of interactions	Play score priority method	Play score all intervals method	Difference	Number of Interactions	Play score priority method	Play score all intervals method	Difference
1	3.37	3.38	0.01	13	3.08	3.25	0.17
1	3.65	3.66	0.01	14	3.30	3.55	0.25
2	3.23	3.30	0.07	14	3.54	3.80	0.26
3	3.82	3.84	0.02	14	3.82	4.00	0.18
4	2.69	2.64	−0.05	16	3.10	3.10	0
5	3.24	3.20	−0.04	16	2.85	3.02	0.17
6	3.03	3.0	−0.03	17	3.44	3.22	−0.22
6	3.12	3.33	0.21	17	2.89	3.41	0.52
6	3.96	3.79	−0.17	17	3.50	3.22	−0.28
7	4.0	4.0	0	18	3.44	2.80	−0.64
7	2.65	2.80	0.15	18	3.33	3.58	0.25
8	2.86	3.02	0.16	18	3.50	3.22	−0.28
8	2.25	2.19	−0.06	19	3.88	3.57	−0.31
9	3.33	3.33	0	21	2.81	3.00	0.19
9	3.59	3.44	−0.15	22	2.93	3.55	0.62
10	2.85	3.05	0.2	23	2.76	3.30	0.54
10	2.81	2.88	0.07	23	2.75	3.60	0.85
10	3.57	3.30	−0.27	24	3.08	3.14	0.06
11	3.0	3.4	0.4	26	2.27	3.25	0.98
11	3.56	3.61	0.05	26	2.10	3.33	1.23
12	3.37	3.75	0.38	28	3.87	4.27	0.4
12	2.96	2.92	0.04	33	5.00	5.00	0

behaviour of a child in a special facility are compared with data collected on children in a regular classroom setting to determine what intervention, if any, would be necessary to facilitate the child's adjustment to the social environment of that mainstream setting. The observation procedures have also been used in the evaluation of a programme designed to teach interaction and play skills to two six-year-olds as part of the regular classroom programme (Ballard & Jenner, 1981).

The procedures involve simultaneous observation of three children and it was intended that one child in particular be of interest while observation of two others provides comparison data. Hartman *et al.* (1979) suggested the value of normative information in behavioural assessment for identification of problematic performance and for indicating the social validity of treatment outcomes. Similarly, O'Leary & Drabman (1971), Johnson *et al.* (1973) and Greenwood *et al.* (1977) have argued for the value of normative peer data against which to compare behaviour considered deviant, or against which to evaluate the effectiveness of intervention for a particular child, while Walker & Hops (1976) argue that comparisons combine with an experimental demonstration of intervention effectiveness to add evidence for practical significance and meaningfulness. Observation procedures providing comparison data and that can be used to generate normative data are also of considerable value in clinical child psychology in such areas as mainstreaming the handicapped in educational settings (Walker & Hops, 1976; Wilton & Densem, 1977). It is, however, important to recognise the warning of Mash & Terdal (1976) that while normative data may provide broad guidelines for terminal levels of behaviour change they should not be used to indicate what an individual should do.

Discussion

This paper has described an observation system and procedures for training observers in its use that gives detailed information on children's social behaviours in natural free play settings. An assessment of children's social involvement in play activities combines with topographic and frequency information on social interactions to give a more complete account of social behaviour than can be achieved by assessing either of these dimensions alone. Simultaneous observation of three children provides for comparison data against which to evaluate the behaviour of a target child.

Results from a study using the procedures showed high levels of observer reliability. The validity of the procedures is suggested in their ability to discriminate children selected by teachers as having low levels of social involvement with peers from children randomly selected within the same setting. Sensitivity to the effects of intervention was also shown, and examples of the use of observation procedures in clinical assessment were given.

A possible threat to validity from the priority coding system was evaluated and shown to exist in the form of a slightly conservative assessment of social involvement in play at high interaction frequency levels. Users of the procedures would need to weigh this effect against additional observer training and work effort demanded by the alternative coding strategy.

Acknowledgements

Research reported here was supported by University of Otago Research Committee Grant No. 37–877, and Mental Health Foundation of New Zealand Research Grant

No. R17. The assistance of the Dunedin Free Kindergarten Association and the participating teachers is gratefully acknowledged. Thanks are due also to Dr L. Nelson, University of Otago and Mr D. Moore, University of Papua New Guinea for helpful comments on this paper.

REFERENCE NOTES

BALLARD, K.D. (1980b) Symbolic modelling for preschool children with low social interactions and low peer involvement in play, *unpublished manuscript*, University of Otago, New Zealand.

HOHAUS, L. & PRIOR, M. (1980) Social behaviour in preschool children: a comparison of measures, *unpublished manuscript*, Department of Psychology, La Trobe University, Australia.

MOORE, D.W. (1978) Time sample observations: an examination of variables affecting naturalistic behaviour observation data obtained by time sampling procedures, *unpublished dissertation*, Department of Education, University of Auckland, New Zealand.

REFERENCES

AUSUBEL, D.P. & SULLIVAN, E.V. (1970) *Theory and Problems of Child Development* (New York, Grune & Stratton).

BAER, D.M., WOLF, M.M. & RISLEY, T.R. (1968) Some current dimensions of applied behaviour analysis, *Journal of Applied Behaviour Analysis*, 1, pp. 91–97.

BALLARD, K.D. (1980a) An assessment of a symbolic modelling procedure in the treatment of socially withdrawn preschool children, in; *Proceedings of the Third Australian Conference on Behaviour Modification* (Melbourne, Australian Association for Behaviour Modification).

BALLARD, K.D. & JENNER, L. (1981) Establishing correspondence between saying and doing as a procedure for increasing the social behaviours of two elementary school children, *The Exceptional Child*, 28, pp. 55–63.

BIJOU, S.W. (1979) Some clarifications on the meaning of a behaviour analysis of child development, *The Psychological Record*, 29, pp. 3–13.

BIJOU, S.W., PETERSON, R.F. & AULT, M. (1968) A method to integrate descriptive and experimental field studies at the level of data and empirical concepts, *Journal of Applied Behaviour Analysis*, 1, pp. 175–191.

BIJOU, S.W., PETERSEN, R.F., HARRIS, F.R., ALLEN, K.E. & JOHNSTON, M.S. (1969) Methodology for experimental studies of young children in natural settings, *The Psychological Record*, 19, pp. 177–210.

CUNNINGHAM, C.E. & BARKLEY, R.A. (1979) The interactions of normal and hyperactive children with their mothers in free play and structural tasks, *Child Development*, 50, pp. 217–224.

DOKE, L. (1976) Assessment of children's behavioral deficits, in: HERSEN, M. & BELLACK, A.S. (Eds) *Behavioral assessment: a practical handbook*, pp. 493–536 (New York, Pergamon Press).

ESSA, E.L. (1978) The preschool: setting for applied behavior analysis research, *Review of Educational Research*, 48, pp. 537–575.

GEWIRTZ, J.L. (1978) Social learning in early human development, in: CATANIA, A.C. & BRIGHAM, T.A. (Eds) *Handbook of Applied Behavior Analysis: social and instructional processes*, pp. 105–139 (New York, Irvington Publishers).

GOTTMAN, J. (1977) The effects of a modelling film on social isolation in preschool children: a methodological investigation, *Journal of Abnormal Child Psychology*, 5, pp. 69–78.

GREEN, E.H. (1933) Friendships and quarrels among preschool children, *Child Development*, 4, pp. 237–252.

GREENWOOD, C.R., WALKER, H.M. & HOPS, H. (1977) Sôme issues in social interaction/withdrawal assessment, *Exceptional Children*, 43, pp. 490–499.

HARTUP, W.W. (1970) Peer interaction and social organisation, in: MUSSEN, P.H. (Ed.) *Carmichaels Manual of Child Psychology*, 3rd edn, Vol. 2, pp. 361–456 (New York, Wiley).

HARTMAN, D.P., ROPER, B.L. & BRADFORD, D.C. (1979) Some relationships between behavioral and traditional assessment, *Journal of Behavioral Assessment*, 1, pp. 3–21.

HAYNES, S.N. (1978) *Principles of Behavioral Assessment* (New York, Gardner Press).

HOPS, H., WALKER, H.M. & GREENWOOD, C.R. (1977) Peers: a programme for remediating social withdrawal in the school setting: aspects of a research and development process, *Report No. 33*, October, Centre at Oregon for Research in the Behavioral Education of the Handicapped, University of Oregon.

JOHNSON, S.M. & BOLSTAD, O.D. (1973) Methodological issues in naturalistic observation: some problems and solutions for field research, in: HAMERLYNCK, L.A., HANDY, L.C. & MASH, E.J. (Eds) *Behavior change: methodology concepts and practice. The Fourth Banff International Conference on Behavioral Modification*, pp. 7–67 (Champaign, Illinois, Research Press).

JOHNSON, S.M., WAHL, G., MARTIN, S. & JOHANSSEN, S. (1973) How deviant is the normal child: a behavioral analysis of the preschool child and his family, in: RUBIN, R.D., BRADY, J.r0P. & HENDERSON, J.D. (Eds) *Advances in Behavior Therapy*, Vol. 4, pp. 37–54 (New York, Academic Press).

JONES, R.R. (1973) Behavioral observation and frequency data: problems in scoring, analysis and interpretation, in: HAMERLYNCK, L.A., HANDY, L.C. & MASH, E.J. (Eds) *Behavior Change: methodology, concepts and practice*, pp. 119–148 (Champaign, Illinois, Research Press).

JONES, R.R., REID, J.B. & PATTERSON, G.R. (1974) Naturalist observation in clinical assessment, in: MCREYNOLDS, P. (Ed.) *Advances in Psychological Assessment*, Vol. 3, pp. 42–95 (San Francisco, Jossey Bass).

KAZDIN, A.E. (1978) Methodology of applied behavior analysis, in: CATANIA, A.C. & BRIGHAM, T.A. (Eds) *Handbook of Applied Behavior Analysis: social and instructional processes*, pp. 61–103 (New York, Irvington Publishers).

KENT, R.M. & FOSTER, S.L. (1977) Direct observational procedures: methodological issues in naturalistic settings, in: CIMINERO, A.R., CALHOUN, K.S. & ADAMS, H.E. (Eds) *Handbook of Behavioral Assessment*, pp. 279–328 (New York, Wiley).

KENT, R.M. KANOWITZ, J., O'LEARY, K.D. & CHEIKEN, M. (1977) Observer reliability as a function of circumstances of assessment, *Journal of Applied Behavior Analysis*, 10, pp. 317–324.

LEITER, M.P. (1977) A study of reciprocity in preschool play groups, *Child Development*, 48, pp. 1208–1295.

LIPINSKI, D. & NELSON, R. (1974) Problems in the use of naturalistic observation as a means of behavioral assessment, *Behavior Therapy*, 5, pp. 341–351.

MANN, R. (1976) Assessment of behavioral excesses in children, in: HERSEN, M. & BELLACK, A.S. (Eds) *Behavioral Assessment: a practical handbook*, pp. 459–492 (New York, Pergamon Press).

MASH, E.J. & TERDAL, L.G. (1976) Observational assessment, in: MASH, E.J. & TERDAL, L.G. (Eds) *Behavior Therapy Assessment: diagnosis, design and evaluation*, pp. 262–278 (New York, Springer).

MOORE, S.G. (1978) Commentary on Thomson, C.L., Holmberg, M.C. and Baer, D.M. An experimental analysis of some procedures to teach priming and reinforcement skills to preschool teachers, *Monographs of the Society for Research in Child Development*, 43, Serial No. 176, No. 4, pp. 74–86.

O'CONNOR, R.D. (1969) Modification of social withdrawal through symbolic modelling, *Journal of Applied Behavior Analysis*, 2, pp. 15–22.

O'LEARY, K.D. & DRABMAN, R. (1971) Token reinforcement programs in the classroom; a review, *Psychological Bulletin*, 75, pp. 379–398.

O'LEARY, K.D. & KENT, R. (1973) Behavior modification for social action: research tactics and problems, in: HAMERLYNCK, L.A., HANDY, L.C. & MASH, E.J. (Eds) *Behavior Change: methodology, concepts and practice: The Fourth Banff International Conference on Behavior Modification*, pp. 69–96 (Champaign, Illinois, Research Press).

O'LEARY, K.D. & KENT, R.M. (1977) Source of bias in observational recording, in: ETZEL, B.C., LE BLANC, J.M. & BAER, D.M. (Eds) *New Developments in Behavioral Research: theory, method and application*, pp. 231–236 (Hillsdale, New Jersey, Lawrence Erlbaum).

PARTEN, M.B. (1932) Social participation among preschool children, *Journal of Abnormal and Social Psychology*, 27, pp. 243–269.

PIAGET, J. (1932) *The Moral Judgement of the Child* (trans. by Marjorie Warden) (New York, Harcourt, Brace & Jovanavich).

REUTER, J. & YUNIK, G. (1973) Social interaction in nursery schools, *Developmental Psychology*, 9, pp. 319–325.

SMITH, P.K. & CONNOLLY, K. (1972) Patterns of play and social interaction in preschool children, in: BLURTON-JONES, N. (Ed.) *Ethological Studies of Child Behavior*, pp. 65–95 (Cambridge University Press).

Strain, P.S., Cooke, T.P. & Apolloni, T. (1976) *Teaching Exceptional Children* (New York, Academic Press).

Strain, P.S. & Shores, R.E. (1977) Social reciprocity: a review of research and educational implications, *Exceptional Children*, 43, pp. 526–530.

Strain, P.S., Shores, R.E. & Kerr, M.M. (1976) An experimental analysis of "spillover" effects in the social interaction of behaviorally handicapped preschool children, *Journal of Applied Behavior Analysis*, 9, pp. 31–40.

Thelen, M.H., Fry, R.A., Fehrenback, P.A. & Frautschi, N.M. (1979) Therapeutic videotape and film modelling: a review, *Psychological Bulletin*, 8, pp. 701–720.

Thomson, C.L., Holmberg, M.C. & Baer, D.M. (1978) An experimental analysis of some procedures to teach priming and reinforcement skills to preschool teachers, *Monographs of the Society for Research in Child Development*, 43, Serial No. 176, No. 4.

Van Hasselt, B., Hersen, M., Whitehill, M.B. & Bellack, A.S. (1979) Social skill assessment and training for children: an evaluative review, *Behavior Research and Therapy*, 17, pp. 413–437.

Wahler, R.G. (1967) Child-child interactions in free field settings: Some experimental analyses, *Journal of Experimental Child Psychology*, 5, pp. 278–293.

Walker, H.M. & Hops, H. (1976) Use of normative peer data as a standard for evaluating classroom treatment effects, *Journal of Applied Behavior Analysis*, 9, pp. 159–168.

Wilton, K. & Densem, P. (1977) Social interaction of intellectually handicapped children in integrated and segregated preschools, *The Exceptional Child*, 24, pp. 165–172.

Wintre, M.G. & Webster, C.D. (1974) A brief report on using a traditional social behavior scale with disturbed children. *Journal of Applied Behavior Analysis*, 7, pp. 345–348.

Wright, H.F. (1960) Observational child study, in: Mussen, P.H. (Ed.) *Handbook of Research Methods in Child Development*, pp. 71–139 (New York, Wiley).

The Use of Serial Correlation in the Analysis of Data from Interrupted Time Series Trials with Single Subjects in Educational Research

R. W. MARSH

ABSTRACT *There is need in educational psychology and elsewhere for a simple but reliable technique for analysing data from baseline/intervention type studies with single subjects. The serial-correlation approach is suitable for this purpose and provides not just a test of statistical significance but also an index of the strength of relationship between intervention and any change, as well as an indication of the proportion of the total variance accounted for by the relationship.*

A considerable amount of discussion has been directed to the proper method of analysis of single subject experiments, in educational psychology and elsewhere, which alternate baseline and treatment conditions for fixed periods (see Kratochwill, 1978, for example). The methods advocated range from inspection of the data for 'substantial' effects, to the application of complex mathematical procedures such as spectral analysis.

The case has already been made elsewhere that inspection by itself is insufficient and can be misleading (Gottman & Glass, 1978). One can also accept that there are situations when the application of spectral analysis is warranted, but this requires access to substantial computing power and a sophisticated knowledge of statistics to understand and interpret the analysis properly. Neither of these requirements is usually met by typical educational psychologists, who are becoming frequent users of single subject trials. Perhaps the experimentalist in educational psychology would appreciate a method which indicated whether or not the extra trouble of an even more sophisticated procedure was required.

What would be helpful is a technique in between the two, which is relatively easy to calculate and interpret, that would indicate the size of an effect, its significance or non-significance and whether further analysis might be called for. Broadly speaking serial correlation fits these requirements, when applied appropriately.

Its most common form is the point-biserial correlation usually used in the analysis of test items. It is derived from the product-moment correlation, which is concerned with the degree of relationship between variables represented by two continuous sets of data, but differs in that while it deals with two sets of data only one of them is continuous and the other is dichotomous. In the extended serial correlation form, it can deal with a variable divided into three or four or more categories, the greater the number of categories the closer it approximates the product-moment correlation (see Appendix).

The form most likely to be of use in the present context, however, is the point-biserial, which may be computed quickly from the following formula

$$r_{pb} = \frac{\bar{x}_1 - \bar{x}_2}{\sigma} \sqrt{pq}$$

where $\bar{x}_1$ and $\bar{x}_2$ are the means on the continuous variable for the two categories, p and q are the respective proportions of the sample in the two categories and σ is the standard deviation of the continuous variable.

Its application to the usual baseline intervention design is quite straightforward. The effect of the intervention against the baseline can be tested by simply calculating the point-biserial correlation using each of the baseline/intervention conditions to represent the two categories in the formula. If the design called for an alternation of baseline with the same intervention characteristics, then one can collect all baseline data for one category and all intervention data for the other category and apply the formula as before. If, however, there is more than one treatment effect, there will be at least three categories, which would require the use of the more general serial correlation formula with the appropriate number of categories (see Appendix).

TABLE I. Levels of on-task classroom behaviour of boy under baseline/reinforcement conditions in an ABAB design type study

	Percentage on-task behaviour																					
Session	1	2	3	4	5	6	7	8	9	10	11	12	13	14	15	16	17	18	19	20	21	22
Baseline	45	44	63	45	51	47									90	75	60	65				
Reinforcement							94	91	75	90	75	98	95	86					90	93	77	80

The efficacy of this method is illustrated by applying it to the demonstration data presented in Table I. These sample data relate to the levels of on-task classroom behaviour of a boy in a classic single subject ABAB design. Application of the point-biserial correlation to these data, after combining the two categories for baseline and combining the two categories for reinforcement effects, produces a coefficient of $r_{pb} = 0.77$. For reasonably large samples, say above 30 observations, we can substitute our value in the usual formula to find t, viz:

$$t = \sqrt{N r_{pb}^2}$$

with about N degrees of freedom. For the example data, this gives $t = 3.61$ with about 22 degrees of freedom which is well beyond the value required for significance at the 0.01 level for a one-tailed test. For samples below about 30 observations, one should either interpret the results conservatively, or calculate the conventional *t*-test for comparing the means of two independent groups.

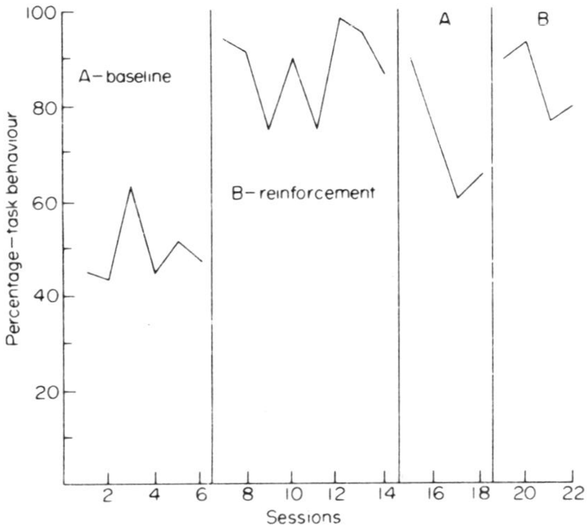

FIG. 1. Levels of on-task behaviour of boy in single subject ABAB design experiment.

Thus we can conclude that nearly 60% (0.77^2) of the variance in the data (found by squaring r_{pb}) is attributable to the experimental effect and that this is highly significant statistically. Clearly serial correlation provides a convenient and useful guide to the meaning of results from studies of this kind. This counters the common criticism of statistical methods, namely that they address themselves only to statistical significance and not to magnitude of effect. It may be particularly valuable in conveying the message of behavioural research to educational researchers, who, whilst familiar with traditional statistical procedures of this kind, are less familiar with behavioural procedures for data analysis.

Acknowledgement

The author is indebted to Ms Christine Ridding for providing the demonstration data used in this paper.

REFERENCES

GOTTMAN, J. & GLASS, G. (1978) Analysis of interrupted time-series experiments, in: KRATOCHWILL, T.R. (Ed.) *Single Subject Research*, pp. 197–235 (New York, Academic Press).

KRATOCHWILL, T.R. (Ed.) (1978) *Single Subject Research* (New York, Academic Press).

Appendix

The formula for the general serial correlation is,

$$r \text{ serial} = \frac{\Sigma\ [(z_l - z_h)\bar{x}]}{\sigma\Sigma \left[\dfrac{(z_l - z_h)^2}{p} \right]}$$

where z_l and z_h = the height of the normal curve ordinate at the lower and upper ends respectively

$\bar{x}$ = the mean of the continuous variable for each category

σ = the standard deviation of the continuous variable and

p = the proportion in the respective category.

Section B.

Antecedent Control

Antecedent Control of Behaviour in Educational Contexts

TED GLYNN

Recently there has been a growing recognition within applied behavioural research of particular dimensions of antecedent control of human behaviour (Risley, 1977; McNaughton, 1980, Glynn, 1982). These dimensions comprise the ecological context or the characteristics of settings within which contingencies of reinforcement operate to shape and maintain behaviour. Contemporary research reviewed in this paper suggests that such ecological conditions or setting events, may exert just as powerful control over human behaviour in developmental and educational situations as do contingencies of reinforcement. Further, in many child development and educational contexts such as classrooms, playgrounds, daycare and residential institutions setting events may be more amenable to modification and hence may yield more efficient strategies for changing behaviour than strategies relying on contingencies or reinforcement alone. Wheldall (1981) argues that a greater concern for ecological variables in classroom management would minimise the 'behavioural overkill' arising from the introduction of unnecessary and time-consuming contingency management procedures. McNaughton (1980) claims that the looser control over learning afforded by the appropriate structuring of settings (rather than the tighter control required for implementing contingent reinforcement procedures) may, in the long term, be more effective and significant for gains in proficiency in reading.

Before reviewing specific studies, it is important to note that antecedent control has been conceptualised in different ways. First the physical properties or stimulus objects present in an environment can in themselves influence human behaviour. The presence of brightly coloured moving objects over an infant's crib might be expected to affect the infant's rate of looking. However, both Kantor (1970) and Bijou & Baer (1978) distinguish between stimulus objects and stimulus functions. For example, Kantor (1970) argues that particular objects can acquire specific functions for an individual neonate as soon as interactions are established with those objects and particular response functions are built up. While the correspondence between stimulus and response in simple reflex behaviour depends on biological evolution, in more complex behaviour situations there is a psychologically evolved mutuality of stimulus and response functions. Those individual response functions may be facilitated or impaired by situational or setting factors. For example using the model of Kantor and of Bijou & Baer it could be predicted that an infant's rate of vocalisation in response to a given stimulus (toy) might be strongly influenced by the presence or absence of a parent who usually reinforces the infant for all vocalisation. Similarly, the rate of child questions and parent responses might vary according to whether child and parent were at home, or in a public setting, e.g. seated on a bus. Increased responding in both these examples, while partly resulting from reinforcement contingencies applied by the adult, *also* results from the availability of the adult as a cue for responding in the particular setting. The essentials of these examples appear to be captured in Bijou & Baer's (1978) definition: "... A setting event influences an interactional sequence by altering strengths and characteristics of the particular stimulus and response functions involved in an interaction" (p. 6).

Wahler & Fox (1981) note that Bijou & Baer (1978) have extended the definition of setting events to cover not only the concurrent presence of a stimulus condition or events (e.g. adult presence as a setting event for interaction) but also to cover two further possibilities. The first extends the definition of setting events to include stimulus-response *interactions* (e.g. presence of an adult playing with a child, so that the adult-child play could be a setting event for cueing and reinforcing child-initiated language). The second possibility includes as setting events stimulus (or stimulus and response) events which occur totally separate in space and time (i.e. may immediately precede, rather than merely overlap with), the stimulus response relationship they influence (e.g. children will display more on-task behaviour following a rest period, than following a period of vigorous activity (Krantz & Risley, 1977).

The conceptual framework provided by Kantor (1970), Bijou & Baer (1978), and Wahler & Fox (1981) thus suggests three different classes of antecedent control of human behaviour, concurrent stimulus events, concurrent stimulus-response events, and prior stimulus or stimulus-response events. Many different educational contexts provide clear opportunities both to describe and to manipulate variables within each of these classes of antecedent control.

Concurrent Stimulus Events

Three important studies examined the effects of large-scale differences in physical environmental variables between schools. Barker & Gump (1964) carried out a broad-scale examination of the relationship between high school size and pupil participation in extra-curricular activities. While numbers of available extra-curricular activities increased as the size of schools increased, as expected, actual rate of participation *decreased*. Increased numbers of activities available did not result in increased participation. Barker & Gump argue that with small numbers there was a greater social pressure on individuals to participate in the smaller number of activities available. Within the context of a small school perhaps, the importance of participation of any one pupil to the success of the activity was much more salient than with the anonymous context of a larger school.

In contrast to the Barker & Gump findings Gill (1977) reported no significant effects on pupil behaviour or achievement of being taught in either conventional classrooms or variable-space (open-plan) classroom settings. Gill reported that differential *teacher* behaviours outweighed the simple effects of the different settings.

Teacher behaviour would seem to be a very powerful factor influencing pupil behaviour, capable of overriding the effects of physical environmental (architectural variables). One further descriptive study by Russell & Bernall (1977) demonstrated clear correlations between rates of appropriate and inappropriate child behaviour at home and time of day, day of week, and rainfall (i.e. child inappropriate behaviour was greater around 3.30–5.00 pm on Fridays, and on wet days rather than dry days). The findings of Barker & Gump and Russell & Bernall point up interesting and important relationships between physical and temporal environmental variables and human behaviour. While these findings have clear implications for the design and management of school and home environments such variables are not easily or readily altered or manipulated experimentally.

Several further studies illustrate the powerful behavioural outcomes arising from the operation of more easily manipulable physical environmental variables. Quilitch, Christophersen & Risley (1977) conducted an analysis of children's use of a wide range of educational toys in child care contexts, and demonstrated that in a free choice situation specific toys varied widely in the amount of child use they occasioned. Risley (1982) has argued for a process of environmental distillation referring to the need to successively select children's play materials according to their ability to engage children at high rates. O'Rourke (1978) reports that merely supplying additional sports equipment and play materials resulted in increased rates of participation and decreased rates of disruptive behaviour on the playground of a large urban Intermediate School. However these effects were not as lasting as those reslting from supplying additional adults to initiate and participate in children's games.

Other studies have manipulated physical environmental variables within individual classrooms, for example by systematically altering seating patterns. Krantz & Risley (1977) demonstrated that disruptive behaviour during story time and during teacher demonstrations could be reduced just as effectively by providing more space between children as by implementing a positive reinforcement contingency for appropriate attending behaviour. Wheldall *et al.* (1981) found that in two separate classrooms on-task behaviour was consistently higher when children were seated at desks arranged in rows than when they were seated at group tables. Wheldall (1982) reports further data from as yet unpublished work which confirm these findings in three separate classes in a special school context. In these classes on-task behaviour was twice as high when children were seated individually in rows than when they were seated at group tables. However, Wheldall also reported that important increases in teacher positive comments and decreases in teachers negative comments occurred when children were seated individually in rows.

Clark (1982) reports data in support of Wheldall's findings. Clark found that individual seating arrangements resulted in increases of on-task behaviour, over the level of on-task behaviour while pupils were seated at group tables and while they were working on a carpeted floor. This pattern was replicated in a variable-space classroom with two groups of children who experienced the different seating arrangements in a different order. Although data from both the Wheldall and Clark studies demonstrate clear effects of seating arrangements on child behaviour, Wheldall's data suggest that this effect may be at least in part mediated through an indirect effect on teacher behaviour. Wheldall (1982) argues that teachers may find it easier to praise and refrain from disapproval when children are seated in rows. Perhaps this results from pupils' on-task behaviour being easier to *monitor* in the rows condition. The task of scanning and discriminating on-task from off-task behaviour may be less complex when children are seated in rows.

Some evidence in support of the claim that changes in seating arrangements affect child behaviour through indirect effects on teacher behaviour is provided in a study by Moore (1980) who demonstrated that the location of children's seats markedly affected the number of questions they were asked by the teacher. In a subsequent study in progress, Moore (1982) reports that switching individual children's seating position from areas receiving either high or low rates of teacher interaction resulted in changes in the rate of interaction in both the predicted directions. This type of manipulation is readily accomplished within individual classrooms with a minimum of effort.

Although seating arrangements can clearly influence the rate of on-task behaviour, their effect on academic work output is not convincing. Neither of the studies reported by Wheldall include data on rate of academic work completed. Clark (1982), however, monitored both rate and accuracy of completed maths problems in her study and found that neither of these measures varied according to change in seating arrangements. This is consistent with other findings that increases on-task behaviour do not necessarily result in increased academic output (Marholin & Steinman, 1977; Henderson, 1976; Glendinning, 1978). Hence, seating arrangements may be a functional ecological variable for attentional behaviours rather than academic output *per se.* It is possible that certain seating arrangements are setting events for high rates of teacher praise for behaviours such as sitting still and working quietly.

One common summary theme emerging from several studies of the behavioural effects of physical environmental stimulus variables on child behaviour is that these effects commonly appear to be mediated through the effects on the behaviour of other people present in the setting. School size influenced participation rates, Barker & Gump argue, because of the greater social pressure to participate generated within small schools.

The studies of the effects of classroom seating arrangements by Wheldall and Moore support the claim that such setting events affected teacher behaviour as well as child behaviour. In the study by Russell & Bernal, child behaviour changes cannot have been *caused* by the day of the week or time of day or by the occurrence of rain, but are likely to have resulted from changes in parent behaviours brought about by the differences in demands of housework and child care duties associated with time and weather conditions. Elsewhere, Sanders & Glynn (1981) argue that competing demands of housework, shopping, attention to visitors and telephone calls may be setting events for non-implementing of behaviour management procedures by parents.

Thus, it would appear that effects on the behaviour of target individuals of changes in specific stimulus setting events are frequently associated with changes in the behaviour of other people present. However, these changes in the behaviour of other people are not explicitly planned, or programmed, as is the case with studies of the second type of setting event.

Concurrent Stimulus and Response Events

The introduction of other people, for example encouraging adults into a pre-school free play context, can influence children's behaviour in two ways. First, familiar adults are likely to have become generalised discriminative stimuli for reinforcement such that child behaviours previously performed and reinforced in the presence of adults (but currently not displayed, or displayed only at a low rate in that pre-school context, e.g. naming objects) will be reinforced in the new context. Secondly, those behaviours specific to the pre-school setting but which have not previously occurred, or have occurred only at a low rate without the presence of adults (e.g. use of climbing equipment), are likely to be cued, prompted and reinforced by the adults. In this way interacting adults can extend antecedent and consequent control over child behaviour. Through these two processes adult presence can be seen both to provide additional opportunities to perform behaviours appropriate to the setting *and* to increase rates of reinforcement for those behaviours. Thus encouraging familiar adults into a pre-school setting may be expected to have a stronger and more lasting effect on child behaviour than either changing the physical stimulus properties of the setting (e.g. introducing new equipment) or merely reinforcing appropriate child behaviour as it occurs.

Several studies of meal-time settings provide clear demonstrations of the effects of the presence of adults on child behaviour. In a pre-school setting, Frewin (1980) manipulated the effects of a physical stimulus change (open display of jigsaw puzzles, versus stacking them together) and introducing an adult into the jigsaw area. Frewin's data show that the adult's presence resulted in more children entering the jigsaw corner, than did displaying the jigsaws, though both manipulations increased the number of children present over baseline rates. Glynn, Glynn & Lawless (1979) examined the amount of different foods eaten and the number of second helpings requested by five children at a family evening meal. Parents either ate their own meal with their children or ate their meal at a later time, leaving the children to eat without adult company. A similar set of menus was presented within each of the four conditions. All children ate more food and required more second helpings when parents ate with them and the effect was greatest for the young children. Baker (1980) describes a child in a day care setting who was a problem eater and who was not responding to systematic procedures for prompting and reinforcing eating. However, Baker found instead that having an adult sit with the child and engage him in conversation during the meal-time resulted in his eating three times as many spoonsful of food as he did on days when the adult supervised from a distance. The two conditions were alternated frequently over three weeks, with the same consistent results. O'Rourke (1978) demonstrated that introducing additional participating adults into a large urban intermediate school playground effected a greater rate of child participation in appropriate activities and a lower rate of disruptive behaviour than did introducing additional play equipment. The effect of the 'adults present' condition was also more lasting than the effect of supplying additional equipment. In these three studies, introducing adults increased the rate of performance of behaviours already occurring in the setting (eating and engagement with play equipment).

Another form of setting event involving stimulus and response effects on behaviour is illustrated in several studies of family style versus institutional style meal service and their effects on other behaviour (language) rather than on eating behaviour. Meal-times, for most people are a generally social context which might be seen as a setting event for language exchange as well as for eating. Unfortunately this is not always the case particularly for people in residential institutions. Risley & Edwards (1978) report greater rates of language interaction among geriatric residents in an institution when they were seated at smaller tables (4–6 persons) than when they were previously seated at larger tables (10–12 persons). Along with the change to smaller tables went a change to self-service from serving bowls for each table. This was in contrast to the former institution style of food service with residents queueing for individual trays on which all food items were pre-served. Risley & Edwards report a gain of 10–15% in interaction and more food eaten with the small table and self-service procedures. VanBiervliet, Spangler & Marshall (1981) compared family style and institutional-style food serving procedures on the language behaviour of five young male retarded adults. In this study only the style of food service and not the number of persons eating together varied across experimental conditions. In a multiple baseline across meals design VanBiervliet *et al.* found a systematic increase in rate of verbalisation with the introduction of family style serving and this increase was largely directed towards peers, rather than towards staff. Baker *et al.* (1982) conducted a meal-time study in a day care setting. Standard procedures in this day care centre involved both having adults seated with children during the meal and children's self-service of food from plates placed on their table. Each of these two components (seated adults and self-service) was individually and systematically withdrawn from the meal-time procedure, in order to examine its separate effect on language interaction. Withdrawing the seated adult (by having the adult supervise from a distance) reduced the occurrence of both total language and child-initiated language far more than did withdrawing the self-service of food. Further, there was little appreciable difference in amount of food eaten under the different conditions in this study. It is clear from these studies in meal-time settings that adult presence as well as influencing the rate of behaviours specific to these settings (eating), can also increase the rate of other behaviours likely to have been previously reinforced by adults (language initiations).

Some further studies are of interest because they not only introduced an interacting adult into a target setting, but in addition required the adult to provide a concurrent model of specific target behaviours appropriate to that setting. Haskett & Lenfestey (1974) studied the pre-reading behaviours (e.g. turning pages in books) of six children in a pre-school setting. Two procedures were compared, introducing stacks of new books (a change in stimulus materials) and introducing adults who modelled individual interested reading of these books (without attempting to engage children's attention or 'read to' the children). Introducing new books resulted in brief increases in pre-reading behaviour in several of the children, whereas introducing the adult models resulted in large and consistent increases in pre-reading behaviours in all of the children. This study was followed up by Pluck (1980), who examined the effects of concurrent teacher modelling of appropriate recreational reading behaviour during classroom recreational reading time in a primary school. Recreational reading involved children selecting their own library books and reading silently for 20 minutes. On different days the teacher either sat on a chair at the front of the room modelling reading her own book silently and with enjoyment or alternatively occupied herself with some other tasks (marking or preparation of work or tidying the room). Observational data show that children's rate of engagement in silent reading was higher on days when the teacher modelled recreational reading than on days when she performed other tasks. Further the five least competent readers were found to have a mean on-task behaviour of 33% on no-modelling days and 65% on teacher modelling days. The corresponding figures for the five most competent readers were 70 and 85%. Interestingly, the mean number of teacher comments contingent on children's inappropriate behaviour on the no-modelling days was 5.0 while the corresponding figure on concurrent modelling days was 1.0. Pluck's data are consistent with previous findings that some setting event effects on child behaviour may be mediated through changes in adult behaviour. In this case acting as a concurrent model for target appropriate behaviour may have reduced the teacher's opportunities to monitor and respond to inappropriate child behaviour. This study raises some interesting questions. What opportunities do schools provide for children to see competent adult models performing with enjoyment the target academic behaviour they are instructing? How often do children see adults enjoying silent reading? Do they see adults engaged in and enjoying writing tasks or engaged in maths work? It is unlikely that concurrent modelling of academic behaviours by adults occurs in schools as often as concurrent modelling of physical education and sporting skills. An important area of research to be explored, is the analysis of the effects of concurrent modelling of target behaviours on children's *academic* performance. Interestingly several graduate student parents who study and write regularly at home have commented that their young children frequently ask to be allowed to write or engage in academic tasks concurrently with their parent's own writing.

A further example of concurrent modelling effects is found in a study of self management approach to training residential staff to implement child behaviour management procedures (Glynn, Vaigro & Lawless, 1982). In this study one particular staff member in one cottage had undertaken to practise two behaviour management skills at a contracted time when a researcher would provide feedback on the correctness of implementation of those two skills (Directed Discussion and Incidental Teaching). It was found that a second staff member who was rostered on duty concurrently with the first, also increased her use of these two skills, though she had not undertaken to practise them at these times. It appeared that the behaviour of the first staff member provided a powerful concurrent model for the second staff member's implementing of behaviour management skills even though this was not the object of the study. The concurrent modelling is likely to have been particularly effective in this case, since targeted 'practices' by the first staff member were necessarily contingent on naturally occurring incidents of child behaviours and since correct implementation of the targeted skills produced an immediate and observable outcome on child behaviour which would be monitored by the second staff member.

Another setting event of major importance in child development and education is the one to one setting in which an adult and child spontaneously interact over a shared task or activity. This context is regarded as a powerful setting event for the naturalistic learning of language. (Bruner, 1977; Risley, 1977). McNaughton (1980) notes that such setting events which operate on both adult and child behaviour are frequently child initiated and have an affective and child-directed basis. This type of child initiated interaction with an adult over a joint task, unfortunately does not often occur in the school context.

In school environments, similar one to one contexts frequently arise though they are not typically child initiated. These occur for example when children read from a reading text to an adult. The important implications of this setting for the three-way interaction between teachers, readers and reading tasks have been discussed extensively McNaughton (1980). McNaughton (1981) presents data to show that the reading behaviour of low progress readers can function as a setting event for instructor behaviour that maintains dependent error correction strategies in these readers. Specifically, teachers in one intensive descriptive study of low progress readers attended to a high rate (74%) of low progress reader's errors with *immediate* intervention, most frequently in the form of providing models (supplying the correct word rather than providing a prompt, or simply pausing). In a second experimental study, teachers reduced their rate of error attention when low progress readers independently increased their reading accuracy, as a result of earlier tutoring sessions. Thus the behaviour of a low-progress reader in a one-to-one reading context can be seen to function as a concurrent stimulus-response setting event for instructor behaviours which leave the reader more dependent on external help.

Within the same one-to-one oral reading context it is also possible for specific instructor behaviours to function as setting events for particular dependent or independent error correction strategies in readers. McNaughton & Glynn (1981), for example, provide data to show that requiring instructors to delay their attention to errors, clearly resulted in marked gains in readers' rates of self-correction of errors and gains in reading accuracy. Thus, one-to-one settings are important because of their potential to influence both instructor and learner behaviour. The McNaughton & Glynn data are consistent with findings by Halle, Marshall & Spradlin (1979) and Halle, Baer & Spradlin (1981) that delaying adult responding resulted in increased use and generalisation of language in retarded children. It seems possible that the behaviours of low-progress, or retarded individuals function as setting events for excessive immediate external support from 'helpers' and 'trainers'. This pattern of support may actually reduce opportunities for low progress or retarded individuals to initiate interactions with adults and to practise independent academic and social skills.

Conditions of extended external control or 'maintained instructional dependence' (McNaughton, 1981) occur not only for low-progress or retarded individuals but also for all children in some situations. In many classrooms teachers initiate almost all instructional interactions with children and these interactions occur under tight stimulus control (i.e. they take place at set times, involve extended interactions with tightly specified stimulus objects or materials and generally occur in group contexts). Thus the opportunities for any one child to be sharing an activity with an adult are limited. The conditions under which much classroom instruction takes place can be seen as counter to the notion of training under 'loose control' over acquisition, which Stokes & Baer (1977) and McNaughton (1980) argue is important for the generalisation of behaviours beyond the confines of the original training setting.

In contrast with instructional interactions at school, instructional interactions in some home settings can be seen (potentially at least), as more often child initiated, typically brief and occurring under loose stimulus control. That is, in the home, instructional interactions are likely to take place at a wide range of different times, involve brief interactions with a variety of stimulus object and materials and are much more likely to occur as one-to-one interactions with an adult. These 'loose' setting events appear to be much more suitable for the process of incidental teaching as described by Hart & Risley (1975, 1980) and also to be more likely to promote generalised learning than those obtaining in school settings. Elsewhere the need for research to exploit the advantages of both home and school settings for teaching academic skills has been argued (Glynn, 1982). Arndt (1980), for example, reports a study in which the rate of words written by a seven-year-old girl was between two and a half and three times as high in story writing at home as it was in story writing at school.

Prior Stimulus or Stimulus-response events

The effect of prior exposure to simple or complex stimulus events is readily illustrated in numerous studies of modelling. A classic study in this area is that of Bandura, Ross & Ross (1963) who demonstrated that prior exposure to a film in which an adult modelled specific aggressive responses towards a doll resulted in young children subsequently displaying these same responses towards an identical doll in a playroom. The efficacy of modelling as a clinical procedure is demonstrated in the following two studies. Bandura, Grusec & Menlove (1967) compared the effects of modelling and systematic desensitisation in the treatment of dog phobia in young children. Children either participated in a typical desensitisation programme in which over repeated sessions, they were slowly moved closer to a dog in a playroom, or they watched a similar-age peer model engage in playful interaction with a dog. All three groups were tested with the target child and the dog in both a neutral and a 'party' context. In both contexts, children who had viewed the child model were markedly less fearful and approached the dog more closely than children who had received the desensitisation procedure. In the second study, Lahey (1971) reported that the use of descriptive adjectives by young children in a Head Start programme was substantially increased by a procedure in which target children watched same aged children model a high rate of descriptive adjectives in their answers to teacher questions.

Prior exposure to a model is also frequently included as a component of programmes of parent training or staff training in the use of behaviour management procedures. However, analyses of the effects of separate training components, e.g. modelling and feedback are seldom carried out. One study which examined the effects of modelling on its own was that of Glastone & Spencer (1977) who modelled the delivery of positive reinforcement (praise) in the context of training retarded adults in self-care skills. Aides were found not only to increase their use of positive reinforcement when supervising subjects in the setting where the modelling took place, but also to generalise this gain to other settings. It is interesting to note that there appear to be no studies comparing the effects of prior modelling with concurrent modelling in training of staff or parents to implement behavioural procedures. Various studies in which modelling formed part of a training package suggest that instructions and modelling components on their own have little influence on behaviour unless complemented by the provision of performance feedback. However, the unprogrammed finding noted by Glynn, Vaigro & Lawless (1982) suggests that concurrent modelling may be a worthwhile procedure for facilitating staff implementation of behavioural procedures.

At a more molecular level, instructions are another form of setting event involving the prior occurrence of stimulus events. Johnson & Lobitz (1974) invited volunteer parents to do what they could to make their child appear either 'good' or 'bad' on different days to independent observers in their homes. Data indicated that one important dimension of parent behaviour which distinguished 'good' days from 'bad' days was the number of instructions given. On 'good' days parents gave far fewer instructions than on 'bad' days, but the rate of child compliance was similar on both good and bad days. However, the rate of negative parental attention was higher on bad days, suggesting that issuing a high rate of instructions may function as a setting event for parents' observing and commenting on non-compliance. Apart from the rate of instruction giving, qualitative aspects of instructions also produce differential effects. Charles (1981) demonstrated that a 34 month old child reduced her rate of non-compliance from approximately 50% to approximately 25% when her mother altered the form of her instruction from commands to polite requests. Reinforcement of compliance occurred at a similarly high rate with each type of instruction.

Less well-known than the effects of simple modelling or instruction giving which involve prior presentation of stimulus material, are the effects of prior stimulus response setting events. Krantz & Risley 1977) demonstrated that children's rate of attention to the teacher or to a story book during story reading was clearly affected by the type of preceding activity the children were engaged in. When story reading followed a quiet rest period children's attention was consistently higher and the time taken to settle and rate of disruption were lower than when story reading followed a period of vigorous activity. In the context of one-to-one oral reading Wong & McNaughton (1980) systematically monitored reading accuracy and rate of self-correction of errors of a seven and a half-year old low-progress reader. This child read a different unfamiliar text each session. Wong & McNaughton found that in sessions which had been preceded by a brief prior discussion of the main events, outcomes and unfamiliar words in the story to be read, this reader's accuracy and self-correction were markedly higher than in sessions where the prior discussion had not occurred. This simple but powerful procedure is commonly used as part of beginning reading programmes in many schools.

In the area of social learning, Fowler & Baer (1981) describe an interesting outcome from children's exposure to a prior stimulus-response setting event. First, pre-school children increased their rate of sharing in an early session following the introduction of contingent reinforcement dispensed at the end of that session. They did not increase sharing in a later session where no reinforcement was dispensed. Next, reinforcement contingent on sharing in the early session was delayed until the end of the later session. However no reinforcement was provided contingent on sharing in the later session. Not only did the rate of sharing continue to remain high in the early session but sharing during the later session also increased. Further analyses showed no changes in teacher or peer social attention contingencies in the later session and no systematic association between sharing in the later session and the number of points obtained. The authors argue that instructions given at the beginning of the school day came to set the occasion for sharing in both early and later session. When reinforcement had occurred after the early session it is likely that children discriminated that sharing in the later session would not be reinforced. With the delay of reinforcement till after the later session the discrimination about when sharing would be reinforced is likely to be blurred. Thus under conditions of delayed reinforcement, the authors argue that instructions about behaviour early in the school day came to set the occasion for sharing in both early and late sessions.

Wahler & Graves (1982) cite an interesting study by Simon, Ayllon & Milan (1982) which reports behavioural contrast effects across settings, resulting from manipulation of token reinforcement contingencies in other settings. The maths performance of seven children was monitored in three different classrooms, each with a different teacher. Following baseline sessions without token reinforcement, a phase in which tokens could be earned at the rate of one per correct response was introduced which produced clear increases in all three settings. Then tokens were withdrawn from two settings, but maintained in the third. Response rate dropped in the first two settings but doubled in the third. When tokens were reinstated in all settings, response rates increased in the first two settings and dropped in the third. Wahler & Graves argue that when these children were subjected to extinction in two settings, they performed in the third setting as if the reinforcement schedule had changed. In this way, the prior extinction experience had served as a setting event in a similar way to that of the prior instruction in the study on sharing by Fowler & Baer (1981).

Wahler & Graves (1982) discuss prior stimulus and response setting events also in the context of training parents in behaviour management. One major issue concerning these authors is why certain parents who demonstrate that they can correctly implement specific behaviour management procedures do not continue to do so outside the confines of the training setting. Using descriptive data from one particular case, Wahler & Graves demonstrated that a woman's rate of initiating aversive interactions with her child was consistently five times as high when she had come from a prior aversive interaction with her own invalid mother. Interestingly, the conditional probability of child-initiated aversive interactions did not vary according to whether or not his mother had had prior aversive interactions. Wahler & Graves suggest mother's reporting of anger and her child-directed aversive behaviour comprise a response class under the control of several different environmental events, e.g. grandmother behaviour and child behaviour. In this way the occurrence of one response in a class will increase the likelihood of another response in that class. Hence, encountering the son's behaviour immediately following an aversive exchange with her mother both heightened the perceptions of anger and incompetence as well as her rate of initiating aversive exchanges with her son. This study highlights the need for persons engaged in training parents and others in implementing behavioural procedures to recognise that other sources of *antecedent* control over their client's behaviour in the target setting may be precluding their client's implementation of behavioural procedures. Removing these sources of antecedent control may not be easy, as Wahler & Graves point out. However, gaining increasing data on the influence of such prior setting events on parents or teachers with their children may result in better use of antecedent strategies in changing children's behaviour. For example, Sanders & Glynn (1981) enhanced generalisation of parent implementation of child behaviour management procedures by requiring parents to formulate plans ahead of time for those home and community settings in which they experience greatest difficulty in managing their children's behaviour. These settings occur, for example, when household tasks, shopping tasks, visits by friends or recreational activities compete with, or are interrupted by, the need to respond to children's appropriate and inappropriate behaviour. These plans include the selection and provision of toys, snacks, and the use of positive instructions to be given prior to inappropriate behaviour arising in any situation. Such advance planning can be viewed as a setting event for subsequent initiation, monitoring and reinforcement of appropriate child behaviour.

Conclusions

In summary, there is an impressive range and variety of evidence to demonstrate the power of antecedent control over adult and child behaviour in educational contexts. The studies reviewed provide clear examples of the behavioural effects of all three types of setting event (concurrent stimulus events, concurrent stimulus-response events, and prior stimulus or stimulus-response events). Several tentative conclusions and research suggestions emerge about each.

(1) Antecedent control through the manipulation of physical stimulus events may influence behaviour in two ways. The first influence is direct, through the availability of new stimulus materials—as in the case of providing additional toys, and the second is indirect, as is the case where the physical stimulus events affect the behaviour of other people present, who in turn influence the behaviour of target children. The indirect effects seem to apply to large-scale physical stimulus changes

(e.g. school size), to small-scale physical stimulus changes (e.g. location of a pupil in a classroom), and to temporal changes (e.g. the time at which stimulus changes are introduced). Of the studies reviewed, only one major research did not find the commonly reported changes in behaviour attributed to physical stimulus variables (Gill, 1977). Nevertheless, Gill reports that individual teachers within classrooms of each architectural type studied (conventional and open plan) varied so greatly in their behaviour, that physical environmental differences were overridden. Clearly the behaviour of adults and other persons exerts a powerful influence, even in contexts where manipulation or intervention is confined to physical stimulus changes. Future research could profitably explore the indirect effects on child behaviour of changing stimulus events, by monitoring for concurrent changes in the behaviour of other people present in a setting.

(2) The presence of an *interacting* adult is a powerful setting event, as it combines elements of antecedent and consequent control of child behaviour. Introducing interacting adults into educational settings resulted in changes not only in those behaviours likely to have been previously reinforced in the presence of the adult, but also in behaviours specific to the setting into which the adult is introduced. Several studies suggest that behaviour change resulting from the presence of an interacting adult may be more effective than that resulting from stimulus changes alone (O'Rourke, 1978; Baker *et al.*, 1982).

Concurrent modelling, where a competent performer provides a continuous model of desired target behaviour in educational contexts appears to be another powerful form of antecedent control over child behaviour, deserving of closer research attention (Haskett & Lenfesty, 1974; Pluck, 1980). It would be interesting to explore the effects of providing, in a classroom context, concurrent modelling of written expression or working at mathematics problems.

(3) The one-to-one instructional setting where adult and child (competent performer and learner) interact over a joint task is of major importance educationally (McNaughton, 1980). Errors made by low-progress learners may set the occasion for *increased* external intervention ('help') by the competent learner. The competent performer's high rate of immediate external assistance may, in turn, restrict the learner's opportunity to learn independent problem solving and self-correction skills.

(4) Where instructional interactions are child initiated and free to occur over a wide range of times, in the presence of a wide variety of different stimulus events, as is the case in incidental teaching episodes (Hart & Risley, 1975, 1980) learning of academic and social skills takes place under 'loose' stimulus control. Learning under such conditions of 'loose' stimulus control is likely to enhance maintenance and generalisation of skills (Stokes & Baer, 1977). Wahler & Fox (1981) have argued that setting event influences have clear implications for the acquisition, maintenance and generalisation of skills, particularly in parent training contexts and recommend increased research attention to these issues.

(5) Recent extension of the term setting events to cover prior stimulus or stimulus-response events and their effects on subsequent behaviour highlights some further interesting research questions. For example, it is important for those involved in remedial or therapeutic interventions with teachers and parents to explore the behavioural outcomes of advance planning, organization and sequencing of educational activities in home and school contexts as illustrated by Krantz & Risley (1977). Another important question is the analysis and manipulation of prior setting events which may prevent people from benefitting from available contingencies of

reinforcement, or from implementing and maintaining a programme of behaviour change.

(6) In contrast with behavioural intervention strategies based on manipulation of contingencies of reinforcement, setting event control over behaviour appears to be much more readily exploitable (McNaughton, 1980). Setting event intervention can be frequently implemented in advance of, or even concurrent with the occurrence of target behaviour. Contingency management intervention must await the occurrence of target behaviour, which might more effectively have been prevented or minimized. When teachers or parents are required to implement response-contingent behaviour change strategies, such strategies have to be implemented in competition with other demands or personal needs, e.g. housework or presenting new teaching material or relaxation.

Further research attention into describing and manipulating the various types of setting events would contribute to better design and construction of educational and living environments for adults and children. Better environmental design and scheduling of activities for adults and children following any of the suggestions from studies reviewed in this paper may reduce the frequency with which we resort to remedial contingency management programmes for adult-child interactions that have gone wrong.

REFERENCES

ARNDT, T. (1980) Effects of timing and feedback on output and legibility in story writing, *unpublished term paper*, University of Auckland, Department of Education.

BAKER, M. (1980) The effect of adult conversation on amount of food eaten by a preschool child in a daycare setting, *unpublished term paper*, University of Auckland, Education Department.

BAKER, M., FOLEY, M.F., GLYNN, T. & MCNAUGHTON, S. (1982) The effect of adult proximity and serving style on eating and social behaviours of preschoolers, University of Auckland, Department of Education, in preparation.

BANDURA, A.R., GRUSEC, J.E. & MENLOVE, F.L. (1967) Vicarious extinction of avoidance behaviour, *Journal of Personality and Social Psychology*, 5, 16–23.

BANDURA, A., ROSS, D. & ROSS, A. (1963) Imitation of film-mediated aggressive models, *Journal of Abnormal and Social Psychology*, 66, pp. 3–11.

BARKER, R.G. & GUMP, P.V. (1964) *Big School, Small School* (Stanford University Press).

BIJOU, S.W. & BAER, D.M. (1978) *Behavior Analysis of Child Development* (Prentice Hall, New Jersey).

BRUNER, J. (1977) Early social interaction and language acquisition, in: SCHAFFER, H.R. (Ed.) *Studies in Mother-Infant Interaction* (New York, Academic Press).

CHARLES, H. (1981) Child compliance in response to maternal commands and requests, *unpublished term paper*, University of Auckland, Education Department.

CLARK, R.M. (1982) The effects of changing seating arrangements on pupil and teacher behaviour in an open-plan unit, *M Soc Sci. thesis (Psychology)*, University of Waikato.

FOWLER, S.A. & BAER, D.M. (1981) "Do I have to be good all day?" The timing of delayed reinforcement as a factor in generalization, *Journal of Applied Behaviour Analysis*, 14, pp. 13–24.

FREWIN, J. (1980) The effect of arrangement of materials and adult presence on number of children present at an activity area in a day care setting, *unpublished paper*, University of Auckland, Education Department.

GILL, W.M. (1977) Classroom architecture and classroom behaviours: a look at the change to open-plan schools in New Zealand, *New Zealand Journal of Educational Studies*, 12(1), pp. 3–16.

GLADSTONE, B.W. & SPENCER, C.J. (1977) The effects of modelling on the contingent praise of mental retardation counsellors, *Journal of Applied Behavior Analysis*, 10(1), pp. 75–84.

GLENDINNING, S. (1978) Reinforcement of attentiveness and academic performance in an adjustment class, *unpublished MA thesis*, University of Auckland, Department of Education.

GLYNN, T. (1982) Building an effective teaching environment, in: WHELDALL, K. & RIDING, R. (Eds) *Psychological Aspects of Learning and Teaching* (London, Croom Helm).

GLYNN, T., GLYNN, V. & LAWLESS, S. (1979) A behavioural approach to nutrition: how we influence what children eat, *Proceedings of the Nutritional Society of New Zealand*, 4, pp. 110–130.

GLYNN, T., VAIGRO, W. & LAWLESS, S. (1982) A self management strategy for increasing implementation of behavioural procedures by residential staff, *paper presented at the Fifth National Conference on Behaviour Modification*, Surfers Paradise, Queensland, May.

HALLE, J.W., BAER, D.M. & SPRADLIN, J.E. (1981) Teachers' generalised use of delay as a stimulus control procedure to increase language use in handicapped children, *Journal of Applied Behavior Analysis*, 14(4), pp. 389–409.

HALLE, J.W., MARSHALL, A.M. & SPRADLIN, J.E. (1979) Time delay: a technique to increase facilitate generalization in retarded children, *Journal of Applied Behavior Analysis*, 12, pp. 431–439.

HART, B. & RISLEY, T.R. (1975) Incidental teaching of language in the preschool, *Journal of Applied Behavior Analysis*, 8(4), pp. 411–420.

HART, B. & RISLEY, T.R. (1980) *In vivo* language intervention: unanticipated general effects, *Journal of Applied Behavior Analysis*, 13(3), pp. 407–432.

HASKETT, G.J. & LENFESTEY, W. (1974) Reading-related behavior in an open classroom: effects of novelty and modelling on preschoolers, *Journal of Applied Behavior Analysis*, 7(2), pp. 223–241.

HENDERSON, M. (1976) Increasing appropriate classroom behaviour and academic performance by reinforcing correct work alone, *Psychology in Schools*, 12(2), pp. 195–200.

JOHNSON, S.M. & LOBITZ, G.K. (1974) Parental manipulation of child behavior in home observations, *Journal of Applied Behavior Analysis*, 7(1), pp. 23–31.

KANTOR, J.R. (1970) An analysis of the experimental analysis of behavior, *Journal of the Experimental Analysis of Behavior*, 13, pp. 101–108.

KRANTZ. P.J. & RISLEY, T.R. (1977) Behavioral ecology in the classroom, in: O'LEARY, K.D. (Ed.) *Classroom Management: the successful use of behavior modification*, 2nd ed (New York, Pergamon Press).

LAHEY, B.B. (1971) Modification of the frequency of descriptive adjectives in the speech of Head Start children through modelling without reinforcement, *Journal of Applied Behavior Analysis*, 4(1), pp. 19–22.

MCNAUGHTON, S.S. (1980) Structuring settings for learning academic skills: applications to oral reading, *Behaviour Therapy in Australia, Proceedings of the Third Australian Conference on Behaviour Modification*, pp. 306–315, Melbourne, May.

MCNAUGHTON, S. (1981) Low progress readers and teacher instructional behaviour during oral reading: the risk of maintaining instructional dependence, *The Exceptional Child*, 28(3), pp. 167–176.

MCNAUGHTON, S. & GLYNN, T. (1981) Delayed versus immediate attention to oral reading errors: effects on accuracy and self correction, *Educational Psychology*, 1(1), pp. 57–65.

MARHOLIN, D.I. & STEINMANN, W.M. (1977) Stimulus control in the classroom as a function of the behavior reinforced, *Journal of Applied Behavior Analysis*, 10(3), pp. 465–478.

MOORE, D. (1980) Location as a causal factor in the unequal distribution of teacher questions: an experimental analysis, *Behaviour Therapy in Australia, Proceedings of the Third Australian Conference on Behaviour Modification*, pp. 316–324, Melbourne, May.

MOORE, D.W. (1982) Variation in teacher question rate as a function of position in the classroom, *paper presented at the Fifth National Conference on Behaviour Modification*, Surfers Paradise, Queensland.

O'ROURKE, M. (1978) Play equipment and adult participation: effects on children's behaviour, in: GLYNN, T. & MCNAUGHTON, S. (Eds) *Behaviour Analysis in New Zealand*, pp. 36–57 (Department of Education, University of Auckland).

PLUCK, M. (1980) The effect of modelling (response facilitation) by classroom teacher on children's recreational reading, *unpublished term paper*, University of Auckland, Education Department.

QUILITCH, H.R., CHRISTOPHERSEN, E.R. & RISLEY, T.R. (1977) The evaluation of children's play materials, *Journal of Applied Behavior Analysis*, 10(3), pp. 501–502.

RISLEY, T.R. (1977) The ecology of applied behavioural analysis, in: ROGERS-WARREN, A. & ROGERS-WARREN, S.F. (Eds) *Ecological Perspectives in Behavior Analysis* (Baltimore, University Park Press).

RISLEY, T.R. (1982) Behavioural design for residential programmes, *keynote address to Fifth National Conference on Behaviour Modification*, Surfers Paradise, Queensland.

RISLEY, T.R. & EDWARDS, A. (1978) Behavioural technology for nursing home care: toward a system of nursing home organization and management, in: GLYNN, T. & MCNAUGHTON, S. (Eds) *Behaviour Analysis in New Zealand*, pp. 1–25 (Department of Education, University of Auckland).

RUSSELL, M.B. & BERNAL, M.E. (1977) Temporal and climatic variables in naturalistic observation, *Journal of Applied Behavior Analysis*, 10(3), pp. 399–405.

SANDERS, M.R. & GLYNN, T. (1981) Training parents in behavioral self management: an analysis of generalization and maintenance, *Journal of Applied Behavior Analysis*, 14(3), pp. 223–237.

SIMON, S.J., AYLLON, T. & MILAN, M.A. (1982) Behavioural compensation: contrast-like effects in the classroom, *Behavior Modification* (in press).

STOKES, T.F. & BAER, D.M. (1977) An implicit technology of generalization, *Journal of Applied Behavior Analysis*, 10, pp. 349–368.

VANBIERVLIET, A., SPANGLER, P.F. & MARSHALL, A.M. (1981) An ecobehavioural examination of a simple strategy for increasing mealtime language in residential facilities. *Journal of Applied Behavior Analysis*, 14(3), pp. 299–305.

WAHLER, R.G. & FOX, J.J. (1981) Setting events in applied behavior analysis: toward a conceptual and methodological expansion, *Journal of Applied Behavior Analysis*, 14, pp. 327–338.

WAHLER, R.G. & GRAVES, M.G. (1982) Setting events in social networks: ally or enemy in child behavior therapy, *unpublished paper*, Child Behavior Institute, University of Tennessee.

WHELDALL, K. (1981) Concluding comments: 'A before C' or the use of behaviour ecology in classroom management, in: WHELDALL, K. (Ed.) *The Behaviourist in the Classroom. Aspects of Applied Behavioural Analysis in British Educational Contexts, chapter 14, Educational Review Offset Publications. No. 2 (University of Birmingham).*

WHELDALL, K. (1982) A positive approach to classroom discipline, in: WHELDALL, K. & RIDING, R. (Eds) Psychological Aspects of Learning and Teaching (London, Croom Helm).

WHELDALL, K., MORRIS, M. VAUGHAN, P. & NG, Y.Y. (1981) Rows versus tables: an example of the use of behavioural ecology in two classes of eleven year old children, *Educational Psychology*, 1(2), pp. 171–184.

WONG, P. & MCNAUGHTON, S. (1980) The effects of prior provision of a context on the oral reading proficiency of a low progress reader, *New Zealand Journal of Education Studies*, 15(2), pp. 169–179

Rows Versus Tables: an example of the use of behavioural ecology in two classes of eleven-year-old children

KEVIN WHELDALL, MARION MORRIS, PAMELA VAUGHAN & YIN YUK NG

ABSTRACT *The effect of different classroom seating arrangements on children's on-task behaviour was examined by observations of two top junior classes of ten- to eleven-year-old children. In both classes mean on-task behaviour was lower for the first two weeks in which children sat around tables compared with the second two-week period spent in rows, and declined again when the children returned to tables for the final two weeks. An analysis of the data broken down into groups of children with low, average and high initial on-task behaviour showed that the rows condition had its most powerful effect on children with low initial on-task behaviour. There was little difference between conditions for the children with high initial on-task behaviour. The results for the average groups of children were similar to those for the classes as a whole. Rising baselines during the first tables condition confused the effect but there was clear evidence for declines in on-task behaviour in the final tables condition.*

There is an increasing movement within the field of applied behaviour analysis in education which rejects the traditional, oversimplistic model of 'behaviour modification' and its emphasis on consequence management techniques, in favour of a more subtle approach which is also more in keeping with the theoretical roots of behaviour analysis. This latter approach is characterised by a concern with the total context in which behaviour occurs; with the antecedent conditions or setting events for behaviours as well as with the naturally occurring, or experimentally manipulated, consequences following behaviours.

We have cautioned elsewhere (Wheldall, 1980, 1981) about the dangers of 'behavioural overkill' in the context of the current preoccupation of behaviour modifiers with often rather crude, unnecessarily heavy, consequence management strategies for controlling children's behaviour. We referred specifically to the over enthusiastic adoption of techniques such as the token economy, time out and overcorrection. 'Heavy' procedures such as these are less likely to lead to generalisation of control to more naturally occurring reinforcers. Behavioural ecology offers alternatives to traditional contingency management procedures and is a potential means of avoiding behavioural overkill.

Behavioural ecology (Risley, 1977; Krantz and Risley, 1977) in the field of education is concerned with classroom environmental variables and their effects on children's behaviour. As Glynn (1981) puts it:

> Within the classroom environment it is known that a wide range of stimulus conditions will influence behaviour, these range from physical events like noise level and seating arrangements or the presence or absence of particular curriculum materials to social events such as the presence or absence of an audience of adults or peers. These social-environmental variables or setting events can strongly influence the quality of teacher child-interaction that can take place. Knowledge of their operation is thus vital to a behavioural approach to teaching.

Ecological or environmental variables influencing children's behaviour in the classroom take many forms. Russell & Bernel (1977), for example, have shown that temporal and climatic variables appeared to influence rates of desirable and undesirable behaviour in five-to-seven-year-old boys. Nor is a concern with such factors new since A. H. Seymour was carrying out research on 'the effects of different conditions of temperature and ventilation on the mental output and mental fatigue of school children' in 1936 (see also W. D. Seymour, 1939). Little research in this area has been carried out subsequently, however, but Axelrod, Hall & Tams (1979) urge that factors in the classroom environment such as room temperature, lighting, background music, etc. should be experimentally assessed for their potential influence on children's behaviour.

Research on setting events or antecedent conditions in schools has tended to focus more on social variables. For example, O'Rourke & Glynn (1978) showed that adult presence in the playground was more effective in increasing playground participation and decreasing inappropriate behaviour, than the provision of extra play equipment. Moss & Childs (1981) report a similar, interesting study on playground behaviour whereby young children's inappropriate and often aggressive behaviour was dramatically improved as a result of teaching the children traditional playground games which they had not previously learned. Glynn and his co-workers have also demonstrated the influence of setting events on academic learning in the classroom (Glynn, 1981). Wheldall & Austin (1980) working with a teacher and a difficult class of 'low ability' secondary aged children have demonstrated that the amount of work set also influences on-task behaviour. The teacher in their study was asked to write on the blackboard a second set of maths problems for the quicker ones to get on with after they had completed the first set. This resulted in an increase in on-task behaviour of nearly 15% overall for the class.

In this paper we are focusing on classroom seating arrangements as an example of a potentially powerful ecological variable, by examining the hypothesis that differing classroom seating arrangements are setting events for different forms of class and teacher behaviour. In the United Kingdom, classroom seating whereby desks or tables are arranged in rows is the norm in secondary schools. This was also the case in most primary schools until the sixties when a less formal approach to primary education came into vogue. This approach favoured learning by discovery, by the use of topic and project work for example, and was accompanied by a move towards less formal seating arrangements, away from rows to a preference for table formations. In this latter arrangement, desks or tables are arranged so that four to eight children sit around a common work area. This seating arrangement was widely adopted and is presently the most commonly found arrangement, being employed for overtly academic, individual, task-orientated work (e.g. workcards), as well as group work. To our knowledge, no empirical evidence was ever adduced to support this change of seating arrangement.

Research has been carried out, however, on seating arrangements and their effects. Early work included observational studies by Griffith (1921) and Dawe (1934). Griffith claimed that the best grades were obtained by pupils who sat in the front centre of the room. Dawe found that the further kindergarten children sat from the teacher when listening to a story, the less likely they were to make verbal contributions.

Schwebel (1969) found that the most common teacher strategy regarding seating was to allow children to sit where they chose initially, but that teachers would subsequently assign seats to children distributing disruptive children to sections of the class where any disruptions would do least harm. This was again, however, only an observational study.

Experimental work has also been carried out on the effects of seating arrangements. Shores & Haubrich (1969) compared seating in rows with seating in individual work cubicles for four 'emotionally disturbed' children. Their experimental manipulation of these conditions revealed that whilst cubicles increased attending behaviour this was not accompanied by improved academic performance. Saunders (1970) obtained inconclusive results when attempting to determine the optimal placement of 'emotionally disturbed' children within a class by comparing the placing of individual children in 'socially acceptable', 'socially unacceptable', and 'socially mixed' groups of children. Rubin (1973) and Ankney (1974) have also compared the effects of various seating arrangements (e.g. rows, horseshoes, circles) on children's behaviour. Rubin found that the verbal interaction and class participation of sixth grade (11- to 12-year-old) children was most affected by changes in seating arrangements whilst Ankney found that the six mentally handicapped children in his study spent more time on task when arranged in a horseshoe figuration than in any other. Moore (1980) has also demonstrated that location (i.e. where children sit in class) markedly effects the number of questions they are asked.

Krantz & Risley (1977) have demonstrated the control of kindergarten children's on-task behaviour by systematic manipulation of spatial density. They showed that during story sessions and demonstrations, on-task behaviour was higher when the children were placed with a space between each child and his neighbours, than when they were allowed to cluster around their teacher. Krantz & Risley's experimental design also allowed comparisons of the power of the control achieved by manipulating the ecological variable with the control achieved by means of a positive reinforcement procedure involving praise and privileges. The ecological intervention proved just as powerful as the reinforcement procedures, whilst being easier and quicker to employ.

The present research, geared towards assessing the effects on classroom behaviour of experimentally manipulated seating arrangements, was inspired by, and is in part a replication of, the work of Axelrod *et al.* (1979). They systematically observed two classes under rows and tables style seating arrangements. In the first study, a class of 17 academically below average second grade children (7- to 8-year-olds) were observed daily and their on-task behaviour sampled whilst they independently completed formal academic work. For nine sessions the children were seated in fours (and one five) around tables, followed by ten days in which they sat in rows of four, followed by a further seven days of tables and, finally, seven more days in rows. On-task behaviour was defined as "orientation toward the appropriate material, attention to the teacher when she was speaking, complying with teacher requests, raising a hand for teacher assistance, and being out of one's seat with teacher permission". Each child was observed successively for one minute per lesson, being rated on- or off-task every ten seconds. The reliability checks throughout indicated good inter-observer agreement of between 92 and 96%. The results clearly demonstrated greater on-task behaviour during rows conditions, the means being 62% during tables 1, 82% during rows 1, 63% during tables 2 and 83% during rows 2.

In their second study, a class of 32 academically average seventh grade children (12–13-year-olds) were observed and 'talk-outs' (disruptions) were recorded. A 'talk-out' was defined as 'any audible, verbal sound made by a student without the teacher's permission'. The number of talk-outs was recorded daily during a 55 minute life sciences lesson in which work book assignments were to be completed. Inter-observer agreement was around 90%. In this study the first five days of observation took place under a tables condition whereby pairs of children sat opposite each other separated by a few feet from similar pairs. This was followed by ten days of rows (as in the first study) and then 5 more days of tables. Again the results were clear, talk-outs averaged 58% under tables 1, 30% under rows and 50% during tables 2. More disruptions occured during tables conditions.

Tables formations appear, therefore, to be associated with more disruptive behaviour and less on-task behaviour, compared with rows. Axelrod *et al.* point out that the reasons for this are obvious since tables formations facilitate eye contact between pairs which can rapidly lead to conversations involving the whole table and also since covert kicking can easily be achieved. They conclude by arguing the case for a greater emphasis to be placed on antecedent events since they require 'less attention from the teacher and less cost to the school systems than contingency arrangements typically used in behaviour modification research'.

Our research was designed to replicate and subsequently to extend Axelrod *et al.'s* findings within a *British* educational context. In the two studies presented here we observed on task-behaviour in two top junior classes of 10–11-year-olds comparing classroom seating arranged around tables with seating in rows.

Method

Subjects and Setting

The subjects in the first study (class A) consisted of a class of 28 mixed ability children (12 girls and 16 boys) aged between ten and eleven years. The school was situated in an urban residential area and the class teacher was female with 13 years teaching experience. Class seating, as detailed later, was normally around tables.

The subjects in the second study (class B) consisted of a similar class of 25 academically mixed ten- to eleven-year-olds (9 girls and 16 boys), attending a school situated on a large urban, council housing estate. The class teacher was again female and had taught for ten years. Class B were generally regarded within the school as 'boisterous' and somewhat difficult to teach. Like Class A they normally sat around tables except for end of term tests.

Design

The design of the experiment was similar for both studies. In both classes, the children were systematically observed daily for two weeks in their usual 'tables' seating arrangement ('tables 1' condition), followed by a further two weeks in which they were seated in rows ('rows' condition) and finally for a further two weeks seated around tables ('tables 2' condition). Daily estimates of on-task behaviour for each child (as described later) were averaged for each class and plotted to compare level of on-task behaviour under the two conditions for both classes.

Conditions/Seating Arrangements

In the first study (class A) the 'tables' conditions involved the class being seated in seven groups of four, in each of which two double desks were placed so that the two pairs were facing each other. During the 'rows' condition, the double desks were arranged in three rows of five double desks (one double desk remaining empty).

In the second study (class B), the arrangements were similar but differed slightly in detail. The 'tables' conditions involved different sized groups, mostly in fours as in class A, but with some in groups of five arranged around three double desks and also with a few individual children seated alone in double desks. (It should be emphasised that in both studies the 'tables' conditions consisted of the seating arrangement normally used by the teacher of that class.) In the 'rows' condition for class B, seating was arranged in three rows of six double desks, in which eight pairs were seated whilst nine children sat alone in a double desk. The remaining double desks were unoccupied. (Again, it should be emphasised that the specific use or interpretation of the 'rows' arrangement was left to the class teacher.) In both studies rearrangement of desks took place during the weekends in between conditions.

Observational Procedure

The classes were observed daily by an independent observer for thirty to forty minutes mainly during academic lessons (see general procedure). In each class every child was observed twice, in a different order each day, for two periods of thirty seconds. Using a stopwatch and a pre-prepared sheet, each child's behaviour was observed and rated every five seconds as to whether (s)he had been 'on-task' for the whole of the preceding five seconds or not. On the observation sheet the observer recorded for each five-second interval, a tick in the appropriate box if the child had been on-task and a cross if for any part of it (s)he had been off-task. (This estimation procedure will, thereby, slightly underestimate on-task behaviour since on task behaviour occurring during a five-second period when a child is off-task, however fleetingly, will not be counted.) This procedure thus gives for each child per lesson two scores out of six (six five-second intervals making up the thirty seconds). These scores are added to give estimates of individual on-task behaviour and then averaged to give percentage estimates of daily on-task behaviour for the whole class and also percentage estimates of on-task behaviour in each condition for each child. 'On-task' behaviour was defined very similarly in both studies as compliance with the teacher's instructions, eye contact with the teacher when requested, eye contact with their textbooks and materials when asked to get on with their set work. 'Off-task' behaviour included calling out, interrupting a neighbour, talking to a neighbour, being out of one's seat without permission, non-compliance with teacher instructions and not getting on with the set work.

Inter-Observer Agreement

In order to provide indications of the reliability of the observation procedure employed, a second observer independently observed and recorded the behaviour of each class once in each of the three conditions. The second observer observed the children alongside, and in the same order as the first observer, but both observers kept separate, independent records. Subsequent inspection of their record sheets allowed a comparison to be made of the decisions of the two observers for each five-second interval. Thus the number of agreements and disagreements between the two observers could easily be counted and an estimate of inter-observer agreement calculated for each child and for the whole class. Inter-observer agreement was expressed as a percentage of number of agreements divided by the total number of observations (agreements plus disagreements).

General Procedural Details

In both studies the classes were initially observed on several occasions prior to the study without records being kept, in order to accustom teachers and children to the presence of an observer.

In the first study, observations over the three conditions were only carried out in the mornings when overtly academic written work was carried out. The children were instructed not to call out, to put up their hands if they needed help and not to interrupt their peers. Class A was observed on ten occasions during 'tables 1', on eight occasions during 'rows' and on seven occasions during 'tables 2'.

In the second study, observations took place at different times during the day and in all lessons except PE, Art and Music. The children were given similar instructions to those in the first study and were observed on ten occasions in each condition.

Absenteeism affected the data collection in both studies. In the first study, out of a total possible number of 700 data collection intervals (25 days multiplied by 28 children), 71 were lost due to absenteeism (10% or an average of 2.8 children absent per day). In the second study 68 out of 750 intervals (30 days multiplied by 25 children were lost (9% or an average of 2.3 children absent per day).

Results

There was evidence of good inter-observer agreement in both studies of around 90%, supporting the reliability of the measures obtained. Inter-observer agreement data for the whole class for the three conditions in the two studies is shown in Table 1, together with comparisons of the estimates of percentage on-task behaviour for the two observers.

Mean on-task behaviour for both classes was higher when the children were placed in rows than when they were seated around tables. Mean on-task behaviour in class A was 72% under 'tables 1', 88% under 'rows' and 69% under 'tables 2'. Similarly for Class B, mean on-task behaviour was 67% under 'tables 1', 84% under 'rows' and 72% under tables 2.

TABLE I. Inter-observer agreement figures and estimates of on-task behaviour by the two observers in the two studies

Condition	% Inter-observer agreement	% On-task behaviour Observer 1	Observer 2
Study 1 (class A)			
Tables 1	93	72	73
Rows	89	85	81
Tables 2	96	73	70
Study 2 (class B)			
Tables 1	90	68	67
Rows	97	92	91
Tables 2	93	73	71

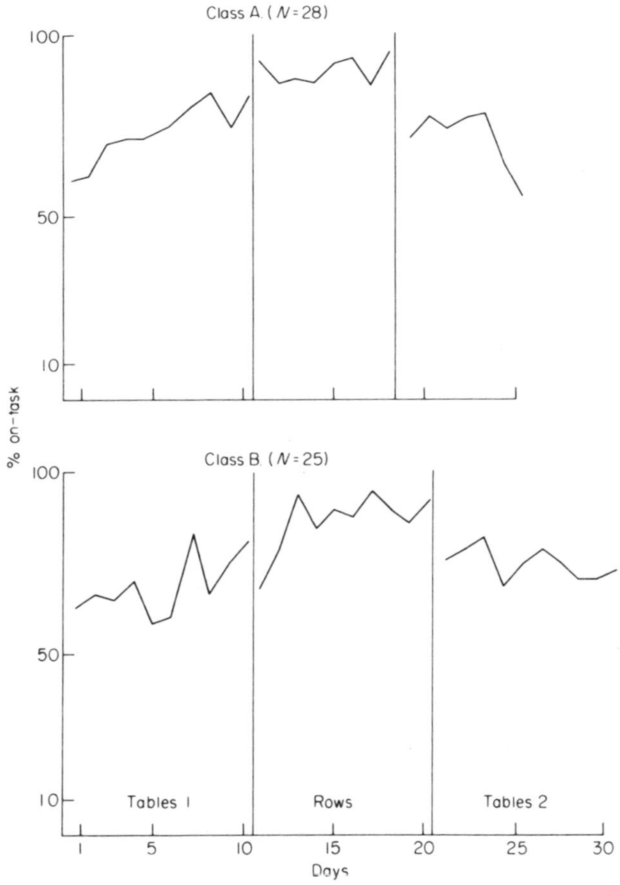

FIG. 1. Mean on-task behaviour for the two classes over the three phases.

Inspection of the (similar) graphs for the two classes suggests that the mean on-task figures cloud a more complicated pattern (see Fig. 1). In both classes average on-task behaviour is characterised by rising baselines during 'tables 1'; this is particularly marked for class A. One interpretation of this is to suggest that the high on-task behaviour during rows is merely due to a continuing general improvement in behaviour. Contrary to this, however, is the clear demonstration of markedly lower on-task behaviour in both classes *immediately* following the reversal, the return to tables. The results of this analysis are, therefore, rather equivocal. Since it was felt that children with high initial on-task behaviour would be reducing the experimental effect (since little further improvement would be posible) it was consequently decided to re-analyse the data, grouping the children with 'high' (80% and over), 'average' (60–79%) and 'low' (under 69%) initial on-task behaviour (during 'tables 1'), separately.

Mean percentage on-task figures for these three groups for both classes are shown in Table 2. As expected, there was evidence for only a small effect for 'high' children a larger effect for 'average' children and a substantial effect for 'low' children. Again, however, these mean percentages must be evaluated in the context of the graphs showing on-task behaviour for each session over the three phases (see Figs. 2, 3 and 4).

TABLE II. Mean percentage on-task behaviour for low (under 60%), medium (60–79%) and high (80% and over) initial on-task behaviour in the two studies

Group	*N*	Tables 1	(Gain)	Rows	(Loss)	Tables 2
Study 1 (class A)						
Low	4	56	(37)	93	(24)	69
Medium	17	71	(17)	88	(23)	65
High	7	84	(2)	86	(7)	79
Total	28	72	(16)	88	(19)	69
Study 2 (class B)						
Low	7	45	(31)	76	(17)	59
Medium	13	72	(11)	83	(11)	72
High	5	86	(10)	96	(6)	90
Total	25	67	(17)	84	(12)	72

The graphs for the 'high' children in both classes (Fig. 2) provide little evidence for any clear effect on behaviour as a result of manipulating classroom seating. There is little separation between the three phases. There is, however, evidence for a decline in on-task behaviour in the reversal to tables in class A. We may conclude that manipulating seating in this way with children whose on-task behaviour is already high does not yield an appreciable effect.

In the graphs for the 'average' groups (Fig. 3) there is, as we might expect, a very similar pattern to that shown in the graphs for the classes overall. The rising baselines again make interpretation difficult, but there is evidence for markedly reduced on-task behaviour in the reversal, particularly in class A. In spite of the rising baselines, we feel that the overall evidence suggests that children whose on-task behaviour when seated around tables is only 'average', benefit from sitting in rows, in terms of increased on-task behaviour.

The graphs for the small number of children in both class with low initial on-task behaviour during tables (Fig. 4) are, it is argued, unequivocal. There is some indication of a rising baseline in class A but this would not account for the immediate leap in on-task behaviour. In class B there is no indication of a rising

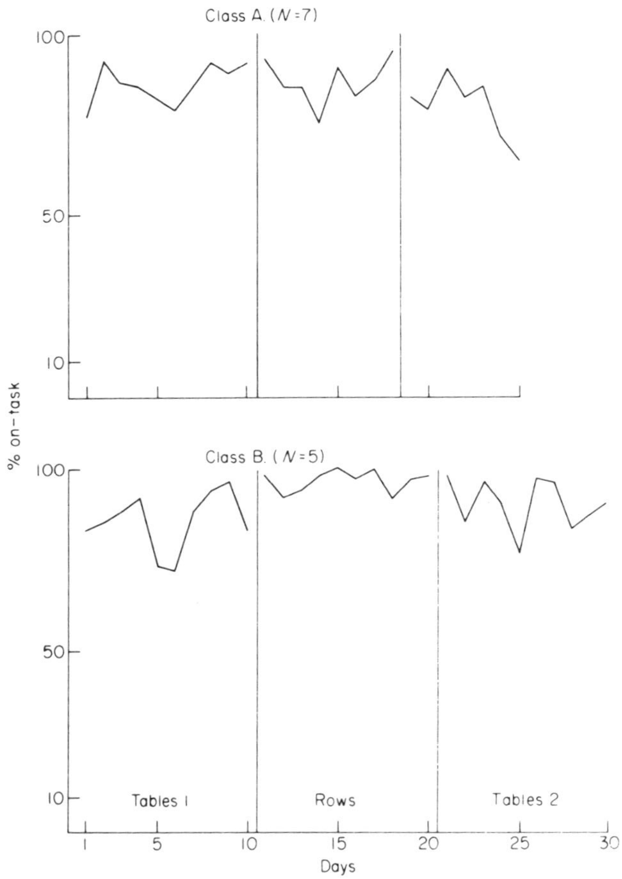

FIG. 2. Mean on-task behaviour for the children in the two classes with 'high' initial on-task behaviour, over the three phases.

baseline and on-task behaviour is shown to rise steadily and appreciably during rows. In class A the reversal shows an immediate decrease in on-task behaviour whereas class B shows a steady decline, except for the fourth session in 'tables 2' when on task behaviour dipped to just over 20% for this one lesson. The overall conclusion is that children whose behaviour is low when seated around tables benefit considerably, in terms of increased on-task behaviour, when seated in rows.

Looking at individual children, the vast majority showed improvement in on-task behaviour in rows except for those whose on task behaviour was already very high where, as already demonstrated, the effect is much reduced. For six children in class 2, on-task behaviour rose during 'rows' and stayed high during 'tables 2, and one child's on-task behaviour *decreased* during 'rows'. He was the lively, noisy ringleader of an anti-school group who consequently spent more time in 'rows' trying to regain contact with his group! Similarly in class A, two children showed lower on-task behaviour in rows, one child's behaviour increased during rows and remained high in 'tables 2', and one child was almost completely unaffected by the changing conditions (averaging over 80%). In both classes, boys and girls were equally affected by the change in seating conditions, with girls showing higher on task figures over all conditions (see Table 3). Further 'fine grain' details of the results are given in unpublished reports by Morris (1981) and Vaughan (1981).

TABLE III. Mean percentage on-task behaviour for boys and girls in each condition in the two studies

Sex	*N*	Tables 1	(Gain)	Rows	(Loss)	Tables 2
Study 1 (Class A)						
Boys	16	70	(16)	86	(14)	68
Girls	12	76	(15)	91	(19)	72
Study 2 (class B)						
Boys	16	64	(16)	80	(11)	69
Girls	9	72	(17)	89	(13)	76

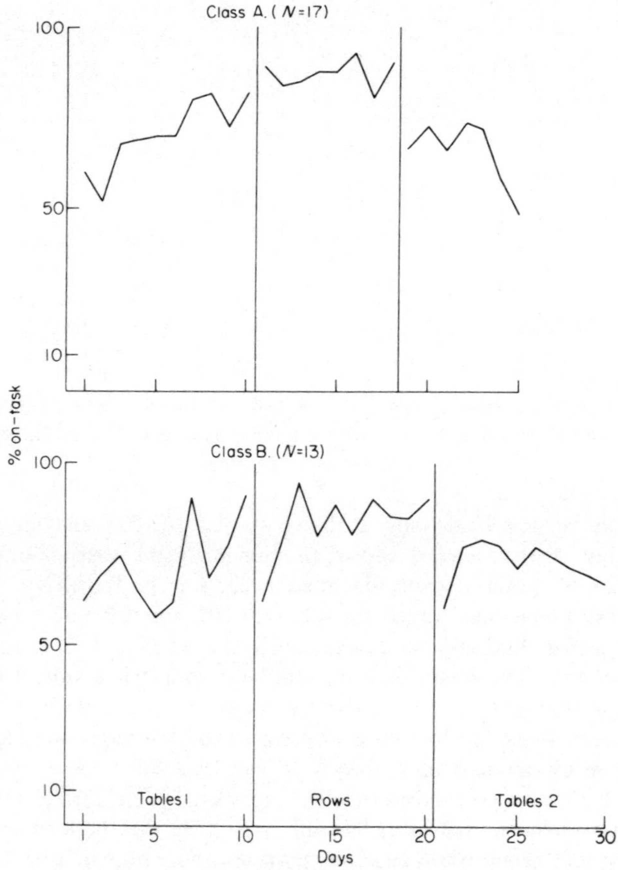

FIG. 3. Mean on-task behaviour for the children in the two classes with 'average' initial on-task behaviour, over the three phases.

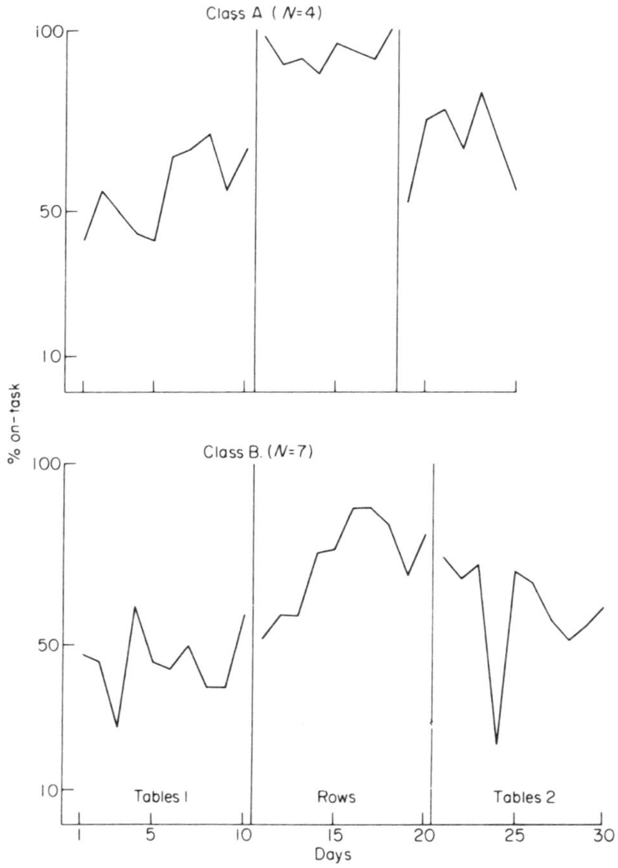

FIG. 4. Mean on-task behaviour for the children in the two classes with 'low' initial on-task behaviour, over the three phases.

Discussion

As the graphs in Figs 1–4 show, control over children's on-task behaviour by the manipulation of seating arrangements is clearly possible, especially with children whose initial on-task behaviour is low. On-task behaviour was around 15% higher in both classes overall during the period whilst children sat in rows. This supports the findings of Axelrod and his colleagues who found 20% higher on task behaviour during rows style seating arrangements in their (American) study of academically below average seven- to eight-year-olds. Moreover, as Axelrod *et al.* emphasised, these substantial increases in on-task behaviour were brought about simply and efficiently with few of the difficulties associated with some behavioural strategies based upon consequence management. We would not wish to minimise the importance of such procedures since we feel it is vital that all teachers should be trained in behavioural approaches to teaching, including such consequence management strategies as the effective use of praise, but here lies the problem. Such procedures do require the careful training of teachers in skills which few already possess or are able to use systematically. Making use of behavioural ecology by control of known setting events for specified behaviours may prove to be a more immediate means of gaining some control over some children's classroom behaviour. This may also prove a useful bridge whilst other behavioural teaching skills are learned and will serve to increase instances of desired behaviour for the teacher to reinforce. In short, our aim is not to suggest an exclusive alternative to more traditional behavioural approaches based on consequence management, but to re-instate and re-assert the importance of setting events in the control of human behaviour.

Turning briefly to the specific question of why does the setting event of classroom seating around tables lead to more off-task behaviour whilst seating in rows leads to improved on-task behaviour, we would concur with the views of Axelrod *et al.*, already mentioned in the introduction. The tables based seating arrangement is, quite simply, geared towards enhancing social interaction. It facilitates eye contact, a prime means of initiating a social encounter, and provides a setting for increased participation in such encounters by involving the whole group. After all, we engineer such seating arrangements in precisely this way when we wish to encourage social interaction, in committees or when playing bridge, for example. Moreover, tables provide ideal cover for covert aggression or teasing by means of kicking or pinching under the table, thereby increasing disruption. Rows formations, on the other hand, minimise either form of social contact, allowing fewer occasions for the teacher to comment adversely and more instances of desirable behaviour for him or her to comment upon favourably. In short, it would be argued that it amounts to little short of cruelty to place children in manifestly social contexts and then to expect them to work independently.

We must immediately emphasise, however, that we are *not* advocating a return to rows for all work. It is offered only as a possible strategy to encourage academic work which requires the child to concentrate on the specific task in hand without distractions. Rows would be totally inappropriate, for example, for small group discussions or group topic work, where table arrangements might prove more effective. Alternatively a horseshoe arrangement of desks around the room facing inwards might well facilitate class discussion sessions as well as allowing children to get on with individual work when necessary. These are empirical questions which we hope to tackle in our future research.

Moreover, we would wish to emphasise that it is the teacher's job to decide on the behaviours which should be encouraged in classrooms; the job of researchers is to attempt to provide the empirical evidence on which to base those decisions. Consequently future research must also seek to demonstrate whether increased on-task behaviour is accompanied by increased quantity and quality of academic work accomplished. As Vargas (1977) has said, "It is possible to produce a class of well mannered, attentive-looking students who don't learn much except the discipline of sitting still" (p. 54). We should be rightly wary of possibly, merely having taught children to "be still, be quiet, be docile", the criticism levelled at earlier behavioural work in the classroom by Winnett & Winkler (1972). The results of our earlier research on classroom management, however, lead us to expect that increased on-task behaviour will lead to greater academic output since the implementation of a 'game' strategy to increase on-task behaviour in one study also resulted in a dramatic increase in the amount of written work produced by the children, with no increase in spelling errors (Merrett & Wheldall, 1978). We must now attempt to demonstrate that the quality of their writing as asssessed by other criteria (e.g. creativity) accompanies increased on-task behaviour.

In a forthcoming paper, Wheldall & Ng (1981) present further studies on the effects of manipulating seating arrangements. These include analyses of disruption rates and of teacher behaviours. Further research is also needed on the long term effects of changing from 'tables' to 'rows'. Do children learn, for example, new ways of being disruptive or off-task to suit their altered circumstances? We would also like to investigate whether the behaviour of children who normally sit in rows deteriorates when they are placed around tables. It can be seen from these few suggestions that the topic of seating arrangements in particular, and behavioural ecology generally, is a most promising field for future research.

Before concluding it is important to stress two other findings from this study. Firstly, the children involved in these studies appeared very interested in the changes of seating arrangement but did not comment on them to the teacher until the rows were changed back to tables. They then complained since they said they *preferred* sitting in rows. Secondly, both teachers subsequently opted for a permanent change to rows following the completion of the studies and many of their colleagues followed their example.

These results on seating arrangements constitute just one lesson to be learned from behavioural ecology when applied to the classroom. Certainly they should cause us to doubt the current preoccupation with fixed classroom seating arrangements and to encourage us to experiment with seating so as to optimise the appropriate behaviour for the task in hand and to discourage unwanted behaviours.

REFERENCES

ANKNEY, R.F. (1974) Effects of classroom spatial arrangement on student behaviour, *Doctoral dissertation*, Ohio State University, 1974, *Dissertation Abstracts International*, 35, pp. 2439A–3940A (University Microfilm No. 74–24289).

AXELROD, D., HALL, R.V. & TAMS, A. (1979) Comparison of two common classroom seating arrangements, *Academic Therapy*, 15, pp. 29–36.

DAWE, H.C. (1934) The influence of size of kindergarten group upon performance, *Child Development*, 5, pp. 295–303.

GLYNN, T. (1981) Building an effective teaching environment, in: WHELDALL, K. & RIDING, R.J. (Eds) *Pyschological Aspects of Learning and Teaching* (London, Croom Helm).

GRIFFITH, C.R. (1921) A comment upon the psychology of the audience, *Psychology Monographs*, 30, pp. 36–47.

KRANTZ, P.J & RISLEY, T.R. (1977) Behavioural ecology in the classroom, in: O'LEARY, K.D. & O'LEARY, S.F. (Eds) *Classroom Management: the Successful Use of Behaviour Modification*, 2nd edn (New York, Pergamon Press).

MERRETT, F. & WHELDALL, K. (1978) Playing the game: a behavioural approach to classroom management, *Educational Review*, 30, pp. 41–50.

MOORE, D. (1980) Location as a causal factor in the unequal distribution of teacher questions: an experimental analysis, *paper* presented to the Third Australian Conference on Behaviour Modification, Melbourne.

MORRIS, M. (1981) A comparison of infant and junior school teachers' behaviour and the influence of classroom seating on children's study level, *unpublished BPhil (Ed) dissertation*, Faculty of Education, University of Birmingham.

MOSS, F. & CHILDS, J. (1981) In-service training for teaching in behavioural psychology: problems of implementation, in: WHEDALL, K. (Ed.) *The Behaviourist in the Classroom: Aspects of Applied Behavioural Analysis in British Educational Contexts* (Birmingham, Educational Review Publications).

O'ROURKE, M. & GLYNN, T. (1978) Play equipment and adult participation: effects on children's playground behaviour, in: GLYNN, T. & MCNAUGHTON, S. (Eds) *Behaviour Analysis in New Zealand* (Department of Education, University of Auckland).

RISLEY, T.R. (1977) The ecology of applied behavioural analysis, in: ROGERS-WARREN, A. & ROGERS-WARREN, S.F. (Eds) *Ecological Perspectives in Behaviour Analysis* (Baltimore, University Park Press).

RUBIN, C.N. (1973) A naturalistic study in proxemics: seating arrangement and its effect on interaction, performance and behaviour, *Doctoral dissertation*, Bowling Green State University, 1972, *Dissertation Abstracts International*, 33, 3071A–4586A (University Microfilm No. 73-01119).

RUSSELL, M.B. & BERNAL, M.E. (1977) Temporal and climatic variables in naturalistic observation, *Journal of Applied Behavior Analysis*, 10, pp. 339–405.

SAUNDERS, B.T. (1970) Modification of emotionally disturbed behaviour in the elementary school child through the manipulation of classroom seating arrangements, *Doctoral dissertation*, University of Connecticut, 1969, *Dissertation Abstracts International 31*, 03–A (University Microfilm No. 70-15552).

SCHWEBEL, A.I. (1969) Physical and social distancing in teacher-pupil relationship, Doctoral dissertation, Yale University, 1969, *Dissertation Abstract International*, 31, 973B–2378B (University Microfilm No. 70-16250).

SEYMOUR, A.H. (1936) The effects of different conditions of temperature and ventilation on the mental fatigue of schoolchildren, *unpublished Doctoral thesis*, University of London.

SEYMOUR, W.D. (1939) *The Heating, Ventilation and Lighting of School Buildings* (London, Oxford University Press).

SHORES, R.E. & HAUBRICH, P.A. (1969) Effects of cubicles in educating emotionally disturbed children, *Exceptional Children*, 34, pp. 21–24.

VARGAS, J.S. (1977) *Behavioural Psychology for Teachers* (New York, Harper & Row).

VAUGHAN, P. (1981) Comparisons of teachers' behaviour across ability groups in the junior school and a consideration of ecological variables in influencing on task behaviour, *unpublished BPhil(Ed) dissertation*, Faculty of Education, University of Birmingham.

WHELDALL, K. (1980) Applied behavioural analysis in British educational contexts (with particular reference to the work of the 'Birmingham Group'), *paper* presented to the Third Australian Conference on Behaviour Modification, Melbourne, May 1980.

WHELDALL, K. (1981) A before C or the use of behavioural ecology in classroom management, in: GURNEY, P. (Ed.) *Behaviour Modification in Education* (Perspectives, No. 5) (School of Education, University of Exeter).

WHELDALL, K. & AUSTIN, R. (1980) Successful behaviour modification in the secondary school: a reply to McNamara and Harrop, *Occasional Papers of the Division of Educational and Child Psychology of the British Psychological Society*, 4, pp. 3–9.

WHELDALL, K. & NG, Y.Y. (1981) Rows versus tables II: the effects of two classroom seating arrangements on disruption rate, on-task behaviour and teacher behaviour in three special school classes (in preparation).

WINNETT, R.A. & WINKLER, R.C. (1972) Current behaviour modification in the classroom: be still, be quiet, be docile, *Journal of Applied Behavior Analysis*, 5, pp. 499–504.

Variation in Question Rate as a Function of Position in the Classroom

DENNIS W. MOORE
TED GLYNN

ABSTRACT *The effect of different seating positions on the frequency with which pupils were addressed questions by the teacher was examined in two primary school classes. Baseline observations identified areas in both classes to which a disproportionately high and low number of questions were directed. Utilising a multiple baseline design six pupils in both classes were systematically moved in and out of these areas. Results indicate that location within the classroom is in itself a causal factor in the question distribution pattern. Concomitant measures of teacher location and pupil on-task levels indicate that changes in these features of the behavioural ecology of the classes did not confound the location effects. Data are discussed illustrating the value of obtaining observational measures on behaviours concomitant with the dependent variable both in order to monitor uncontrolled variables which it is anticipated may confound the experimental effects, and to assist in the identification of other potentially significant ecological setting events within the classroom.*

With increasing recognition of the interdependence of behaviour and the environment (Gump, 1977), the experimental analysis of antecedent stimulus conditions, including setting events, has become a major focus in applied behavioural psychology (Hamerlynck, 1979; Rogers-Warren & Warren, 1977; Wahler & Fox, 1981; Willems, 1974). Relative ease of implementation and maintenance of change are two pragmatic benefits of attending to the arrangement of antecedent events instead of concentrating exclusively on the consequence management more typical of behaviour modification research (Axelrod, Hall & Tams, 1979; Van Biervliet, Spangler & Marshall, 1981). Furthermore, as argued previously (Glynn, 1981), the implimentation of such eco-behavioural research in educational settings yields evidence of the influence of numerous social-environmental variables on teacher-pupil interaction, knowledge vital to a behavioural approach to teaching.

Wong & McNaughton (1980) and McNaughton & Glynn (1981) have shown that marked gains in oral reading proficiency can be obtained through quite simple but very precise changes in instructional setting conditions. Similarly, direct instruction, an educational technology entailing a comprehensive specification of curriculum materials and their presentation, has been demonstrated to contribute significantly to children's academic attainments (Becker *et al.*, 1981).

Researchers have also demonstrated a marked effect of different seating arrangements on pupils' attention and/or participation rates in preschool (Krantz & Risley, 1977), primary (Axelrod *et al.*, 1979; Schwebel & Cherlin, 1972; Wheldall *et al.*, 1981; Clark *et al*, 1982 [1], and university settings (Sommer, 1967).

Pupil location within the class is another variable which several writers have observed to correspond with differential behaviour and attainments. Adams (1969) reported an observational study of primary and secondary level classes in which teacher attention and pupil participation in verbal interaction were both highly concentrated in the centre front and middle sections of the room. So powerful was this phenomenon that Adams coined the term 'zone of influence' to describe this area of the classroom. Sommer (1969) replicated this finding in undergraduate university classes and posited a hypothesis of maximal visual contact/expressive contact as explanation for this unequal distribution of teacher-student interaction.

Two systematic replications of Adams' (1969) study have been reported. Delefes & Jackson (1972), although they did not observe a 'zone of influence' centre front and middle of the room, did note a disparity in the distribution of teacher attention in that pupils seated further from the teacher were not singled out for communication as often as those seated at the front of the class. Bates (1973) conversely reported little evidence of higher participation rates in the front centre locations. Unfortunately Bates' results are insufficiently detailed to permit a more complete analysis of the relationship between pupil location and participation in the classes he studied.

Together these studies clearly demonstrate that differences in seating position correspond with non-equivalent pupil participation in classroom interaction. However such observational studies necessarily leave unaddressed the possibility of a causal relationship between location and pupil behaviour and, more specifically, the direction of such a hypothesised relationship. Do teachers initiate more interaction with pupils in their immediate physical and/or visual field, or do pupils with a predisposition to participate verbally in class activities and to attract teacher attention choose certain seats or get placed in particular areas? Alternatively, is the teacher's attention unknowingly differentially distributed under the stimulus control of some other characteristics within the classroom thereby in turn consequating unequal pupil participation?

Several studies have produced data of relevance to these questions. Dykman & Reis (1979), Morrison & Thomas (1975), and Walberg (1969) all found significant differences between students seated in various regions of classrooms in their responses to pencil and paper measures of self-concept and attitude to school. Dykman & Reis report that in their sample of high school students, all of whom were seated in self-selected positions, responses . . .

> indicative of feelings of vulnerability and inadequacy showed a marked tendency to be located in the rear and far-side regions of the class-

> room . . . [whereas] . . . students with the most positive self-concepts tended to sit in front. (p. 352)

These findings support the hypothesis that students with particular predispositions select seats that favour their expression. However, as Dykman & Reis observed, all the teachers in their sample, when questioned, reported differences in the appropriate direction between front and rear seated students on a number of academically oriented descriptors. Consequently the possibility of differential treatment of these students compounding their attitudinal and behavioural characteristics cannot be ruled out. Dykman & Reis suggested that causality may be multi-directional; self-concept affecting seat choice, and seating location producing different teacher-student interactions which in turn influence the students' self-concept.

Researchers have also manipulated seating position in a number of experimental investigations of the effect of location on student behaviour. Studies employing between-subjects designs (Koneya, 1976; Sommer, 1967; Stires, 1980) and within-subject methodology (Levine *et al.*, 1980) with changes in student attitude, behaviour and attainments serving as dependent measures, have all shown that location within the class does affect student performance. Stires (1980) concluded that "while it is physically possible to pay attention from any place in the room, some locations facilitate attending while others make it more difficult" (p. 252).

Although it is now clear that the physical location of pupils within a classroom can significantly affect both their behaviour and academic attainment levels, the authors of two recent literature reviews (Ornstein & Levine, 1981; Weinstein, 1979) both noted that the mechanisms responsible for these effects have not yet been identified. Weinstein hypothesised that differential teacher attention to pupils in different positions could partially account for this phenomenon.

This hypothesis presupposes a causal relationship between classroom location *per se* and unequally distributed teacher attention. As outlined above, observational studies of classroom interaction have found teacher attention to be unequally distributed across the classroom (Adams, 1969; Delefes & Jackson, 1972). However these studies can do no more than suggest the possibility of a causal relationship between this setting variable and the teacher's behaviour. Weinstein's hypothesis would be strengthened considerably by empirical evidence that different classroom positions directly influenced the rate of occurrence of some educationally significant teacher behaviour. Lesson-related questions are one such behaviour which has been the focus of two recent studies.

Moore & Smith (1980) monitored the distribution of teacher questions in a sample of secondary school classes. They reported an unequal distribution, with a disproportionately high number of questions being addressed to pupils in the back corners of the rooms, and the side sections proving to be comparatively neglected areas. It should be noted that this finding does not conform either with Adams' 'zone of influence', or Sommer's maximal visual contact/expressive contact hypothesis.

Moore (1981a) reported an experimental investigation of the effect of pupils' location within a classroom on the proportion of teacher's questions they received. This study, in which a within-subjects ABAB design was employed (Hersen & Barlow, 1976) in a single primary school class, provides some evidence that location within the classroom may in itself be a causal factor in the unequal distribution of teachers' questions.

However as data from only one teacher and classroom are reported, generalisation to other teachers or settings is at present unwarranted. Furthermore, Moore's presentation of his results in a grouped format prevents assessment of the experimental effects on individual pupils within the class thereby also restricting the internal generalisability of this result.

The present study was designed as a systematic replication of Moore (1981a). The aim of the study was to gain information concerning the inter-teacher/inter-class generalisability of the earlier results and also to obtain more idiographic data relating to the effects of location on the rate at which questions were directed at individual pupils within the classroom.

Method

Subjects and Setting

The subjects in this study were the teachers and pupils in a grade 2 and a grade 3 class in an urban International Primary School. The grade 2 class consisted of 27 children (14 girls and 13 boys) and a female teacher, while the grade three class had 29 children (12 girls and 17 boys) and a male teacher. Both classes were heterogeneous ability groupings and the school principal described both teachers as experienced and competent. The teachers agreed to participate in the study on the condition that they would only be informed of the nature of the hypotheses investigated after all observations had been completed.

In both classes the children were seated in individual desks and both the overall seating pattern and the location of individual pupils had been determined by the class teacher. The grade 2 children were seated in five clusters of from four to six children. In the grade 3 class the seating was arranged in five rows across the room (see Fig. 1). Both teachers reported that the positioning of individuals was on the basis of their experience with the children and was intended to reduce disruption and maximise the class's attention to lesson activities.

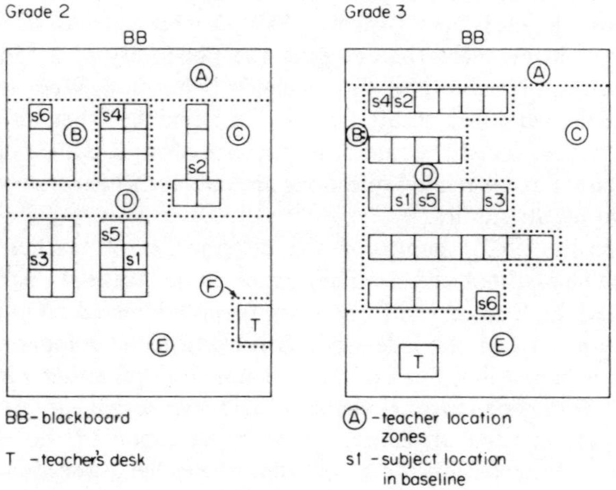

FIG. 1. Class plans showing teacher location zones and baseline seating positions of experimental subjects.

Procedure and Experimental Design

The general procedure in this study involved identifying areas within the two classrooms in which pupils were the targets of a disproportionately high and low number of the teacher's questions, then systematically shifting individual children in and out of these areas while continuing to monitor the frequency with which they received questions.

In the grade 2 class a multiple baseline across subjects design incorporating two time-lags (Hersen & Barlow, 1976), or serial replications, was utilised. Baseline data were used to map the distribution of teacher questions across the room and identify areas of relatively high and low question density in addition to serving their conventional function of providing base rate measures of the frequency with which the teacher addressed questions to each child. At each experimental intervention point the first author selected an individual pupil from a high question area and one from a low question area who then exchanged seats. Overall this design therefore provides two independent tests of the experimental hypothesis at each time-lagged intervention. No explanation was given to the teacher or pupils for these seating rearrangements which were carried out by the teacher in the absence of both the investigators and the regular observers.

Identical procedures were employed in the grade 3 class except that following the second time-lagged intervention a reversal phase was added in which six experimental subjects were simultaneously returned to their original seating position. Inclusion of this reversal component provides a final within-subjects replication of the experimental effect, thereby further strengthening the experimental design.

Concomitant Measures

Several writers have recommended the measurement of concomitant behaviour in applied behaviour analysis (e.g. Hersen & Barlow, 1976; Willems, 1974). Birnbrauer (1981) argued that as changes in specific uncontrolled features of an applied setting may have a confounding effect on treatment outcomes researchers should attempt to measure such potential confounds in order to make their results more comprehensible.

Unfortunately there are no straightforward rules to be applied in the *a priori* identification of appropriate concomitant measures. However there were three factors which could not be controlled in the present study which we considered could confound the effect of location on teacher question distribution and therefore warranted observation.

Firstly, any systematic changes in overall rate at which the teachers asked questions—particularly if such a change coincided with an experimental intervention—could obscure the effects of the independent variable. As described above, each intervention point involved an experimental manipulation of two subjects, one moving into a high question density area, the other being placed in a low question density area. On the basis of the experimental hypothesis one would predict an increase in rate of questions received by one and a decrease for the second. Therefore a systematic change in the overall rate of questions asked, be it an increase or a decrease, would confound by increasing the apparent experimental effect with one subject while camouflaging the effect with the other.

Secondly, any consistent changes in the children's attention to the lesson which could be associated with a change of seating position could confound the experimental effect. If, for example, moving closer to the teacher resulted in an increase in on-task behaviour, this changed pupil characteristic might alter the probability of that pupil being questioned independent of his or her location.

Thirdly, a direct relationship has been suggested between physical proximity and teacher-student interaction levels (Adams, 1969). Thus a systematic change in the teacher's location within the room which coincided with an experimental intervention could arguably also function as an experimental confound.

Concomitant measures of each of these variables were taken throughout the study to assay the possibility of their confounding the experimental effect.

Observational Procedures

The observation system was developed as part of a continuing research project (Moore, 1981a, b, 1984; Moore & Smith, 1980;). This system entails the continuous frequency recording of five discrete aspects of the classroom interaction on a form representing the physical layout of the room such that overall class rates, and each pupil's individual engagement in these can be subsequently ascertained. The five behaviours thus quantified are [3]:

teacher verbal praise directed at specific individuals;
teacher verbal disapproval directed at specific individuals;
teacher emitted questions addressed to a particular child, regardless of the outcome of the question;
teacher's use of individual pupil's names; and
any pupil-initiated interaction with the teacher.

The observation system also incorporated a 15 second interval, momentary time sampling procedure detailed by Thomas *et al.* (1977) which yields a simultaneous measure of the time spent attending to the lesson by a subset of 10 pupils in each class. Similarly, momentary time samples of the teacher's location in the room were also recorded at 15 second intervals throughout the observation session.

Four third-year university students acted as observers throughout the study. Prior to the commencement of data collection the students undertook a minimum of five one-hour training sessions involving both video recordings of class lessons and practice in live classrooms, and attained a minimum criterion level of 80% agreement (total agreement formula) with the first author. None of the observers were informed of the purpose of the study.

Daily 25 minute observation sessions were scheduled during the Mathematics lesson in both classes. Pairs of observers were time-tabled to take simultaneous but independent observations of all sessions, enabling calculation of inter-observer agreement levels for all data. Observation partners were regularly rotated to minimise differential observer drift effects (Johnson & Bolstad, 1973).

Recordings were only made when the class was operating as a single instructional or interacting group. On those occasions when the class divided into subgroups the observers simply stopped recording and waited until the class resumed its whole group status. Furthermore, no observations occurred during the first and last five minutes of a lesson, during which time lesson activity was often disrupted by a variety of organisational and administrative matters.

Results

Inter-observer Agreement

Although two observers were scheduled to be present for all sessions, a combination of unreliable transportation and other commitments resulted in both being present on only 18 of 37 days (49%) and 14 of 35 days (40%) in the grade 2 and 3 classes respectively. These days were distributed across the entire study such that inter-observer agreement was assessed at least twice in each experimental phase in both settings.

Inter-observer agreement was calculated separately for both teacher questions and the pupil on-task data using the weighted combined agreement formula (Harris & Lahey, 1978). In the grade 2 class this produced an index of 51.7% agreement for teacher questions (occurrence probability=24.7%) and 71.3% agreement for the pupil on-task measure (occurrence probability=88.3%). The equivalent figures for the grade 3 class were: teacher questions, 59.1% agreement (occurrence probability=56.7%); pupil on-task 50.7% agreement (occurrence probability=84.8%).

It has been argued elsewhere [2] that this method of calculating inter-observer agreement is one of the most conservative and least susceptible to chance variation with high and low rate behaviours. Unfortunately no empirically founded guidelines or *de facto* rules have yet emerged as to what levels of agreement may be considered acceptable when using the weighted combined formula. Interestingly, the same data when recalculated using the more familiar total agreement formula (Kelly, 1977) produced inter-observer agreement scores of 80.5% (teacher questions) and 96.5% (pupil on-task) in the grade 2 class, and in the grade 3 class 96% and 91.7% respectively.

Agreement levels on the teacher location data were determined by dividing the class into six (grade 2) and five (grade 3) unequal zones reflecting the spatial organisation of each room (see Fig. 1) and assessing occurrence agreement (Kelly, 1977) between observers as to the location of the teacher within these areas at each observation. Occurrence agreement scores of 76.5% and 69.3% were obtained in the grade 2 and 3 classes.

Concomitant Measures

The teacher's mean number of controlled questions per session across each experimental phase are presented in Table I. A chi square test indicated no statistically significant differences between phases in the grade 3 class ($\chi^2=8.54$, df 4, $p>0.05$) but showed a significant difference across phases in question rate in the grade 2 class ($\chi^2=20.24$, df 3, $p<0.001$).

A further split middle trend analysis (Kazdin, 1976) of the grade 2 data showed the only significant increase in rate of questioning to occur between treatment (time lag 1) and treatment (time lag 2).

TABLE I. Mean controlled question rate per session across experimental phases

	Baseline	Treatment			Reversal	χ^2
		Initial	Time lag 1	Time lag 2		
Grade 2	11.2	14	11.8	18.3	NA	$p<0.001$
Grade 3	22.6	27	22.4	18.3	20.6	$p>0.05$

As these data show a relatively constant question rate in both classes it appears reasonable to conclude that, overall, fluctuations in question rate did not confound with the independent variable. The only subjects whose data may have been affected by a variation in total teacher question rate were the two subjects in the grade 2 class who underwent the experimental treatment at time lag 2 (grade 2 subjects 5 and 6).

Given the design of this experiment, if the increase in question rate did confound with seating location for these subjects it will have artificially inflated the treatment effect for one (subject 6) and decreased the effect on the other (subject 5).

Mean on-task levels across experimental conditions for the subject pupils in both classes are presented in Table II. The multiple baseline data from both classes were subjected to Revuskys' Rn test for differences between phases in both level and slope (Wolery & Billingsley, 1982). No significant differences were obtained in either level or slope for both classes (grade 2: level changes Rn = 12, N6, $p > 0.05$; slope changes Rn = 9, N6, $p > 0.05$. Grade 3: level changes Rn = 11, N6, $p > 0.05$; slope changes Rn = 12, N6, $p > 0.05$).

TABLE II. Individual children's mean time on task across experimental conditions

Subject	Baseline	Treatment (Time lagged)	
Grade 2			
1	88.9	94.2	
2	83.5	84.2	
3	95.5	95.4	
4	82.6	90.0	
5	91.7	91.4	
6	81.7	83.6	
Grade 3			
1	95.6	82.9	92
2	82.6	79.0	—
3	78.6	78.9	74
4	92.3	87.8	84
5	84.0	45.0	72
6	75.7	70.0	42

The fact that, overall, the observed pupil on-task levels did not differ significantly in the baseline and experimental conditions might simply reflect insufficient sensitivity in the observation procedure. It does not completely eliminate the possibility that some subtle changes in pupil behaviour brought about by their relocation affected the frequency with which they were the target of the teacher's questions. However, within the limitations of the observation system, these data do provide some evidence of between phase stability in the pupils' on-task behaviour running counter to the hypothesis that changes in pupil behaviour systematically confounded the experimental variable.

An interesting adjunctive feature of the behavioural ecology of the grade 3 class was exposed by the pupil on-task data. During baseline the teacher reported that the seat in the extreme back right corner was reserved for a particularly disruptive pupil as in that position he had less access to other children and was therefore less distraction to others and also concentrated more on his work. Subject 6 occupied this position during baseline and reversal phases. Subject 5 exchanged seats with him during the experimental manipulation. Visual inspection of his data clearly shows that, contrary to the teacher's belief, movement into this seat brought about a marked and experimentally reversable deterioration in his attending behaviour. This result was replicated with subject 6 during the reversal phase although previously his average on-task level had not been so depressed.

The proportion of time the teacher spent in each of six (grade 2) and five (grade

3) zones (see Fig. 1) across experimental phases is presented in Table III. Chi square tests showed significant differences between phases in the proportion of time the teacher spent in five of the grade 2 zones and in three of the grade 3 zones.

TABLE III. Proportion of time teacher spent in each zone across experimental phases

Grade 2			Phases			
Zone	Baseline	Treatment (initial)	Treatment (lag 1)	Treatment (lag 2)	χ^2 (df=3)	
A	22.5	21.0	19.3	19.6		
B	5.2	10.0	5.8	7.0	**	
C	6.6	9.9	13.1	11.2	**	
D	11.8	11.7	17.8	15.0	*	
E	31.3	26.4	32.0	39.4	**	
F	22.6	21.0	12.1	7.8	**	
Grade 3						
						(df=4)
A	64.2	57.7	56.3	55.1	60.5	
B	17.0	26.3	23.6	15.7	17.1	**
C	16.4	14.5	15.3	19.4	13.3	
D	3.2	1.2	4.6	7.9	8.4	**
E	0.2	0.3	0.2	1.9	0.8	**

* $p<0.01$.
** $p<0.001$.

The finding of significant differences between experimental phases in the proportion of time both teachers spent in particular areas within their classes supports the possibility of systematic changes in teacher location confounding the experimental variable. Exactly how changes in teacher position might affect the distribution of teacher attention, or more specifically teacher questions, is at present largely a matter of conjecture. However, reasoning on the basis of evidence of a proximity effect (Adams, 1969; Delefes & Jackson, 1972) one could postulate that if teacher position changes do affect the distribution of questions, an increase or decrease in the proportion of time the teacher spends in a specific pupil's proximity would be accompanied by an equivalent increase or decrease in the rate of questions addressed to a specific pupil. Accordingly a treatment phase increase in teacher time in the experimental zone for subjects 2, 4 and 6 (both classes) and decrease in teacher time in the experimental zone for subjects 1, 3 and 5 (both classes) might suggest a positive confound of the experimental effect. Conversely a decrease in time spent near subjects 2, 4 and 6 and an increase of time in the new locations for subjects 1, 3 and 5 could work against the experimental hypothesis.

The relevant figures for all 12 subjects are presented in Table IV. A Test of Significance of Differences Between Proportions (Ferguson, 1959) performed on the raw scores from which these figures are derived revealed statistically significant differences in nine cases. Of these, five (grade 2 subjects 4, 6; grade 3 subjects 1, 2, 6) are in the direction predicted by the teacher proximity as confound hypothesis whereas the remaining four differences (grade 2 subjects 1, 2, 3, grade 3 subject 5) were in the direction opposite to that expected if teacher location change confounded with student position to affect frequency of teacher questions.

TABLE IV. Proportion of time teacher spent in experimental zones

	Subject	Pre-treatment	Treatment	
	1	6.6	9.9	**
	3	11.7	17.8	**
Grade 2	5	5.8	7.0	
	2	31.3	26.4	**
	4	26.4	32.0	*
	6	32.0	39.4	**
	1	64.2	57.7	**
	3	26.3	23.6	
Grade 3	5	4.6	7.9	**
	2	17.0	26.3	**
	4	14.5	15.3	
	6	0.2	1.9	*

* $p<0.005$.
** $p<0.0001$.

To summarise these data, significant differences across experimental phases were observed with both teachers in the proportion of time they spent in particular areas in the room. Assuming the previously reported proximity effect, these differences were such that for three pupils (grade 2 subject 5; grade 3 subjects 3, 4) they should have had no effect on question rate as teacher proximity did not vary significantly for them. With subjects 4 and 6 (grade 2) and 1, 2 and 6 (grade 3) the observed changes in teacher location may have confounded additively with the changes in pupil location, while for subjects 1, 2 and 3 (grade 2) and subject 5 (grade 3) if changes in teacher location did function as an experimental confound, it would have been to decrease the observed effect.

Finally, a completely unanticipated ecological feature of the grade 2 classroom became evident as a result of the concomitant measurement of teacher location. Across the entire study the teacher was seated in her desk (zone F) on average 17.9% of the time. However this figure varied widely across sessions. When plotted, the variation in time the teacher spent at her desk appears to conform to a regular pattern (see Fig. 2). The two peaks in this graph, obtained in observation sessions 5 and 21, occurred 28 calendar days apart.

Main Results

Data from the first 15 days of baseline showed a markedly uneven distribution of teacher questions in both classrooms. The grade 2 teacher addressed proportionately more questions to pupils seated in the back two groups of desks than to pupils in the front ($\chi^2=5.45$, df 1, $p<0.05$). In the grade 3 class the teacher asked a proportionately higher number of questions to pupils seated in the middle two rows, followed by the back two rows with the front row pupils receiving fewest questions ($\chi^2=26.7$, df 2, $p<0.001$).

Table V presents the mean number of questions per session directed at each subject for each phase of the study. Individual cumulative records of the number of questions addressed to the experimental subjects are also presented in Figs. 3 and 4. These being cumulative graphs the experimental effect is best assessed by analysing the change in slope between experimental phases. In both classes subjects 1, 3 and 5 were moved after baseline from high to low question areas. The experimental

TABLE V. Mean questions per session across experimental phases for individual subjects. Treatment predicted to decreased question rate for S1, S3, S5; increased rate for S2, S4, S6

Grade 2 Subject	Baseline	Treatment (Time lagged)	
1	1.06	1.68	
2	0.22	0.63	
3	0.71	0.53	
4	0.05	0.85	
5	1.23	0.57	
6	0.40	1.57	
Grade 3			
1	1.47	0.60	—
2	0.19	1.14	0.20
3	1.29	0.67	1.20
4	0.48	1.89	0.20
5	2.45	1.00	2.20
6	1.17	1.75	1.80

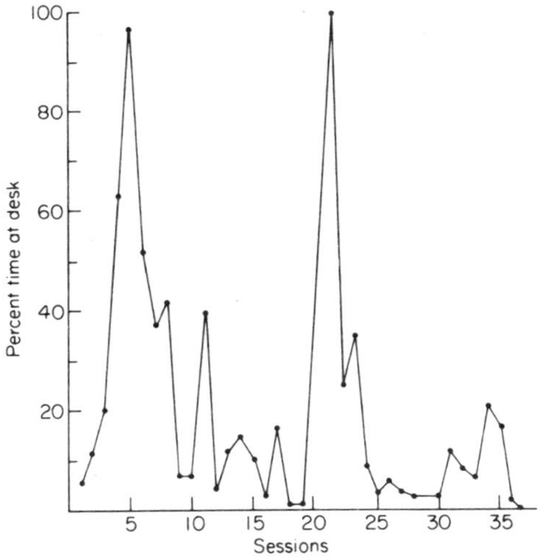

FIG. 2. Percentage of time per session the grade 2 teacher spent seated at her desk.

prediction for these subjects was therefore a decrease in question rate as a function of the experimental manipulation. Conversely, subjects 2, 4 and 6 were moved to high question areas; consequently an increase in questions asked of them during the treatment condition—reflected by an increase in slope of the graph—was predicted. In the grade 3 reversal phase (Fig. 4) a return to baseline trends was predicted for all subjects.

Within phase gaps in the data, including the whole reversal phase for subject 1 in the grade 3 class, indicate the pupils's absence from class during those observation sessions.

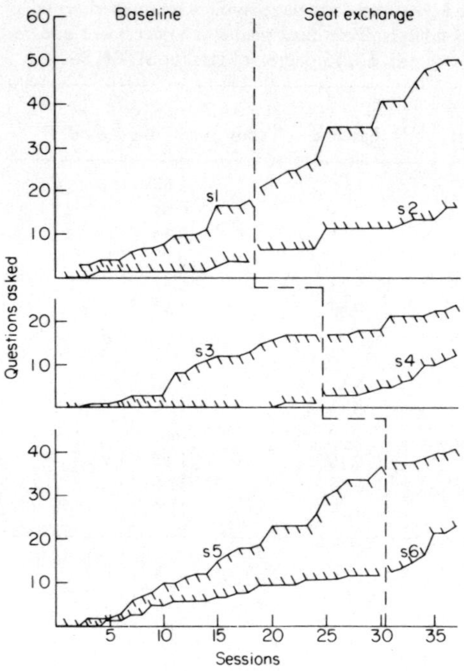

FIG. 3. Cumulative record of the number of questions addressed to individual subjects (grade 2). Seat exchange was predicted to decrease question rate for S1, S3, S5; increase rate for S2, S4, S6.

Analysis of changes in slope between baseline and experimental conditions by Revusky's Rn test revealed significant differences in the predicted direction in both classes (grade 2, Rn=8, N6, $p<0.05$; grade 3, Rn=7, N6, $p<0.05$). Visual inspection of the individual data confirms this effect overall although two of the subjects, grade 2 subject 1, and grade 3 subject 6, appear not to have been affected by the experimental manipulation.

Discussion

Since Adams (1969) first reported different rates of pupil participation in classroom interaction corresponding with differences in position within the room many researchers have explored the relationship between location and pupil performance. Alternative accounts positing firstly that different personality types select or are selected to sit in particular positions—thereby predetermining differential interactions, and secondly that location differences function in themselves as causal setting variables for unequal pupil participation and attainment, have both obtained empirical support (see for example: Dykman & Reis, 1979; Morrison & Thomas, 1975; Walberg, 1969; Koneya, 1976; Levine *et al.*, 1980; Schwebel & Cherlin, 1972; Stires, 1980).

Exactly what the mechanisms are for this location effect remain unclear. Weinstein (1979) hypothesised that differential teacher attention to pupils in different positions could partially account for the phenomenon. This obviously presupposes that teacher attention is differentially distributed across classroom locations *per se*,

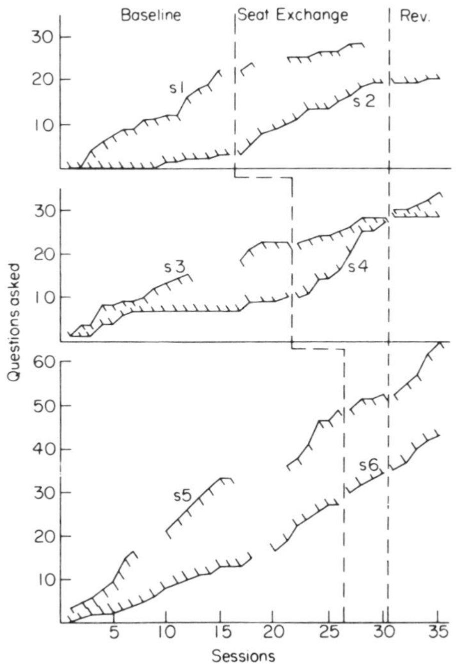

FIG. 4. Cumulative record of the number of questions addressed to individual subjects (grade 3). Seat exchange was predicted to decrease question rate for S1, S3, S5; increase rate for S2, S4, S6.

not across pupils alone. That pupils' position in the class significantly affected the frequency with which they were addressed questions by both teachers in this study is a clear demonstration that at least this aspect of teacher attention may be differentially distributed across locations within the room in conformity with Weinstein's hypothesis.

Subsequently both teachers independently expressed surprise at the results and reported that they were not conscious of any differences in their treatment of the pupils. Clearly changes in the probability of questions being targeted to the individual pupils did take place. Identification of specific stimulus properties or other setting events (Wahler & Fox, 1981) within the room which brought about these changes is beyond the scope of this study. However the concomitant measures included in the observation schedule do provide evidence that changes in overall question rate, teacher location and/or levels of pupil on-task behaviour were not likely to be primary controlling variables.

The concomitant measures proved valuable, not only in providing a quasi-control over three elements of the classroom setting we considered potential experimental confounds, but also in yielding interesting ancillary information regarding the behavioural ecology of both classes. Firstly, in the grade 3 class the pupil on-task measure provided evidence that—contrary to the teacher's stated intention and subjective impression—being seated in the back right corner seat resulted in a reduction in attending to the lesson, not an increase. This illustrates once again the potential significance of the applied analysis of antecedent setting events in classroom control rather than focusing exclusively on consequence management (Rogers-Warren & Warren, 1977; Wheldall *et al.*, 1981).

The second unanticipated product of our concomitant measures was the observation of systematic and apparently cyclic changes in the time the grade 2 teacher spent at her desk. The importance of adequate baseline data in within-subjects experimental designs is now routinely emphasised (Baer, Wolf & Risley, 1968; Hersen & Barlow, 1976; Kazdin, 1980, and Sidman (1960) first suggested that researchers, when confronted with marked variability in baseline measures, look for patterns in the data which might suggest causal relationships accounting for the observed changes.

We can at best only speculate as to the causes of the periodic changes in the proportion of time this teacher remained seated at her desk. Fortunately alteration in this aspect of her behaviour did not materially effect the experimental outcome. However such rhythmic patterns could seriously confound experimental effects in research of this type, especially in designs employing baseline and treatment phases of only three of four days' duration. Furthermore such changes may prove to be particularly significant features of the behavioural ecology of classrooms in their own right and therefore deserve further empirical investigation.

Acknowledgements

This research was supported by the University of Papua New Guinea. The assistance of the participating teachers and children is gratefully acknowledged. Thanks are due also to Paul Asukusa, Peter Kanjui, Burt Uglinga and Tinoi Vui for their help with data collection.

NOTES

[1] Clark, R., Parsonson, B.S., Smith, J.F. & Temple, B. (1982) The effects of classroom seating arrangements on the on-task and academic behaviour of elementary school students in an open plan unit, *paper presented to the 5th Annual Conference of The Australian Behaviour Modification Association*, Surfer's Paradise.

[2] Moore, D.W. & Glynn, T. (1982) Interobserver agreement; further consideration of the effects of behaviour rate, *paper presented to the 5th Annual Conference of the Australian Behaviour Modification Association*, Surfer's Paradise.

[3] Although this paper only reports data pertaining to one of these categories—teacher questions—the others are listed to provide some indication of the dimensions of the observer's workload. Full details of the observation system are available from the first author on request.

REFERENCES

Adams, R.S. (1969) Location as a feature of instructional interaction, *Merrill Palmer Quarterly*, 15, pp. 309–321.

Axelrod, S., Hall, R.V. & Tams, A. (1979) Comparison of two common seating arrangements, *Academic Therapy*, 15, pp. 29–36.

Baer, D.M., Wolf, M.M. & Risley, T.R. (1968) Some current dimensions of applied behaviour analysis, *Journal of Applied Behaviour Analysis*, 1, pp. 91–97.

Bates, R.J. (1973) Classroom location, learning and status, *New Zealand Journal of Educational Studies*, 8, pp. 142–153.

Becker, W.C., Englemann, S., Carnine, D. & Maggs, A. (1981) Direct instruction technology—recent developments and research findings, in: Karolz, P. & Steffen, J. (Eds) *Child Behaviour and Therapy* (Vol. 2) (New York, Gardiner Press).

BIRNBRAUER, J.S. (1981) External validity and experimental investigation of individual behaviour, *Analysis and Intervention in Developmental Disabilities*, 1, pp. 117-132.

DELEFES, P. & JACKSON, P. (1972) Teacher-pupil interaction as a function of location in the classroom, *Psychology in the Schools*, 9, pp. 119–123.

DYKMAN, B.M. & REIS, H.T. (1979) Personality correlates of classroom seating position, *Journal of Educational Psychology*, 71, pp. 346–357.

FERGUSON, G.A. (1959) *Statistical Analysis in Psychology and Education* (New York, McGraw-Hill).

GLYNN, T. (1981) Building an effective teaching environment, in: WHELDALL, K. & RIDING, R.J. (Eds) *Psychological Aspects of Learning and Teaching* (London, Croom Helm).

GUMP, P.V. (1977) Ecological psychologists: critics or contributors to behaviour analysis, in: ROGERS-WARREN, A. & WARREN, S.F. (Eds) *Ecological Perspectives in Behaviour Analysis* (Baltimore, University Park Press).

HAMERLYNCK, L.A. (Ed.) (1979) *Behavioural Systems for the Developmentally Disabled (Vol. I). School and Family Environments* (New York, Brunner/Mazel).

HARRIS, F.C. & LAHEY, B.B. (1978) A method for combining occurrence and non-occurrence inter-observer agreement scores, *Journal of Applied Behaviour Analysis*, 11, pp. 523–527.

HERSEN, M. & BARLOW, D.H. (1976) *Single Case Experimental Designs. Strategies for Studying Behaviour Change* (New York, Pergamon Press).

JOHNSON, S.M. & BOLSTAD, O.D. (1973) Methodological issues in naturalistic observation; some problems and solutions for field research, in: HAMMERLYNK, L.A., HANDY, L.C. & MASH, E.J. (Eds) *Behaviour Change; Methodological Concepts and Practice* (Champaign, Research Press).

KAZDIN, A.E. (1976) Statistical analyses for single-case experimental designs, in: Hersen, M. & BARLOW, D. (Eds) *Single Case Experimental Designs: Strategies for Studying Behaviour Change* (New York, Pergamon Press).

KAZDIN, A.E. (1980) *Behaviour Modification in Applied Settings*, revised edn (Homewood Illinois, The Dorsey Press).

KELLY, M.B. (1977) A review of the observational data-collection and reliability procedures reported in the Journal of Applied Behaviour Analysis, *Journal of Applied Behaviour Analysis*, 10, pp. 97–101.

KONEYA, M. (1976) Location and interaction in row-and-column seating arrangements, *Environment and Behaviour*, 8, pp. 265–282.

KRANTZ, P.J. & RISLEY, T.R. (1977) Behavioural ecology in the classroom, in: O'LEARY, K.D. & O'LEARY, S.G. (Eds) *Classroom Management; The Successful Use of Behaviour Modification*, 2nd edn (New York, Pergamon Press).

LEVINE, D.W., O'NEAL, E.C., GARWOOD, S.G. & MCDONALD, P.J. (1980) Classroom ecology: the effects of seating position on grades and participation, *Personality and Social Psychology Bulletin*, 6, pp. 409–412.

MCNAUGHTON, S. & GLYNN, T. (1981) Delayed versus immediate attention to oral reading errors: effects on accuracy and self-correction, *Educational Psychology*, 1, pp. 57–65.

MOORE, D.W. (1981a) Location as a causal factor in the unequal distribution of teacher questions: an experimental analysis, in: HORNE, D.J. & MCMURRAY, N.E. (Eds) *Behaviour Therapy in Australia: Proceedings of the Third Australian Conference on Behaviour Modification*, Melbourne, Australian Behaviour Modification Association.

MOORE, D.W. (1981b) Teacher expectations and interaction with Papua New Guinean and expatriate children, *Papua New Guinea Journal of Education*, 17, pp. 92–101.

MOORE, D.W. (1984) Disparate teacher attention favouring the more able; some data from Papua New Guinean community and provincial high schools, *Australian Journal of Education*, 28(2), pp. 19–28.

MOORE, D.W. & SMITH, P. (1980) Teacher questions: frequency and distribution in a sample of Papua New Guinea high schools, *Australiun Journal of Education*, 24(3), pp. 315–317.

MORRISON, T.L. & THOMAS, M.D. (1975) Self-esteem and classroom participation, *Journal of Educational Research*, 68, pp. 374–377.

ORNSTEIN, A.C. & LEVINE, D.U. (1981) Teacher behaviour research: overview and outlook, *Phi Delta Kappan*, 62, pp. 592–596.

ROGERS-WARREN, A. & WARREN, S.F. (Eds) (1977) *Ecological Perspectives in Behaviour Analysis* (Baltimore, University Park Press).

SCHWEBEL, A.J. & CHERLIN, D.L. (1972) Physical and social distancing in teacher-pupil relationships, *Journal of Educational Psychology*, 63, pp. 543–550.

SIDMAN, M. (1960) *Tactics of Scientific Research: Evaluating Experimental Data in Psychology* (New York, Basic Books).

SOMMER, R. (1967) Classroom ecology, *Journal of Applied Behavioural Science*, 3, pp. 489–503.

Sommer, R. (1969) *Personal Space: the Behavioural Basis of Design* (Englewood Cliffs, Prentice-Hall).

Stires, L. (1980) Classroom seating location, student grades, and attitudes: environment or self-selection?, *Environment and Behaviour*, 12, pp. 241–254.

Thomas, J.D., Presland, I.E., Grant, M.D. & Glynn, T.L. (1977) Natural rates of teacher approval and disapproval, *Journal of Applied Behaviour Analysis*, 10, pp. 91–94.

Van Biervliet, A., Spangler, P.F. & Marshall, A.M. (1981) An ecobehavioural examination of a simple strategy for increasing mealtime language in residential facilities, *Journal of Applied Behaviour Analysis*, 14, pp. 295–306.

Wahler, R.G. & Fox, J.J. (1981) Setting events in applied behaviour analysis: toward a conceptual and methodological expansion, *Journal of Applied Behaviour Analysis*, 14, pp. 327–338.

Walberg, H. (1969) Physical and psychological distance in the classroom, *School Review*, 77, pp. 64–70.

Weinstein, C.S. (1979) The physical environment of the school: a review of the research, *Review of Educational Research*, 49, pp. 577–610.

Wheldall, K., Morris, M., Vaughan, R. & Ng, Y.Y. (1981) Rows versus tables: An example of the use of behavioural ecology in two classes of eleven-year-old children, *Educational Psychology*, 1, pp. 171–181.

Willems, E.P. (1974) Behavioural technology and behavioural ecology, *Journal of Applied Behaviour Analysis*, 7, pp. 151–165.

Wolery, M. & Billingsley, F.F. (1982) The application of Revusky's Rn Test to slope and level changes, *Behavioural Assessment*, 4, pp. 93–103.

Wong, P. & McNaughton, S. (1980) The effects of prior provision of context on the oral reading proficiency of a low progress reader, *New Zealand Journal of Educational Studies*, 15(2), pp. 169–175.

The Effect of Adult Proximity and Serving Style on Pre-schoolers' Language and Eating Behaviour

MARY BAKER, MARY F. FOLEY, TED GLYNN & STUART McNAUGHTON

ABSTRACT *This study examined the effects on child language and amount of food eaten by five pre-school children in a day care setting of withdrawing two components of the regular mid-day meal routine. The two components were having an adult seated at the table with the children and allowing children to serve their own food. Child language was more affected by withdrawal of the two components than was amount of food eaten. Withdrawal of the seated adult had a more powerful effect in reducing child language, than did withdrawal of self-serving of food. Amount eaten was reduced only when both components were withdrawn simultaneously. Findings were discussed in terms of the implications of setting events for theory and practice of applied behaviour analysis.*

Recent research in applied behaviour analysis has emphasised the powerful influence of ecological variables and setting events on human behaviour (Risley, 1977; Bijou & Baer, 1978; Wahler & Fox, 1981). There is growing research evidence to support the claim that in many child development and educational contexts, analysis and modification of behavioural antecedents such as setting events may yield more efficient strategies for behaviour change than reliance on analysis and modification of contingencies of reinforcement alone (McNaughton, 1980; Glynn, 1982). In the context of classroom management, Wheldall (1981) argues that increased concern with ecological variables will minimise 'behavioural overkill' from the introduction of unnecessary and time-consuming contingency management procedures.

The concept of 'setting events' recognises that both stimulus functions and response functions will be altered by situational or setting factors (Kantor, 1970; Bijou & Baer, 1978). For example, a child's rate of vocalisation to a specific toy might differ according to whether or not a parent is present at the same time as the toy. Similarly, the amount of food eaten and the rate of language displayed by a child at mealtimes might differ according to whether or not a parent or familiar adult is present. In these examples, adult presence can be seen as a setting event influencing language behaviour and eating behaviour. The stimulus function of the toy (in the first example) and the meal (in the second) as well as the response function of language and eating are likely to be altered by the presence of a parent. The presence of a familiar adult would usually have a facilitating influence on child behaviour, for two reasons. First, behaviours which are specific to a setting (e.g. eating at mealtimes) and behaviours which are not so setting specific (e.g. language) are likely to have been previously reinforced by that adult. Secondly, the availability of an interacting adult may result in a greater opportunity for child-initiated language to occur. Hart & Risley (1968, 1974, 1975, 1980) have clearly demonstrated the power of their procedure for incidental teaching of language. These studies show that adult-child interactions that were child-initiated resulted not only in marked increases in specific target language but also in overall language use. The family meal can thus be seen as an important context for language development, in that it is a regular and frequently occurring pleasant social setting which provides children with opportunities for incidental learning of language. Several descriptive studies of adult-child interaction concluded that such interaction occurred at greater frequency and with greater duration in home settings than in centre-based day care, including 'family day care' in which one caregiver looked after a small group of 2–5 children (Cochran, 1977; Golden *et al.*, 1978). Differences between day care and home settings were particularly marked at the noon-day meal (Golden *et al.*, 1978).

One possible reason for lower rates of adult-child interaction at mealtimes in day care settings could be an excessive concern by staff with eating behaviour *per se.* When children refuse to eat or display problematic eating (e.g. throwing food or messing with food) staff frequently respond by providing massive attention for this inappropriate behaviour. Children are given additional instructions, prompts and pleadings to eat the food provided, as well as increased rates of extrinsic reinforcement for eating and punishment for not eating. Under such contingencies it is not surprising that independent eating declines and eating problems persist. Further, with increased time spent in prompting and cueing eating and in providing extrinsic consequences, adults are less available to respond to child-initiated language and social approaches. As a result, the essentially pleasant *social* character of the meal may be lost, and the setting becomes aversive to both children and adults. This view is supported in a report by Baker (1980) where a problem eater in a day care setting was not responding to systematic procedures for prompting and reinforcing of eating. Baker found that having an adult sit with the child and engage him in conversation on intermittent days resulted in his eating three times as many spoonsful of food as he did on days when the adult prompted and reinforced from a distance. This finding is consistent with those of Glynn, Glynn & Lawless (1979) who reported that all children in a family of five tasted and finished more food and requested more second servings at meals when their parents ate with them than they did at meals when their parents were absent from the table (though present in an adjacent room). The differential effect on amount eaten was greatest for the youngest two of the five children. In this study parents did not engage in prompting, reinforcing or any way commenting on children's eating but, instead, concentrated on holding regular conversations about the events of the day. Clearly, the availability of a conversational adult rather than a supervisory adult was an important setting event for eating in these two studies. Unfortunately, child language was not measured in either study.

Another ecological variable influencing mealtime behaviour is the manner in which food is served. Several studies have examined the effects of family style and institutional style meal service. Hall & Holmberg (1974) found in a day care setting that 'family style' serving (i.e. allowing two preschool problem eaters to help themselves) resulted in both children tasting more food items than they did under a staff implemented positive reinforcement procedure. Van Biervliet, Spangler & Marshall (1981) compared family style and institutional style food serving on the language behaviour of five young male retardates. These authors found a systematic increase in rate of verbalisation with the introduction of family style serving across different meals and that most of this increase involved interaction with peers rather than with institutional staff. These findings are consistent with those of Risley & Edwards (1978) who found increased language interaction among geriatric residents when they were seated at small rather than large tables and when they served themselves rather than when they had their food pre-served by staff. The family style meal procedure in allowing pre-schoolers, retardates and elderly residents to serve their own food, thus provided them with more opportunities to make choices and thus to exert some control over their environment. In this way their behaviour was less directly dependent on staff behaviour, so that increased opportunities for language initiation were possible and staff were more free to respond to these.

Hence two ecological variables, proximity of an interacting or conversational adult and self-service of food appear to be important setting events for both eating and language behaviour at mealtimes. The present study took place in a day care setting which incorporated both of these variables in its mealtime routines. Each of these variables was systematically withdrawn from the mealtime routine in order to examine the effects on both language and eating behaviour.

Method

Subjects and Setting

The subjects were four girls and one boy aged between two years six months and four years seven months (mean three years eight months), who attended an urban day care centre. The study was conducted during the 11.30 a.m. to 12.00 noon mealtime over a period of three months. The total number of children present at mealtime ranged from eight to 20, sitting at three or four separate tables with no more than six children per table. All target children sat at the same table throughout the study. Three or four adult staff members were present each day.

Experimental Design

A seven phase within-subjects A B A C A D A design was employed. During the four A phases the normal lunchtime meal procedures operated, such that an adult was seated at the table with the children and children served their own food. During each of the B, C and D phases one of these two conditions was altered. In phase B the adult was standing apart from the table, and the food was pre-served by the staff. In phase C the adult was seated at the table, but the food was pre-served by the staff. In phase D, the adult was standing apart from the table but the children served their own food.

Measures

Child Language. Two observers independently scored the language responses of each child over a four-minute interval, so that all five subjects were observed once every 20 minute daily observation session. Each child's place in the recording schedule was rotated so that a subject was not observed at the same time each day. Within a four-minute interval observers recorded and classified all language responses of the target child as either child-initiated language (Hart & Risley, 1975) or language in response to an adult comment or question. Observers were instructed to score any language response which followed after an interval of five seconds from a previous response as a new response. From these event records, the number of child-initiated language responses and the total language responses was calculated for each child each day.

Food Eaten. Observers also recorded the amount of food eaten by children each day. This was calculated by subtracting the number of ladles of food left over by each child from the number of ladles served (either by the child during the self-service phases or by the staff during the pre-service phases). A 'ladle' was a plastic kitchen utensil which was marked grossly into four levels, '$\frac{1}{4}$', '$\frac{1}{2}$', '$\frac{3}{4}$' and '1'. The main course food served at these meals was generally of a mushy consistency. The detailed menus for 10 days is shown in Table I. This menu was cycled through four times during the study. The level of food in each ladle could be easily observed and recorded, when either children or staff served the food. At the end of the meal plates were returned to the kitchen and food remaining on each child's plate was spooned back into the ladle for measurement and recording.

TABLE I. Detailed menu for each successive ten day cycle over 40 days

Day 1	Mince, carrots, potatoes (stew)
Day 2	Vegetarian stew
Day 3	Spaghetti
Day 4	Milk puddings, jelly
Day 5	Fish and potato pie
Day 6	Vegetarian stew
Day 7	Chicken and rice casserole
Day 8	Tomato and mince casserole
Day 9	Thick soup with luncheon chunks
Day 10	Macaroni cheese

Inter-observer Agreement. Inter-observer agreement was calculated on four (10%) of the 40 language observation sessions, one from each type of experimental condition, for two of the five children (S1 and S3). Due to staff workload around preparing, serving and supervising the meals a second observer could be spared for only a fraction of the observation sessions. The occurrence agreement formula (Hartmann, 1977) was used to express the number of intervals in which the two observers completely agreed on the number and classification of language responses as a percentage of intervals in which one or other recorded some language as having occurred. Inter-observer agreement on the number of ladles of food eaten was calculated on four (10%) of the 40 observation sessions, one from each of the four experimental conditions, for the same two children. The whole session agreement formula was employed, i.e. placing the smaller number recorded by one of the two observers over the larger number and expressing this as a percentage.

Procedure

A Phases (Baseline). These phases involved *adult seated* and *self-service* conditions. The adult seated condition involved one staff member being seated at the table with the children. Both adult and children were free to engage in conversation begun by either party. The adult was given no explicit instructions to engage children in conversation or to introduce particular topics of conversation. The self-serve condition involved a family style service arrangement whereby food for the meal was placed in large dishes, in the centre of the table and when children helped themselves. Children were free to take second helpings of food if they wished.

Phase B. This phase involved the *adult standing* and the *pre-serve* condition. During the adult standing condition, the adult staff member who normally sat at the table with a group of children, was instructed to stand and supervise the meal from a distance of about two feet. No other instructions were given to the staff member who was free to interact socially with the children, so long as she remained standing at a distance of about 1–2 feet away from the table. None of the children in this experiment needed assistance with feeding, and during the study no very young toddlers who required help with feeding were seated at the same table as children participating in the experiment. During the 'pre-serve' condition, food was pre-served in the kitchen on to each child's individual plate before being placed before the child at the table. In order to gauge how much food to pre-serve, a guide was provided from an estimate based on the average amount of food eaten during the first A phase (baseline). Children could make requests for more food, if they wished. This involved a staff member taking the child's plate to the kitchen and serving out the food in the kitchen.

Phase C. This phase involved the *adult seated* condition as described for the A phases, and the pre-serve condition as described for the Phase B.

Phase D. This phase involved the *adult standing* condition as described for phase B, and the *self-serve* condition as described for the A phases.

Results

Data on inter-observer agreement are presented in Table II, which shows the inter-observer agreement scores for language responses and amount eaten, across the four types of experimental condition, for S1 and S3 separately. The occurrence agreement across the four conditions on language responses ranged from 83 to 94% (mean, 88%) for S1 and from 78 to 92% (mean 87%) for S3. The whole session agreement across the four conditions on amount of food eaten ranged from 73 to 83% (mean, 76%) for S1 and from 68 to 85% (mean 77%) for S3. The per cent agreement is lower for the whole session data, since the numbers recorded were typically small (ranging from 0.5 to 3.0 ladles), so that a difference of one ladle would markedly lower the level of agreement. However, in general these levels of occurrence and whole session agreement are considered satisfactory, with the qualification that inter-observer agreement was sampled only on 10% of occasions for two of the five subjects.

TABLE II. Mean inter-observer agreement on language responses and amount eaten for two subjects across all phases

	Language responses*		Amount of food eaten†	
	S1	S3	S1	S3
A Phases: (adult-seated, self-serve)	87%	92%	83%	72%
Phase B: (adult standing, pre-serve)	83%	92%	80%	85%
Phase C: (adult seated, pre-serve)	94%	87%	74%	68%
Phase D: (adult standing, self service)	89%	78%	73%	81%

*Occurrence agreement formula.
†Whole session agreement formula.

Data on children's language responses are shown in Fig. 1. Total language responses are represented by closed circles and child-initiated language responses are represented by open circles. The highest levels of total language and child-initiated language occurred during the A phases (i.e. under the adult seated and self-serve condition). This pattern holds for all subjects (though S5 left the centre at the end of phase B). The lowest rates of total language and child-initiated language occurred during phase B. This held for all subjects. The next lowest rates of total language and child-initiated language occurred during phase D. Phases B and D were the two phases in which the adult was standing apart from the table. Fig. 1 also shows that for S1, S2, and S4 the levels of total language and child-initiated language appear somewhat higher during phase D than during phase B, though in both these phases the levels are markedly lower than during any of the A phases. In phase D the self-serve condition operated, while in phase B the pre-serve condition operated. Taken together these data suggest that withdrawing the seated adult exerted a stronger effect on child language than did withdrawing the self-serve procedure. This is supported from the data for phase C, during which adult seated condition operated, but food was pre-served. The level of total language and child-initiated language during phase C was very similar to that during the A phases. Thus, given the high levels of child language under the seated adult condition, altering the serving style from self-serve to pre-serve had no further effect. However, given the lower level of child language under the adult standing part condition, altering the serving style from pre-serve to self-serve resulted in increased child language for three of the four subjects. The one exception, S3, was the youngest of the five subjects. These effects are summarised in the upper and middle sections of Table III. On both language measures the mean levels across all subjects show minimal differences between phase C and any of the A phases. In contrast, the mean levels across all subjects are markedly higher for phase D than for phase B, while both of these mean levels for phase D and phase B are well below the means of all the A phases.

Data on children's eating are shown in Fig. 2. Generally there is far less difference between phases in eating behaviour than in language behaviour. In only one phase

TABLE III. Phase by phase mean scores for total language, child initiated language and amount eaten for individual children

Conditions	A	B	A	C	A	D	A
Adult:	Seated	Standing	Seated	Seated	Seated	Standing	Seated
Service:	Self	Pre-	Self	Pre-	Self	Pre-	Self
Total language responses							
S1	11.5	4.2	10.6	10.8	11.3	7.2	13.3
S2	16.7	2.7	12.2	12.2	12.2	6.0	14.0
S3	6.3	6.0	5.7	6.0	7.3	3.2	6.3
S4	6.6	1.2	9.0	9.8	7.4	5.8	9.5
S5	9.2	1.8	abs	abs	abs	abs	abs
X	10.1	3.2	9.4	9.7	9.6	5.6	10.8
Child initiated language responses							
S1	7.35	1.7	7.4	5.8	6.3	4.3	7.5
S2	9.0	2.0	8.8	8.0	6.0	4.5	8.0
S3	3.7	2.8	1.3	2.8	4.5	1.2	2.3
S4	3.0	1.0	8.2	6.2	5.6	3.3	5.8
S5	3.2	0.8	abs	abs	abs	abs	abs
X	5.2	1.7	6.4	5.7	5.6	3.3	5.9
Amount of food eaten (ladles)							
S1	2.1	1.1	2.3	2.0	2.3	2.1	2.3
S2	1.8	0.8	1.7	2.3	1.9	1.7	1.5
S3	1.5	0.9	1.8	1.3	1.5	1.5	1.4
S4	1.5	1.6	1.8	1.7	1.8	1.7	2.0
S5	1.2	0.6	abs	abs	abs	abs	abs
X	1.6	1.0	1.9	1.8	1.9	1.8	1.8

did children eat less than they did during the A phases when adult seated and self-serve conditions were in effect. In this one phase, phase B, when adult standing apart and pre-serve conditions operated, four of the five children ate less than during any other phase. No other between phase differences are evident from Fig. 2. Thus withdrawing either seated adult or self-service of food had little impact on the amount of food children ate. However, withdrawing both seated adult and self-service of food simultaneously did result in a reduction in amount of food eaten for four of the five children. This effect is summarised in the bottom line of Table III, where it can be seen that the mean amount eaten across all children, was 1.0 ladles during phase B, in comparison with 1.6, 1.8, and 1.9 ladles eaten during the other phases. Also since the amount of food pre-served on the children's plates in phases B and C was based on the child's average intake during the first A phase, the drop in amount eaten in phase B meant children were leaving some food on their plates. Thus, in phase B there was not only a decrease in the amount eaten but also an increase in the amount wasted. Hence, the impact of adult proximity and style of food serving was much less on the amount of food eaten than it was on the amount of child language occurring. Only when both variables were withdrawn from the lunchtime routine was there a marked decrease in the amount of food children ate.

Discussion

These results add to the growing body of evidence concerning the influence of

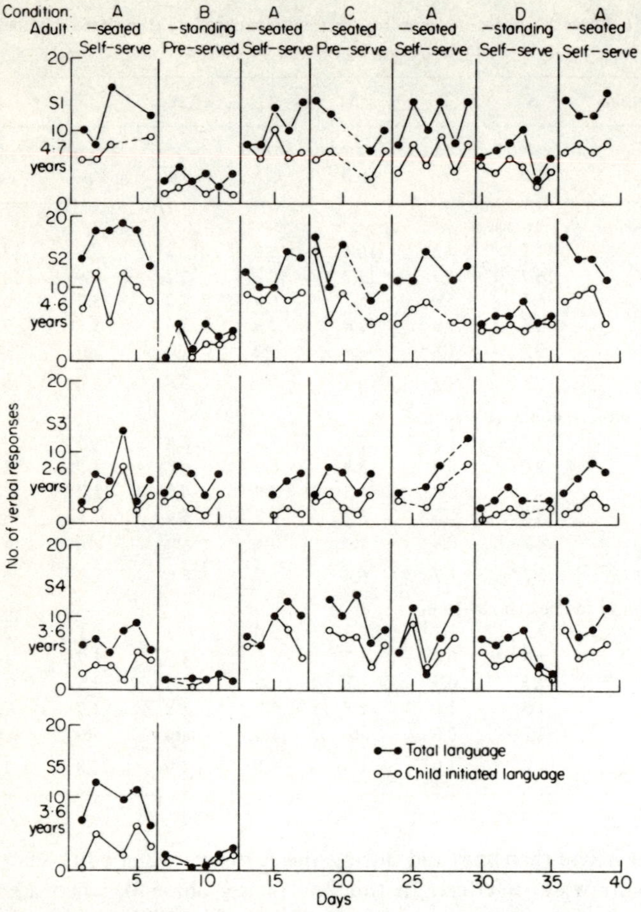

FIG. 1. Child initiated language responses and total language responses for each subject across all phases of the study.

ecological variables or setting events on human behaviour (Bijou & Baer, 1978; Risley, 1977; Glynn, 1982). In this study, adult proximity (seated *v.* standing apart) had a stronger effect on both measures of child language, total language and child initiated language than did the serving style of food. However, given the markedly lower levels of child language which occurred when the adult was standing apart, self-service of food resulted in increased language and language initiations for the oldest three of the four subjects, but not for the youngest. Perhaps the older children had a greater repertoire of language skills which could be put to use in the self-serve condition when adult proximity was withdrawn whilst the younger children need to rely more heavily on the adults' attention and 'scaffolding' or tutoring functions (Kaye, 1979). The effects of either variable on amount of food eaten were far less than the effects on child language. However, when both adult proximity and self-serve variables were withdrawn simultaneously, there was a marked drop in amount eaten for three of the four subjects.

The findings of this study, when considered along with other research on the influence of setting events (McNaughton, 1980; Glynn, 1982) have both theoretical

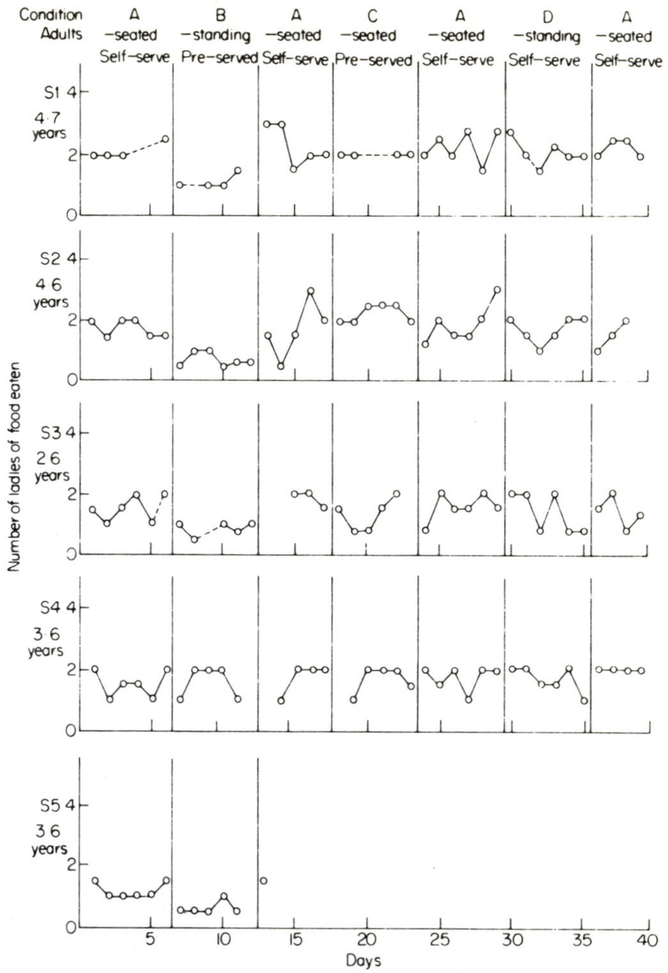

FIG. 2. Amount of food eaten by each subject across all phases of the study.

and practical implications for applied behaviour analysis. In terms of theory, the results lend support to the notion that the structuring of settings needs to be incorporated in, and to form an integral part of, our theoretical framework for understanding and intervening in human learning and development. Bronfenbrenner (1979) argues the importance for child development of two complementary contexts which he terms primary and secondary developmental contexts. These two contexts, which occur regularly and consistently for the developing child, are contexts which establish the primacy of adult-child interpersonal processes and take into account the power of particular settings in enhancing or stifling children's development. Bronfenbrenner describes these two contexts in the form of two propositions.

> *Proposition 1.* A primary developmental context is one in which the child can observe and engage in ongoing patterns of progressively more complex activity jointly with or under the direct guidance of persons who possess knowledge and skill not yet acquired by the child and with whom the child has developed a positive emotional relationship.

> *Proposition 2.* A secondary developmental context is one in which the child is given opportunity, resources, and encouragement to engage in the activities he or she has learned in primary developmental contexts, but now without the active involvement or direct guidance of another person possessing knowledge and skill beyond the levels acquired by the child. (Bronfenbrenner, 1979, p. 845)

The data from this study support the notion that mealtimes may provide important primary and secondary developmental contexts. For example, the regular lunchtime routine conditions in this study (i.e. adult seated and self-serve) were such that a positive adult was readily available for responding to child initiated language and engaging the child in progressively more complex language (Proposition 1). Further, the self-serve procedure may be seen as providing both opportunities and incentive for the children to engage in previously learned complex activities such as independent eating and independent language use (Proposition 2). Data for the oldest three children during phase D suggest that the self-serve procedure could be conceptualised as a secondary developmental context. These three children were able to capitalise on previously learned language skills and maintain a higher level of social interaction without the proximity of the adult, whereas the youngest child (S3) could not. It is likely that the youngest child had not yet acquired sufficient language skills, with the support of the adult, for language to be used independently.

The present study also points to some interesting practical implications for staff training and improving the effectiveness of the day care environment. As noted earlier, day care environments may provide fewer opportunities when compared with home environments for adult-child interaction (Cochran, 1974; Golden *et al.*, 1978). An alternative view is that staff in day care environments may not be capitalising on all opportunities available for adult-child interaction. Essa (1978) reviewing applied behaviour analysis in the pre-school concludes that it is a setting where very often intuition and tradition determine the environment. The findings of the present study suggest that if the environment is reorganised so that the adult can be more available to children particularly during regularly occurring contexts such as mealtimes, children's language usage will increase. The data from this study also indicated that increasing the availability of a conversational adult also increased *child-initiated* language. An increased rate of child-initiated language clearly increases the opportunity for incidental teaching of language to take place. This possibility would allow for adults involved in day care to make a strong positive contribution to children's learning of language and social skills without engaging in inappropriate formal instruction or structured teaching of language.

However, this study did not measure the frequency of adult language behaviour so that one cannot make conclusions about differences in staff language behaviour across the different phases. It would be interesting to know whether and/or how adults' language behaviour changed across phases. Informally, it was observed that this was the case (i.e. that adults appeared to talk more when seated). When looking at effective staff training procedures, it is important to consider those setting variables which optimise appropriate staff behaviour. This strategy becomes particularly important in settings such as day care centres which rely heavily on unqualified staff with little knowledge of relevant human development and behaviour management principles. The hypothesis that the seated adults engaged the children in 'progressively more complex language' is not supported by the data since such functional aspects of language were not measured. Further research, undertaking such a functional analysis, could provide useful information.

It is important to recall also that in this study under conditions where the adult sat with the children during the lunchtime meal and where children served themselves, there was no noticeable reduction in the amount of food eaten. In fact, children ate less when the adult was standing apart and food was pre-served. Although the children in this study were not problem eaters it was seen as necessary to measure the amount of food eaten as a check that capitalising on readily available contexts such as meals for enhancing children's language need not occur at the expense of other behaviour such as eating. Taken together with the findings from other studies with children who *are* problem eaters (Hall & Holmberg, 1974; Baker, 1980) these findings suggest that ecological interventions such as allowing children to serve their own food and providing a conversational adult may be just as effective in improving children's eating as are response contingent procedures. Implementation of response contingent procedures demand more staff time and attention which leaves fewer opportunities for positive adult-child interaction. If the findings from this study are confirmed by further research, then such ecological interventions for problem eating will be preferable since they can preserve or even enhance the function of mealtime settings as important primary and secondary developmental contexts.

Data in this study suggest that increases in child language resulted from both the adult being seated with the children and from consequent increases in adult language. The seated adult, it is argued, functioned as a setting event for child-initiated language and that this increased adult language which in turn promoted further child language. Further research is needed to clarify this process.

REFERENCES

BAKER, M. (1980) Influence on an interacting adult on amount of food eaten by a pre-schooler in a day care setting. *Unpublished term paper,* Department of Education, University of Auckland.

BIJOU, S.W. & BAER, D.M. (1978) *Behavior Analysis of Child Development* (New Jersey, Prentice Hall).

BRONFENBRENNER, U. (1979) Contexts of child rearing, problems and prospects, *American Psychologist,* 34, pp. 844–850.

COCHRAN, (1977) A comparison of group day care and family child-rearing patterns in Sweden, *Child Development,* 48, pp. 102–107.

ESSA, E.L. (1978) The preschool: setting for applied behaviour analysis research, *Review of Education Research,* 48, pp. 537–575.

GLYNN, T. (1982) Building an effective teaching environment, in: WHELDALL, K. & RIDING, R.J. (Eds) *Psychological Aspects of Teaching and Learning* (London, Croom Helm).

GLYNN, T., GLYNN, V. & LAWLESS, S. (1979) A behaviour analysis approach: how we influence what children eat, *Proceedings of the Nutrition Society of New Zealand,* 4, pp. 110–130.

GOLDEN, M., ROSENBLUTH, L., GROSS, M.T., POLICARE, H.J., FREEMAN, H. & BROWNLEE, M. (1978) *The New York City Infant Daycare Study* (New York, New York Medical and Health Research Association).

HALL, J.S. & HOLMBERG, M.C. (1974) The effect of teacher behaviour and food serving arrangements on young children's eating in a day care centre, *Child Care Quarterly,* 3, pp. 97–108.

HART, B.M. & RISLEY, T.R. (1968) Establishing use of descriptive adjectives in the spontaneous speech of disadvantaged pre-school children, *Journal of Applied Behavior Analysis,* 1, pp. 109–120.

HART, B.M. & RISLEY, T.R. (1974) Using preschool materials to modify the language of disadvantaged children, *Journal of Applied Behavior Analysis,* 7, pp. 243–256.

HART, B.M. & RISLEY, T.R. (1975) Incidental teaching of language in the pre-school, *Journal of Applied Behavior Analysis*, 8, pp. 411–420.

HART, B.M. & RISLEY, T.R. (1980) In vivo language intervention: unanticipated general effects. *Journal of Applied Behaviour Analysis*, 13, pp. 407–432.

HARTMANN, D.P. (1977) Consideration in the choice of interobserver reliability estimates, *Journal of Applied Behavior Analysis*, 10, pp. 3–116.

KANTOR, J.R. (1970) An analysis of the experimental analysis of behavior, *Journal of the Experimental Analysis of Behavior*, 13, pp. 101–108.

KAYE, K. (1979) The development of skills, in: WHITEHURST, C.J. & ZIMMERMAN, B.J. (Eds) *The Functions of Language and Cognition*, pp. 23–55 (New York, Academic Press).

MCNAUGHTON, S.S. (1980) Structuring settings for learning academic skills: applications to oral reading, *Behaviour Therapy in Australia: Proceedings of the Third Australian Conference on Behaviour Modification*, Melbourne, May 1980, pp. 306–315.

RISLEY, T.R. (1977) The ecology of applied behavior analysis, in: ROGERS-WARREN, A. & ROGERS-WARREN, S.F. (Eds) *Ecological Perspectives in Behaviour Analysis* (Baltimore, Baltimore University Press).

RISLEY, T.R. & EDWARDS, A. (1978) Behavioral technology for nursing home care: toward a system of nursing home organisation and management, in: GLYNN, T. & MCNAUGHTON, S. (Eds) *Behavior Analysis in New Zealand* (Auckland, University of Auckland).

VAN BIERVLIET, A., SPANGLER, P.F. & MARSHALL, A.M. (1981) An ecobehavioural examination of a simple strategy for increasing mealtime language in residential facilities, *Journal of Applied Behavior Analysis*, 14, pp. 299–305.

WAHLER, R.G. & FOX, J.J. (1981) Setting events in applied behavior analysis: toward a conceptual and methodological expansion, *Journal of Applied Behavior Analysis*, 14, pp. 327–338.

WHELDALL, K. (1981) Concluding comments: 'A before C' or the use of behaviour ecology in classroom management, in: WHELDALL, K. (Ed.) *The Behaviourist in the Classroom: aspects of applied behavioural analysis in British educational contexts*, Ch. 14 (Birmingham, Educational Review Publications, University of Birmingham).

Section C.

Control of Social Behaviour by its Consequences

Behaviour Modification in the Secondary School: issues and outcomes

E. McNAMARA

ABSTRACT *The dearth of behaviour modification research carried out in secondary school situations is recognised and an emphasis on 'heavy' behavioural interventions in both North America and UK research literature is identified. Additionally attention is drawn to a lack of repeated replication studies in single-case experimental design in general—a shortcoming that reduces the case for claiming generalisability of findings of many research outcomes.*

This paper reports the effects on Secondary school classroom on-task behaviour of a number of 'light' behavioural interventions. Six whole class studies are reported. Increase in pupil on-task behaviour resulted in three cases—though in one situation a return to baseline phase was not attempted. In two further cases inconclusive outcomes resulted and the reasons for this are discussed. In one case initial levels of on-task behaviour were so high that little room for improvement was possible.

The lack of demonstration of the effect of the interventions on any individual pupil's behaviour is recognised, although positive outcome data for one pupil are reported.

The conclusion is drawn that 'light' behavioural strategies can effect change in the behaviour of secondary aged pupils in a positive direction.

The dearth of behaviour modification research carried out in secondary school situations has been commented on in the literature (Wheldall & Austin, 1980) and possible reasons for this have also been discussed (McNamara & Harrop, 1979). These range from lack of response from teachers to participate in such research (Presland, 1980) to negative outcome—the latter resulting in either failure of the researchers to submit the findings to journals or failure of the submitted articles to gain acceptance for publication. The possible reasons for both lack of research and/or positive outcomes have been listed (McNamara & Harrop, 1979) and the problems associated with setting up and implementing such research have also been described (McNamara, 1982).

Research using behaviour modification techniques with secondary age pupils has been reported, particularly from educational settings in the USA. This research has been catalogued by Presland (1980). A feature of the research listed is the preponderance of 'heavy' and/or intrusive behavioural interventions making up the management procedures. 'Heavy', in the context of this article, is used to refer to any teacher management strategy other than social reinforcement, reproof or other teacher verbal behaviour—these exceptions being considered 'light' (Wheldall & Austin, 1980). 'Intrusive' is the term used to indicate any intervention strategy which involves great change in teacher behaviour—the greater the change required the more intrusive is the intervention. An exception to this is pupil self-recording, which is not intrusive from the teacher's perspective but may be so with respect to pupil behaviour. Thus the terms 'heavy' and 'intrusive' are used to refer to initiated management practices which call for changes in classroom routine, usually directly on the part of the teacher, but occasionally on the part of the pupil.

Those studies listed by Presland included the use of (i) tokens (Main & Munro, 1977); (ii) time-out (Webster, 1976); (iii) self-determined reinforcement (Glynn, 1970); (iv) daily report card (Schumaker, Hovell & Sheerman, 1977); (v) self-recording (Broden, Hall & Mitts, 1971); (vi) peer reinforcement (Solomon & Wahler, 1973) and (vii) tokens plus teams (White-Blackburn, Semb & Semb, 1977).

Examination of the less extensive research carried out in UK secondary school settings reveals a similar preponderance of heavy and/or intrusive behavioural procedures, e.g. token points with an individual pupil (Presland, 1980) or classes of children (Lane, 1978); plastic tokens (Merrett, 1982); contracts (Lane & Miller, 1977); self-recording (McNamara, 1979; Blundell & Merrett, 1982).

Lobitz & Burns (1977) in a consideration of the intrusiveness of interventions suggest that the optimal intervention strategy for teachers is to begin with the least intrusive method and add more powerful procedures only if needed. They express the view that behaviour modification techniques are not readily accepted by teachers because they are disruptive of normal classroom procedures (Abid, 1975) or are perceived of as having no utility in the classroom (McNamara, 1975).

Such intervention procedures as are listed earlier can be termed 'intrusive' in that they represent, to varying degrees, departures from normal classroom management practices. As such, these intrusive strategies can be contrasted with the least intrusive, i.e. the technique of using teacher approval or disapproval in a systematic contingency-determined manner: to promote pro-social/academic behaviour by using contingent teacher approval and to reduce anti-social disruptive and/or off-task behaviour by using contingent teacher disapproval.

The work of McAllister *et al.* (1969) is a much quoted exception to the heavy interventions referred to earlier. This study reported how, in a High School in the USA, a three component light behavioural intervention substantially reduced the occurrence of two categories of unwanted behaviour in a class of 16–19-year-olds. The target behaviours were inappropriate talking and turning around. Unlike most intervention packages utilised with younger children, that of McAllister *et al.* (1969) did not contain an 'ignore inappropriate behaviour' element. Teacher disapproval was a component and it was both personalised and explicit, e.g. 'Johnny, stop talking'. This negative control technique was coupled with teacher praise of appropriate behaviour and an evaluative statement to the whole class at the end of the lesson. In the UK, Wheldall & Austin (1980) report the effective use of teacher praise and attention coupled with ignoring inappropriate behaviour. In the investigation of Wheldall & Austin, the pupils involved were aged 14–15 years and were described as being below average academically; the lesson was mathematics. These two studies do provide evidence that light behavioural strategies can successfully change the behaviour of secondary aged pupils—but without further research they are an inadequate basis from which to claim generality of findings. By this is meant that one single-case experimental design outcome does not constitute sufficient evidence to suggest that in similar circumstances there is a reasonable probability that the same intervention will result in an analogous outcome. However, if researches demonstrating a similar outcome are reported regularly, the power of demonstration of the effect and hence the grounds for claiming generalisability of findings are progressively strengthened.

The general case for the equivalence of the replicated single case design to the group design in terms of generalisability of findings has now gained widespread acceptance. However, often the successful outcome of a single-case experimental research design study subsequently becomes widely cited in the absence of replication of findings having been demonstrated, i.e. generality of findings is taken for granted. For example, the work of O'Leary *et al.* (1970) demonstrated a differential effect of loud and soft reprimands. Subsequently the findings were widely cited, e.g. Kazdin (1980, p. 164), yet a successful replication of the study has not been located in the literature by the writer. This is not to claim that the findings have not been replicated—for such research would not be original and might therefore either not be submitted for publication or alternatively not be accepted for publication by the journal editor. Sometimes a study is frequently cited without evidence of systematic replication being available—only for an eventual replication to fail to support the initial findings. An example of this kind was the demonstration of the generalisation of self-instruction report by Bornstein & Quevillon (1976). This is frequently cited, e.g. O'Leary & O'Leary (1977, p. 303), again in the absence of evidence of repeated replication. However, evidence of failure to replicate the findings is available (Friedling & O'Leary, 1979). Therefore, on the basis of the published evidence, an equal case can be made for the failure of the self-instructional technique as that for its success. Other examples exist. Patterson's (1974) work on the successful treatment of conduct problem children is widely cited, yet Ferber, Keeley & Shemberg (1974) failed to replicate the reported successful outcomes.

The need for repeated replication to justify the claim for generalisability of findings is not necessarily met by the publication of a number of successful single-case design studies. Journals selectively publish successful outcome research and therefore the accumulation of a number of such successful outcome researches is not necessarily evidence of generalisability of findings. This is because the number of unsuccessful interventions attempted is unpublished and therefore unknown. An example of such a situation is to be found in the literature on behavioural contracting. A number of case-studies exist which report successful outcomes for this method of intervention, e.g. Bristol & Sloane (1974), Cantrell *et al.* (1969) and White-Blackburn *et al.* (1977). Such evidence could be used to claim generalisability of findings viz a viz the effectiveness of behavioural contracting, yet larger scale research, e.g. Weathers & Liberman (1975) and Stuart *et al.* (1976) gives grounds for less optimistic conclusions to be drawn.

This issue of generalisability of findings is relevant to research into the success or otherwise of light behavioural procedures in the control of pupil behaviour in the secondary school classroom. For example, in the American literature successful replications of the study of McAllister *et al.* (1969) are not readily found—yet evidence confounding claims to generalisability exist. For example, Cormier &

Cormier (1975, p. 7) claim that non-contingent praise and attention increased pupil on-task behaviour; in addition, evidence exists suggesting that the use of teacher praise and attention can be counter productive—McCullough (1972) reported that praise was disliked by older pupils.

It can be seen from this discussion that single case-studies do need to be repeated and equally that there is a need for the results of such investigations to be published whether they support or *do not support* the original findings. Accordingly, the use of light behavioural strategies referred to earlier in this article needs to be subjected to this process, since the findings, if they are positive and give grounds for suggesting generalisability, could have a considerable impact on the use of behaviour modification techniques in the Secondary school.

Hence the aims of the research reported in this paper were two-fold. Firstly, to assess the effects, if any, of light behavioural interventions on the on-task behaviour of Secondary aged pupils. Secondly, to assess the extent to which the demonstrated effects, if any, could be replicated in a number of different Secondary school classroom situations.

In addition, in view of the scarcity of research publications in the area, it was decided to report the outcome of *all* the case studies embarked upon, regardless of methodological shortcomings, e.g. absence of a return to baseline phase in one case and low levels of off-task behaviour in two further cases.

Method

Research Hypothesis

The research reported in this paper attempted to (i) investigate the effects of a number of 'light' behavioural interventions on the on-task behaviour of secondary school pupils and (ii) to generate sufficient data in terms of a number of systematic replications to allow some judgments on the generalisability of findings to be made. The problems associated with setting up the research have been described elsewhere (McNamara, 1982) and the details are described in the following paragraphs.

Settings

Three mixed sex comprehensive schools were used. In the first school three studies were carried out, in the second two, and in the third one. These schools had very similar catchment areas of mixed middle-class and working-class catchment areas.

Observers

Nine third year students from two Colleges of Higher Education were recruited. They were following BA and BEd Ordinary Degree Courses in Psychology.

Pupils

The selection of classes of pupils and the difficulties encountered in matching observers, teachers and difficult classes have been described fully elsewhere (McNamara, 1982). Briefly, observers were assigned to volunteer teachers; after joint consultation, a decision was reached as to which class of pupils should be involved. Decisions regarding choice of classes were largely dictated by the availability of the observers and the times of the week when the teachers concerned were taking difficult classes. The teachers and class situations are summarised in Table I.

TABLE I. Brief details of teachers, lessons and pupil year group

Case	Year group	Lesson	Teacher
1	5th year	GCE English group	30-year-old male BEd qualification. Nine years' teaching experience
2	5th year	Mixed CSE and non-examination group History	27-year-old male graduate. Four years' teaching experience
3	4th year	CSE Chemistry	25-year-old male graduate. Three years' teaching experience
4	2nd year	Chemistry (below average ability)	24-year-old female BEd in second year of teaching
5	3rd year	French: mixed ability group	34-year-old female: following a part-time BEd course. 12 years of teaching
6	1st year	Science: mixed ability group	24-year-old female BEd in her second year of teaching

Data Collection

The data collection was carried out by classroom observers. In three studies (cases 1, 2 and 3) two observers were present throughout the course of the investigations. In the remaining studies one observer was present for the duration of each study and each had available a second observer to call on occasionally to carry out inter-observer agreement checks. A consecutive five-second interval recording method was used to collect the following data:

(i) pupil on-task and off-task behaviour,
(ii) teacher approving and disapproving behaviour.

The definitions of these behavioural categories were those of Madsen, Becker & Thomas (1968)—on-task/off-task behaviour—and White (1975)—teacher approving and disapproving behaviour. These definitions are described in Appendix A. Teacher behaviour was restricted to the verbal domain because of the problems encountered in observing and recording non-verbal behaviour—see McNamara (1984).

The above categories of behaviour represented the minimum data collection requirements necessary for the achievement of the research objectives. Separate observation sheets for teachers and pupils were used and teachers and pupils were observed for alternate three-minute periods for the duration of each observation session—usually a lesson of 35 or 70 minutes. Each pupil in the class was observed in a predetermined order for five seconds. The order of pupil observation was followed repeatedly for the duration of the observation period.

In the three studies in which two observers worked together, this arrangement could have provided measures of agreement for *all* observations made if the two observers had been instructed to observe at the same time either the teacher or the pupils. On the other hand, if the observers observed the teachers and pupils out of phase, i.e. observer one→pupils, observer two→teacher, and then changed over, a 100% increase in observation time would be achieved—at the expense of no observer agreement data being obtained. In view of the indications from earlier research (McNamara, 1978) that student observers with limited training and experience of classroom observation work could achieve high levels of inter-observer agreement (87–93%), it was decided to utilise a compromise observation schedule. Observers one and two were to observe teacher and pupils respectively for three-minute periods and then change over. Occasionally (once per observation session) both observers were to observe the teacher and then the pupils at the same time. These probes of inter-observer agreement of teacher and pupil behaviour were thus designed to yield the data on a sampling basis across the duration of the study.

Baseline

Before establishing a baseline, the observers watched their assigned classes for two lessons. This was aimed at orientating the observers to the task and to allow the classes to habituate to the observers' presence. The baseline was planned to consist of at least three separate observation sessions. While three points of measurement are usually accepted as the minimum requirement for a baseline (Hersen & Barlow, 1977, p. 76), the actual pragmatic criterion generally used, or at least aimed for (see Baer & Parsonson, 1981), is a demonstration that stability of baseline rates of behaviour is indicated. The baselines in the present study range from four to eight lessons.

Intervention

The intervention consisted of a multi-component package arrived at from a review of the literature on applied behaviour analysis in the classroom with particular emphasis being paid to contingency management procedures. The components of the intervention procedure were arrived at after a consideration of:

(i) the most influential study of this type (Madsen *et al.*, 1968);
(ii) the most successful and perhaps widely read study of this type carried out with a teenage population (McAllister *et al.*, 1969);
(iii) one of the few UK studies carried out in a secondary school classroom (Wheldall & Austin, 1980).

At the completion of the baseline assessment, four possible components of an intervention package were presented to the teacher and discussed with him/her. The consultation was carried out by the writer, but the observers were present and joined in the discussion. (Photostat copies of the three papers referred to above were made available to the teachers.) A copy of the actual list of possible interventions, as presented to the teacher, is contained in appendix B. This involved four components, (i) rules, (ii) praise, (iii) disapproval of inappropriate behaviour and (iv) an evaluative statement at the end of the lesson. The teachers were requested to implement as many of the strategies as they could—but were told that it was only expected that they should implement those strategies which they felt were 'reasonable' and consistent with their teaching style. The reasons for presenting the teachers with this opportunity to opt out from any aspect of the intervention with which they did not agree were:

(a) continued teacher co-operation was more likely assured,
(b) it enhanced the likelihood that those interventions agreed to by the teachers would actually be implemented.

The strategies agreed for use in the case-studies are summarised in Table II.

TABLE II. Summary of intervention strategies used in cases 1 to 7

	Intervention			
	Praise	Personalised disapproval: unacceptable behaviour labelled	Rules	Evaluative statement
Case 1	√	√	—	√
Case 2	√	—	—	√
Case 3	√	√	√	√
Case 4	√	√	√	√
Case 5	√	√	—	√
Case 6	√	√	√	√
Case 7	√	√	√	√

Unlike cases 1 to 6, which involved the on-task behaviour of classes of pupils, case 7 involved the behaviour of an individual pupil. This pupil was a member of the class for which the data are reported in case 4. The baseline level of on-task behaviour for this class was high—about 70%. For this reason, it was felt that there might not be a great deal of room for improvement. It was, therefore, decided both to focus the interventions on the class in general and also on one select pupil, Patrick, who evidenced much off-task behaviour. The data related to this individual are reported as case 7.

Results and Discussion

Inter-observer Agreement

The summarised data are reported in Table III. Less data on observer agreement were obtained than was planned for. Some of the reasons for this have been described in a paper published earlier (McNamara, 1982). All the obtained levels of inter-observer reliability except one (case 6) approximated to or exceeded that generally deemed to be satisfactory, i.e. 80% or more (Axelrod, 1977, p. 89). However, level of inter-observer agreement is a function of the method of calculation (Harrop, 1979) and in the present research two different methods were used, one for pupil data and one for teacher data. Inter-observer agreement of pupil behaviour was calculated using the equation:

$$\text{Percentage agreement} = \frac{\text{No. of agreements}}{\text{No. of agreements and disagreements}} \times 100.$$

As *all* pupil behaviour observed was either on-task or off-task, this method produced results not biased by the method of calculation. In contrast to pupil behaviour, the teacher behaviour observed, verbal approval and disapproval, was of low frequency. Therefore, to have used the above method to calculate inter-observer agreement would have resulted in an inflated measure of inter-observer agreement—by including those observation intervals in which no recordable teacher behaviour occurred. For this reason, the method of calculation was identical to that for pupil behaviour—with the exception that intervals in which both observers recorded no teacher behaviour were omitted.

TABLE III. Mean inter-observer percentage agreement for observation of pupil and teacher behaviour

Case	Teacher behaviour	No. of three-min probes	Pupil behaviour	No. of three-min probes
1	96.9	9	94.8	4
2	89.7	5	85.8	3
3	79.5	4	82.2	5
4	98.4	5	88.6	3
5	87.5	2	88.0	2
6	68.2	2	94.6	2

Interventions

The intervention strategies agreed to by the teachers are reported in Table II. All six teachers agreed to give the pupils feedback at the end of the lesson in the form of an evaluative statement. All teachers complied with this for all lessons during the intervention phase. Changes in teacher verbal behaviour (praise and personalised disapproval) are reported in Table VI. The number of observation intervals in which each behaviour occurred was counted for each observation session. These data were then extrapolated to give an indication of the frequency of these behaviours during 35 minute lessons.

Effect of Interventions

The data are summarised in Table IV and are reported in terms of the average pupil on-task behaviour for the baseline and experimental phases. The reporting of data in this way is a contentious issue (see Baer & Parsonson, 1981). However, in that the data presented in graphs 1 to 7 tend to indicate changes in levels rather than slopes across the two phases, this method of presenting data is legitimate.

TABLE IV. Summary of effects of intervention. Increase in average on-task behaviour from baseline to intervention phases

	Average on-task behaviour (%)		
	Baseline	Intervention	Average increase in on-task behaviour (%)
Case 1	60.33	83.5	23.17
Case 2	67.1	83.63	16.53
Case 3	68.53	79.52	10.99
Case 4	73.75	81.66	7.91
Case 5	68.13	85.88	17.75
Case 6	83.39	84.69	1.3
Case 7	24.42	54.09	29.67

Evaluation of Interventions

Inspection of Table IV of the baseline levels of on-task behaviour in cases 1 to 6 indicates that in general the level was quite high; the lowest average level was 61% (case 1); four baseline measures of on-task behaviour were in the range 60–70% (cases 1, 2, 3 and 5); one baseline level was over 70% (case 4), while case 6 yielded a baseline level of over 80%.

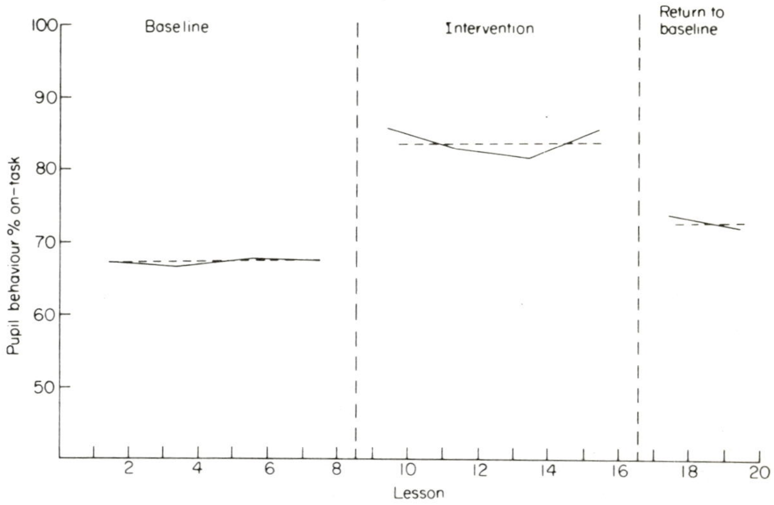

FIG. 1. Case 1.

The lesson by lesson levels of on-task behaviour are presented in Figs 1–7. The arithmetic mean of the on-task behaviour has been indicated on the graphs by a pecked line. The critique of this practice (Baer & Parsonson, 1981) has already been referred to. One of the criticisms is that such a practice may deflect the readers' attention from methodological shortcomings in the data. For example, in case 3 of this report the data points for lessons 7 and 8 indicate that a rising baseline situation may prevail—a situation which has implications for outcome assessment, yet one whose importance may be masked by reporting and superimposing the average data level on the graphs. Nonetheless, such a practice, i.e. superimposing mean levels on graphed data, can be helpful in the visual analysis of data—provided the possible pitfalls are recognised and avoided. Such considerations demand that a cautious interpretation be put forward for the difference in *mean* levels of on-task behaviour between the baseline and intervention phases.

Reference has already been made to the rising baseline of case 3 but stability of baseline was achieved for the remaining cases, although only cases 1, 6 and perhaps 7 present baselines whose stability is unequivocally demonstrated. Case 2 contains two data points (lessons 7 and 8) whose value is very similar to those for the experimental phase. However these data were obtained in atypical situations for an examination was in progress in both lessons. Therefore it was felt legitimate by the writer to exclude these data from the calculation of mean baseline level of on-task behaviour. Cases 4 and 5 generated baselines which appear reasonably stable; but the *range* of on-task behaviour assessed during the baseline phase in both cases was high—65 and 85% for case 4 and 52 and 80% for case 5. Had the investigation not been time-

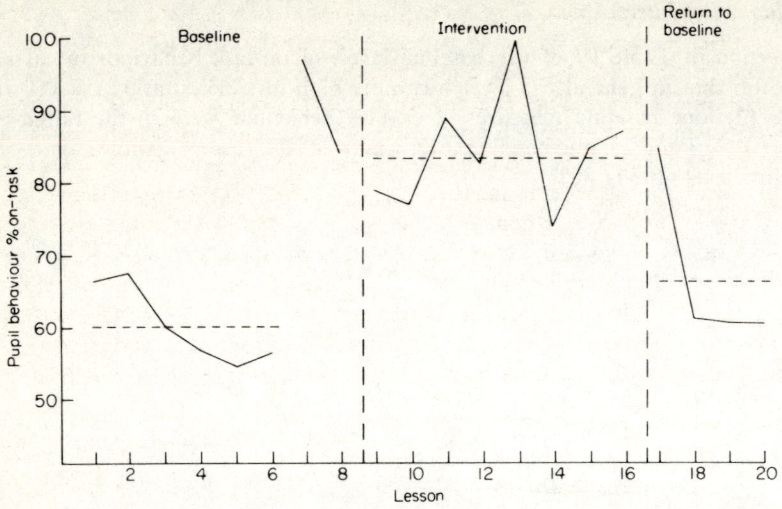

FIG. 2. Case 2.

constrained because of the limited period for which the observers were available a more extensive baseline would have been preferable to demonstrate beyond doubt that both stability and representativeness has been achieved. While the range for baseline on-task behaviour in case 7 was also extensive—3–34%—the five data points do seem to indicate stability and reflect the range of on-task behaviour evidenced by the pupil. The mean rate of on-task behaviour was calculated omitting the data for lesson 4. The pupil was on-task for 67% of the time in this lesson; however, the situation was atypical in that the pupil had been isolated; he was seated by himself at a desk at the back of the class. With the above reservations and observations about the 'quality' of the baseline data noted, attention is now turned to the relative values of the mean on-task behaviour for the baseline and experimental conditions.

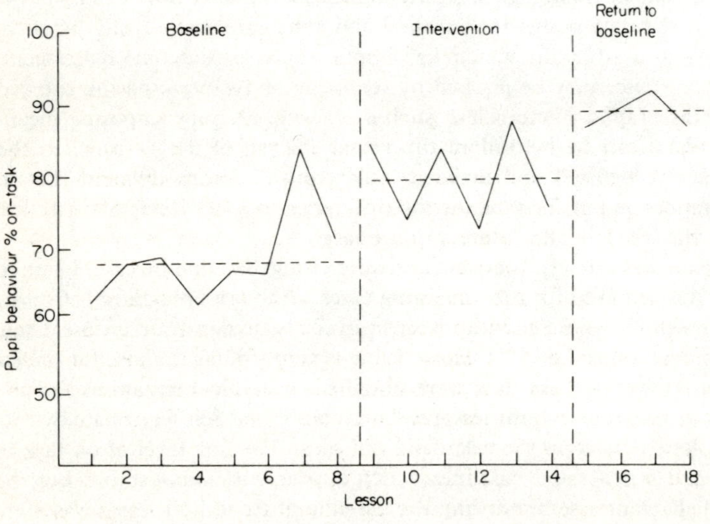

FIG. 3. Case 3.

In cases 1 to 5 an increase in average on-task behaviour occurred. In case 6 no such increase occurred—but it should be noted that the baseline level of on-task behaviour in this instance was above 80% so that little room for improvement existed. Examination of Figs 1, 2 and 5 indicates a marked effect on baseline levels of behaviour of the intervention procedures. Thus for three of the six cases involving whole classes of pupils the light behavioural interventions listed in Table II appear to have effected a significant increase in the level of on-task pupil behaviour. For cases 1 and 2 the power of demonstration of the effect of intervention is enhanced because a return to baseline phase followed the intervention phase and resulted in a reduction in on-task behaviour. For case 5 no return to baseline phase was implemented for reasons described elsewhere (McNamara, 1982); this shortcoming seriously reduced the power of demonstration of the effect of intervention because of all the limitations associated with the AB design (see Hersen & Barlow, 1976, p. 169).

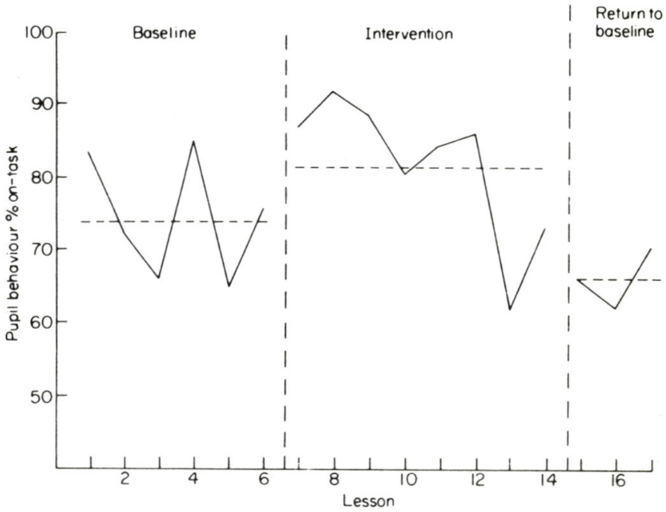

FIG. 4. Case 4.

Examination of the results for case 6 (see Fig. 6) indicated that this case-study constituted something of a redundant exercise, for the mean level of baseline on-task behaviour was above 80%, leaving little room for improvement. This obstacle to completing the research as planned for in this case has been discussed more fully (McNamara, 1982) in the context of implementation problems to setting up school based behaviour modification studies. Cases 3 and 4 pose problems of evaluation of effect by the method of visual inspection. For case 3 the calculation of mean on-task behaviour across the baseline and intervention phases indicates an increase of on-task behaviour of about 12%. However, examination of the baseline indicates that stability is far from certain. It is an example of a rising baseline and an implication of this is that the intervention strategies should not have been implemented until baseline stability had been established. Inspection of the levels of on-task behaviour during the return to baseline phase is supportive of the writer's cautious interpretation of the data. The return to baseline phase yielded on-task levels above that of the intervention phase.

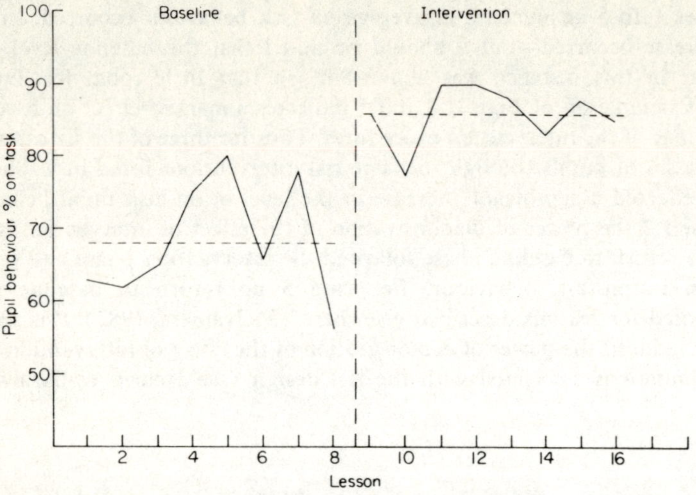

FIG. 5. Case 5.

Visual inspection of Fig. 4 indicates an increase of on-task behaviour between baseline and intervention phases of about 8%. The average on-task level during intervention phase is depressed by return to baseline levels of on-task behaviour during the final two lessons of this phase. This leads to the conclusion that the effect of intervention, in this case, is equivocal. The reason for the shortfall between the planned experimental design and that actually implemented in cases 3 and 4 has been described in the paper referred to earlier. Briefly the observers were time constrained in as much as the amount of time they had available to participate in the study was limited. This fact, together with their uncertain grasp of the rigorous requirements of single-case experimental research design, resulted in a premature entry into the experimental phase in case 3 and a premature return to baseline phase in case 4.

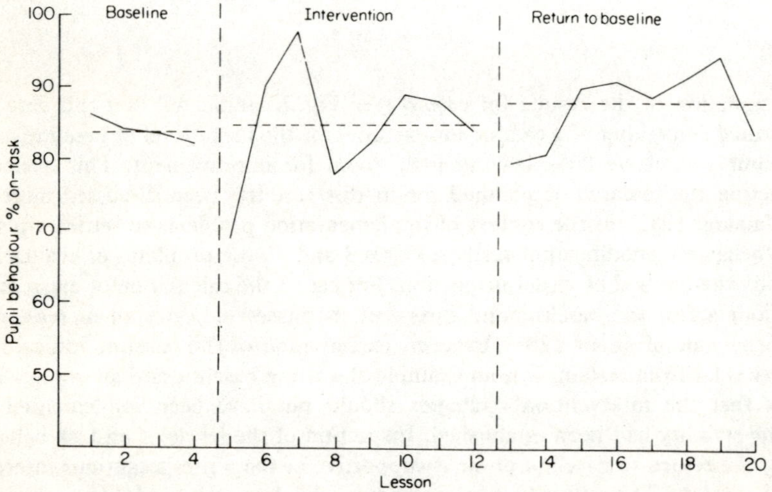

FIG. 6. Case 6.

Effect of Intervention on the Individual

Case 7 represents the percentage on-task behaviour of an individual pupil in the class for which the class data is presented in Fig. 4 (case 4). The data for this particularly troublesome pupil (Patrick) were collected as the observer feared that the baseline level of on-task behaviour for the class as a whole was so high that there was little room for improvement. Fig. 4 indicates that the baseline levels of on-task behaviour was high (74%), yet nonetheless was susceptible to the intervention strategy—the level being increased to 82% during the intervention phase. The effect of focusing the intervention on Patrick increased the pupil's on-task behaviour from a baseline level of 24% to an intervention phase of 54%.

The conclusion is that in two cases (1 and 2) the light behaviour interventions described were effective in increasing the level of pupil on-task behaviour. The pupils concerned in these studies were fifth year classes. The classes were at the extremes of the continuum of attainment. Case 1 involved a class of fifth year pupils preparing for a GCE English examination. The second class, i.e. case 2, involved a group of pupils, about half of whom were preparing for a CSE examination in History, the remaining pupils were not considered of sufficient ability to be entered for this examination. Thus this limited evidence indicates that the practice of behaviour modification *may* have some utility in the secondary school sector.

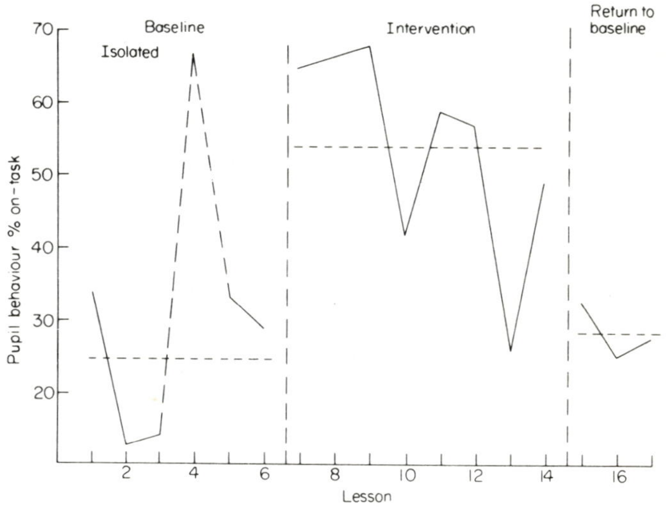

FIG. 7. Case 7.

The outcomes of the remaining four cases involving whole classes of pupils did not contraindicate the cautious positive interpretation and conclusion drawn. However, methodological considerations limited the support that could be drawn from the outcomes of cases 4 and 5, while the high baseline level of on-task behaviour for case 6 left little room for improvement. In case 3 there is a rising baseline and the general trend of rising levels of on-task behaviour from the baseline through the intervention phase to the return to baseline phase gives grounds for believing that some other factor(s) may have been at play. The class teacher concerned felt that the major factor in increasing the level of pupil on-task behaviour over the weeks of the study was the pupils' increasing awareness of an approaching end of term assessment. While this is perhaps a speculative interpretation of the data, it is one that warrants consideration for curriculum matters are possibly of more importance in secondary school settings than in primary. It may well be that a self-regulation model such as that of Kanfer & Spates (1977) which can involve target setting can be used to good effect in the Secondary school and such a model is compatible with the operant model.

Data Collection

Table IV indicates that in all six cases average pupil on-task behaviour increased while Table V indicates in which cases the increase is claimed to be functionally related to the intervention strategy. In two cases (1 and 2) it has been claimed that a functional relationship exists between pupil on-task behaviour and the implementation of the intervention. The practical conclusion that might be drawn from this finding is that the teacher practices making up the intervention package can be successful in managing disruptive Secondary school children. However, off-task behaviour is not synonymous with disruptive behaviour; therefore the increase in on-task behaviour could have been achieved without a reduction of disruptive behaviour. In other words, the average increase in pupil on-task behaviour could have been achieved by the industrious children being even more industrious, the less industrious pupils being unchanged—or alternatively the increase in average on-task behaviour may have been achieved by general reduction in *non-disruptive* off-task behaviour.

TABLE V. Evaluation of effects of intervention. Effect of intervention on pupil on-task behaviour

	Effects of intervention	Comments
Case 1	Increase in pupil on-task behaviour	Withdrawal of intervention resulted in a reduction of pupil on-task behaviour
Case 2	Increase in pupil on-task behaviour	Withdrawal of intervention resulted in a reduction of pupil on task behaviour
Case 3	Inconclusive	(i) Rising baseline (ii) Withdrawal of intervention resulted in a *further increase* of pupil on-task behaviour
Case 4	Inconclusive: *temporary* increase in pupil on-task behaviour	Withdrawal of intervention resulted in a return to baseline levels of pupil on-task behaviour—but the last two lessons of the treatment phase had already returned to baseline levels
Case 5	Increase in pupil on-task behaviour	No return to baseline phase implemented
Case 6	No effect	Very high baseline level of pupil on-task behaviour
Case 7	Increase in pupil on-task behaviour	Data for an *individual* pupil reported

The method of data collection used (which focused on the whole class) was not conducive to indicating how the behaviour of one individual pupil or small group of pupils altered from baseline to intervention phases, yet clearly these data would have been useful.

In case 2, for example, the observer reported that much of the disruptive behaviour was generated by a small group of pupils:

> It was always the same pupils by and large who caused classroom disruption. They were four boys who always got at the back of the classroom. They seemed a lot bigger physically and somehow a lot older than the other boys. The nature of their disruption was not malicious but took the form of talking amongst themselves and shouting out comments and jokes. (Observer i)

The observer went on to comment that not infrequently the pupils would be observed for data collection periods when on-task—indicating that much off-task (and often disruptive) behaviour was being 'missed'. A similar comment was made by the observer in case 3, viz:

> The girls, however, tended to be the noisiest and the teacher tended to direct most of his negative behaviour towards them. The same girls chatted and moved out of their seats, but off-task behaviour sometimes was not recorded for several three minute periods until the trouble spots were "hit" and then it was not always the case that the unruliness would be recorded: by the time the observer reached the disruptive pupils they may have been on-task. (Observer i)

These observers were indicating that in the classes observed there were present a minority of pupils who were responsible for the majority of the off-task behaviour. They were also indicating their opinion that this off-task behaviour was under-represented in the data reported for the class as a whole.

Considerations such as these led the writer to consider retrospectively if the pupil behaviour data could have been collected in a way which (a) gave more weight to the influence on the class of a small number of difficult pupils and (b) which would enable the behaviour of small groups of individuals in the class to be monitored. With hindsight, both considerations (a) and (b) could have been met, to a certain extent, by utilising a method of observation described by Merrett (1980). This method involved grouping the class into a number of convenient observation groups: each group was observed in turn and the number of pupils in the group who were off-task in the observation period noted. If, for example, there were four groups then each pupil would be observed very fourth observation interval: this is in contrast to the method used in the present study, for in this research each pupil was observed every 24th or 25th observation interval—depending on the number of pupils present.

In contrast to the method used in this research, that described by Merrett allows the behaviour of a small number of frequently off-task pupils to be reflected quite accurately in the data for the class. Additionally, Merrett's method would allow for the effect of the intervention on a group of children within the class to be monitored.

Thus, the methodological limitations discussed above indicate that the effect of the intervention on any given individual in the class studies is unknown. However, the data for Patrick (case 7) indicates that the light behavioural strategies used *can* influence the behaviour of particularly disruptive individuals.

Extent of Interventions

Two of the four elements of the multi-component light behavioural intervention package involved specific teacher behaviour at the beginning (rules) or end (evaluative statement) of the lesson. These were easy to monitor and the teachers did implement these behaviours during the intervention phase and cease to use them during the return to baseline phase. The behaviour of the pupils (on-task/off-task) and teacher verbal behaviour (praise and reproof) were recorded using a sampling method described earlier.

The intent of this latter aspect of the investigation was to shift the balance of control in favour of positive teacher verbal behaviour. This was to be achieved by increasing the frequency of teacher positive verbal behaviour and reducing the frequency of teacher negative verbal behaviour.

TABLE VI. Rates of teacher approving and disapproving verbal behaviour per 35 minute lesson (prorated)

	Approval		Disapproval	
Case	Baseline	Intervention	Baseline	Intervention
1	6.6	16.25	13.61	16.59
2	15.25	26.46	27.85	18.06
3	27.55	45.15	21.08	31.16
4	16.17	44.35	57.54	51.66
5	80.35	52.0	33.1	24.7
6	53.76	44.86	52.29	44.94

It might therefore seem relevant to discuss the contents of Table VI in relation to this intent. However, there are grounds for believing that the sampling of teacher verbal behaviour was inadequate—to the extent that the data are unreliable. The basis for this view is as follows. Each lesson was of 35 minutes' duration. In this time the observers were expected to record alternatively four three-minute observation periods of pupil and teacher behaviour. Such an observation schedule would yield 12 minutes of observational data on both pupils and teachers. Thus, in cases 4, 5 and 6 12 minutes of observation of teacher and pupils per lesson was planned for. These cases involved only one observer per case: cases 1, 2 and 3 involved two observers. Therefore, up to 24 minutes of observational data per lesson on both pupils and teacher were anticipated. In fact, only one observer achieved the target of 12 minutes of observation of pupils and teacher per lesson. Three further observers approached the target and the remainder fell short to varying degrees. This shortfall in sample size of pupil and teacher behaviour is not too crucial with respect to the pupil behaviour observed. These behaviours—on-task/off-task—are of high frequency, for necessarily the pupil must be either on-task or off-task. There is evidence available that small samples of high frequency behaviour can be representative. For example, Kubany, Bloch & Sloggett (1971) reported that a teacher using a four-minute observational interval for pupil behaviour obtained very similar results to those obtained by independent observers yet the latter generated their results from a 50 day, 20 minutes per day, 15 second interval observation schedule.

However, teacher positive and negative verbal behaviour are low-frequency behaviours and the likelihood of obtaining unrepresentative data increases as the length and number of observation periods decreases. For progressively the observer will obtain less data on the full range of target teacher behaviour over the course of the lesson. For these reasons it is felt that the data obtained on teacher verbal behaviour may not be representative of teacher behaviour over the course of a lesson. Although the data do suggest that the teachers did increase the frequency of approval while little change was seen in the number of disapproving comments. In retrospect, this shortcoming could have been overcome by recording teacher positive and negative verbal behaviour using a frequency count method throughout the lesson. Teacher verbal behaviour was not observed in the return to baseline phases.

Conclusions

The effects of intervention on pupil on-task behaviour are summarised in Table IV. These indicate that in three cases (1, 2 and 5) the intervention strategies produced increases in pupil on-task behaviour, and outcome in two cases was inconclusive (cases 3 and 4) and no functional relationship was established between the intervention and pupil on-task behaviour in the remaining case (case 6). Further, in case 4 (inconclusive outcome for the class as a whole) it was demonstrated that the on-task behaviour of an individual pupil was increased by the intervention strategies (case 7).

The results obtained from the studies reported do support the finding of Wheldall & Austin (1980) that 'light behavioural strategies' can effect change in the behaviour of Secondary school pupils and yielded no evidence to support the view that such teacher behaviour may elicit inappropriate pupil behaviour (cf. McCullough, 1972). The target behaviour in this research has been 'on-task'; however, there is an increasing body of research indicating that promoting on-task behaviour may not promote a concomitant increase in academic product, e.g. Hay, Hay & Nelson (1977). In view of this, further research on the efficacy of contingent teacher social behaviour in increasing academic product as well as on-task behaviour might be fruitfully pursued.

Acknowledgement

The writer would like to thank Dr L. A. Harrop for his helpful comments on the draft form of this article.

REFERENCES

ABID, R.R. (1975) Negative effects of behaviour consultation: "I know I ought but it hurts too much", *Journal of School Psychology*, 14, pp. 89–94.

AXELROD, S. (1977) *Behaviour Modification for the Classroom Teacher* (New York, McGraw-Hill).

BAER, D.M. & PARSONSON, B.S. (1981) Applied changes from steady state: still a problem in the visual analysis of data, in: BRADSHAW, C.M., SZABADI, E. & LOWE, C.F. (Eds) *Quantification of Steady State Operant Behaviour* (Elsevier/North-Holland).

BLUNDELL, D. & MERRETT, F. (1982) The successful application of behavioural methods in the secondary school. *Behavioural Approaches with Children*, Vol. 6, No. 3, pp. 17–27.

BORNSTEIN, P.H. & QUEVILLON, R.P. (1970) The effects of a self-instructional package on over-active pre-school boys, *Journal of Applied Behavior Analysis*, 9, pp. 179–188.

BRISTOL, M.M. & SLOANE, H.N. (1974) Effects of contingency contracting on study rate and test performance, *Journal of Applied Behavior Analysis*, 7, pp. 271–280.

BRODEN, M., HALL, R.V. & MITTS, B. (1971) The effects of self-recording on the classroom behaviour of two eighth grade students, *Journal of Applied Behavior Analysis*, 4, pp. 191–200.

CANTRELL, R.P., CANTRELL, M.L., HUDDLESTON, M.C. & WOOLDRIDGE, R.L. (1969) Contingency contracting with school problems. *Journal of Applied Behavior Analysis*, 2, pp. 215–222.

CORMIER, L.S. & CORMIER, W.H. (1975) *Behavioral Counselling: Operant Procedures* (Boston, Houghton Mifflin & Co.).

FERBER, H., KEELEY, S.M. & SHEMBERG, K.M. (1974) Training parents in behavior modification: outcome of and problems encountered in a programme after Patterson's work, *Behavior Therapy*, 5, pp. 415–419.

FRIEDLING, C. & O'LEARY, S.G. (1979) Effects of self-instructional training on second and third-grade hyperactive children. A failure to replicate, *Journal of Applied Behavior Analysis*, 12, pp. 211–219.

GLYNN, E.L. (1970) Classroom applications of self-determined reinforcement, *Journal of Applied Behavior Analysis*, 3, pp. 123–132.

HARROP, L.A. (1979) Unreliability of classroom observation, *Educational Research*, 21, pp. 207–211.

HAY, W.M., HAY, L.R. & NELSON, R.O. (1977) Direct and collateral changes in on-task and academic behaviour resulting from on-task versus academic contingencies, *Behavior Therapy*, 8, pp. 431–441.

HERSEN, M. & BARLOW, D.H. (1977) *Single Case Experimental Designs: strategies for studying behavior change* (Oxford, Pergamon Press).

KANFER, F.H. & SPATES, C.R. (1977) Self-monitoring, self-performance and self-reinforcement in children's learning: a test of multi-stage self regulation model, *Behavior Therapy*, 8, pp. 17–24.

KAZDIN, A. (1980) *Behavior Modification in Applied Settings* (The Dorsey Press).

KUBANY, E.S., BLOCH, L.E. & SLOGGETT, B.B. (1971) The good behavior clock. A reinforcement/time-out procedure for reducing disruptive classroom behavior, *Journal of Behavior Therapy & Experimental Psychiatry*, 2, pp. 173–179.

LANE, D.A. (1978) *The Impossible Child*, Vol. 2 (London, ILEA Publication).

LANE, D.A. & MILLAR, R.R. (1977) Dealing with behaviour problems in school: a new development, *Community Health*, 8, pp. 155–159.

LOBITZ, W.C. & BURNS, W.J. (1977) The "least intensive intervention" strategy for behavior change procedures: the use of public and private feed-back in school classrooms, *Psychology in the School*, 14, pp. 89–94.

MCALLISTER, L., STACHOWIAK, J.G., BAER, M. & CONDERMAN, L. (1969) The application of operant conditioning techniques in a secondary school classroom, *Journal of Applied Behavior Analysis*, 2, pp. 277–285.

MCCULLOUGH, J.P. (1972) An investigation of the effects of model group size upon response facilitation in the high school classroom, *Behavior Therapy*, 3, pp. 561–566.

MCNAMARA, E. (1978) Management of problem behaviour through self-recording techniques: *unpublished MSc thesis*, University of Manchester.

MCNAMARA, E. (1979) The use of self-recording in behaviour modification in a secondary school, *Behavioural Psychotherapy*, 7, pp. 57–66.

MCNAMARA, E. (1982) Reality problems in classroom research, *Occasional Papers of the Division of Educational and Child Psychology of the British Psychological Society*, 6, pp. 50–53.

MCNAMARA, E. (1984) Classroom contingency management and teacher non-verbal behaviour. *Occasional Papers of the Division of Educational and Child Psychology of the British Psychological Society* (in press).

MCNAMARA, E. & HARROP, L.A. (1979) Behaviour modification in the secondary school: a cautionary tale. *Occasional Papers of the Division of Educational and Child Psychology of the British Psychological Society*, 3, pp. 38–41.

MCNAMARA, J.R. (1975) Ways in which outcome measures influence outcomes in behaviour modification, *Journal of School Psychology*, 13, pp. 104–113.

MADSEN, C.H., BECKER, W.C. & THOMAS, D.R. (1968) Rules, praise and ignoring: elements of elementary classroom control, *Journal of Applied Behavior Analysis*, 1, pp. 130–150.

MAIN, G.C. & MUNRO, B.C. (1977) A token reinforcement programme in a public junior high school, *Journal of Applied Behavior Analysis*, 10, pp. 93–94.

MERRETT, F. (1980) Application of behaviour modification in the primary school classroom, doctoral thesis, *Collected Original Resources in Education*, 4, (3), 11 fiches.

MERRETT, F. (1982) 'Encouragement works better than punishment': an in-service behavioural workshop for teachers, *Behavioural Approaches with Children*, 6, pp. 27–33.

O'LEARY, K.D., KAUFMAN, K.F., KASS, R.E. & DRABMAN, R.S. (1970) The effects of loud and soft reprimands on the behaviour of disruptive students, *Exceptional Children*, 37, pp. 145–155.

O'LEARY, K.D. & O'LEARY, S.G. (1977) *Classroom Management: the successful use of behavior modification* (Oxford, Pergamon Press).

PATTERSON, C.R. (1974) Interventions for boys with conduct problems: multiple settings, treatments and criteria, *Journal of Consulting and Clinical Psychology*, 42, pp. 471–481.

PRESLAND, J.L. (1980) Behaviour modification and secondary schools, in: GOBELL, A. & UPTON, C. (Eds) *The Challenge of Adolescent Behaviour in Schools*, Faculty of Education, University College, Cardiff.

SCHUMAKER, J.B., HOVELL, M.F. & SHEERMAN, J.A. ((1977) An analysis of daily report cards and parent managed privileges in the improvement of adolescents' classroom performance, *Journal of Applied Behavior Analysis*, 110, pp. 449–464.

SOLOMON, R.W. & WAHLER, R.G. (1973) Peer reinforcement control of classroom problem behaviour, *Journal of Applied Behavior Analysis*, 6, pp. 49–56.

STUART, R.B., TRIPODI, I., JAYARATNE, S. & CAMBURN, D. (1976) An experiment in social engineering in serving the families of predelinquents, *Journal of Abnormal Child Psychology*, 4, pp. 243–261.

WEATHERS, L. & LIBERMAN, R.P. (1975) Contingency contracting with families of delinquent adolescents. *Behavior Therapy*, 6, pp. 356–366.

WEBSTER, R.E. (1976) A time-out procedure in a publish school setting, *Psychology in the Schools*, 13, pp. 72–76.

WHELDALL, K. & AUSTIN, R. (1980) Successful behaviour modification in the Secondary school. A reply to McNamara & Harrop, *Occasional Papers of the Division of Educational and Child Psychology of the British Psychological Society*, 4, pp. 3–8.

WHITE, M.A. (1975) Natural rates of teacher approval and disapproval in the classroom, *Journal of Applied Behavior Analysis*, 8, pp. 367–372.

WHITE-BLACKBURN, G., SEMB, S. & SEMB, G. (1977) The effects of a good-behaviour contract on the classroom behaviors of 6th grade students, *Journal of Applied Behavior Analysis*, 10, pp. 31–37.

Appendix A: behavioural coding categories

I *Off-task pupil*

A. *Gross Motor.* Getting out of seat, standing up, running, hopping, skipping, jumping, walking around, moving chair etc.

B. *Object Noise.* Tapping pencil or other objects, clapping, tapping feet, rattling or tearing paper, throwing book on desk, slamming desk. Be conservative, only rate if you can hear the noise when eyes are closed. Do *not* include accidental dropping of objects.

C. *Disturbance of Other's Property.* Grabbing objects or work, knocking neighbour's books off desk, destroying another's property, pushing with desk (only rate if someone is there). Throwing objects at another person without hitting them.

D. *Contact (high and low intensity).* Hitting, kicking, shoving, pinching, slapping, striking with object, throwing object which hits another person, poking with object, biting, pulling hair, touching, patting, etc. Any physical contact is rated.

E. *Verbalization.* Carrying on conversations with other children when it is not permitted. Answers teacher without raising hand or without being called on; making comments or calling out remarks when no questions have been asked; calling teacher's name to get her attention; crying, screaming, singing, whistling, laughing, coughing, or blowing loudly. These responses may be directed to teacher or children.

F. *Turning Around.* Turning head or head and body to look at another person, showing objects to another child, attending to another child. Must be of four-seconds duration, or more than 90 degrees using desk as a reference. Not rates unless seated. If this response overlaps two time intervals and cannot be rated in the first because it is less than four-seconds duration, then rate in the interval in which the end of the response occurs.

G. *Other Inappropriate Behaviour.* Ignores teacher's question or command. Does something different from that directed to do, including minor motor behaviour such as playing with pencil or eraser when supposed to be writing, colouring while the record is on, doing spelling during the arithmetic lesson, playing with objects. *The child involves itself in a task that is not appropriate.* Not rated when other Inappropriate Behaviours are rated. Must be time off-task.

H. *Mouthing Objects.* Bringing thumb, fingers, pencils, or other objects in contact with the mouth.

II *On-task*

Time on task; e.g. answers question, listens, raises hand, works on assignment. Must include whole five-seconds interval except for Turning Around responses of less than four-seconds duration.

Teacher Verbal Behaviour

All teacher verbal approval and disapproval were recorded verbatim.

Appendix B: classroom management—intervention strategies

I *Rules*

Identify up to four basic rules of *your* classroom, e.g.
when the teacher is talking to us we look at him/her;
we get on with our work quietly;
we try not to stop others from working;
we try to pay attention to our work and try not to daydream.
(N.B., The above examples define appropriate on-task behaviour and attempt to be *specific.*)

Print your rules on a card and read out at the beginning of each lesson: refer to them occasionally during the lesson.

II *Praise*

Accentuate the positive! Look for individuals keeping the rules, either individually or collectively and emphatically praise those pupils: use names where possible, e.g. 'It is good to see Joe, David and Arthur getting on with their work'; or to a group, 'This is good, I can see you are all working well'.

III *Attention to Inappropriate Behaviour*

If not already the case, ensure that more attention is paid to pupils *working* than to pupils *not working.*

When correcting a pupil (or pupils) use their name(s) and identify the unwanted behaviour, e.g. 'John, stop talking', 'Jane, do not interrupt when I am talking'. etc.

IV *Evaluative Statement*

At the end of each lesson make a summary statement concerning the general behaviour of the class, e.g. 'You've done a good morning's/afternoon's work today, well done', 'You've worked quite well today, let's see if you can do better still tomorrow', 'Your work (behaviour) has been disappointing today, let's see if you can improve on it next lesson', etc.

Self-recording as a Means of Improving Classroom Behaviour in the Secondary School

FRANK MERRETT & DOROTHY BLUNDELL

ABSTRACT *Two experiments are reported in which children's study behaviour was manipulated systematically within a behavioural paradigm. Both studies were carried out in the remedial department of a large, modern Secondary school in England by a woman teacher. The first involved an individual, a boy whose study behaviour was controlled using self-recording in a reversal design. On-task behaviour increased whilst maladaptive responses were reduced and there was a pronounced improvement in the boy's attitude to school work. The second study was a group intervention employing self-recording which was again successful in improving the on-task behaviour rate. At the same time it proved possible to gain measures which show clear evidence of improvement in both the quality and quantity of written work produced by the group. In both studies there was some evidence of generalisation of effects.*

Following the pioneering work carried out in the United States there has recently been a great deal of interest in Britain in the possibilities opened up by the behavioural approach to classroom teaching. However, much of practical work has been accomplished in Primary schools. Published studies reporting the use of the behavioural approach in this country up to the beginning of 1981 numbered 56 at the Primary level compared with only 24 at the Secondary stage (Merrett, 1981). This is strange, since at first sight it would appear that it is in the Secondary schools that the most troublesome and more anti-social behaviour is to be found (Upton & Gobell, 1980). Accordingly, one might reasonably suppose that in such schools teachers would be disposed to use any promising method that came to their notice.

This does not seem to be so and McNamara & Harrop (1979) refer to the dearth of studies at the Secondary level suggesting that, "methods of proven success and acceptable to teachers may not be as successful in the Secondary school as in the Primary sector" (p. 38).

In the paper quoted and in McNamara (1977) an attempt is made to set out some of the reasons for this. They include the facts that in Secondary schools pupils come under the influence of a large number of teachers for relatively short periods (unlike those in Primary schools), that lecture-type lessons do not lend themselves to interventions and that the greater sophistication of older children, together with strong peer-group influences, make them less likely to respond to teachers' manipulation of contingencies.

We should not fail to note, however, that Holland (1978), after carrying out some careful observations, made useful suggestions about behaviour change in an assessment centre whilst Brown (1977) has successfully applied behavioural methods with adolescent boys in trouble. Both of these groups contained boys of Secondary age with severe behaviour problems. Rose (1981) has used the behavioural approach successfully with maladjusted boys of Secondary age. Milward (1981) reports an individual study with a 13-year-old whilst the Barnsley Special Education Team (1981) give several case-studies of the successful use of behaviour modification at the Secondary level. Kolvin *et al.* (1981) report a large-scale project where some 72 children of Secondary age treated with behavioural methods were compared with a control and two other treatment groups. Behavioural methods were found to bring about many desirable outcomes and, whilst comparing very favourably with other treatments, were shown to be economical in teachers' time and effort. In addition, we have Lawrence's (1980) account of work in a Secondary school in London and the studies of Friedman (1978), Appleton (1979) and Masterson, Earls & Taylor (1981) which report the use of behavioural methods in improving specific academic behaviours in Secondary schools, all within the British context.

Cormier (1969) commenting upon findings in the USA reported that 'rules, praise and ignoring', a useful and popular device, works just as well with adolescents as with younger children. Wheldall & Austin (1980) found reason to support Cormier's position after carrying out an interesting and successful intervention through a teacher in a Secondary school in the English Midlands. Their paper goes on to answer many of the points made by McNamara & Harrop. Presland is another very experienced worker in the field who suggests that behavioural methods have an important place at the Secondary level (Presland, 1980). Despite his misgivings about the use of the behavioural approach in Secondary schools, McNamara nevertheless reports some successful outcomes, especially where children have been involved in self-recording and self-management (McNamara, 1979a, b). The two interventions described in this paper were carried out in the remedial department of a Secondary school and both used self-recording. In a remedial department there is a more continuous contact between pupils and teachers and this perhaps gave a better chance of success.

Experiment One: the modification of the deviant behaviour of an individual in a remedial class

Setting

The first experiment was carried out in a modern co-educational school in the West Midlands, England. The school houses 780 pupils from 11 to 16 years, many coming from a council housing estate which borders the site on two sides. A remedial department, which employs three teachers, was established five years ago. Children are selected for remedial treatment on the results of a battery of tests administered in the last year of the Primary school. Pupils in the department spend 50% of their time working with teachers whom they know and trust. Subsequent movement in or out of the department depends upon general classwork and the results of the annual survey of reading ability undertaken throughout the school.

The Subject

Timothy, aged 13 years at the time of the intervention, was the youngest of three children in his family and the only boy. He was rather small and under-weight for his age. Since babyhood he has suffered from urinary tract problems which have necessitated hospital treatment and subsequent periods of absence from school. In June 1978 Timothy took a battery of tests just prior to his transfer to Secondary School. These included tests of the National Foundation for Educational Research in English and maths and a non-verbal intelligence test. In all of these he registered norms between 71 and 83 whilst his reading ability was also low (6.9 years: Burt Word Recognition Test). Accordingly, he was placed in the remedial department on entry to Secondary school.

Timothy was very aware of his limitations and tended to display a number of avoidance strategies. These included making a great deal of fuss before settling down to work and taking any opportunity to stop. He took pains to set himself up as a 'funny man' to gain attention and approval from his peer group. He would become very anxious if asked to work alone (on the Language Master, for example) and would soon begin to interact with others, usually to their annoyance and detriment. His behaviour became disruptive if he encountered the slightest difficulty and the teacher was not immediately available.

His progress in the remedial department was very slow and when he reached the third year his teacher realised that if he were to succeed in the next year, when examination options would be started, it was necessary to improve his persistence and concentration and to reduce the extent of his deviant behaviour. She felt that this was the time for action if he were to make progress socially and academically.

Method

The teacher allowed three weeks of the new term to pass, as a settling in period, before any attempt was made to collect baseline data. The operational definitions of inappropriate behaviour for this purpose were:

(i) getting out of seat and moving two paces or more to touch another child's work, and
(ii) unrequested verbalisations which could be heard over a distance of two metres.

A sampling technique was employed for observation so that the teacher could get on with her job of teaching for most of the time. A tape-cassette was played which gave an audible cue 30 times during a half-hour period but at variable intervals (i.e. variable interval schedule of 60 seconds). The signal was loud enough for the teacher to hear but not loud enough to distract the class. Every time she heard the signal the teacher would look at Timothy and tally his behaviour as 'on-task' or as one of the categories of deviance, as defined above. On-task behaviour was defined as getting on with the work he had been given to do and varied according to the task. In general terms, it included writing in his book, looking at the work sheet, reading his book and so on. Baseline data were collected on five successive days for 30 minutes during the time set aside for English, which occurred at a different period on each day.

During this phase the records indicated that Timothy had been on-task for 30.4% of the sampled times. Physical interference with other children's work and verbal outbursts accounted for a large proportion of the remaining cued samples. He was very shocked when he saw a graphical representation of these data. He had not realised that he 'wasted so much time', as he put it and obviously saw this as a problem in which he had a responsibility. Because of this and his relative maturity it was decided that he should be involved in the monitoring of the intervention, by self-recording. It was believed that in this way he would become aware immediately of any improvements made.

The intervention programme was aimed at increasing on-task behaviours by using the Premack principle, i.e. increasing the incidence of a low-priority behaviour through the manipulation of a high-priority behaviour (Premack, 1959, 1971). Timothy was very fond of using a 'Doodle Art' sketch pad to colour in a cartoon picture and this was made contingent upon on-task behaviour, as defined above. The boy was accordingly given the opportunity to tally his on-task behaviour using the same definition, observation schedule and signal as his teacher. He knew that the teacher would be recording at the same time and understood that only those tally marks for on-task behaviour which were agreed between them would count. Ten such agreed tally marks could be exchanged for two minutes of the reinforcing activity, i.e. colouring in the 'Doodle Art' picture. At the end of the third week Timothy expressed dissatisfaction with this method of recording. He found having to stop working to tally his on-task behaviour a distraction and he was allowed to use a pocket counter instead.

During weeks seven and eight the teacher arranged a return to baseline conditions so that Timothy did not record his on-task behaviour and was not told his 'score' until the end of the week. He continued to earn time for the reinforcing activity, however. During weeks nine and ten Timothy once again recorded his on-task behaviour every time the signal was heard.

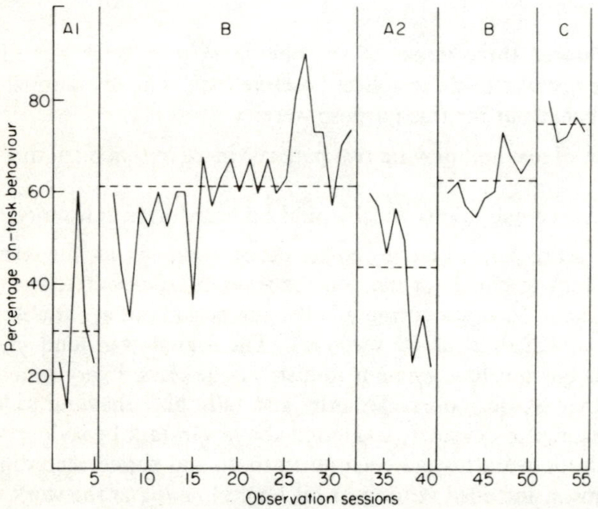

FIG. 1. Graph to show percentage on-task behaviour tallied for each (daily) observation session (teacher's scores). A1—baseline, A2—reversal, B—self-recording, C—follow-up checks (6 weeks after). Dashed lines show mean levels for each phase.

Results

As can be seen from Fig. 1, on-task behaviour during the baseline conditions was at a mean level of approximately 30%. During the first intervention period it rose to over 70% with a mean level of 62%. For the two weeks when the boy ceased recording his own on-task behaviour this level fell to a mean of 40% rising again to a mean level of approximately 61%, for the last two weeks. The graphical representation of the results from the A B A B C design demonstrates that the target behaviour (on-task) was clearly controlled by the manipulation of the contingencies. It has been suggested by McNamara (1979a, b) that self-recording can be very effective in bringing about changes in pupils' behaviour once a simple procedure can be devised for them to operate. This experiment seems to be in accord with McNamara's suggestion. When the boy first began to record his own behaviour the level of agreement between his results and those of his teacher was just over 90%. After the first week the level of agreement never fell below 93% and the mean level for the eight weeks was 96.5%. This may be considered satisfactory (Gelfand & Hartmann, 1975).

The intervention was brought to an end naturally at the end of the school term. After the holiday the contingencies were not reinstated. Instead, the boy and his teacher had an agreement according to which he was to try to maintain his pre-holiday level of on-task behaviour without extra help. She, on her part, continued to provide contingent positive reinforcement, mainly social. After six weeks of the new term the teacher carried out covert observations, as in the original baseline conditions, for a period of one week. Results showed an on-task level of 74.6% of sampled observations. This is good objective evidence of generalisation of effects after the cessation of the intervention.

Discussion

Analysis of the baseline data showed no obvious setting events but Timothy appeared to be responding chiefly to attention from the peer group and the teacher. Once it was seen that the boy was willing to improve his 'attending' behaviour, his cooperation was made effective through self-recording. His lack of concentration and distractibility were the behaviours to be improved and this was done by providing positive reinforcement for alternative and incompatible behaviours which were classed as 'on-task'. The rewarding consequence was time to engage in a favoured occupation, namely colouring in. The graph of the results shows a good measure of control through differential reinforcement with self-recording in a reversal design.

Improvement in agreement rates in tallying, achievement of minutes of earned time and completion of the colouring task all gave opportunities for the teacher to deliver social reinforcement in the form of praise, approval and other encouragement. This was added to by the interest and cooperation of the rest of the class and other members of the staff and culminated when the picture was completed and displayed in the school corridor for everyone to see. It was later taken home so that the parents also could register approval and praise. Thus, one of the chief effects of the intervention was that Timothy began to receive positive reinforcement for well-defined acceptable behaviours instead of for 'clowning' and other avoidance strategies. This could be looked upon as the first stage on the way to his becoming subject to the natural, intermittent schedules of reinforcement which keep most of us in line with the expectations of our group and the first step towards the generalisation of effects.

It should be noted that whilst Timothy was improving his on-task score his teacher was manipulating the nature of the tasks being set. By degrees she made the tasks more difficult in the sense that they tended to be those that Timothy found less to his taste and more likely to arouse his anxiety. These were mainly tasks which called for him to work alone and to solve his own problems.

In addition to generalisation over time there was subjective evidence of generalisation to other situations and a change of attitude in the boy. His anticipation of involvement in the mainstream of school work after the choice of subjects had been made for the last two years of Secondary schooling had a marked effect upon his attitude towards his schoolwork. He showed much greater confidence and application and his self-reliance was seen to increase. These changes were maintained until the end of the summer term when the option subjects for the next year were finally decided upon by the staff. Since Timothy was from the remedial department his choices did not carry much weight and, in fact, he was able to follow none of his chosen studies. The effect of this was predictable and he quickly reverted to his former patterns of behaviour. He is not particularly troublesome or disruptive but now takes little or no interest in his school work and is just waiting to leave.

Experiment Two: a group programme for improving academic output in a remedial class

Setting and Subjects

The second experiment was carried out in the same Secondary school as the first and by the same teacher (the second author). In this case the subjects were a class of eight girls and eight boys who had been placed in the remedial group after the administration of a battery of standardised tests. Some details of the group are given in Table I.

TABLE I. Details of chronological and reading ages (Schonell, Silent B) for the remedial class

	N	Mean ages	Mean reading ages
Girls	8	12.65 (0.33)	9.72 (1.04)
Boys	8	12.66 (0.28)	9.34 (0.55)
All	16	12.65 (0.30)	9.53 (0.80)

The general feeling of the staff was that the class members were too noisy, that they did not get down to work quickly enough and that when they did, their work output was below what it should have been. The teacher approached the class about these issues with which they showed general agreement. They agreed also with the suggestion that an intervention should be set up to improve their work output.

Method

A simple recording sheet was provided for each child for the week (see Appendix). For the whole of one session per day (it was always an English lesson) a tape was played which emitted an audible signal on a variable interval schedule of 60 seconds. The signal thus occurred 30 times during the half hour but with a variable interval between each 'ping' of from 15 to 95 seconds. To the class it appeared to sound at irregular and unpredictable intervals. The children were told that if they were working, i.e. concentrating upon whatever task had been set, when the signal occurred they could make a tally mark in the appropriate line. The marks were totalled at the end of the session and at the end of the week. The teacher hoped to be able to regard this first week's score as a baseline but it can be seen from the records (Table II) that scoring was high from the start. From the outset the 'ping' became a highly discriminative stimulus for getting on with work. Since they never knew when it would sound next, the only way that the children could be sure of scoring was to work constantly and that is just what they did. Scores for the first week averaged 133.5. The teacher used the lowest score of all (86) as a guide for setting the target for week two. Accordingly, she set this target at 80 as being realisable and promised a reward. This was a 30 minute period on Friday afternoon in which all children who met the target could follow activities of their own choosing. The weekly target was raised by small steps to 120 for the fifth week. No child ever failed to meet the target set. The teacher asserts that since the children sat in small groups around tables they could easily check up on each other when marking the tallies and that the incidence of cheating was low. The teacher herself was also able to keep a check on cheating. The children were aware that she could observe some of them every time the signal sounded and note whether they marked their sheets or not.

Results

It can be seen from Table II that all the children in the class maintained very high rates of on-task behaviour in the recorded sessions during the intervention. Especially for the girls there was little fluctuation in the scores from week to week.

TABLE II. Mean scores for on-task behaviour (self-recorded)

	Week 1	Week 2	Week 3	Week 4	Week 5
Boys	126.9	134.5	144.9	134.8	138.7
Girls	141.0	141.6	142.0	141.9	141.6
All	133.5	138.1	143.5	137.9	140.0
Targets		80	100	110	120

Subjective evaluation of the effects of the intervention made by the class teacher and other members of the staff suggested that there was a considerable improvement in noise levels during working whilst the amount and standard of work completed seemed to have improved. The Christmas holiday brought about a natural break in the experiment and the class agreed to try to maintain both behaviour and work levels without the help of the signal after the new term began. Although this was not entirely successful there was general agreement among the staff concerned that much of the improvement in work and behaviour was carried over into the new term. Thus there was some subjective evidence for generalisation.

Many experimenters using the behavioural approach have been able to demonstrate improved on-task rates and so on and it has been assumed that work output will have improved in quantity and quality as a consequence. This is not necessarily so, however, and has to be examined empirically. One such experiment (Ferritor *et al.*, 1972) showed little relationship between on-task behaviour and work output. Since some of the products of the present experiment were in written form it was possible to take a *post-hoc* evaluation of a more objective kind. Samples of work done by members of the group before and after the intervention during similar 35 minute periods of English were available and from these two measures were obtained. A crude, but objective measure of quantity was obtained through a word count whilst a more subjective measure of quality was obtained by having a teacher-colleague award marks for neatness and presentation. The teacher-marker awarded these marks 'blind', i.e. without knowing which set of papers related to which stage of the intervention nor of the purpose of the evaluation. This was an attempt to avoid bias in the marking. The fact that the evaluation of the work was decided *post-hoc* removes one source of experimental error since the outcome could not have been prejudiced by foreknowledge that it was to be put under scrutiny. The means and standard deviations for these measures are given in Table III.

TABLE III. Mean scores for work in English lessons

		Before intervention	At end of intervention	df	*t*	*p**
Boys:	neatness scores	5.57 (5.57)	6.71 (1.11)	6†	2.07	n.s.
	word count scores	132.57 (25.44)	178.86 (15.50)	6†	3.61	<0.02
Girls:	neatness scores	6.38 (1.30)	7.25 (1.04)	7	2.97	<0.05
	word count scores	129.88 (18.69)	199.0 (18.96)	7	10.05	<0.001
All:	neatness scores	6.07 (1.41)	7.0 (1.07)	14	3.87	<0.01
	word count scores	131.13 (21.30)	189.6 (19.77)	14	7.90	<0.001

**p* values are two-tailed.
†Data incomplete for one boy.

Table III shows a shift in the predicted direction (better outcomes) for all of the measures for both boys and girls and for both combined. The movements were statistically significant in all cases except one. These findings support the subjective evaluation of the teachers reported above and give credence to their opinion about the improvement in work output.

Discussion

Several important issues arise from the second study. To begin with it is interesting to note that the children accepted the intervention as reasonable and were able to carry out the self-recording effectively and conscientiously. The effects were felt immediately, the signal for recording becoming a discriminative stimulus for on-task behaviour straight away. The high scores which were made at the outset were maintained throughout. The raising of the target score was ineffective because the children almost always managed to exceed it. Some of the girls and one of the boys actually had a lower score during the last week of the intervention than in the first so the pacing of the target setting was clearly at fault.

General Discussion

In both experiments reported we have demonstrated that behaviour change took place. Whilst we must not overlook the fact that the novelty of a new approach may be a potent factor, the evidence of the reversal procedure in the first experiment and of some generalisation effects in both, help to discount this as a prime cause. In both experiments, social reinforcement in the form of praise and approval was used systematically in order to bring about generalisation of effects and in both there was a measure of success, albeit judged somewhat subjectively. This would suggest that it is not the level of sophistication of the subjects which prevents the successful application of behavioural methods at the Secondary stage of education. Indeed, from some aspects, the method is easier to apply at this level. In both of the experiments reported we have evidence that the subjects themselves were aware of their problems, desired change and were prepared to cooperate. They showed further that they could reliably record their own responses and were ready to respond to a simple rewarding strategy. Adolescents certainly respond to peer-group reinforcement. Perhaps the fault is that teachers, reflecting society, do not provide a context in which it can be directed appropriately. In the first experiment reported here, the peer-group were undoubtedly reinforcing the subject's 'clowning' and other maladaptive behaviours. When the teacher provided a different and clearly structured context they co-operated by reinforcing other, much more constructive forms of behaviour, thus bringing about changes of benefit to all.

The second experiment is of particular interest because it contains evidence, rare in British studies, that not only was on-task behaviour increased but that the quantity and to some degree the quality of the work output was also improved. This is a great step forward. For too long applied behaviour analysts have had to accept criticisms that the behaviour change which they manage to demonstrate is merely cosmetic. Teachers have always known intuitively that to work well, children need peace and quiet and the opportunity to concentrate on the task in hand without distraction. If teachers are able to use behavioural methods to bring about these necessary conditions with ease and confidence then they will be able to engage in their principal task of teaching more effectively.

Both of these experiments were carried out in the remedial department of a Secondary school where the stability of relationships between staff and pupils and teaching styles resemble those which operate in Primary schools. It may appear that we have thereby avoided some of the issues raised by McNamara & Harrop (1979). Theoretically, by the time that pupils reach the Secondary stage of schooling they should be in total command of the tools of scholarship, i.e. the three R's. For children who are confident in the use of such tools, specialisation of teaching, with its need for short-term contact with a variety of 'experts' and for self-organisation and application to the drudgery of learning the rudiments of many new subjects may be exactly what they need. Such children are able to respond quickly to the challenge of new subjects, finding in them fresh purpose for the exercise of their well-developed skills so that before long they begin to receive intrinsic reinforcement from these new activities; poetry and prose read, experiments carried through, calculations successfully completed, stories and essays written and so on. Some official reports, e.g. Newsom (1963, especially chapters 13 and 14), however, would suggest that the majority are not so equipped at the age of 11. In which case it is easy to see that for most children academic learning will be slow and the accompanying drudgery prolonged. The postponement of intrinsically reinforcing outcomes will, in many cases, lead to disillusionment and lack of interest in such activities. The children then begin to respond to other reinforcing outcomes, probably provided by the peer-group, as in the case of Timothy. These responses tend to be counter-productive academically and at variance with the aims of the school.

The lack of success in academic pursuits and the consequent frustration experienced by so many children at the Secondary level may thus be seen as the failure of an inflexible system to cope with the needs of the majority of its customers. The same system, through its sheer size and complex structure delimits the closeness and permanence of human contact which would enable behavioural and scholastic remediation to take effect. The conclusion to be drawn then is that few applications of behavioural methods have been seen at the Secondary level of education not because they are not called for and not because they are inappropriate but because the organisational structure makes them very difficult to apply. We are suggesting further that the same organisational system may itself be the cause of at least some of the problems.

Timothy was not given the chance to pursue any of his chosen subjects into the final years of his Secondary schooling. For many of his classmates in the remedial department the same was true. By and large, the successful are well-catered for and are given their first-choice subjects. Where there is a shortage of space and facilities not all can be satisfied but it is daunting for devoted, enthusiastic and innovative teachers who manage to bring about changes in 'failed' students to see these gains dissipated through the actions of an inflexible system. It may be issues like these which deter teachers from using behavioural methods in Secondary schools rather than difficulties inherent in the age group or in the methods themselves.

REFERENCES

APPLETON, C. (1979) Con man smiles: contingency management in a Secondary Maths. individualised learning experiment, paper read at *Conference of Association of Teachers of Psychology*, Bulmershe College of Higher Education, May 1979.

BARNSLEY SPECIAL EDUCATION TEAM (1981) A team approach to disruption, *Special Education—Forward Trends*, 8, pp. 8–10.

BROWN, B.J. (1977) Gilbey House: a token economy management scheme in a residential school for adolescent boys in trouble, *Bulletin of the British Association for Behavioural Psychotherapy*, Vol. 5, No. 3, pp. 79–89.

CORMIER, W.H. (1969) Effects of teacher random and contingent social reinforcement on the classroom behaviour of adolescents, *Dissertation Abstracts International*, **31**, pp. 1615–1616.

FERRITOR, D.E., BUCKHOLT, D., HAMBLIN, R.L. & SMITH, L. (1972) The non-effects of contingent reinforcement for attending behaviour on work accomplished, *Journal of Applied Behaviour Analysis*, 5, pp. 5–17.

FRIEDMAN, E. (1978) Increasing spelling proficiency and attentiveness in a Secondary school classroom, *Newsletter of the Association for Behaviour Modification with Children*, 2, pp. 10–11.

GELFAND, D.M. & HARTMANN, D.P. (1975) *Child Behaviour and Analysis* (Oxford, Pergamon Press).

HOLLAND, J.M. (1978) Observation and planned intervention programme in an assessment centre classroom, *Newsletter of the Association for Behaviour Modification with Children*, 2, pp. 21–23.

KOLVIN, I., GARSIDE, R.F., NICOL, R.A., MACMILLAN, A., WOLSTENHOLME, F. & LEITCH, I.M. (1982) *Help Starts Here: the maladjusted child in the ordinary school* (London, Tavistock Press).

LAWRENCE, J. (1980) A behaviour modification project with class three boys in a Secondary school, *Education Monograph II* (London, Goldsmith's College).

MCNAMARA, E. (1977) Results and impressions of using behaviour modification in a schools psychological service, *Bulletin of the British Association for Behavioural Psychotherapy*, 5, No. 3, pp. 55–62.

MCNAMARA, E. (1979a) Pupil self-management in the Secondary school—the goal of behavioural intervention, *A.E.P. Journal*, 5, pp. 26–29.

MCNAMARA, E. (1979b) The use of self-recording in behaviour modification in the Secondary school, *Behavioural Psychotherapy*, 7, No. 3, pp. 57–66.

McNamara, E. & Harrop, L.A. (1979) Behaviour modification in the Secondary school—a cautionary tale, *B.Ps.S. D.E.C.P. Occasional Papers*, 3, No. 2, pp. 38–41.

Masterson, J.F., Earls, H. & Taylor, D. (1981) The effects of instructions and reinforcement on the handwriting of a 13 year-old child in a remedial school, *Behavioural Psychotherapy*, 9, pp. 167–176.

Merrett, F.E. (1981) Studies in behaviour modification in British educational settings, *Educational Psychology*, 1, pp. 13–38.

Milward, I. (1981) Behavioural contracting: some theoretical and applied issues, *Behaviour Modification with Children*, 5, pp. 12–15.

Newsom, D.H. (1963) *Half our Future* (London, HMSO).

Premack, D. (1959) Towards empirical behaviour laws: 1 positive reinforcement, *Psychological Review*, 66, pp. 219–233.

Premack, D. (1971) Catching up with common sense, or two sides of a generalisation; reinforcement and punishment, in: Glaser, R. (Ed.) *The Nature of Reinforcement* (New York, Academic Press).

Presland, J. (1980) Behaviour modification and Secondary schools, in: Upton, G. & Gobell, A. (Eds) *Behaviour Problems in the Comprehensive School* (Cardiff, Faculty of Education).

Rose, R. (1981) The effect of the use of behaviour modification techniques upon the social and academic performance of maladjusted boys, *Behavioural Approaches with Children*, 5, No. 2, pp. 6–20.

Upton, G. & Gobell, A. (Eds) (1980) *Behaviour Problems in the Comprehensive School* (Cardiff, Faculty of Education).

Wheldall, K. & Austin, R. (1980) Successful behaviour modification in the Secondary school—a reply to McNamara and Harrop, *B.Ps.S. D.E.C.P. Occasional Papers*, 4, No. 3, pp. 3–9.

Appendix: the scoring schedule used to record on-task behaviour in the second experiment

W/E	30 minute session (English)	Total
Monday		
Tuesday		
Wednesday		
Thursday		
Friday		
	Weekly Total	

During the course of each half hour English lesson the signal would sound 30 times, the intervals between signals being variable and unpredictable. Every time the children heard the signal they had to decide whether they were working according to the definition, i.e. paying attention to the task that they had been set to do. If they were, they were permitted to put a stroke in the line for the day, to be tallied at the end of the lesson and again for the week. Thus, the maximum for the week would be 150 tally marks.

The Establishment and Decline of a Token Reinforcement Program with Three Emotionally Disturbed Pre-school Children

WALTER J. MUSGROVE

ABSTRACT *This paper describes the initiation and evaluation of a behavioral program designed to increase command following and to decrease out-of-seat behavior in three emotionally disturbed pre-school children. The children were two girls and a boy, each 4 years of age, attending a private facility for retarded children, but the children in this study were of average intelligence. The program succeeded in increasing command following to 95% compliance, and in reducing out-of-seat behavior to 1.5 times per 15 minute session. The children were then transferred to a public school and the behaviors targeted deteriorated to only slightly better than initial base rate. Some reasons for regression in behavior of the children based upon observational data are presented and possible ways of correcting the problems are posited.*

The maintaining of classroom control has long been a topic of concern for both novice and experienced teachers, and a special emphasis has been placed upon pupil behavior which tends to be aggressive and/or disruptive. Not only is the effectiveness of the teacher impaired, but also there tends to be a lessening of learning by the disruptive as well as the non-disruptive pupil in the class as a result of the undesired behavior patterns. Feldhusen, Thurston & Benning (1970) reported that a 5-year follow-up of elementary school children showed a significantly lower school achievement of children considered as aggressive-disruptive when compared to a control group not so considered. The variable of IQ was statistically ruled out as a contributing factor by an analysis of covariance technique.

It will follow, then, that intervention as early as possible with disruptive behavior would not only benefit the teacher and the non-disruptive pupil, but could also serve as a cumulative factor in aiding the disruptive pupil's scholastic accomplishments.

The literature is replete with studies which have established the efficacy of the utilization of behavior modification technology to assist the classroom teacher.

Novy *et al.* (1973) employed an A-B-A design to evaluate the efficacy of a token system with a 9-year old boy in a class of learning disabled children with a target behavior of attending to work. A baseline (based on 30-minute observation sessions) of 60% attending to work time was obtained. A reinforcement program increased attending to work behavior to 88%, and a reversal produced a drop in target behavior to 67%. The authors concluded that attending to work behavior was subject to change by a token system.

Token economies have also been applied to elementary pupils who have been classified as emotionally disturbed (ED). Fjellstedt & Sulzer-Azaroff (1973) supplied tokens contingent upon several separate behaviors, one of which was direction following. The subject was an 8-year old boy selected from a class of ED children, and the results of the study indicated that the subject's direction following was changed in the desired direction as a result of the token reinforcement program.

A cursory review of a few journals has yielded sufficient precedent to indicate that the initiation of a behavior modification program based upon a token system with pre-school age children is a viable procedure.

Three children enrolled in a retardation facility located in a mid-size urban area in west central Florida were the subjects of this study. Approximately 30 persons ranging in age from 6 months to 43 years attend this facility. Class size varied with age and ability level. Each of the four classes had a teacher's aide, and an assistant aide. Three of the teachers had Bachelor of Arts degrees, two of whom were certified by the State Board of Education in the field of retardation. One teacher held an Associate of Arts (Junior College) degree in Mental Retardation Technology. Teachers' aides had an average of 6 years of practical experience working with retarded children. Assistant aides, sponsored by The State Division of Vocational Rehabilitation, had little or no formal training and were themselves diagnosed as retarded. The teacher in this study held the Associate of Arts degree. She was responsible for the initiation and maintenance of the behavioral program for the children. Her aide had almost 2 years of practical experience working with retarded children.

Eight children, three of whom were diagnosed as emotionally disturbed with no physical abnormalities, were the population from which the subjects of this study were drawn. Two of the three children selected were 4-year old twin females, and the other a 4-year old male. Binet IQ scores of the twins were 80 and 93, and 69 for the male. Although the one score was fairly low, the tester did not feel that he was truly mentally retarded. Ages of the other children in the class ranged from 3 years, 3 months to 4 years, 6 months, and tested IQs from 42 to 98 were reported. One of the children in the class had multiple handicaps and another was physically handicapped. The three subjects in this study were treated as a separate unit in teaching sessions, but grouped for music, lunch, and outdoor activities with the rest of the class.

The focus of the program was to increase to 90% the percentage of commands by the teacher followed by the children, and to decrease the children's out-of-seat behavior to zero. The changes in these behaviors were used to assess the efficacy of the token system.

Baseline data were obtained from several 15 minute observation sessions conducted over a period of 4 weeks. Data obtained from all the subjects for each observation session were grouped to obtain a mean for each behavior observed. A token system was then implemented for 2 weeks and the reactions of the children were recorded. Each child was given a card to wear with his/her name on it at the beginning of each teaching session. Stickers, in the form of cut-up address labels, were used as tokens to be placed on the card. Tokens (along with praise) were given to the children on a variable-interval schedule for remaining in seat and following instructions given by the teacher. If a child left his/her seat or did not follow the teacher's instruction after being asked twice, other children who remained in their seats or who followed the instruction of the teacher, were reinforced with praise and a sticker token. There was no limit placed on the number of stickers given during the 15-minute teaching sessions. Back-up reinforcers of candy and trinkets were available at the end of each session for redemption of the tokens, or tokens could be accumulated as desired. Initially the children were receiving about 15 tokens per session. By the end of the treatment period, the children were receiving as few as five tokens while maintaining the desired behavior. In addition, the children were beginning to use their tokens for special activities as well as tangible back-ups. After employing this system for 2 weeks, a 1-day reversal was undertaken, and then the same token system as before was reinitiated. This procedure represented the standard A-B-A-B design.

These data indicate that the utilization of the token system produced a marked effect in the desired direction in both in-seat behavior and in command following. The behavior rate of the group prior to the implementation of the token system was represented by an average of 3.3 times per session of out-of-seat behavior, and the group, as a whole, followed 43% of the commands given by the teacher on either the first or second request.

Following a 2-week application of the token reinforcement program, the out-of-seat behavior was reduced to a mean of 1.6 times per session. The ratio of commands followed on either the first or second request was increased to 74%. During the 1-day reversal, the group mean of out-of-seat behavior increased to 3.5 times per session; the percentage of commands followed on either the first or second request decreased to 67%.

When the token system was reinstituted, out-of-seat behavior of the group was reduced to a mean occurrence of 1.5 times per session, and the following of the teacher's commands was increased to 95% compliance on either the first or second request.

The subjects in this study were transferred to a public school ED class at the beginning of the school year. After 2 months, follow-up data were taken. There was a deterioration of performance levels in both target behaviors when compared to final baseline performance. The occurrence of out-of-seat behavior increased to a mean of 5 times per 15 minute session and the number of commands followed was reduced to 68% per session. These data suggest that there had been an improvement over initial baseline rate, but the improvement was not significant. Fig. 1 shows the average performance of the group during the baseline, reinforcement period, reversal, reinforcement, and follow-up periods for the out-of-seat behavior and for the command-following responses.

As with most programs involving a number of individuals of different disciplines over a period of time, this program met with a considerable number of difficulties. The problems encountered are not felt to be atypical or unusual in any sense, but the author feels they are worthy of some discussion, for each contributed to the program's overall lack of success.

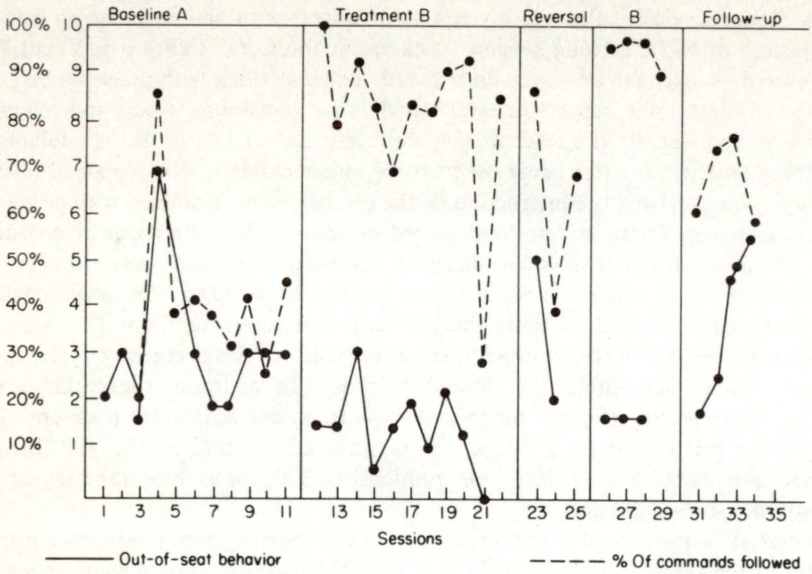

FIG. 1. Out-of-seat behavior, command following performance and follow-up data for three pre-school ED children.

Perhaps the most salient factor of all the difficulties met was the lack of understanding by the teachers of the purposes and procedures of behavior modification. It was found that the public school classroom instructional personnel involved in this project tended to employ reinforcers, especially primary ones, haphazardly. The use of reinforcers was not only inconsistent, but there was no effort made to wean the children from the primary reinforcers to tokens, to non-systematic social reinforcers, or to the natural reinforcers consequent to the behavior. There was often blatant non-contingent use of reinforcers and there were several examples seen of the teacher giving the child his/her reinforcer before the desired behavior was emitted, and, if the child failed to exhibit the behavior, he/she still kept the reinforcement.

Also closely related to the above was a marked lack of structure in the children's program. This facet produced a non-integrated curriculum without clear-cut objectives and behavioral outcomes stated. With these lacking, systematic progress could not be realistically expected.

The author feels that appropriate inservice or pre-service training could do much to reduce the lack of understanding on the part of the contingency managers. The school psychologist or a representative of a local university could serve as the instructor of the training program.

Another problem was the lack of adequate staff to implement the program throughout the day. This situation, however, could be quite easily remedied by utilizing reliable volunteers or by hiring and training para-professional personnel.

Finally, the reinforcers employed in the public school quickly lost their value to the children and there was not a sufficient variety of either primary or back-up reinforcers to be effective. The reinforcers themselves held no value, and the children seemed either to reject the available reinforcers or did not seem to care if they received the reinforcers or not. While the cause of this reaction has not been fully investigated, the author hypothesizes that it may stem from a lack of sophistication on the part of those selecting the reinforcers and/or a lack of financial support necessary to purchase appropriate reinforcers. Since the heart of any behavior modification program is the reinforcer, a program is doomed to failure if the reinforcers are, in fact, not reinforcing.

The project described in this paper served not only to demonstrate the practical application of a behavior modification program with pre-school ED children, but also it has shown how an effective program can deteriorate as a result of the breakdown of standard, accepted behavior modification practices. The author has shown the need for articulation between behavior management programs initiated in the non-public pre-school systems and the public schools as well as pointed out a need for further pre-service and in-service training programs designed to offer instruction in the principles and practices of systematic contingency management.

REFERENCES

FELDHUSEN, J., THURSTON, J. & BENNING, J. (1970) Longitudinal analysis of classroom behavior and school achievement, *Journal of Experimental Education*, 38, pp. 4–10.

FJELLSTEDT, N. & SULZER-AZAROFF, B. (1973) Reducing the latency of a child's responding to instructions by means of a token system, *Journal of Applied Behavior Analysis*, 6, pp. 125–130.

NOVY, P., BURNETT, J., POWERS, M. & SULZER-AZAROFF, B. (1973) Modifying attending-to-work behavior of a learning disabled child, *Journal of Language Disabilities*, 6, pp. 217–221.

Carryover Effects of Multielement Manipulations: enhancement of preschoolers' appropriate rest-time behavior

MICHAEL A. MILLER, C. SUE McCULLOUGH, & JEROME D. ULMAN

ABSTRACT *Carryover effects associated with the use of the multielement design were investigated within the context of a preschool classroom of eight boys. A reversal design incorporating a multielement-manipulation phase was used to analyze possible multiple treatment interference generated by the experimental manipulation. The results of the first three phases (corresponding to a conventional ABA design) indicated that token reinforcement was effective in increasing the target behavior: appropriate rest-time behavior of the class as measured by planned activity checks. Following introduction of the multielement manipulation the target behavior sharply increased during non-treatment days as well.*

In the field of applied behavior analysis, experimental designs are usually employed to evaluate the effectiveness of a particular intervention procedure. A major task of the applied researcher is to draw valid inferences about functional relationships between a socially significant behavior and the treatment under investigation. But, as Campbell & Stanley (1973) have pointed out, the validity of such inferences may be threatened by a number of factors. One of the factors they enumerate—multiple treatment interference—is the focus of this article. Multiple treatment interference may occur whenever more than one treatment is applied to the same individual. It is observed when differential responding under one condition is brought about by an individual's exposure to a prior condition. Obviously, complex behavior analyses involving single-subject (intrasubject replication) comparisons of two or more treatments, components of a treatment package, or different 'dosages' of a single treatment, are subject to multiple treatment interference. The particular concern of this study is the threat of multiple treatment interference to one member of the family of intrasubject replication designs, the multielement design.

Also called a multiple schedule design, alternate treatments design, and simultaneous-treatments design (see Sparzo & Ulman [1] for a discussion of appropriate terminology and a bibliography of multielement studies), this design is based on discrimination learning principles, i.e. if a behavior is treated differentially in the presence of different stimuli, it will exhibit different characteristics in the presence of those stimuli. The basic feature of the multielement design is the relatively rapid alternation of two or more different treatments or conditions, each associated with a distinct (potentially discriminative) stimulus. The multielement design is especially useful for comparing different treatments; additional advantages offered by this design have been discussed in length elsewhere (Barlow & Hayes, 1979; Ulman & Sulzer-Azaroff, 1975).

The multielement design is susceptible to three types of multiple treatment interference (Barlow & Hayes, 1979): *alternation effects*—interference resulting from the rate at which the conditions are alternated in a fixed order; *sequence effects*—differential responding solely produced by the order in which the conditions are presented; and *carryover effects*—the behavioral effects of one condition on adjacent conditions regardless of the overall sequencing of conditions. Carryover effects may actually be the greatest single threat to the internal validity of the multielement design.

Carryover effects have traditionally been studied in the operant conditioning laboratory as behavioral contrast and induction effects of multiple or concurrent schedules of reinforcement. Such effects are observed when a change in one schedule produces a behavioral change within another schedule that is not being manipulated. When the two patterns of responding change in the same direction, the phenomenon is usually called *induction*, or if in the opposite direction, it is called *contrast* or *behavioral contrast*. Reviews of the extensive basic operant research literature dealing with induction and contrast suggest that carryover effects are reliable, but relatively small (Dunham, 1968; Freeman, 1971). In the applied behavioral literature, on the other hand, the topic of carryover effects has been discussed (Bailey & Bostow, 1979; Barlow & Hayes, 1979; Ulman & Sulzer-Azaroff, 1975), but has received scant attention in empirical investigations. And as Ulman & Sulzer-Azaroff (1975) have stated, "In the absence of systematic investigation, however, such interaction remains unspecified, and any generalization based on this design should be qualified accordingly" (p. 389). That this warning continues to be of serious concern to applied researchers is shown by the fact Ollendick *et al.* (1980), in their recent multielement analyses of spelling remediation procedures, found it necessary to conclude: "We are unsure to what extent such interference was operative in the present studies" (p. 653), pointing out that "such effects would have a direct bearing on the validity of the obtained findings" (p. 653).

The purpose of the present study was to conduct one such systematic investigation; that is, to empirically assess possible carryover effects resulting from multielement manipulations [2]. Sidman (1960) has described two intrasubject replication techniques for analyzing carryover effects: *independent verification*—conducting control experiments in which each condition is presented alone so that the results can be compared to those of an experimental situation in which the conditions have been alternated; *functional manipulation*—varying the parameters of the treatment(s) being administered to the same individual. The functional manipulation technique offers several advantages: it eliminates the problem of intersubject variability; it can assess the extent of carryover effects at different points along the scale of manipulated parameter values; and it is considered to be a more precise and elegant technique than that of independent verification (Barlow & Hayes, 1979; Ulman & Sulzer-Azaroff, 1975). In the present study, possible carryover effects were analyzed by means of the functional manipulation technique within the context of a preschool classroom. The dependent variable was appropriate rest-time behavior, and the independent variable was token reinforcement.

Method

Subjects and Setting

The subjects were a preschool class of eight boys, ages four and five years, from middle-class homes and enrolled in a five-day morning preschool. In the preschool classroom there were tables, chairs, and shelves of toys and children's books. The class was observed daily during the 15-minute rest-time period. At rest time rugs were spread on the floor two or three feet apart; each boy was to remain on his rug, look at a previously selected book, and not bother the other children. The observer was seated in a corner of the classroom and did not interact in any way with the children during rest-time.

Response Definition, Recording, and Reliability

The target behavior, appropriate rest-time, was defined as: (a) sitting or lying with at least half of one's body on the rug, (b) not touching another boy or his rug, and (c) no vocalizations nor other noise-making. Rest-time behavior not satisfying all of these criteria was considered inappropriate.

Planned Activity Check class recording (Doke & Risley, 1972) was used to measure the average percent of appropriate rest-time behavior per day. At the exact end of each 15-second interval, sampled from the 15-minute observation period, the observer rapidly counted the number of children engaged in appropriate rest-time behavior, and divided the count by the number of children present. From the resulting quotients a mean was computed and multiplied by 100 to yield an "average percent of appropriate rest-time behavior" of the class per day—the dependent variable.

Interobserver reliability was assessed in every experimental condition by a second observer seated across the classroom from the primary observer, but able to view the sweep-second hand of the wall clock, thereby enabling both to determine identical 15-second observation intervals. The second observer simultaneously and independently observed once during each of the five phases of the study (once in each condition of the fourth phase). A check-by-check reliability coefficient was derived by dividing the lower count of each planned activity check by the larger, averaging these quotients, and multiplying the result by 100 to obtain the present of interobserver agreement. Reliability was assessed on Days 2, 11, 15, 21, 25, 30, and 43 and averaged 91% (range: 85–98%). Each reliability assessment is indicated by an 'x' in Fig. 1.

Baseline

Just prior to rest-time periods the children were instructed about appropriate behaviour; e.g. 'Look at your books very carefully; look at each picture, each word, quietly.' During baseline the teacher occasionally praised children for appropriate behavior.

Treatment

Token reinforcement on a 2-minute variable-internal schedule (VI 2-min) was used to increase appropriate rest-time behavior. Prior to treatment sessions the teacher also instructed the children regarding how they could earn tokens (plastic chips);

e.g. 'Those who are really looking at their books will get a chip.' The class was informed that each chip could be exchanged for half of a cookie when rest-time was over. According to a prearranged schedule, the observer cued (by a head-nod or raised finger) the teacher to dispense praise and chips to children demonstrating appropriate rest-time behavior. Other behaviors were ignored.

Experimental Design

A reversal design incorporating a multielement manipulation was employed in the following order: a 5-day baseline, an 8-day treatment phase, a second 4-day baseline, a 10-day multielement-manipulation phase (5 treatment days interspersed with 5 non-treatment days), a second 5-day treatment phase, and finally a 12-day maintenance phase (in which the treatment was gradually phased-out) with postchecks on Days 55 and 82. This reversal design could thus be designated at A–B–A–C–B–C where A is baseline, B is the token-reinforcement treatment, and C is the multielement manipulation of treatment and non-treatment conditions.

Results

Each data point in Fig. 1 represents the daily average of the planned activity checks of appropriate rest-time behavior for the entire class (the target behavior) during the six experimental phases. During the first baseline the target behavior averaged 32% and was very stable, not varying from the mean by more than 2%. During the first treatment phase the target behavior increased to a mean of 78%. With the introduction of the second baseline the mean decreased to 44% and the target behavior tended to continue to decrease during this phase.

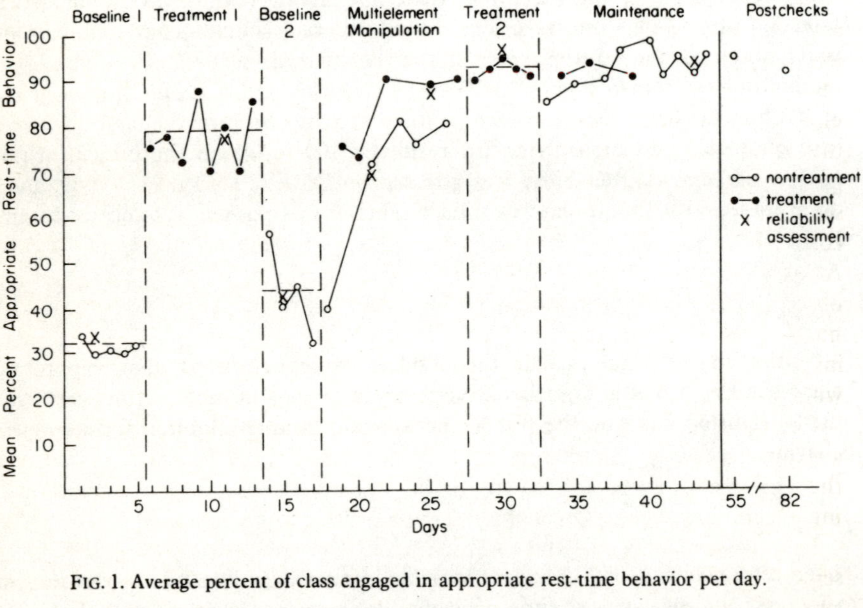

FIG. 1. Average percent of class engaged in appropriate rest-time behavior per day.

The multielement-manipulation phase followed the second baseline. As treatment and non-treatment conditions were alternated there was a sharp increase in the target behavior under both conditions. The treatment mean was 84% (range: 74–90%). The non-treatment mean was 69% (range: 40–80%). The overall levels of the target behavior in the two conditions were comparable (medians: 88 and 75% respectively).

In the second treatment phase, the level of the target behavior remained high, averaging 93% (range: 90–95%). The level of the target behavior was 90% or higher for the remainder of the study; i.e. twelve days of maintenance (in which the treatment was phased out by the eighth maintenance day) and the postchecks on Days 55 and 82.

Discussion

The results clearly indicate that token reinforcement was effective in increasing appropriate classroom behavior of a group of eight preschoolers. In the first three phases—which in themselves constitute a common ABA reversal design—the results were as expected: When the treatment was introduced there was a sharp increase in the target behavior; and when removed, the behavior returned to the initial baseline level.

In the multielement manipulation the effects in the non-treatment conditions (open-circles in Fig. 1) are of particular interest. It can be seen that in the second baseline phase the level of the behavior decreased to that observed in the initial baseline phase. But in the subsequent multielement manipulation phase, there was an abrupt and enduring increase in the behavior in the *non-treatment condition.* These results suggest the presence of a carryover effect. More specifically, since the behavioral change in the nontreatment condition was in the same direction of that in the treatment, this type of carryover effect is termed induction or generalization (Reynolds, 1975, p. 50).

It should be noted, however, that the results of the present study are inconclusive as to whether carryover (enhancement) effects were actually operating. The problem here is analogous to that of comparing two treatments, B and C, in a ABAC reversal design: how does one control for possible confounding due to sequence effects? Thus, if the level of behavior in the C phase is, say, higher than in B, the difference could be due either to the greater effectiveness of Treatment C or to the prior experience with B. One strategy often used to deal with the problem of sequence effects is to employ a counterbalanced reversal design. That is, conduct a concurrent replication, but with the conditions presented in the reverse order—ACAB. Since this study did not implement a counterbalanced reversal strategy, the observed carryover effects cannot be attributed exclusively to the introduction of the multielement manipulation. Sequence effects have been found in other multielement investigations (Johnson & Bailey, 1977) and they have even been shown to interact with carryover effects (O'Brien, 1968).

Carryover effects generated by a multielement-manipulation can also be viewed as a treatment strategy. In the present study, for example, the dramatic improvement in the children's rest-time behavior under non-treatment conditions following the introduction to the multielement manipulation is noteworthy.

In sum, the results of this study suggest that multielement manipulation may serve a dual purpose for the applied behavioral researcher: (a) as an experimental strategy for evaluating treatment effectiveness, and (b) as a therapeutic strategy for enhancing treatment effectiveness. Regarding the latter purpose, more systematic research is needed to investigate the potential advantages of programming multielement manipulations to deliberately generate treatment-enhancing carryover effects.

NOTES

[1] Sparzo, L. & Ulman, J.D. (1981) Multielement design—alias "multiple schedule," "simultaneous treatment," and "alternating treatment": Some comments on terminology, *paper presented at the meeting of the Association for Behavior Analysis*, Milwaukee, Wisconsin, May.

[2] The term 'Multielement manipulations'—a term originally coined by Sidman (1960)—is used here to denote that conditions were alternated within the context of, say, a ABACB reversal design in which C consisted of the repeated alterations of A (non-treatment) and B (treatment) conditions.

REFERENCES

Bailey, J.S. & Bostow, D.E. (1979) *Research Methods in Applied Behavior Analysis* (Tallahassee, Copygrafix).

Barlow, D.W. & Hayes, S.C. (1979) Alternating treatments design: one strategy for comparing the effects of two treatments in a single subject, *Journal of Applied Behavior Analysis*, 12, pp. 199–210.

Campbell, D.T. & Stanley, J.C. (1973) Experimental and quasi-experimental designs for research, in: Gage, N.L. (Ed.) *Handbook of Research on Teaching* (Chicago, Illinois, Rand McNally).

Doke, L.A. & Risley, T.R. (1972) The organization of day care environments: required vs. optional activities, *Journal of Applied Behavior Analysis*, 5, pp. 405–420.

Dunham, P.J. (1968) Contrasted conditions of reinforcement: a selected critique, *Psychological Bulletin*, 69, pp. 295–315.

Freeman, B.J. (1971) Behavioral contrast: reinforcement frequency or response suppression? *Psychological Bulletin*, 75, pp. 347–356.

Johnson, M.S. & Bailey, J.S. (1977) The modification of leisure behavior in a half-way house for retarded women, *Journal of Applied Behavior Analysis*, pp. 273–282.

O'Brien, F. (1968) Sequential contrast effects with human subjects, *Journal of the Experimental Analysis of Behavior*, 11, pp. 537–542.

Ollendick, T.H., Matson, J.L., Esreldt-Dawson, K. & Shapiro, E.S. (1980) Increasing spelling achievement: an analysis of treatment procedures utilizing an alternating treatments design, *Journal of Applied Behavior Analysis*, 13, pp. 645–654.

Reynolds, G.S. (1975) *A Primer of Operant Conditioning*, 2nd edn (Glenview, Illinois, Scott, Foresman & Co.).

Sidman, M. (1960) *Tactics of Scientific Research* (New York, Basic Books).

Ulman, J.D. & Sulzer-Azaroff, B. (1975) Multielement baseline design in educational research, in: Ramp, E. & Semb, G. (Eds) *Behavior Analysis: areas of research and application* (Englewood Cliffs, New Jersey, Prentice-Hall).

Section D.

Control of Academic Behaviour

Childcare Workers' Use of Talking Up and Incidental Teaching Procedures under Standard and Self-management Staff Training Packages

HELEN CHARLES
TED GLYNN
STUART McNAUGHTON

ABSTRACT *Two childcare workers in a daycare setting were trained in the use of Talking Up and Incidental Teaching procedures, designed to increase children's language. Training was introduced in two stages. The first was a standard training package comprising oral and written instructions, roleplay, modelling and feedback. The second was a modified package comprising a self-management component (the formulation by childcare workers of specific plans to implement each procedure, and a correspondence training component in which they received feedback on correspondence between their performance and their plans). Following a baseline period in which rates of child-initiated language were monitored the standard training package was introduced for both Talking Up and Incidental Teaching. Next, the modified (self-management) training package was introduced, first for Incidental Teaching, and subsequently for Talking Up. Introducing the standard training package resulted in markedly increased use of Talking Up by one worker and Incidental Teaching by both workers. However there was a concomitant decrease in child-initiated language (and hence opportunities to use Incidental Teaching). When the modified (self-management) package was introduced for Incidental Teaching, there was a resultant increase in the use of that procedure as well as a marked increase in child-initiated language. When the modified (self-management) package was introduced for Talking Up, there was a resultant increase in the use of that procedure but in contrast, there was a decrease in child-initiated language. With the introduction of each training package, nevertheless, both workers responded to increased proportions of child initiations over baseline. Results are discussed in terms of the confounding effects of the two procedures in this study and their relative usefulness in improving child language.*

The amount and quality of adult-child social interaction is increasingly seen as crucial for the development of language and cognitive skills in young children. Bronfenbrenner (1979) stresses the importance of adult-child interpersonal processes in providing two complementary contexts (primary and secondary developmental contexts) in which children acquire, elaborate and practise cognitive and social skills. When young children are placed in day care settings for long periods it is thus critical that childcare workers appreciate and exercise an educative role in addition to their custodial role. In particular it is important for them to create and capitalise on opportunities for young children in their care to develop and practise language.

Where childcare workers become almost exclusively concerned with their custodial role, many opportunities for children's cognitive and language development may be lost. For example, excessive concern about children's eating behaviour may result in a great deal of time going into prompting, cueing and reinforcing of eating—perhaps occasioned by the fixed routines and custodial schedules of the centre. Under such conditions, childcare workers have less time available to respond to child-initiated language and social approaches, so that the essentially *social* character of these interactions may be lost (Baker *et al.*, 1983).

Descriptive studies of adult-child interaction have found that such interactions occurred more often and with greater duration in home settings than in centre-based daycare, particularly around the midday meal (Cochran, 1977; Golden *et al.*, 1978). Of course, some home settings may have several clear advantages over daycare settings. There are usually fewer children per adult. The adult has detailed knowledge of each particular child's language and has a strong positive relationship with, and commitment to that child. The home setting is less constrained by schedules and routines. Under these conditions, both more language interactions and interactions around a wider variety of content might be expected, than in daycare. However, it is clearly possible to train childcare workers to improve greatly the rate and content of their language, even given the constraints of the larger numbers of children and centre routines. One approach which such training might take is the implementing of specific procedures designed to engage childcare workers in increased language interaction with children beyond that occasioned by the needs of custodial care. O'Brien *et al.* (1977) describe two such procedures which address both rate and content of interaction, Talking Up and Incidental Teaching.

The first procedure, *Talking Up*, is adult-initiated. It is implemented when a child is clearly engaged in some appropriate activity. Hence the content is based on appropriate task engagement rather than on inactivity or on some inappropriate activity. Talking Up requires the adult to make a comment or ask a question about the child's involvement in the activity, to pause to allow the child the opportunity to respond, and to obtain some language response from the child. Talking Up is seen as an attempt both to reinforce the child's involvement in appropriate activity and to provide increased opportunities for child language via contingent conversation.

The second procedure is *Incidental Teaching*. In contrast with Talking Up, this procedure is child-initiated. It is implemented when a child attempts some language utterance, such as making a request for an object or toy, or for help with a task or activity. Incidental Teaching can be implemented no matter how minimal or how brief the child's original utterance. Incidental Teaching requires the adult to respond immediately to the child's initiation. The adult is required either to prompt or model a language response that is just a little more elaborate than the language initiated by the child. The child then imitates, or tries to imitate, the more elaborate response. The adult in turn immediately reinforces the child's use of the new response by providing the requested object, information, or assistance with the task or activity. Thus, Incidental Teaching can be seen as an attempt both to reinforce and elaborate child-initiated language use, as well as to reinforce participation in a specific activity. In addition, however, the reinforcement is not restricted to adult attention but also incorporates the salient and powerful reinforcer specified in the child's initial request. The power of Incidental Teaching in the teaching of language has been amply demonstrated by a series of studies by Hart & Risley (Risley & Hart, 1968; Hart & Risley, 1975, 1980; Risely, 1977).

Talking Up and Incidental Teaching both appear to be viable procedures for including in training programmes for childcare workers. Both would appear to result in increased language use by children. Since the two procedures share several common features, it appeared appropriate to introduce them concurrently. Taken together the procedures appeared to offer childcare staff a two-pronged strategy for increasing children's language. The two procedures appeared to enable childcare workers both to prompt children to use language and to respond constructively to children's self-initiated language. This study attempted to train two childcare workers in the use of both Talking Up and Incidental Teaching procedures, and to monitor their implementation of these procedures in a daycare setting. Limited information on children's language initiations was also monitored.

A standard staff training package incorporating written instructions, modelling by the trainer, and specific positive and negative feedback on staff performance was employed. These standard components have all been established as functional components in a review of staff training research by Clark (1983). The study also examined whether the addition of a self-management package had an additive effect over and above the standard training package. The self-management package involved two components. The first component was advance planning and self-selection by staff of specific times for implementing each procedure with individual children. This component was adapted from a procedure for training parents to implement behavioural procedures with their own children (Sanders & Glynn, 1981). Advance planning and self-selection of implementation targets was found by Sanders & Glynn to enhance generalisation of parents' use of procedures. The second component was adapted from the correspondence training procedure devised by Risley & Hart (1968). Correspondence training appears to offer promise as a means of effecting behaviour change in settings where direct contingency management is not possible or desirable. In the present study, correspondence training took the form of first encouraging each childcare worker regularly to make 'should statements' about their intended use of the Talking Up and Incidental Teaching before an 'audience' comprising the other childcare worker and the first author. Next, within this non-threatening context, the first author provided each childcare worker with specific session by session feedback on the correspondence between her own planned 'should statements' and observed use of each procedure with individual children.

Method

Subjects

Subjects were two female full-time childcare workers who had been employed at the centre for six months and had no other experience of training in childcare.

Setting

The childcare centre in which observations were made, was Church administered and licenced to cater for 35 children by New Zealand Department of Social Welfare Regulations. During the observation period attendance varied between 30 and 35 children. Ages ranged from 15 months to 4 years 11 months for full- and part-time attenders. Children were divided into two groups, under and over 3 years, and cared for in two separate rooms. The number of staff available to children during observation times arranged seven. Staff were rostered to work with under or over 3-year-olds in 2-hour blocks. Each staff member took responsibility for supervision of activities available, rather than for specific children. The organisation can thus be defined as 'zone to zone' (LeLaurin & Risley, 1972).

Observation Procedure

Three observation sessions were scheduled per week over 7 weeks. Thirty minutes' data were taken for each childcare worker during each observation session. Subjects wore transmitter microphones so that language interaction could be tape recorded. Data were collected for subject one, over 21 days, and over 20 days for subject two. Generalisation data were recorded on six observation days across all treatment phases and constituted 15-minute recordings taken at a random time across the observation morning or afternoon. Subjects continued wearing microphones and another staff member switched on the tape recorder (during observer absence and without subject's knowledge) at a randomised time during the morning or afternoon of the observation. During observation sessions children were served morning or afternoon tea and then involved in free play. Subject one was always with the over-3-year-old children and subject two with the under-3-year-olds. The first author served as the main observer, and used a stop-watch to time observation intervals when playing the tapes.

Observation sheets were divided into thirty 30-second intervals. For purposes of giving accurate positive and negative feedback during training the following setting events were coded using momentary time sampling of 5 seconds at the beginning of each 30-second interval:

Setting categories: location (area of centre and part of room);
number of adults present in room;
number of children within 4 feet of subject;
participation of subject (not exclusionary).

The following language behaviours were coded using event recording:

Verbal behaviour: AA —verbal interaction subject and another adult;
~~Ch~~ —child initiation not answered;
Ch —child initiation answered but not incidental teaching;
Ch+—child initiation, incidental teaching;
TA —adult initiation, talking up.

Each event was bounded by any or all of the following: a 3-second pause, a change in topic, a change in conversational partner. While this procedure allowed for individual analysis of data on caregiver implementation of Talking Up and Incidental Teaching the data on child initiations were not analysed for individual children.

Hence data on child-initiated language are pooled from whichever children were present during the session with each caregiver.

Experimental Design

During a baseline phase of five sessions each childcare worker's rate of use of Talking Up and Incidental Teaching, and children's language initiations were recorded. The standard staff training package was then introduced, and recording of Talking Up, Incidental Teaching and children's language initiations continued. Next, the modified training package incorporating staff planning and correspondence training was introduced for Incidental Teaching, but the standard training package alone continued to operate for Talking Up. Finally, the modified training package was introduced for Talking Up, but the Standard training package alone was reinstated for Incidental Teaching. Thus the experimental design employed was an intra-subject A, B, B&C, B, sequence for Incidental Teaching (incorporating a partial withdrawal) and an A, B, B&C, sequence for Talking Up. The design was replicated across the two childcare staff.

Inter-observer Agreement

An independent graduate student observer who was experimentally naive but experienced in behavioural observation conducted inter-observer agreement checks on 20% of the observation sessions. Inter-observer agreement checks occurred across all phases of the study. The presence of an independent observer at the centre was found to be too intrusive for the childcare workers so the independent observer used taped data. Thus agreement checks were carried out on verbal behaviour only. Information on incidents of child initiation directed at caregivers and on child involvement in activity when caregivers initiated interaction with children was not available from tapes alone, so the independent observer had access to the setting event information recorded by the first author. Observer agreement was also obtained from 30% of the generalisation data tapes. The occurrence agreement formula (Hartmann, 1977) was used to express the number of intervals in which the two observers completely agreed on the number and classification of language responses as a percentage of intervals in which one or other observer recorded some language as having occurred.

Procedure

Baseline: Observations were taken for 5 days. During this time subjects were not aware of the specific behaviours being coded.

Standard Training Package: A 2-hour training session was arranged for both childcare workers. A manual was provided based on O'Brien *et al.* (1977) describing Talking Up and Incidental Teaching, together with the use of open questions and elaborations as part of these procedures. After workers had read the relevant section of the manual the first author discussed and modelled each procedure. Childcare workers then gave examples from their own experience of when and how they might use each procedure. These examples were role played with each subject acting both as child and as childcare worker. Prior to the next session the author interacted with the children in the centre and modelled the target procedures, with childcare workers observing. Workers were given cue cards summarising each procedure which they carried and consulted when they felt it necessary. Thereafter, individual feedback occurred daily. This constituted pointing out firstly successful use of procedures (positive feedback) and then occasions when it would have been possible to use the procedures but when this had not occurred (negative feedback). At all times the amount of positive feedback exceeded that of negative feedback. Workers were shown graphs on which the incidence of Incidental Teaching and Talking Up were plotted continuously.

Modified (Self-management) Training Package: Approximately 10 minutes prior to each observation session in this phase, the author asked the childcare workers to describe the setting, activity and children who would be available during the ensuing observation session. When Incidental Teaching was targeted the childcare workers were then required to make specific plans as to how they would facilitate child initiations by specific children and what sort of content they would use in response to this initiation. The steps on the cue cards were then used to outline an Incidental Teaching episode using the suggested content. When Talking Up was targeted the childcare workers were required to suggest specific topics for individual children. The steps on the cue cards were then used to outline a Talking Up episode using the suggested topic. Individual childcare worker feedback was provided by the first author, according to the observed correspondence between the specific plans of that worker for implementing either Talking Up or Incidental Teaching with individual children and the data obtained from the author's observation and from the tape recording. A child careworker would first be praised for instances of match between her planned and her actual implementation, and then differences between plans and actual implementation would be pointed out in a non-threatening manner.

Withdrawal of Modified (Self-management) Package: The modified (self-management) package was discontinued for Incidental Training, and the Standard Training Package was reinstated as described above.

Generalisation: On some sessions from all training phases, 15-minute generalisation tapes were taken at random times across the morning or afternoon. During the modified (self-management) package phases each childcare worker was required to formulate a specific plan that would be operational over the entire morning or afternoon (and not just during the observation session when the first author was present). Feedback was given on the following observation day, on the basis of data from the tapes.

Follow Up: Follow-up tapes were taken on two days after the end of the study when neither standard training nor the modified (self-management) training packages operated, and without the presence of the first author.

Results

Inter-observer Agreement

Occurrence agreement rates on language response data were calculated separately for each childcare worker. These ranged from 87 to 93% with a mean of 89% over four Training sessions, and from 72 to 79% with a mean of 75% over four of the Generalisation sessions. The lower occurrence reliability figures for the Generalisation session reflect an additional difficulty arising from the fact that both observers were working only from tape-recorded data, without the aid of setting event information recorded at the time language interactions occurred. Given this restriction and the more stringent occurrence agreement formula, the reliability figures are considered adequate.

Childcare Worker 1

Data for childcare worker 1 are presented in the upper half of Table I which is read downwards. Session by session data are presented in Fig. 1. Data are presented in terms of rate per 15-minute session to allow direct comparison of rates from Training sessions to Generalisation sessions. Table I shows that during baseline a mean of 9.20 child language initiations to childcare worker 1 occurred per 15-minute session and that this childcare worker implemented the Talking Up and Incidental Teaching procedures a mean of 0.60 and 0.70 times per session, respectively. With the introduction of the standard training package, this childcare worker increased her rate of Talking Up to 2.85 per session but decreased her rate of Incidental Teaching to 0.35 per session. Thus, she increased her use of Talking Up by more than four times her baseline rate, but decreased her use of Incidental Teaching to half her baseline rate. With the introduction of the modified (self-management) training package to Incidental Teaching in the next experimental phase, this worker now increased her rate of Incidental Teaching to 2.90 per session, while her rate of Talking Up (still under conditions of the standard training package only) decreased to 0.90 per session. In the final experimental condition when the modified (self-management) package was introduced for Talking Up and the standard training package was reintroduced for Incidental Teaching, this childcare worker dramatically increased her rate of Talking Up to 3.30 per session, and decreased her rate of Incidental Teaching to 1.70 per session.

It is clear that the standard training package was effective in increasing this childcare worker's rate of implementation of Talking Up (but not Incidental Teaching) relative to baseline. In contrast, the modified (self-management) training package introduced sequentially to Incidental Teaching and Talking Up resulted in substantial gains in her use of each procedure over and above baseline, and, in the case of Talking Up, over and above gains made with the standard training package.

However, an unexpected confounding effect of the two procedures is also evident. This can be seen by inspecting the data on child initiation of language in both Table I and Fig. 1. When childcare worker 1 displayed major increases in Talking Up (during the second and the fourth experimental conditions) the rate of child initiations decreased to less than half its baseline level (from a rate of 9.20 per session during baseline to 4.20 and 4.40 during the second and the fourth phases). These data suggest that for childcare worker 1, increased Talking Up resulted in fewer opportunities for children to initiate language interactions, an essential antecedent for Incidental Teaching to occur. The introduction of the modified (self-management) training package for Incidental Teaching resulted in a sharp reduction in this childcare worker's use of Talking Up, and a restoration of baseline rates of child-initiated language.

Given the large changes in rate of child-initiated language across experimental conditions, an appropriate measure of childcare workers' implementation of Incidental Teaching is the percentage of child initiations responded to with Incidental Teaching, rather than simply the number of Incidental Teaching episodes which occurred. Table 1 shows that childcare worker 1 responded to an increased percen-

TABLE I. Mean rates of talking up, incidental teaching, child initiations, and percentage child initiations responded to, across all experimental conditions

	Talking up			Incidental teaching		Child initiations	Percentage initiations responded to
Training		Generalization	Training		Generalization	—	—
Childcare worker 1							
Rate per 15-minute tape							
(A) :	0.60	—	(A) :	0.70	—	9.20	4.4
(B) :	2.85	2.50	(B) :	0.35	1.00	4.20	7.0
(B) :	0.90	4.00	(B&C):	2.90	1.00	9.30	31.6
(B&C):	3.30	4.50	(B) :	1.70	2.00	4.40	19.8
Follow Up	1.50	—	Follow Up	2.00	—	—	—
Childcare worker 2							
Rate per 15-minute tape							
(A) :	1.00	—	(A) :	0.90	—	10.20	12.6
(B) :	3.45	4.50	(B) :	1.90	1.00	4.70	43.4
(B) :	3.50	2.50	(B&C):	3.90	2.00	8.00	53.3
(B&C):	7.40	6.00	(B) :	1.75	1.50	4.25	28.5
Follow Up	11.00	—	Follow Up	3.50	—	—	—

Note: A refers to baseline (no training package).
B refers to standard training package.
C refers to modified (self-management) training package.

tage (7%) of child initiations over baseline (4.4%) with the introduction of the standard training package, despite the reduction in number of child initiations from 9.20 to 4.20 per session. With the introduction of the modified (self-management) package, there was a further and major increase to 31.6% of child initiations responded to (compared to 4.4% at baseline and 7.0% with standard training). With the reinstatement of the standard training package for Incidental Teaching the percentage of child initiations responded to by childcare worker 1 reduced to 19.8%, but still remained at over four times the baseline rate, even though the number of child initiations (4.40) was now half that of baseline (9.20).

Data from generalisation tapes recorded following the standard training sessions suggest that childcare worker 1 generalised her increased rates of Talking Up and Incidental Teaching. Rates of 2.50 and 1.00 per session were obtained for Talking Up and Incidental Teaching respectively. These compared favourably with corresponding baseline rates of 0.60 and 0.70 and with rates from the standard training sessions of 2.85 and 0.35 respectively. However, there appeared to be little evidence of an additive effect of the self-management component in the generalisation data to match the additive effect evident in the Training data. Nevertheless, allowing for the very limited number of generalisation tapes, and the amount of session by session variability evident in Fig. 1, it is clear that childcare worker 1's gains in implementation of both procedures were not constrained to the training sessions, but carried over to sessions where the first author was absent.

Follow-up data collected from two sessions over two weeks after the final experimental phase, indicated childcare worker 1 was using Talking Up and Incidental Teaching a mean of 1.50 and 2.00 times per session, respectively, both rates being well over twice those at baseline.

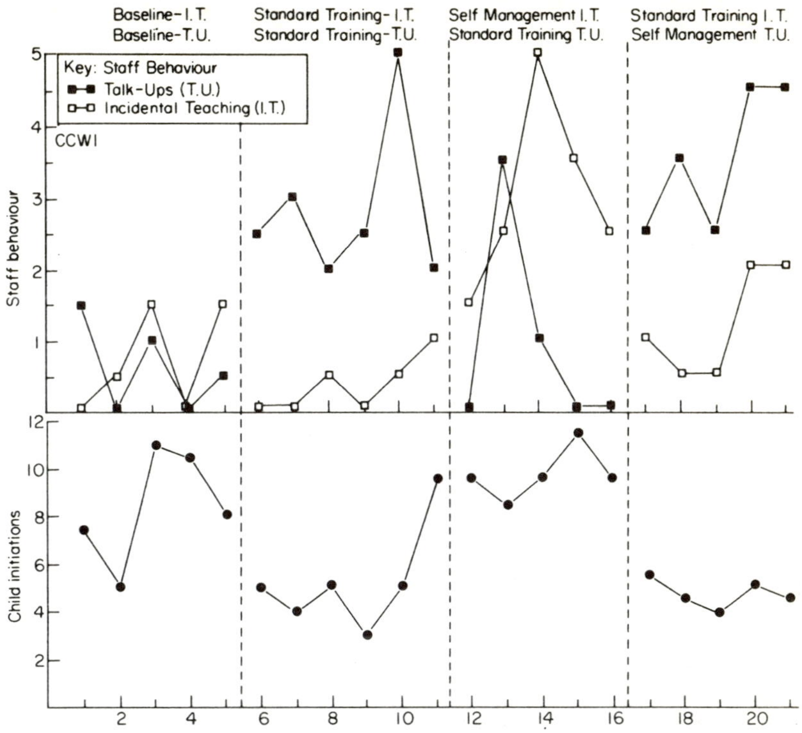

FIG. 1. Rate of Talking-Up and Incidental Teaching by childcare worker 1 and rate of child-initiated language directed at childcare worker 1 per 15-minute session.

Childcare Worker 2

Data for childcare worker 2 are presented in the lower half of Table I and session by session data are presented in Fig. 2. Patterns in the data for this childcare worker are very similar to those for childcare worker 1 but with additional evidence of generalisation effects of the modified (self-management) training package.

Table I shows that during baseline a mean of 10.20 child language initiations occurred per 15-minute session, and that childcare worker 2 implemented the Talking Up and Incidental Teaching procedures a mean of 1.00 and 0.90 times per session respectively. With the introduction of the standard training package childcare worker 2 increased her rate of Talking Up to 3.45 per session, and increased her rate of Incidental Teaching to 1.90 per session, both figures indicating clear increases over baseline rates. With the introduction of the modified (self-management) package for Incidental Teaching in the next experimental condition, this worker further increased her rate of Incidental Teaching to 3.90 per session, while her rate of Talking Up (still under conditions of standard training package only) remained stable at 3.50 per session.

In the final experimental condition when the modified self-management package was introduced for Talking Up and standard training package only was reinstated for Incidental Teaching, this childcare worker dramatically increased her rate of Talking Up to 7.40 per session, and decreased her rate of Incidental Teaching to 1.75 per session. It is clear that the standard training component was effective in increasing childcare worker 2's rate of implementation of both Incidental Teaching

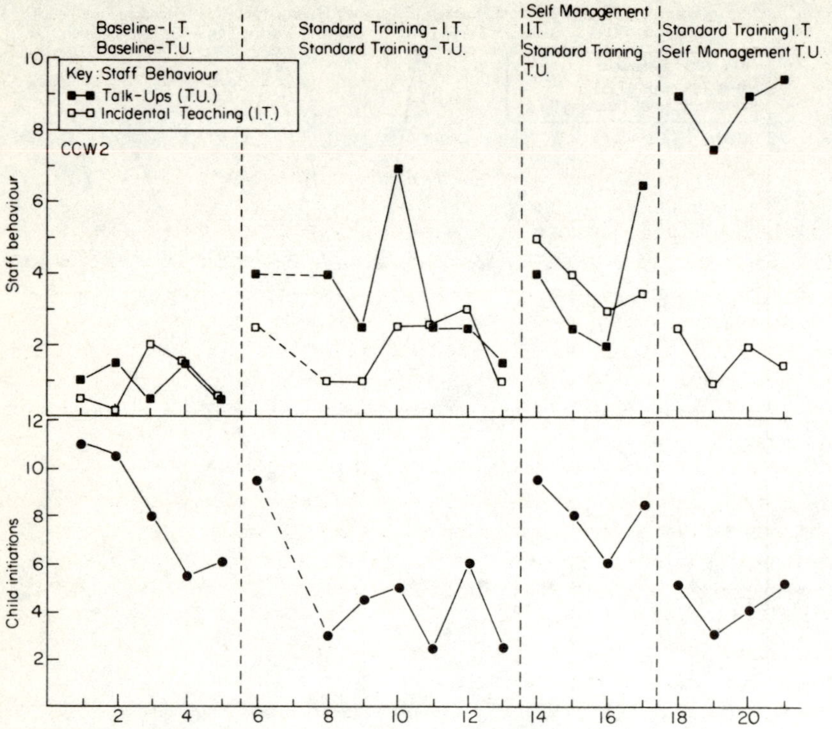

FIG. 2. Rate of Talking-Up and Incidental Teaching by childcare worker 2 and rate of child-initiated language directed at childcare worker 2 per 15-minute session.

and Talking Up procedures relative to baseline. However, as was the case with childcare worker 1, the addition of the modified (self-management) package sequentially to Incidental Teaching and Talking Up resulted in substantial gains in her use of both procedures over and above baseline and over and above the gains made with the standard training package.

Again, the unexpected confounding effect of the two procedures is evident. This can be seen by inspecting the data on child initiations of language in both Table I (lower half) and Fig. 2. When childcare worker 2 displayed major increases in Talking Up but not Incidental Teaching (during the second and the fourth experimental conditions) the rate of child-initiated language decreased to below half its baseline rate (from a rate of 10.2 per session during baseline to 4.7 and 4.25 during the second and the fourth experimental conditions). These data suggest that, as with childcare worker 1, increased use of Talking Up by childcare worker 2 resulted in markedly fewer instances of child-initiated language, an essential antecedent for Incidental Teaching to occur. The introduction of the modified (self-management) package for Incidental Teaching resulted in a marked increase in incidence of Incidental Teaching (3.90 per session) and a major increase in child-initiated language (8.0 per session) though not quite restoring it to baseline levels (10.20 per session).

On the measure of percentage of child initiations responded to, Table I shows that there is a major increase in percentage of child initiations responded to with the introduction of the standard training package (from the baseline level of 12.6%, to

43.4%) despite the reduction in number of child initiations occurring. With the introduction of the modified (self-management) package for Incidental Teaching there was a further increase to 53.3%. With the reinstatement of the self-management component the percentage of child initiations responded to by childcare worker 2 reduced to 28.5%. However this pattern remained at over twice the baseline rate, even though the number of child initiations was less than half that of baseline.

Data from the generalisation session tapes for childcare worker 2 (Table I, lower half) provide stronger evidence for generalisation of increased rates of Talking Up and Incidental Teaching than those for childcare worker 1. Rates of 4.50 and 1.00 per session for Talking Up and Incidental Teaching, respectively, were obtained from generalisation tapes following the standard training sessions. These compared very favourably with corresponding baseline rates of 1.00 and 0.90 and with rates from tapes following the standard training sessions of 3.45 and 1.90 respectively. From generalisation tapes which followed the modified (self-management) package, childcare worker 2 displayed strong evidence of generalisation of the additive effect in the training data. Rates of generalisation of Talking Up and Incidental Teaching in sessions following the standard training package alone were 4.50 and 1.00. Corresponding rates of generalisation in sessions following the modified training (self-management) package were 6.0 and 2.0 respectively. Again, allowing for the very limited number of generalisation sessions and for the amount of session by session variability evident in Fig. 2, it is clear that child care worker 2 displays strong generalisation of training effects.

Follow up data collected from the two sessions two weeks after the final experimental condition, indicated that childcare worker 2 was using Talking Up and Incidental Teaching a mean of 11.00 and 3.50 times per session, respectively, both rates being very much above baseline rates.

Adult-adult Interaction

From the analysis of setting event data across all observation sessions, it was found that one adult only was present during 30% of the observation intervals, two adults were present in 38% of the intervals, three adults in 20% of the intervals, four adults in 10% of the intervals and five adults in 2% of the intervals. Levels of adult-adult interaction (which can be seen as reducing the opportunity for either Talking Up or Incidental Teaching to occur) were also calculated from the observational data. These ranged from zero (when only one adult was present), through 16% when two adults were present, 29% with three adults present, to 50% with four or five adults present.

Discussion

Both childcare workers in the present study increased their use of Talking Up, but only one increased her rate of Incidental Teaching following the introduction of the standard training package. This package incorporated oral and written instructions, modelling and individual feedback. In accord with the intra-subject experimental design, both childcare workers markedly increased their use of Talking Up and Incidental Teaching following the sequential introduction of the modified (self-management) package. This package involved childcare workers in formulating specific plans to practise each procedure, and receiving feedback on the correspondence between their performance and their plans. The increase in use of each procedure following the sequential addition of the modified (self-management) package to the standard training package was greater than the increases in use from baseline to standard training package. Thus it is claimed that the modified (self-management) package of staff training not only contributed something over and above the standard training package but also was the more powerful contributor to the childcare workers' increased use of target procedures. Data from within the separate designs of A, B, B, B&C (for Talking Up) and A, B, B&C (for Incidental Teaching) strongly support this claim (Table I). The specific self-management strategies of self-selection of target children and advance planning of occasions to implement target behaviour (Sanders & Glynn, 1981) together with feedback on correspondence between plans and behaviour (Risley, 1977) was highly effective in this study. This supports an earlier preliminary study which included the same strategies in training residential staff to implement behavioural procedures (Glynn *et al.*, 1983). However it must be acknowledged that the present study cannot address the question of the differential contributions of advance planning and correspondence feedback to the modified (self-management) package. Such analyses require further research.

While the use of Talking Up and Incidental Teaching increased in response to the staff training packages in this study, there was however a confounding effect between the two procedures. This confounding effect showed up in the data on child-initiated language. For both childcare workers phases of increased use of Talking Up generally coincided with phases of low rates of child-initiated language. Conversely, phases of lowest rates of Talking Up (baseline) coincided with phases of highest rates of child-initiated language. These data suggest that during phases when childcare workers increased their rate of Talking Up (between three to seven to times baseline rates) children would have less time available to initiate language due to being engaged in increased staff initiated Talk Ups. Alternatively, children may have perceived staff as 'not available', or busy with other children, and hence lowered their rate of language initiation even if it were still possible for them to initiate language.

While the study indicates that the two procedures can be introduced concurrently in staff training, there may be theoretical and practical reasons for not doing so. Talking Up may offer the child more frequent opportunities for language interaction with an adult, but these may well occur at times inappropriate for the child's performance of a task (i.e. an adult's comments or questions may interfere with task performance. Further, the content of language interactions in Talking Up is under the control of the adult, since the child is always expected to respond to language selected by the adult. In contrast, Incidental Teaching offers the child a means of learning to use language to gain some control over the environment through learning how to engage an adult's assistance. However, since the procedure is always child initiated, the adult-child interaction would occur only at times when such interaction is important and functional for the child. In addition to preferring Incidental Teaching over Talking Up because Incidental Teaching offers the child a means of gaining control over the environment through engaging adult assistance, the data suggest that increased use of Talking Up may restrict the occurrence of child-initiated language, which is a major antecedent for adult use of Incidental Teaching.

With the introduction of the standard training package for Talking Up, less than half the child-initiated language opportunities were available than were available at baseline. Nevertheless one childcare worker increased her rate of Incidental Teaching per session and both responded to a greater proportion of child initiations than they did at baseline. With near baseline rates of child-initiated language restored when the modified (self-management) training package was introduced for Incidental Teaching both childcare workers responded to a further increased proportion of child initiations. These data support the claim for separate and additive effects of both staff training packages in the present study.

Although the generalisation data in this study were limited, these data at least demonstrate that the increases over baseline rates of Talking Up and Incidental Teaching for both childcare workers were retained outside of the formal training sessions from which the first author provided feedback. Given two childcare workers, two separate procedures, and two stages of training the intra-subject design of the study afforded eight opportunities to compare generalisation data from the standard training package (B phases) with baseline data (A phases) and four opportunities to compare generalisation data from the modified (self-management) package (B&C phases) with those from standard training alone (B phases). Table I shows that all eight comparisons of generalisation rates of Incidental Teaching and Talking Up following standard training with their corresponding baseline rates yielded markedly higher rates in the generalisation data. Three of the four comparisons of generalisation rates of Talking Up and Incidental Teaching following the modified (self-management) training package with those following the standard training package indicated further support for the claim for separate and additive effects of each training package. Thus the modified (self-management) package appears to contribute incrementally to generalisation as well as to training. This is consistent with data reported by Sanders & Glynn (1981), which showed that a self-management component within a parent training programme resulted in generalised use of target parenting procedures from training settings at home into community settings.

Data from two follow-up sessions collected two weeks after the end of the training programme, under conditions essentially similar to baseline show that rates of Talking Up and Incidental Teaching remained at levels well above baseline rates. In the case of Talking Up for childcare worker 2, the follow up rate was eleven times the baseline rate. This demonstrates that each childcare worker was able to maintain both procedures at higher than baseline levels without further assistance from the first author.

This study suggests that although the procedures of incidental Teaching and Talking Up can be introduced concurrently in training childcare workers, it may be better not to do so. This claim is made on the grounds that Talking Up indirectly inhibited opportunities for using Incidental Teaching.

Finally, important contextual variables relating to the introduction and successful use of both Talking Up and Incidental Teaching in this study may qualify the generalising of findings to other daycare centres. These variables comprise some specific setting factors or setting events which were in place in this daycare centre. The importance of such setting events in influencing adult and child behaviour has been stressed by various writers (Kantor, 1970; Bijou & Baer, 1978; Wahler & Fox, 1981; Glynn, 1982). In the present study the specific setting events were: (1) the provision of a suitable range of appropriate tasks and activities which engaged children effectively; (2) allowing children a free choice among these activities; and (3) the presence of an adult who was available to engage children in language interaction. The presence of more than one adult, it was noted, may mean *less* adult availability for interacting with children rather than more, if those adults spend time interacting with each other.

Furthermore, in contexts where appropriate tasks or activities are limited, or where children are required to perform tasks prescribed or directed by adults, rather than being allowed free choice of activities, the adults are more likely to be heavily occupied with prompting, reinforcing and monitoring children's performance of these tasks. Under these conditions the adults are less likely to be available either to initiate appropriate language interactions or to respond competently to child-initiated language interactions.

REFERENCES

BAKER, M., FOLLEY, M., GLYNN, T. & MCNAUGHTON, S. (1983) The effect of adult proximity and serving style on pre-schoolers' language and eating behaviour, *Educational Psychology,* 3(2), pp. 137–148.

BIJOUR, S.W. & BAER, D.M. (1978) *Behaviour Analysis of Child Development* (New Jersey, Prentice-Hall).

BRONFENBRENNER, U. (1979) Contexts of child rearing, problems and prospects, *American Psychologist,* 34, pp. 844–850.

CLARK, B. (1983) Training residential childcare staff: a self management strategy, *unpublished thesis in Education,* University of Waikato.

COCHRAN, M.M. (1977) A comparison of group day care and family child rearing patterns in Sweden, *Child Development,* 48, pp. 702–707.

GLYNN, T. (1982) Antecedent control of behaviour in educational contexts, *Educational Psychology,* 2(3–4), pp. 215–229.

GLYNN, T., CLARK, B., VAIGRO, W. & LAWLESS, S. (1983) A self-management strategy for increasing implementation of behavioural procedures by residential staff, *The Exceptional Child* (1984), 31(3).

GOLDEN, M., ROSENBLUTH, L., GROSS, M.T., POLICARE, H.J., FREEMAN, H. & BROWNLEE, M. (1978) *The New York City Infant Day Care Study* (New York, Medical and Health Research Association).

HART, B.M. & RISLEY, T.R. (1975) Incidental teaching of language in the pre-school, *Journal of Applied Behaviour Analysis,* 8, pp. 411–420.

HART, B.M. & RISLEY, T.R. (1980) In vivo language intervention: unanticipated general effects, *Journal of Applied Behavior Analysis,* 13, pp. 407–432.

HARTMANN, D.P. (1977) Consideration in the choice of interobserver reliability estimates, *Journal of Applied Behavior Analysis,* 13, pp. 407–432.

KANTOR, J.R. (1970) An analysis of the experimental analysis of behavior, *Journal of the Experimental Analysis of behavior,* 13, pp. 101–108.

LELAURIN, K. & RISLEY, T. (1972) The organisation of day care environments: zone to zone vs man to man staff assignments, *Journal of Applied Behavior Analysis,* 5, pp. 225–232.

O'BRIEN, M., PORTERFIELD, J., HERBERT-JACKSON, E. & RISLEY, T. (1977) *The Toddler Center: a complete guide to organising and maintaining day care* (Lawrence, Kansas, Living Environments Group).

RISLEY, T. (1977) The social context of self control, in: STUART, R.B. (Ed.) *Behavioral Self Management: strategies, techniques and outcomes* (New York, Brunner Mazel).

RISLEY, T. & HART, B. (1968) Developing correspondence between the nonverbal and verbal behavior of preschool children, *Journal of Applied Behavior Analysis,* 1, pp. 267–281.

SANDERS, M.R. & GLYNN, T. (1981) Training parents in behavioural self-management: an analysis of generalisation and maintenance, *Journal of Applied Behaviour Analysis,* 14, pp. 223–237.

WAHLER, R.G. & FOX, J.J. (1981) Setting events in applied behavior analysis: toward a conceptual and methodological expansion, *Journal of Applied Behavior Analysis,* 14, pp. 327–338.

Training Low Progress Readers to Use Contextual Cues: generalised effects on comprehension, oral accuracy and rate

ELIZABETH LIMBRICK, STUART McNAUGHTON & TED GLYNN

ABSTRACT *A Cloze procedure was used in combination with training in problem solving difficulties encountered in texts to increase three nine-year-old problem readers' attention to syntactic and semantic cues. The multiple-baseline across subjects design showed that this package increased readers' attention to cues on Cloze exercises. Classroom performance on comprehension exercises also improved and tested Reading Ages increased by several months over the seven week experimental period. Results are discussed in terms of the usefulness of the exercises for developing attention to context and the importance of training in problem-solving skills to facilitate generalisation.*

Discrepancies between low readers' performance on reading skills such as oral reading accuracy and comprehension have been noted by both classroom teachers (Holdaway, 1972) and researchers (Guthrie, 1976). Uncontroversially, despite differing remedial programmes and different theories of reading acquisition, reading ultimately implies gaining meaning from (i.e. comprehending) a text. The discrepancies, therefore, pose important questions for remedial instruction. The identification of remedial techniques which might lead directly to the improvement of all aspects of reading, but particularly comprehension, is an important task for educational research.

Previous behavioural research has attempted to increase comprehension both through manipulation of consequent events, via procedures such as token economies (Knapczyk & Livingston, 1973; Lahey, McNees & Brown, 1973); and through manipulation of antecedent events using procedures such as 'skipping and drilling', change in difficulty level of texts, and 'previewing' (Hansen & Lovitt, 1978). However, these studies typically do not show that the motivational or instructional procedures used produced independent readers. Independent readers are those whose skills generalise to comprehension tasks other than the training tasks and whose skills are not dependent on consistent and immediate external support.

Psycholinguistic theorists (e.g. Clay, 1979; Goodman, 1976; Smith, 1978) tend to see the development of proficient and independent reading as the utilisation of strategies of anticipation and problem solving based on contextual information. Readers draw on linguistic and cognitive knowledge and selectively use syntactic and semantic cues in the test to predict, search and confirm or reject aspects of the upcoming text. Research supporting this position indicates that contextual information is important in *both* reading accuracy and reading comprehension. Inexperienced or poor readers are more reliant on graphic cues to identify words when reading texts while more proficient readers effectively anticipate by using semantic and syntactic cues in texts (Clay, 1979; Goodman & Burke, 1973).

From this perspective it would be important to identify techniques for increasing or improving use of syntactic and semantic information within texts. This information will also enable a reader to relate a particular text to previously encountered texts, to prior knowledge of the world, and to experience with language. The Cloze procedure developed by Taylor (1953), which has been used for *measuring* comprehension, might also provide the basis for a technique to enhance comprehension.

The Cloze procedure requires that sentences with one or more words missing be completed by adding words that will make the sentence conform to the intended meaning, thus generating a word which is consistent, semantically and syntactically, with the available words in the sentence. This procedure has been shown to correlate well with other tests of reading comprehension (Bormuth, 1967; McLeod, 1965; Schneyer, 1965). It has been suggested that since Cloze procedures measure the use of contextual cues, training using Cloze techniques in classroom instruction could increase effective utilisation of such cues (Dulin, 1970; Balyeat & Norman, 1975).

Two studies which used Cloze procedures to increase comprehension produced conflicting results. Schneyer (1965) found that an experimental group using Cloze exercises did not make a significant improvement in comprehension, while Kennedy & Weaver (1973) claimed significant increases in both listening and reading comprehension when auditory and visual Cloze training processes were used for underachieving readers. One possibility for the discrepancy is that Schneyer did not use underachieving readers, and did not carry out instruction in small groups as did Kennedy & Weaver (1973).

In the present study underachieving students were given Cloze type exercises in an attempt to improve attention to and use of contextual cues. Students also verbalised their reasons for choices of words to complete the Cloze exercises and were given training in how to approach and solve difficult words in ordinary texts.

The latter feature of the training package was aimed at solving the interference with contextual cues brought about by words left unsolved or incorrect during reading. Readers received training in the deliberate use of anticipation and problem-solving strategies to maintain meaningful context. This training was predicted to facilitate improvement and generalisation into the classroom setting by giving the readers skills for regulating their own performance after training. In behavioural terms this method of training for generalisation has been termed 'mediated generalisation' (Stokes & Baer, 1979). Similar rationales for training are found in concepts of 'metacognitive' skills (Brown & DeLoache, 1978) and cognitive-behavioural training (Meichenbaum & Asnarow, 1979). These writers stress the use of self-instructions both to cue and to evaluate performance on academic tasks.

Method

Subjects and Setting

The subjects were three nine-year-old children (mean age, 8.9) whose reading ages, as measured by the Metropolitan Achievement Test (1970) administered by the school, were all approximately a year below their chronological ages (mean Reading Age, 7.6). Two of the three subjects had substantially higher scores for Listening Comprehension than for Reading Comprehension, suggesting that their deficits were not conceptually based. All three children were judged by the classroom teacher as not efficiently attending to and utilising the syntactic and semantic cues available in their reading texts.

The programme was school based, with all assessment and training administered in a resource room or the staff room. Both training and the primary measure of Cloze performance were taken by the first author and the school Principal in either of these two settings. The generalisation measure was based on classroom performance on comprehension questions during the classroom reading programme.

Design

A multiple baseline across subjects was used (Hersen & Barlow, 1976) which involved the successive introduction of Cloze training to each subject. Training outside the classroom involving Cloze exercises followed a baseline of ordinary classroom instruction.

Measures

(1) *Cloze Measure* Children's use of strategies was measured by Cloze exercises constructed from Readers Digest (1971) Graded Readers, Part 3 (New Reading Skills Builders). These exercises were constructed according to the following specifications.

(a) The reading level of the exercises was selected as approximately six months above that of the three subjects. This decision was based on the need to select material which would allow for improvement without having to change book levels throughout the study, and yet would not prove too difficult initially.
(b) The exercises were constructed using exact length blanks. Anderson (1970) reports no difference in performance between exact and standard length blanks. Since it is easier to construct exercises with exact length blanks, the procedure was selected because it is clearly more suited to use by the classroom teacher.
(c) First and last sentences in each passage were left undeleted. Otherwise every fifth word was deleted. Although it is more usual to delete every tenth word, data from Elley (1977) indicated no difference in performance on passages with deletions of every fifth and every tenth words.
(d) There were minimal adjustments to the number of deletions to avoid deleting a disproportionate number of nouns. Elley (1977) notes that disproportionate deletion of nouns resulted in increasing the difficulty levels of the passage.
(e) Passages were prepared with between 35 to 39 deletions even though Culhane (1970) suggested 50 deletions allowed for a greater range in scoring. Passages with 50 deletions were considered to render the task too long for these subjects.

Measures of syntactically appropriate and semantically appropriate errors were taken in addition to measures of exact replacements. This was done in order to assess the extent to which syntactic and semantic cues were utilised even though the exact word was not always produced.

(2) *Comprehension Measure* The classroom reading programme, which was based on a graded series of books (Wardlock 6–10; Wardlock, 1975), periodically required the children to complete comprehension exercises. Successive unfamiliar exercises provided a means of probing for the generalisation of training in Cloze techniques. Each child was reading at a different level and they remained on that level throughout the study. The exercises contained referential and recall questions for a text passage plus questions on vocabulary knowledge and word usage.

(3) *Standardised Reading Measures* Pre- and post-test measures utilising different forms of standard reading tests were also administered. These could also be considered measures of generalisation as well as providing statements of normative gains. These were (1) 'GAP' (McLeod, 1965), a standardised Cloze-type comprehension test and (2) the Neale Analysis of Reading Ability (Neale, 1966), which provides measures of oral reading rate and accuracy, as well as comprehension on graded passages. Alternate forms of each test were used for the pre- and post-test measure.

Reliability

Reliability of observations was assessed on 18 randomly selected Cloze exercises, six from each subject, and on all Wardlock comprehension exercises. At least two Cloze observations were taken from baseline measures for each subject. Reliability checks were carried out by a teacher at the school for the Cloze exercises and by the first author for the classroom comprehension measures.

Percentage exact substitutions and percentage semantically and syntactically appropriate substitutions from each observer were compared and agreement calculated by dividing the smaller percentage by the larger percentage and multiplying by 100. Agreement percentages ranged from 83 to 100% ($\bar{x}=95\%$) for appropriate substitutions, and from 99 to 100% on exact substitutions. Agreement on the measures of answers on the Wardlock comprehension exercises completed in the classroom was calculated using the same procedures and found to be 100%.

Procedure

Baseline During baseline, Cloze exercises were administered three times a week by the experimenter. All three subjects were tested together. No feedback or discussion was given other than instructions on how to complete the tests. Instruction consisted of a demonstration of a sentence completion followed by an orally worked completion on the first two sessions, thereafter just directions to 'fill in the spaces with the lines underneath with a word you think fits'. Baseline consisted of six sessions for Subject 1, eight sessions for Subject 2; and nine sessions for Subject 3.

Training Training was conducted for 30 minutes each session on two days each week, i.e. the days on which no Cloze exercises were given. The first session was to provide a basis for the generalisation of Cloze training to other comprehension tasks (i.e. regular texts). For each subject, training consisted of a discussion of the cues available to the subject in reading, i.e. syntactic, semantic and graphic. The first author discussed this with the subjects in terms of: (1) the meaning of the sentence and the story, (2) whether it sounded right, that is 'fitted' grammatically, and, (3) the letters in the word, e.g. first letter, letter sound associations.

Subjects and experimenter then constructed a chart, for the subject to keep, of 'Things I can do when I don't know a word' when reading normal texts. Subjects were encouraged to phrase 'instructions' in their own words but were guided to include the following.

(1) Read on to the end of the sentence,
(2) Read from the beginning of the sentence again,
(3) Think what the word might be from the meaning of the sentence and what the story is about,
(4) Try to see if a tentative response fits with the first letters of the text word,
(5) Try it out to see if it sounds right,
(6) Check that the word makes sense with the sentence and with the story.

It was stressed in discussion that these are all cues available to a reader when reading. But when completing a Cloze exercise the absence of graphic cues means the reader must use 'sounding right' and 'making sense of the sentences and the story' as the major cues to determine the missing word.

The first session was completed by a review of the previous day's Cloze exercise, and a discussion of correct and incorrect completions and reasons why such words were chosen and why alternatives might be better. The first training session for each subject was conducted individually, thereafter training sessions were group sessions. This was designed to approximate a classroom situation as closely as possible.

Subsequent training sessions consisted of review and discussion of previously completed Cloze exercises. Reasons for word choices and alternatives were discussed. Each training session included a Cloze exercise worked orally with different form words deleted (as suggested by Culhane, 1970). Terms for the form words were congruent with classroom usage, e.g. words that tell the name of something; words that describe what someone or something is doing.

Passages used in training sessions were constructed from the same reading level, i.e. the 8 year level, with the following deletions: prepositions, verbs, pronouns, nouns, adjectives, adverbs and one with alternating verbs and nouns. The reason for each completion was discussed as it was considered important to minimise guessing. Training for Subjects 1, 2 and 3, consisted of ten, eight and six sessions respectively, in accordance with the multiple-baseline design.

Results

Cloze Measure

The effects of training on the Cloze exercises completed three times per week are presented in Fig. 1. For exact substitutions there is a marked change following the beginning of training with each subject. After the baselines, which show variable responding with no trend (Subjects 2 and 3), or a downward trend (Subject 1), subjects became increasingly accurate in supplying the exact word. All three subjects showed variable responding but within clearly ascending trends (mean percent correct for baseline = 32%; for training = 54%).

For Subjects 1 and 3, the data for semantically and syntactically appropriate substitutions parallel the exact word data. With training the baseline responding (Subject 1 mean = 35%; Subject 3 mean = 45%) changed to variable but increasingly more accurate responding (Subject 1 mean = 60%; Subject 3 mean = 77%). In

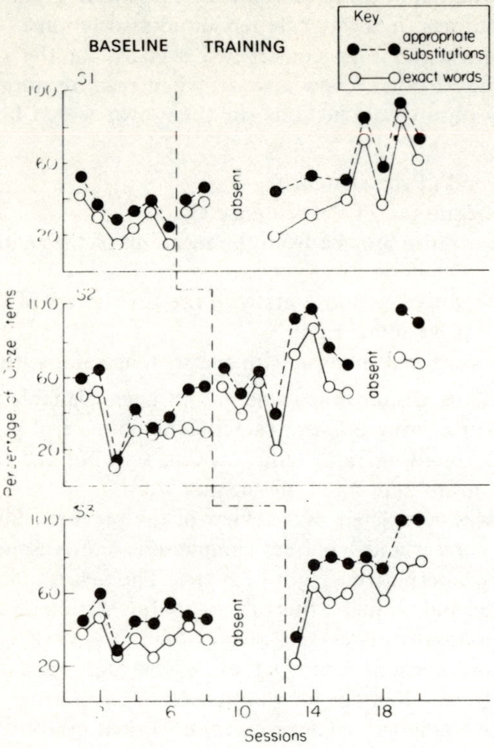

FIG. 1. Percentages of Cloze items filled in with exact words and with appropriate substitutions across sessions.

Subject 3's case the last two sessions were both at 100%. For Subject 2 ascending data points in the latter half of the baseline make it difficult to attribute further gains to the effects of training.

TABLE I. Percentage of comprehension questions correct in classroom exercises (from series: Wardlock 6–10) during different phases

Subject	Percentage correct on comprehension	
	Baseline*	Cloze training†
1	70.7	96.4
2	65.0	87.3
3	53.0	74.6
$\bar{x}$	63.0	86.0

*Average of two exercises.
†Average of five exercises.

Comprehension Measure

The classroom reading comprehension results are presented in Table I. Two measures were obtained for each reader during baseline and five during training. The percentages of answers correct (out of a total number of 33 questions on each exercise) show considerable differences between phases. Under baseline conditions with regular classroom instruction, but no further training, the subjects averaged 63% of the questions answered correctly. With training, accuracy increased to 86% questions answered correctly on new exercises at the same level. Only one exercise for one subject after training was less accurate than a baseline exercise.

TABLE II. Reading ages (years;months) on standardised reading tests administered before and after Cloze training

			Neale†					
			Rate		Accuracy		Comprehension	
	GAP*							
Subject	Pre	Post	Pre	Post	Pre	Post	Pre	Post
1	7;0 (8;1)	7;8 (8;6)	7;4	8;3	8;5	8;7	8;1	9;6
2	7;8 (8;4)	8;10 (9;10)	7;0	8;2	8;1	8;7	8;8	10;1
3	7;10 (8;7)	9;6 (10;4)	8;1	8;2	7;9	8;0	9;10	10;8

Note: Test-retest interval = 7 weeks.
*GAP reading comprehension test (McLeod, 1965; New Zealand norms plus British norms in brackets).
†Neale analysis of reading ability (Neale, 1966).

Standardised Reading Measures

The standardised test measures are contained in Table II. Marked gains occurred in reading comprehension, beyond those expected for 'normal' progress over a two month period. All three subjects showed considerable improvement on measures similar to the Cloze exercises (gains of between 5 and 21 months on the GAP test) and on standard comprehension measures (Neale comprehension results show gains between 10 and 17 months). British norms are also given for the GAP comprehension test because the Neale Reading test is also based on British norms.

There was some indication also that related reading skills of oral reading accuracy and reading rate improved, over the two month period, although gains are less consistent across subjects. Subjects 2 and 3 gained give and three months respectively in reading accuracy, while Subject 1 gained the expected two months. Reading rate gains of 11 and 14 months were made by S1 and S2, respectively, while S3 gained only one month.

Discussion

The instruction given to low progress readers consisted of practice and feedback on Cloze exercises, and training in problem solving to gain meaning. This 'package' produced gains in performance on the training task such that all three students were much more able to use semantic and syntactic cues to 'predict' correct words. These skilful performances on the training tasks produced generalised changes for each reader, both in performance on classroom comprehension questions and on standardised tests of reading skills.

Gains on the latter two sets of measures were clearly educationally significant. Classroom reading performance became much more accurate, and measures of reading age, particularly those based on comprehension skills, showed substantial gains of five or more months over a two month period.

The basis for this generalised effect cannot be completely differentiated in the present research but there are two possible causes. First, the skills involved in using contextual cues are likely to be similar to those involved in answering inferential and recall questions. Obviously proficiency in both tasks is dependent on gaining and maintaining meaning in the tasks.

Secondly, there was a deliberate attempt to train problem-solving strategies. These strategies were intended to function as self-regulatory or metacognitive skills (Brown & DeLoache, 1978; Meichenbaum & Asarnow, 1979). These skills should increase the generalised proficiency of readers on tasks similar to the ones they were trained on, and which demanded the same sort of executive skills. The problem-solving strategies would work in combination with the increased sensitivity to contextual cues brought about by the Cloze exercises. In this way the subjects would learn to control and maintain performance independently on unfamiliar tasks.

It is interesting to note that although Schneyer (1965) provided feedback for Cloze performance during his training there was no discussion by students on reasons for choice for possible alternatives. He suggested verbalisation of reasons for appropriate responses is essential. This study tends to confirm the importance of controlling performance via deliberate (perhaps verbally mediated) strategies.

The results of this study also suggest that at least some underachieving readers, rather than being overdependent on contextual cues and thus unable to process visual cues effectively (as Juel, 1980 has claimed), need to increase their use of contextual cues. For these readers improvement in the use of contextual cues in addition to their current skills for using graphic and graphophonemic information will lead to improvement in reading comprehension. In addition, there is evidence that under appropriate conditions increasing attention to contextual cues can also increase oral reading accuracy (McNaughton & Glynn, 1981; Wong & McNaughton, 1980).

In the present study, improvements in reading accuracy from a training 'package' based on use of context were also found. But these gains were not as substantial as those for comprehension. The study does not show whether this smaller increase in accuracy was merely transient or if continued training might further accelerate the gains in accuracy.

The training package in the present study seems to be a promising remedial technique. This is particularly so given the ease of administration and small amount of time required in the Cloze training procedures to supplement the classroom reading programme. Small group discussions are both economical and feasible in a busy classroom. Further research is needed to determine its applicability with different groups of students and when used in combination with other techniques.

REFERENCES

ANDERSON, J. (1970) Research on comprehension in reading, in *Improving Reading Around the World* (Newark, Delaware; International Reading Association).

BALYEAT, R. & NORMAN, D. (1975) LEA-Cloze-comprehension test, *The Reading Teacher*, 28, pp. 555–560.

BORMUTH, J.R. (1967) Cloze readability: criterion reference scores, *Journal of Educational Measurement*, 6, pp. 189–195.

BROWN, A.L. & DELOACHE, J.S. (1978) Skills, plans and self regulation, in: SIEGLER, R. (Ed.) *Children's Thinking: What Develops?* (Hilldale, New Jersey, Erlbaum).

CLAY, M.M. (1979) *Reading: the Patterning of Complex Behaviour*, 2nd edn (Auckland, Heinemann).

CULHANE, J.W. (1970) Cloze procedures and comprehension, *The Reading Teacher*, 23, pp. 410–413.

DULIN, K.L. (1970) Using context clues in word recognition and comprehension, *The Reading Teacher*, 23, pp. 440–442.

ELLEY, W. (1977) A close look at Cloze, in *Set 77* (Wellington, New Zealand Council for Educational Research).

GOODMAN, K.S. (1976) Reading: a psycholinguistic guessing game, in: SINGER, H. & RUDDEL, R.G. (Eds) *Theoretical Models and Processes of Reading* (Newark, International Reading Association).

GOODMAN, K.S. & BURKE, C. (1973) Theoretically based studies of patterns of miscues in oral reading performance, *Report on Project 90357*, United State Office of Education Bureau of Research.

GUTHRIE, J.T. (1976) Operational definitions of reading, in: BRIGHAM, T., HAWKINS, R., SCOTT, J.W. & McLOUGHLIN, T.F. (Eds) *Behaviour Analysis in Education: self control and reading* (Dubuque, Iowa, Kendal/Hunt).

HANSEN, C. & LOVITT, T. (1978) An applied behaviour analysis approach to reading comprehension, in: GUTHRIE, J.T. (Ed.) *Cognition Curriculum and Comprehension* (Newark, Delaware, International Reading Association).

HERSEN, M. & BARLOW, D.H. (1976) *Single Case Experiment Design* (New York, Pergamon Press).

HOLDAWAY, D. (1972) *Independence in Reading* (Auckland, Ashton).

JUEL, C. (1980) Comparison of word identification strategies with varying context, word type, and reader skill, *Reading Research Quarterly*, 15, pp. 358–376.

KENNEDY, D.K. & WEAVER, P. (1973) Visual and auditory training with the Cloze procedure to improve reading and listening comprehension, *Reading Research Quarterly*, 8, pp. 524–541.

KNAPCZYK, D.R. & LIVINGSTON, G. (1973) Self-recording and student-teacher supervision. Variables within a token economy structure, *Journal of Applied Behavioural Analysis*, 6, pp. 481–486.

LAHEY, B.B., McNEES, M.P. & BROWN, C.C. (1973) Modification of deficits in reading for comprehension, *Journal of Applied Behaviour Analysis*, 6, pp. 475–480.

McLEOD, J. (1965) *GAP Reading Comprehension Test*, 2nd edn (Melbourne, Heinemann).

McNAUGHTON, S. & GLYNN, T. (1981) Delayed versus immediate attention to oral reading errors: effects on accuracy and self correction, *Educational Psychology*, 1, pp. 57–65.

MEICHENBAUM, D. & ASNAROW, J. (1979) Cognitive-behavioural modification and metacognitive development: implications for the classroom, in: KENDALL, P.C. & HOLLON, S.D. (Eds) *Cognitive-Behavioural Intervention: Theory, Research and Procedures* (New York, Academic Press).

METROPOLITAN ACHIEVEMENT TESTS (1970) (New York, Harcourt, Brace & Jovanovich).

NEALE, M.D. (1966) *Neale Analysis of Reading Ability*, 2nd edn (London, McMillan).

READERS DIGEST (1971) *New Reading Skill Builders Part 3, Stories for Young Readers* (Readers Digest Services).

SCHNEYER, J.W. (1965) Use of Cloze procedure for improving reading comprehension, *The Reading Teacher*, 19, pp. 265–268.

SMITH, F. (1978) *Understanding Reading: a Psycholinguistic Analysis of Reading and Learning to Read*, 2nd edn (New York, Holt, Rinehart & Winston).

STOKES, T.F. & BAER, D.M. (1979) An implicit technology of generalisation, *Journal of Applied Behaviour Analysis*, 10, pp. 349–368.

TAYLOR, W.L. (1953) Cloze procedure, *Journalism Quarterly*, 30, pp. 415–433.

WARDLOCK (1975) *Reading Workshop* (London, Wardlock).

WONG, P. & McNAUGHTON, S. (1980) The effects of prior provision of context on the oral reading proficiency of a low progress reader, *New Zealand Journal of Educational Research*, 15, pp. 169–175.

Behavioural Peer Tutoring: training 16-year-old tutors to employ the 'pause, prompt and praise' method with 12-year-old remedial readers

KEVIN WHELDALL & PAUL METTEM

ABSTRACT *Eight 16-year-old, low achieving pupils were trained to tutor reading using the 'Pause, Prompt and Praise' method. The effectiveness of training such tutors was investigated through a tutorial programme in which these eight older pupils tutored eight 12-year-old remedial children who were retarded in reading. The programme consisted of 24 tutorial sessions conducted over eight weeks. Two matched control groups of remedial readers were also included in the experiment. One consisted of eight pupils tutored by a group of eight untrained tutors who tutored during the same sessions using the same materials. The second control group consisted of a third group of remedial readers who read silently, without a tutor. The experimental group of tutees, who had a mean pre-test reading age of 8 years 4 months, made a mean gain of 6 months in reading accuracy by the end of the programme. The tutees of control group I who had received tutoring from untrained tutors made a mean gain of 2.4 months. The pupils of control group II who read silently without a tutor made a mean gain of .8 months. Analysis of covariance showed the gains of the experimental group to be statistically significantly different from the gains of the two control groups.*

Introduction

An impending teacher shortage in the United States in the early 1960s, precipitated renewed interest in the pedagogic device of peer-tutoring, previously employed in the Bell-Lancaster Monitorial System during the Industrial Revolution. Intensive research has subsequently been carried out in the U.S.A. over the past 20 years (reviewed Paolitto, 1976; Strain, 1981; Allen, 1976; Goodlad, 1979). Goodlad has also reviewed studies carried out in the U.K. which tend, however, to be more anecdotal in nature. Although peer-tutoring has been carried out in a number of school subjects the present paper will consider only research concerned with the most frequently selected subject for peer tutoring, reading. Further, whilst acknowledging that many benefits of a tutorial programme may acrue to the *tutor*, this paper will be concerned only with the possible gains of the *tutee*.

Research in the 1960s and early 1970s was primarily concerned with establishing whether the reading abilities of tutees who were retarded in reading could be improved by their participation in a tutorial programme. In a variety of peer-tutoring programmes, Ellson, Barber, Engle & Kampworth (1965), Niedermeyer (1976), Klosterman (1970) and Shaver & Nuhn (1971), all found that the reading ability of such tutees could be significantly improved in comparison with non-tutored control subjects.

During the early 1960s two large scale peer-tutoring programmes were organised and are reported by Cloward (1967). The Mobilisation of Youth Inc. took place in New York in 1963 and included 2500 tutees who were low achieving high school pupils. After five months of the programme it was discovered that a mean gain of six months in reading ability has occurred which was found to be statistically significant when compared with a mean gain of 3.5 months in control subjects. Similar gains were found to have occurred in tutees as a result of their participation in the second large programme, the High School Homework Helpers Programme which took place during 1962 and 1963. Despite the positive findings of these studies there have been studies which have produced non-significant findings forcing Feldman, Devin-Sheehan & Allen (1976) to conclude that "empirical support for generalisations about the effect of tutoring on tutors and tutees has often been inconclusive . . .".

More recent research has been concerned with increasing the effectiveness of the tutors involved in peer-tutoring programmes. This has been conducted in two ways. First, attempts have been made to structure both the content of the tutorial programme and the behaviour of the tutor so that the tutor's attention is maximally effective and error free. Structured tutoring, according to Harrison (1976), consists of setting instructional goals as a result of pre-tests, the validation of tutoring techniques with systematic review, and record keeping. Significant gains have been reported by Harrison (1976) and Niedermeyer (1976) as a result of structured tutoring programmes. Feldman *et al.* (1976) describes a similar method, Programmed Tutoring, in which "the tutors' behaviour is controlled in a highly specific manner, analogous to computer programmes". Ellson, Barker, Engle & Kampworth (1965) and Ellson, Harris & Barber (1968) found that Programmed Tutoring was more effective than Directed Tutoring, that is tutoring similar to that of a normal teacher.

The second way of increasing the tutor's effectiveness has been by the training of tutors in specific skills. Harrison (1976) reports the failure of a project which was devised to tutor Mexican-American children. It was discovered that the tutors lacked a large number of tutoring skills such as dealing with various error responses or praising the tutee, and that they failed to establish a rapport with the tutee. Niedermeyer (1970) developed a Tutor Observation Scale and used it to observe trained and untrained fifth grade pupils who acted as tutors. He found that the trained tutors performed significantly better in conversing, confirming responses, supplying correct responses, eliciting correct responses and praising. In fact, the untrained tutors were found to use no praise.

The effectiveness of training tutors in appropriate skills has been further shown by Niedermeyer (1976) and Allen & Boraks (1978) who report significant gains in the tutees' reading ability as a result of tutor training. With regard to the procedure for training tutors Harrison (1976) reports that "several different procedures for training tutors have been compared empirically. The most effective procedure was found to consist of three parts". This procedure requires the tutors to first read written instructions of their tasks. The instructions are then discussed and the tasks clarified. Finally role play is conducted where the trainer plays the learner and the tutors take turns in practising the skills. Following the use of these procedures Harrison (1976) concluded that almost all upper-grade elementary pupils could be trained to use effective tutoring skills.

Thus research indicates that pupils who are retarded in reading ability can gain by participating as a tutee in a peer-tutoring programme. Further, such gains can be increased as a result of structuring the content of the programme and by training the tutors in specific tutoring skills.

Peer tutoring is not, however, without its problems, not least the problem of adequately training tutors in pedagogically sound, but relatively simple, tutoring skills. It is our contention that the behavioural tutoring method summarised as the 'pause, prompt and praise' technique (reviewed below) may prove to be one answer to the quest for an appropriate tutoring model for use by children to teach other children.

Behavioural Tutoring

Research at the University of Auckland, New Zealand, inspired by the earlier work of Marie Clay (1972, 1979), has resulted in the development of a behavioural method for turoring oral reading by McNaughton, Glynn & Robinson (1981) which may best be termed the 'Pause, Prompt and Praise' method. The Prediction Model of reading assumes that a reader relies heavily on syntactic and semantic clues to predict ahead so that only enough graphic information need be sampled to support those predictions. Thus errors in prediction will occur and will result in reading errors or miscues which should then be corrected. Clay (1972) established that the self-correction of errors was not only a natural reading behaviour but a desirable one which was more frequent in better readers. The more able 25% of her sample self-corrected one in three or four errors whilst the least able 25% self-corrected only one in every 20 errors.

McNaughton & Glynn (1981) investigated the effects upon tutees' reading of immediate attention to errors, that is attention that occurs within five seconds of the error, versus delayed attention, that is attention that is delayed five seconds or until the end of a sentence. It was discovered that by delaying attention not only was the tutee encouraged to self-correct more errors but that reading accuracy was also improved. Thus the first part of the tutoring procedure, 'Pause', requires the tutor to delay attention to a tutee's reading error for more than five seconds or until the end of a sentence.

McNaughton & Delquadri (1978) investigated the effects of modelling and prompting as methods of achieving a correct response following no self-correction. It was discovered that although modelling was more effective with very poor readers, prompting was effective with better readers whose error rates were not high. It was felt that such readers were able to incorporate the prompts with the self-correction strategies already learned. Thus the second part of the procedure 'Prompt' requires the tutor to supply a prompt if no self-correction occurs. It is recognised that the miscue can result from failure to attend to graphic or contextual cues so if the miscue is a meaningful substitution the prompt is aimed at the graphical features of the word and vice-versa. If no correct response is elicited following two prompts, in the interest of continuity, a model is supplied.

The final part of the procedure 'Praise' requires the tutor to reinforce verbally positive behaviours by the tutee and to encourage the development of independent and self regulatory skills. Therefore, apart from general praise for such behaviours as reading a whole page, the tutor is required to praise self-corrections and prompted corrections made by the tutee.

This method supplies the tutor with a procedure for dealing with both correct and error behaviour by the reader and also for reinforcing desired behaviours. Equally importantly it allows the reader to develop self-correction strategies and independence. The effectiveness of the 'Pause, Prompt and Praise' method as a procedure for tutoring oral reading has been shown in two studies in which parents were trained to tutor their offspring who were retarded in reading (Glynn, McNaughton, Robinson & Quinn, 1981; and Glynn, 1981). Both studies were conducted using a multiple base line design. In the former study a mean gain of 1.4 months in book level occurred in the tutee during the one month period of untrained baseline observations. Following 2.5 months of trained tutoring the tutees had made a 6.5 month gain in book level. Further it was found that the mean proportion of self-corrected errors rose from 20.2% to 34.4%. The second study was on a smaller scale but showed similar results. Both studies attempted and succeeded in achieving a rapid increase in the reading ability of retarded readers by training their parents as tutors. We felt that for such pupils at secondary school age an alternative and possibly more effective and efficient source of tutors might lie in the non-examination groups of pupils in the final year of school. Furthermore there is evidence (reported by the reviewers of peer-tutoring research mentioned earlier) which suggests that such pupils might gain in a number of ways by acting as tutors.

The aim of the present study is to attempt to incorporate the advantages of peer tutoring with the advantages of the 'Pause, Prompt and Praise' method in order to improve significantly the reading ability of secondary age remedial readers. More specifically, the present study attempts to evaluate the feasibility of training 16-year-old tutors in the 'praise, prompt and praise' technique and to determine whether this results in measurable gains in the reading performance of their 12-year-old tutees.

Method

Subjects and Setting

The pupils selected as subjects in this experiment all attended a large mixed, comprehensive school situated near the centre of a West Midlands industrial town. The school is streamed into seven classes for each year intake, the lower two classes being designated as remedial. It was from these two classes of the 1st year intake that 24 remedial readers were selected. The most retarded pupils, with respect to reading, were selected, having a mean chronological age of 12 years 0.25 months (age range 11 years 5 months to 12 years 3 months) and a mean retardation in reading age, as measured by the Neale Analysis of Reading Ability (1966) (Form A) of 3 years 5.8 months (range 2 years 2 months to 4 years 10 months).

The basic approach to the teaching of reading by the Remedial Department is phonetically based with emphasis on comprehension and reading experience. Reading experience is organised on a Book Box system where the pupils selected reading material from a box appropriate to their reading level. (These boxes range from Box A, which is appropriate for children of a reading age of 6 years to 6 years 5 months, to Box H, which accommodates children of a reading age of 9 years 6 months to 10 years.)

A group of 16 fifth year pupils were selected to act as reading tutors. All had been taught within the Remedial Department during their first three years at the school and some were still being taught English by the specialist remedial teachers. Eight boys and eight girls were selected so that each reader in the two tutored groups would be tutored by an older pupil of the same sex, in line with the recommendations of Devin-Sheehan & Allen (1976). Tutors were selected on the criteria of having a reading ability considered sufficient for the role of tutoring less able children (i.e. at least six months of reading age higher than the lowest tutee), having an attitude which was sympathetic to the remedial reader and having an excellent attendance record. The mean age of these pupils was 15 years 7 months (range 15 years 3 months to 15 years 9 months) with a mean reading age of 9 years 9 months (range 8 years 6 months to 10 years 6 months) as measured by the Salford Sentence Reading Test.

Design

The experiment was designed to evaluate experimentally the effectiveness of 'Pause, Prompt and Praise' based peer tutoring and hence required a standard control group and an untrained peer tutored control group to counter possible alternative explanations of results in terms of 'reading drive' or 'Hawthorne' effect. Further this additional control group would allow a comparison of the effectiveness of untrained tutoring with the standard (untrained) control group. Consequently, three equivalent/matched groups were established which were designated as experimental group (trained tutoring), control group I (untrained tutoring,) and control group II (no tutoring).

The experimental group received a programme of reading tuition from tutors trained in the 'Pause, Prompt and Praise' method. Control group I received an identical programme from similar tutors but who had received no training. Control group II pursued their usual reading activity of silent reading during the tutoring sessions, so that all the young remedial readers were receiving identical reading time. (The importance of equal instruction time is emphasised by Devin-Sheehan & Allen (1976) who comment that "most studies have compared tutoring and classroom instruction to classroom instruction alone; thus confounding tutoring with the total amount of instructional time").

The pool of 24 pupils selected to be reading tutees was found to consist of nine boys and six girls from the lowest ability class and three boys and six girls from the next lowest ability class. This facilitated the grouping of pupils into eight units of three, or triads, which contained subjects of the same school class and sex and as similar a reading age as possible (as measured by Neale Analysis of Reading Ability: Reading Accuracy). The matched pupils of each unit were then randomly assigned to one of the three groups. The mean reading ages of the three groups was found to be highly similar ranging from 8 years 4 months to 8 years 4.6 months with mean reading retardation ranging from 3 years 5.3 months to 3 years 7.5 months.

The eight boys and eight girls selected to act as reading tutors were allocated randomly to either the experimental group or control group I so that each group contained four boys and four girls. The mean reading age (Salford Sentence Reading Test) of the two groups of tutors was very similar with the experimental group tutors averaging 9 years 8.5 months (S.D. 9.1 months) compared with the control group I tutors 9 years 11 months (S.D. 7.3 months). Tutors were then paired with tutees of their group so as to establish same sex dyads, as previously described.

Materials

The Trend reading scheme was selected since it allows pupils to progress through levels whilst maintaining a reasonable level of difficulty and whilst also sustaining their interest. This scheme was also used by McNaughton *et al.* (1981) and was found to be highly satisfactory. This Australian series provides a number of high interest stories for pupils of 10 to 14 years of age who have previously failed in reading. It is graded into levels from 6.5 years to 12.5 years. This scheme was available within the school but none of the remedial readers had previously used the scheme before.

As the performance of both the tutors and tutees had to be monitored, battery operated cassette recorders were used to record tutoring sessions.

Procedure

Training of tutors. The tutors of the experimental group received two training sessions of 30 minutes in the use of the 'Pause, Prompt and Praise' method and were also given (as a summary) a copy of the written instruction sheet shown in Fig. 1, which was taken from McNaughton *et al.* (1981). Subsequent discussion of the method (which followed every recorded session) allowed the children to question certain parts of the procedure. Training in the form of role play was employed in which the experimenter acted as the tutee and the tutors took turns in tutoring in the 'Pause, Prompt and Praise' method, followed by the tutors working in pairs, taking it in turns to act as the tutee. Group discussion again followed this training. These trained tutors were told briefly of the exact nature of the study and informed that the untrained group should remain ignorant of their special training.

The control group I tutors received one 30-minute session in which they received a general talk on reading tuition. They were informed that their task was to help the tutees read. The talk consisted of encouraging them to insist on clear reading from the tutee, of placing the book between them both and in being friendly and patient. They were then allowed to practise tutoring each other with no intervention from the experimenter. It was explained to them that due to the size of the groups involved, the two groups of tutors would meet separately with the experimenter for further instruction and feedback.

Each tutor group receive feedback regarding their performance following each recorded session. The experimental group tutors received feedback related to the 'Pause, Prompt and Praise' method. The control group I tutors were given general feedback concerning their attitude to the tutee and were questioned about how they thought their tutee was performing in order to elicit general discussion.

Monitoring and analysis of tutor performance. Audio recordings were made of tutoring during alternate tutoring sessions so as to analyse both tutor and tutee performance. The analysis procedures carried out were those of McNaughton *et al.* (1981). Each tutor group was monitored on different days, thereby supplying data on half of the sessions attended. The programme was planned to consist of 24 sessions and hence

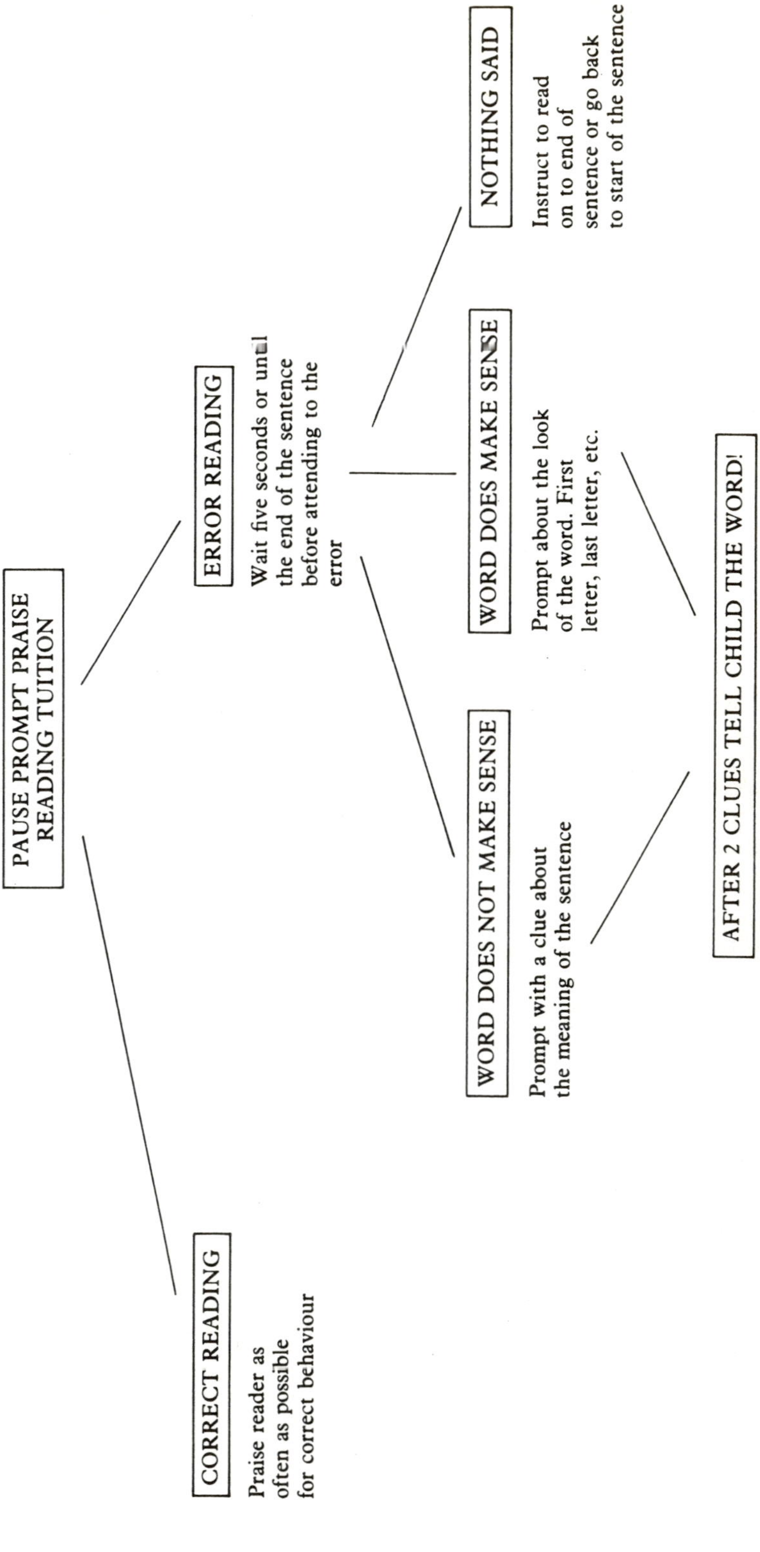

FIG. 1. 'Pause, Prompt, Praise' instruction sheet.

data was available on all dyads for 12 sessions. From the recordings of tutorial interactions the following measures of behaviour were obtained.

(A) Reader Behaviour

(1) Percentage of words read correctly. This was a measure of the accuracy of the reading, i.e. all words intially read correctly. Errors were defined as any deviation between the written word and the oral response of the child. In addition Omission or Non-Attempts and Substitution or Addition errors were included. This measure was computed by the formula,

$$\frac{\text{Total Words Read} - \text{Errors}}{\text{Total Words Read}} \times 100$$

(2) Percentage of self-corrected errors. Self corrected errors were defined as spontaneous independent correction of errors without tutor attention to the error. This measure was calculated by the formula,

$$\frac{\text{Total Self Corrections}}{\text{Total Number of Errors}} \times 100$$

(B) Tutor Behaviour

(1) Percentage error attention. This was the number of errors made by the child (not self corrected) which received some form of attention from the tutor. This measure was calculated to form a percentage by the formula,

$$\frac{\text{Total Tutor Error Attention}}{\text{Total Errors} - \text{Self Corrections}} \times 100$$

(2) Percentage of delayed tutor attention. Each instance of tutor attention to an error was regarded as delayed if it occurred more than five seconds after the child's error or at the end of the sentence in which the error occurred. The formula to calculate this was,

$$\frac{\text{Tutor Delayed Attention Instances}}{\text{Total Tutor Error Attention}} \times 100$$

(3) Percentage of prompts used. Prompts were defined as clues given about the meaning of the word, directions to think about context or to look at graphic cues in the word. The formula to calculate this was,

$$\frac{\text{Number of Prompts Used}}{\text{Total Tutor Error Attention}} \times 100$$

(4) Percentage prompted corrections. This is a measure of the effectiveness of the prompts given by the tutor and is calculated by the formula,

$$\frac{\text{Number of Prompted Corrections}}{\text{Number of Prompts Used}} \times 100$$

(5) Praise. Three measures of verbal reinforcement were made in the form of a tally.

(a) Praise following self-corrections.
(b) Praise following prompted corrections.
(c) General praise statements.

These measures were recorded for later analysis but also were used to provide specific feedback to the trained tutors. Untrained tutors only received general feedback on attention to errors, with regard to its adequacy or inadequacy.

Placement and Promotion in Book Level

The procedures for placement and promotion in book level for the tutee were identical to those used by McNaughton *et al.* (1981). These procedures were felt to have been successful and the use of them would facilitate direct comparison of the results of this study with the previous studies of the 'Pause, Prompt and Praise' method.

The Trend series is based on levels of approximate reading ages but these ages are neither satisfactory for placement, due to variations between reading tests, nor for promotion to a higher book level as a result of testing. The level at which children were placed needed to be sufficiently low so as to allow the children to gain meaning and thus be able to use contextual cues for the self-correction of errors. On the other hand the level had to be high enough to provide a sufficient number of errors for the tutee to learn such strategies and for the tutor to be able to respond to error attention adequately (i.e. to have sufficient errors to work on).

Consequently, as in McNaughton *et al.* (1981), a criterion of 90% accuracy of words read initially correct was adopted for promotion to a higher book level. McNaughton *et al.* observed that promotion at 95% accuracy is suggested by Clay (1979) but that this regards self corrections as correct words. As most children will self-correct to some extent, it was felt that both criteria would, in the end, be equal. Thus where tutees were found, from the recorded sessions, to perform above the 90% reading accuracy criterion, they were promoted to the next book level in the Trend series in the following session.

For the initial placement of book level it was necessary, therefore, to discover the highest book level at which each tutee could not read at the 90% reading accuracy criterion. This was carried out at the pre-test stage by the tutees reading samples of a book at each level. When each tutee reached the criterion they were placed on the previous book level for the commencement of the programme. These procedures were followed for the placement of the readers in the experimental group, control group I and control group II. Control group II were subsequently promoted in book level on the recommendation of the relevant class teacher as would occur in the normal classroom situation.

Tutoring procedure. The tutoring programme consisted of three sessions per week for eight weeks giving a total of 24 tutoring sessions. The sessions took place on Mondays, Wednesdays and Fridays when the children were released from their normal lessons at 11.30 a.m. in order to begin tuition at 11.35 a.m. This allowed 15 minutes before the children were released for the lunchtime break.

Before each session the tape recorders were tested and placed ready for the scheduled tutor group to use. The box of reading books for each group was placed in the session room. Promotions in book level were required from the previously recorded session were made, and where any books were almost completed another book of the same book level was supplied.

At the end of each session the book boxes were stored, to prevent tutees practicing between sessions. The group tutors who had used the tape recorders returned them to the store, whilst the other tutor group assembled for their feedback from the previous sessions. Feedback was given to all tutors orally and it was felt that by giving both tutor groups such sessions the possibilities of a Hawthorne effect were equalised between them.

The absence from tutoring sessions, of both tutors and tutees, was very low. The class teachers of the tutees were asked to encourage full attendance and on the days when tutoring was scheduled many tutors would return from 'illness'. An extra week of tuition was arranged to allow for absence. Although many needed one additional session to achieve attendance for a full 24 sessions only dyads needed a whole week of extra sessions to complete the programme.

At the end of the programme all tutees were given another form (Form B) of the Neale Analysis of Reading Ability (1966) as a Post Test. The final form of the test (Form C) was administered two months later as a Delayed Post Test. Each form was administered over two days of testing by the second author. The Neale test of reading is not without it's critics and it must be conceded that it is now nearly twenty years old. However, there is little doubt that it is a sound measure of reading *accuracy* (a main concern of this study) and there appears to be no real alternative, not least in terms of its three parallel forms, an important design requirement of this study.

A final de-briefing session was subsequently held for all tutors. In this the untrained tutors were informed that the other group had received special training. Their reaction confirmed that they had no prior knowledge of this. This untrained group were promised (and later given) the special training.

Results

Baseline observations were not made of the experimental group's tutoring skills prior to training and hence pre/post comparisons of their tutoring behaviours cannot be made. Tutors were, however, randomly allocated to groups and hence we can compare the tutoring behaviours of the eight experimental group tutors over the 12 recorded sessions following training with the tutoring behaviours of the eight untrained control group tutors. Attention to errors in both groups was very similar over the twelve sessions as Fig. 2 demonstrates, with experimental tutors attending to a mean of 77% of errors compared with 78% in the control group. Moreover, this level was fairly uniform over the 16 tutors. For delayed attention to errors, however, the picture is markedly different, as Fig. 3 shows. Whereas a mean of 58% of attention to errors was delayed in the experimental tutors, for the control group it was almost non-existent (mean of less than 1%). All experimental tutors delayed attention to at least 50% of errors.

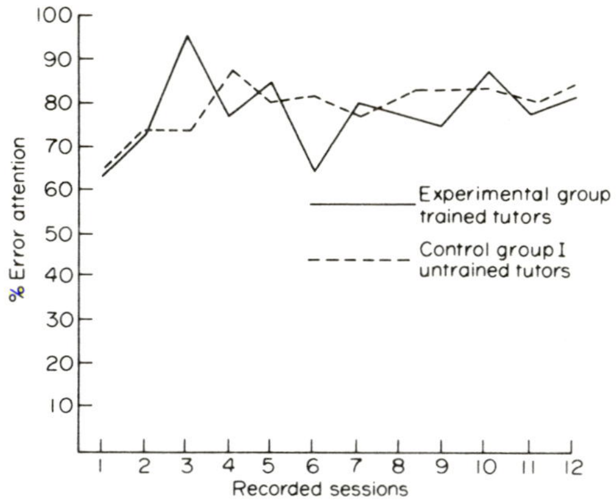

FIG. 2. Group mean percentage error attention per recorded session.

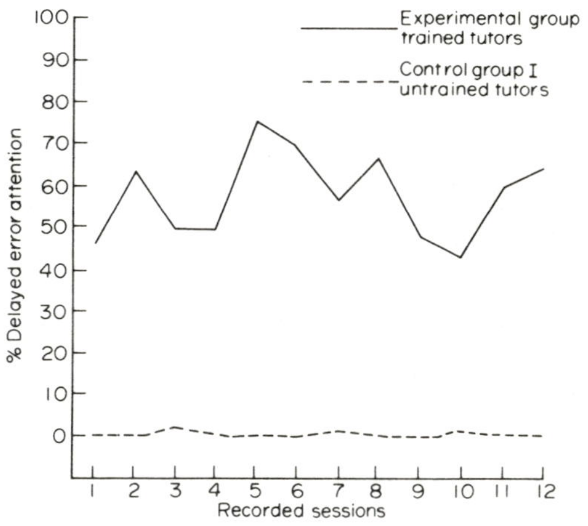

FIG. 3. Group mean percentage delayed attention to errors per recorded session.

As can be seen in Figs. 4 and 5 prompting almost never occurred in the untrained control group and was never successful (mean less than 1%). Trained tutors, however, used prompts in 27% of their attention to errors (range 17–54%) and were successful in 49% of these prompts. (Successful use of prompts, however, varied from 36% to 72% between tutors.)

Finally, use of praise was observed on average 8.8 times per tutor per session in the experimental group (see Fig. 6) but hardly ever in the control group (once by one tutor in one session). Praise in the experimental group was mostly general (mean 5.1) with some use of praise for self-corrections (mean 2.1) and prompted corrections (mean 1.6).

From the above results it can reasonably be claimed that the experimental group tutors were trained successfully in the 'Pause, Prompt and Praise' procedure,

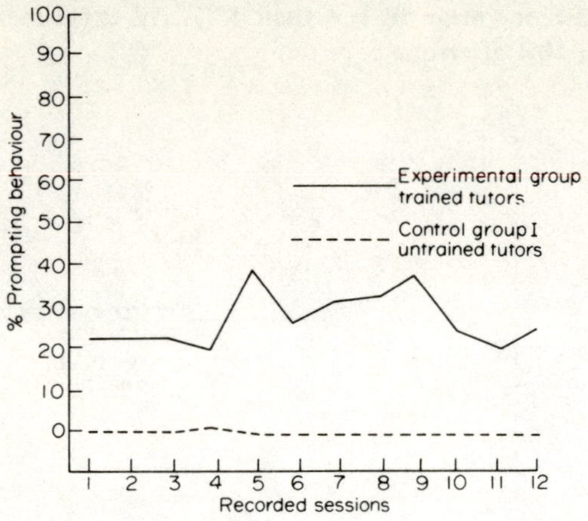

FIG. 4. Group mean percentage prompting behaviour per recorded session.

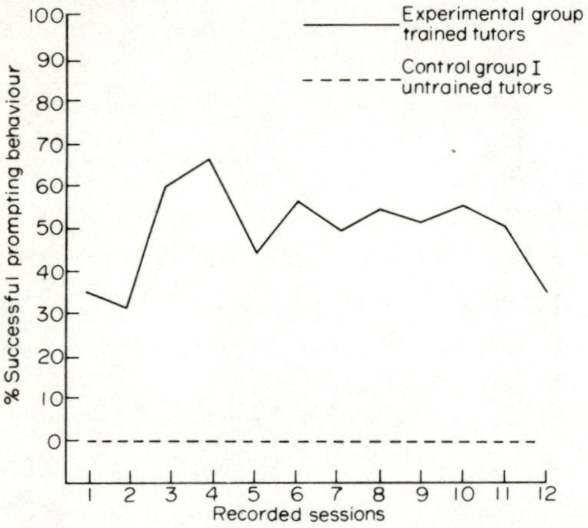

FIG. 5. Group mean percentage successful prompting behaviour.

exhibiting markedly different behaviour from the control group on each of these three tutoring skills. Given that it is possible to train 16-year-old tutors in this technique, however, how effective are they in terms of improving the reading skills of their tutees?

Fig. 7 shows the percentage of self corrections made by the tutees in the two groups. For the experimental group children self corrections were around 20% but in the control group this figure never rose above 10%. It must be pointed out, however, that the experimental group had far more opportunities to self-correct since their tutors were trained to pause.

Reading progress may also be measured by promotion in book level, since promotion to a substantial level is dependent upon reading accuracy of 90% or over in terms of words read correctly. The experimental group progressed through a total of 36 levels during the programme compared with 29 levels for the control group I and 24 levels for Control Group II. Looking at these data more individually, six

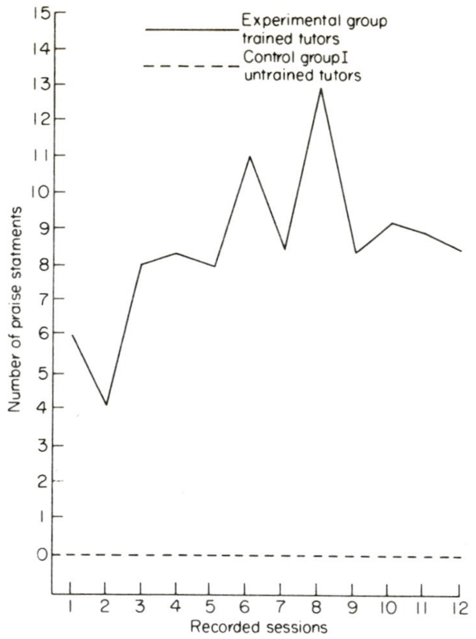

FIG. 6. Group mean number of praise statements per session.

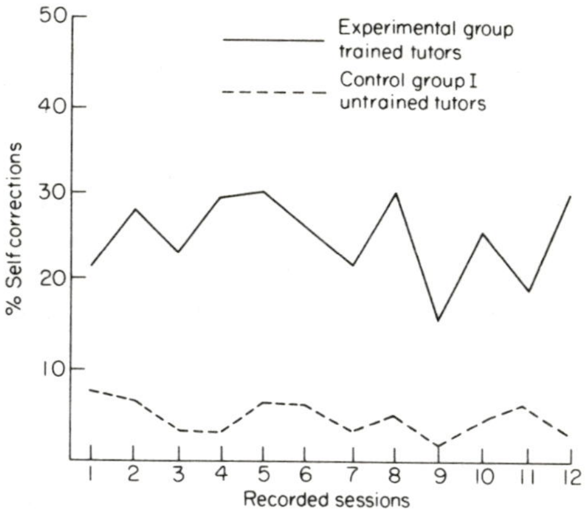

FIG. 7. Group mean percentage of tutee self-correction per recorded session.

children progressed through four book levels in the experimental group compared with only two children in control group I and none in control group II.

Finally, the results of standardised reading testing are shown in Table I for the three groups for both accuracy and comprehension at pre-test, post-test and delayed post-test stages. It can be seen that the experimental group tutees made a mean gain of 6 months in reading accuracy at the post-test stage which was maintained at the delayed post-test stage. This can be directly compared with the mean gain of 2.4 months by the control group I tutees and the mean gain of 0.9 months by the control group II readers. Again looking at this more individually, half of the experimental group made gains in excess of six months whilst none of the children did so in the control groups I or II. The gains in mean comprehension scores are in line with the gains in reading accuracy. The large mean gain by the experimental group tutees is reduced at the delayed post-test stage and it was noted that the control group II readers had improved.

TABLE I. Mean group performance on Neale analysis of reading ability for reading accuracy, and comprehension, at pre, post and delayed post-test stages

Group	Pre Test	Post Test	Delayed Post Test
Reading accuracy (months)			
Experimental	100.0	106.75	106.75
	(S.D.8.52)	(S.D.9.95)	(S.D.11.56)
Control I	100.63	103.00	103.63
	(S.D.5.04)	(S.D.5.6)	(S.D.6.44)
Control II	100.50	101.38	101.00
	(S.D.7.50)	(S.D.7.01)	(S.D.7.69)
Comprehension (raw score)			
Experimental	10.38	15.25	14.25
	(S.D.2.45)	(S.D.4.71)	(S.D.4.59)
Control I	10.38	13.88	13.38
	(S.D.4.63)	(S.D.3.18)	(S.D.6.02)
Control II	9.75	12.50	13.50
	(S.D.2.60)	(S.D.4.17)	(S.D.5.83)

Analysis of variance on the pre-test scores in reading accuracy showed that the three groups were not significantly different ($F2,21=0.02$, N.S.). A subsequent analysis of covariance on post-test scores, covarying pre-test scores, showed that the observed differences between the groups were statistically significant ($F2,20=5.80$, $P<.025$). A series of planned comparisons revealed that the mean experimental group gain was significantly different from the mean of control group I and control group II gains ($F1,20=10.89$, $P<005$). The second planned comparison of control group I gains with control group II gains was not significant ($F1,20=0.71$, N.S.). These results can be appreciated more fully by considering the mean group scores in reading accuracy at the post-test stage when adjusted for any initial differences in pre-test scores: experimental group, 107.1 months; control group I, 102.8 months; and control group II, 101.3 months.

A covariance analysis was also carried out on the results obtained from the delayed post-test and the findings were very similar. Analysis of covariance showed the differences in scores between groups to be significant ($F2,20=5.86$, $P<0.025$) and the first planned comparison was again highly significant ($F1,20=10.89$, $P<.005$).

With regard to comprehension scores, the experimental group made the largest mean gain of 4.9 on the post-test compared with the respective mean gains of 3.5 and 2.8 by the control group I tutees and control group II readers. These gains were not maintained by the tutored groups. Analyses of covariance showed that the groups were not significantly different at the post-test stage ($F2,21=0.91$, N.S.) nor at the delayed post-test stage ($F2,21=0.069$, N.S.).

Discussion

The control group of untrained tutors provided information about what might be regarded as the 'natural' tutoring behaviours of older children. (It should be remembered, however, that the tutors were also poor readers themselves.) They attended to over 78% of errors and this was usually immediate. In fact only three untrained tutors displayed any delayed attention and this was exceedingly small. As a group, these tutors delayed their attention to only one in every 230 reading errors. A similar situation was found with regard to their use of prompts. For this behaviour only two untrained tutors displayed its use at all and as a group only one prompt was used in attention to every 500 reading errors. These results support observations, made during the analysis of recordings, that the untrained tutors employed a 'modelling' method. Their perceived role as tutor appears to have been the detection and immediate correction of reading errors. It was observed in the recordings that attention was so immediate on many occasions that the tutor appeared to anticipate the words with which their tutee would have difficulty, by supplying a model as the error was made.

With regard to the use of verbal reinforcement, the findings of Harrison (1976) and Niedermeyer (1976) are supported. The untrained tutors were found to make almost no use of praise at all. Only one untrained tutor made praise comments and this was less than one per session. As these tutors displayed a knowledge of their tutees' reading ability by anticipating the words they would have difficulty with, one might have expected praise to have occurred when the tutee read such a word. It must, therefore, be concluded that the tutors expected good reading and regarded it as normal. They were concerned almost exclusively with inappropriate behaviour and its correction.

An interesting comparison with these tutors may be made with the untrained parents acting as tutors in the McNaughton *et al.* (1981) study. The levels of error attention of both groups in this study was lower than the levels shown by the parents in the McNaughton *et al.* study which reports 85% for trained parent tutors and 88% for untrained parent tutors. These untrained tutors also displayed higher levels of specific behaviours than those in this study. Their mean proportion of delayed attention was 15.9%, prompts were used in 28% of error attention and praise statements occurred at a mean of 1.5 per session. The differences between these two groups, although small, may well be a function of the relationship of the members of the tutoring dyad. Parents may, quite simply, have a greater desire for the tutee (their own child) to perform well. The untrained tutors of this study, it would appear, perceive their role as teacher to be as a corrector of error behaviour.

In comparison with the children in control group II, the tutees of control group I benefitted in a number of ways from the presence of their (untrained) tutors. They received feedback on about threequarters of their errors, many of which would otherwise have remained undetected. Further, with each error or non-response they were given a model which might have helped to prevent that error occurring again. Finally by the *non-response* of the tutor they also received confirmation of correct responses.

The results of the trained tutors' tutoring behaviour indicates that their training was successful. The group mean attention to errors was similar to that of the untrained tutors (77%). (It is recognised that the tutors in both this study and the McNaughton *et al.* study would tend to ignore very minor errors in favour of continuity but the element of failure by tutors in this study (trained and untrained) in not detecting more errors, may have been due to their own reading limitations.) The trained tutors were successful in delaying their attention to over 50% of the tutees' errors. In many cases this was over 60% in individual tutors and as a group the proportion of delayed attention is nearly identical to the trained parents in the McNaughton *et al.* study. Of the 40%+ of the attention to errors which was not delayed, some was probably due to a failure to allow the minimum of five seconds but instead to delay for a shorter period.

The group mean for prompting behaviour is far lower than that of the trained parents of McNaughton *et al.*, being 27.1%. Moreover, unlike other behaviours, there was a large range between the tutors, from 17% to 54%. This figure is slightly masked by a tendency for tutees to correct their error following the tutors' attention but before a prompt could be given. Thus, although it can be stated that prompts occurred approximately once in every four occasions of error attention, this does not mean that models were supplied in the others. Overall it must be stated that the proportion of prompting behaviour by trained tutors was lower than desired but the prompts that were administered by the trained tutors were successful in obtaining a correct response from the tutee on nearly 50% of the occasions they were given. The overall relative success of prompting behaviour by trained tutors questions the avoidance of such a behaviour by Niedermeyer (1970), in his programmes. While it is acknowledged that prompting behaviour needs to be trained far longer and may not suit those interested in a highly rigid procedure, it was in this study successful.

The contrast between the performance of trained and untrained tutors in their use of praise was particularly dramatic. A possible explanation for the absence of praise by the untrained tutors, may lie in the view held by some teachers that appropriate behaviour is to be expected and hence deserves little recognition. The untrained tutors were possibly modelling their behaviour on the non-positive behaviour of teachers they had experienced.

The use of verbal reinforcement has been analysed here in three categories. The trained tutors varied in their mean scores for general praise from 3.5 to 7.0 occasions per session with a group mean of 5.0. Although contingent upon positive behaviour this form of praise is open to use by the tutor for clarity of speech or effort made. The other two categories, though, are highly contingent upon the performance of the specific behaviours of self correction and corrections following prompting. The reinforcement of these behaviours is important in establishing the use of such strategies and self regulatory skills in the reader. Tutors are dependent in their use of this type of reinforcement upon performance by the tutee. For example, the tutor who used the highest number of praise statements for self correction had the tutee with the highest rate of self corrections. It could be argued, however, that the tutee is self-correcting at a higher level due to the praise he is receiving for this behaviour. Therefore, although it can be concluded that high self-correction behaviour by the tutee and high praise of self-corrective behaviour by the tutor tend to occur together, no suggestion of causality with regard to the source of such a relationship can be made.

Melaragno (1976) commented that, "most programmes are designed to satisfy the cognitive need of the tutees, but, not surprisingly, the tutors become bored with repeating the same type of instruction" (p. 192). At a de-briefing meeting the tutors stated unanimously that, although they had enjoyed the experience, a shorter programme of say 5–6 weeks length would have been preferable. If it were to be extended they stated that they would require an extension of their duties by the gradual introduction of new, additional tasks for the tutor. (It has also been suggested by Glynn (personal communication) that this slight lowering of enthusiasm by tutors might be avoided "if tutors were to see gains for themselves as a result of time tutoring others".) From the above it may reasonably be concluded that older secondary pupils are capable of being trained to tutor oral reading effectively using the 'Pause, Prompt and Praise' method. We turn now to the effect of such tutoring on the tutees.

The gains of the experimental group tutees are substantial in view of the mean gain of *six* months in reading accuracy following *two* months of tutoring. In comparison with the mean gains made by the control group I tutees of 2.4 months in reading accuracy and the 0.8 months mean gain of the control group II readers, these differences were highly significant and this was confirmed by the delayed post test. Children with reading deficits improved more in their reading accuracy when tutored by trained tutors than by untrained tutors. The difference between the two control groups was not statistically significant.

The study by McNaughton *et al.* (1981) considered the promotion of children across book levels as a measure of the tutees' reading improvement. The results of this study have shown that the tutees of the trained tutors were promoted more rapidly than those of untrained tutors, and were promoted to a mean of almost one more book level. This, in itself, is good evidence for the effectiveness of the behavioural peer tutoring.

The small gains made in comprehension scores by the different groups, although not statistically significant are in line with the gains in reading accuracy. The tuition of the tutees was aimed primarily at increasing reading *accuracy* and for the tutees of the Experimental Group this included the use of strategies that utilise context. As reading accuracy improves, the ability to use meaning, as a clue to word identification, should also improve. An increase in reading accuracy will facilitate greater understanding of the text which will in turn assist greater reading accuracy. Thus the small gains made by the Experimental Group tutees suggests that they were perhaps more aware of meaning.

The results for the tutees' self-corrective behaviour show that the tutees of control group I performed at a low level compared to the Experimental Group tutees. This suggests that the tutees trained in the 'Pause, Prompt and Praise' method achieved a higher level of independence than the other groups.

McNaughton & Glynn (of McNaughton *et al.*, 1981), who pioneered the 'Pause, Prompt and Praise' method, have subsequently also been involved in a successful study demonstrating clear gains on a behavioural peer tutoring programme (Limbrick, McNaughton & Glynn, 1983, unpublished). This study, however, involved two groups of only three trained and three untrained tutors aged 10–11 years tutoring 6–8 year olds in a multiple baseline design. Their peer tutoring method was based on the paired reading technique of Morgan & Lyon (1979) rather than their own 'Pause, Prompt and Praise' procedure, and hence comparisons with the present study are precluded. Our successful demonstration of peer tutoring of reading using the behavioural 'Pause, Prompt and Praise' technique appears to be the only study on this so far completed. Our findings recommend its use to a wider audience of researchers and practitioners of peer tutoring in schools. The behavioural 'Pause, Prompt and Praise' technique offers a clearly specified and relatively easily trainable set of key tutoring behaviours which are shown to be effective and which can be readily monitored.

REFERENCES

ALLEN, R.A. & BORAKS, N. (1978) Peer tutoring: putting it to the test *The Reading Teacher*, 32, pp. 274–278.

ALLEN, V.L. (Ed.) (1976) *Children as Teachers: theory and research on tutoring* (New York, Academic Press).

CLAY, M.M. (1972) *Reading: the patterning of complex behaviour*, 2nd edn 1979 (London, Heinemann Educational).

CLOWARD, R.D. (1967) Studies in tutoring, *Journal of Experimental Education*, 36, pp. 14–25.

DEVIN-SHEEHAN, L. & ALLEN, V.L. (1976) Implementing tutoring programs: some alternatives for practitioners and researchers, in: V. L. Allen (Ed.) *Children as Teachers: theory and research on tutoring* (New York, Academic Press).

ELLSON, D.G., BARBER, L., ENGLE, T.L. & KAMPWERTH, L. (1965) Programmed tutoring: attaching aid and a research tool, *Reading Research Quarterly*, 1, pp. 71–127.

ELLSON, D.G., HARRIS, P. & BARBER, L. (1968) A field test of programmed and directed tutoring, *Reading Research Quarterly*, 3, pp. 307–367.

FELDMAN, R.S., DEVIN-SHEEHAN, L. & ALLEN, V.L. (1976) Children tutoring children: a critical review of research, in: V. L. Allen (Ed.) *Children as Teachers: theory and research on tutoring* (New York, Academic Press).

GLYNN, T. (1981) Behavioural research in remedial education: more power to the parents, in: K. Wheldall (Ed.) *The Behaviourist in the Classroom: aspects of applied behavioural analysis in British educational contexts* (Birmingham, Educational Review Publications).

GLYNN, T., MCNAUGHTON, S.S., ROBINSON, V. & QUINN, M. (1979) *Remedial Reading at Home: helping you to help your child* (Wellington, New Zealand Council for Educational Research).

GOODLAD, S. (1979) *Learning by Teaching: an introduction to tutoring* (London, Community Service Volunteers).

HARRISON, G.V. (1976) Structured tutoring: Antidote for low achievement, in: V. L. Allen (Ed.) *Children as Teachers: theory and research on tutoring* (New York, Academic Press).

KLOSTERMAN, R. (1970) The effectiveness of a diagnostically structured reading program, *The Reading Teacher*, 24, pp. 159–162.

LIMBRICK, E., MCNAUGHTON, S. & GLYNN, T. (1983) Reading gains for underachieving tutors and tutees in a cross age peer tutoring program, *Unpublished manuscript*, Department of Education, University of Auckland.

MCNAUGHTON, S. & DELQUADRI, J. (1978) Error attention tutoring in oral reading, in: T. Glyn & S. McNaughton (Eds) *Applied Behaviour Analysis in New Zealand* (Auckland, Education Department, University of Auckland).

MCNAUGHTON, S. & GLYNN, T. (1981) Delayed versus immediate attention to oral reading errors: effects on accuracy and self-correction, *Educational Psychology*, 1, pp. 57–65.

MCNAUGHTON, S., GLYNN, T. & ROBINSON, V.M. (1981) *Parents as Remedial Reading Tutors: issues for home and school* (Wellington, New Zealand Council for Educational Research).

MELARAGNO, R.J. (1976) The tutorial community, in: V. L. Allen (Ed.) *Children as Teachers* (New York, Academic Press).

MORGAN, R. & LYON, E. (1979) 'Paired Reading': a preliminary report on a technique for parental tuition of reading retarded children, *Journal of Child Psychology*, 20, pp. 151–160.

NEALE, M.D. (1966) *Neale Analysis of Reading Ability* (London, MacMillan).

NIEDERMEYER, F.C. (1970) Training of tutors, *Journal of Educational Research*, 64, pp. 119–123.

NIEDERMEYER, F.C. (1976) Development or selection of school-based tutorial system, in: V. L. Allen (Ed.) *Children as Teachers: theory and research on tutoring* (New York, Academic Press).

PAOLITTO, D.P. (1976) The effect of cross-age tutoring on adolescents: an inquiry into theoretical assumptions, *Review of Educational Research*, 46(2), pp. 215–237.

SHAVER, J.P. & NUHN, D. (1971) Underachievers in reading and writing, *Journal of Educational Research*, 65, pp. 107–112.

STRAIN, P. S. (Ed.) (1981) *The Utilisation of Classroom Peers as Behaviour Change Agents* (New York, Plenum Press).

Teaching Self-management Strategies for Independent Story Writing to Children with Classroom Behaviour Difficulties

INGRID RUMSEY & KEITH D. BALLARD

ABSTRACT *Seven primary school children with behaviour difficulties showed low levels of on-task writing behaviour, high levels of off-task disruptive behaviour and a low number of words written during regular classroom story writing sessions. Introduction of self-recording of work behaviours during story writing for the whole class of 34 children was associated with increased on-task, decreased off-task disruptive behaviour and an increased number of words written for target children. There was also an increased number of words written by six other children for whom story writing data was collected. Introduction of say-do correspondence training for five of the target children showed further increases in independent story writing behaviour and reductions in off-task behaviours that disrupted the written language sessions.*

A primary function of the classroom teacher is to facilitate learning. When children in a class behave in ways that interrupt the classroom programme then some form of intervention can be justified. Children experiencing behaviour difficulties can interfere with the academic progress of other pupils as well as impede their own learning (Rutter, 1975), while classroom problems have been shown to be a major cause of stress among primary school teachers (Galloway, Boswell, Panckhurst, Boswell & Green, 1982).

When disruptive behaviour is evident in a classroom, first consideration for both educational and ethical reasons must be given to evaluating the appropriateness of the curriculum, the competence of the teacher and the efficacy of instructional strategies and materials. If these critical areas are being well managed, then it may be necessary to focus attention on the children. An intervention programe that directly targets child behaviour should aim at developing positive skills, preferably in a way that encourages children toward independence through monitoring and managing their own behaviours.

The present study took place in a primary school classroom comprising 34 children. Seven of the children in the class experienced difficulties in working independently, particularly during story writing time, when they showed limited attendance to the written assignment and tended to disturb the work of others. When children are asked to generate their own writing they are being required independently to perform a complex academic task. Writing involves focusing attention on a topic and on the content of the written communication, producing the written script and executing various dictionary and proof-reading skills. Assuming that these behaviours are part of the child's repertoire, then their performance is largely a matter under the control of the individual.

Teaching children self-management skills would seem to be a positive strategy that develops independence and could lead to increased attention and application to classroom assignments. An essential component of self-management involves identifying and monitoring one's own responses. Self-monitoring alone has been shown to produce behaviour change in some (e.g. Broden, Hall & Mitts, 1971) but not all (e.g. O'Leary & Dubey, 1979) self-management studies. The present study evaluated self-monitoring alone as an initial intervention. Children who showed no response to this strategy were then to be involved in a second intervention.

The second self-management strategy evaluated in the present study involved establishing correspondence between children's verbal descriptions of desired behaviours (saying) and their actual performance of the response (doing). The essential training components for this strategy were identified in research by Risley (1977) and involve description of the behaviours required; teacher comment on the correspondence between saying and doing; predictable occurrence of training sessions; guidance of verbal statements so they contain required behaviours and not just those already being performed; and feedback to the teacher so that she or he can provide accurate comment.

Most studies of this procedure for using verbal self-statements to control behaviour have involved preschool children (e.g. Israel & Brown, 1977; Rogers-Warren & Baer, 1976), although Ballard & Jenner (1981) increased the social interaction and social play behaviours of two children in an elementary school setting by teaching intention statements and praising for correspondence between these and the child's social performance, and Whitman, Scibak, Butler, Richter & Johnson (1982) used say-do training to improve the classroom behaviour of some 9- to 12-year-old children in special education classes.

The present study evaluated the use of self-monitoring and correspondence training as procedures for helping children to engage in appropriate academic and social classroom behaviours, thereby indirectly reducing rates of disruptive non-learning behaviours. Seven pupils were observed through five phases of the study for 50 sessions over a period of two school terms. On-task writing behaviour, off-task disruptive behaviour and work product (number of words written) were the dependent variables. Data on amount written is important, as studies have shown students to increase on-task behaviour without increasing work product, and also that the reverse can be true, with work output increasing without an increase in observed on-task behaviours (Klein, 1979). Another measurement issue involves the need to evaluate the quality as well as the quantity of written work. This was achieved in the present study by obtaining independent subjective evaluations of the children's stories from experts in the area of children's written language.

Method

Subjects

The study was undertaken in a State primary school, in a class into which some children with a past history of behaviour difficulties had been placed so that they would be with an experienced senior teacher. This teacher agreed to participate in the study and the first author then observed the class on three occasions to note possible subjects. On-task and off-task disruptive behaviour for 12 pupils was recorded and seven of these children with the highest incidence of off-task disruptive behaviour were identified as potential subjects. Independent teacher evaluation of pupil behaviour confirmed this selection as including the children most in need of help toward independent work. Off-task behaviour typically exhibited during the observations included, loud talking, calling out to teacher or to pupils in another section of the room, being out of seat for no useful or appropriate reason, flicking paper and touching or pushing other children.

The children selected were six boys and one girl (S7) who ranged in age from nine years two months to eleven years one month.

Story writing data was also collected from a group of children other than the target subjects. This was to provide information on work product current amongst other children in the classroom during written language sessions throughout the study. A group of five girls with ages ranging from nine years one month to ten years three months formed this comparison group. These children were selected for administrative reasons, and may not be representative of the class. Nevertheless, the group provides some data on responses of children other than those in the target group.

Setting

All observations were carried out in the classroom during a 25-minute written language session (story writing) which took place three mornings a week between approximately 9.20 a.m. and 9.50 a.m. There were 34 children in the class, 18 boys and 16 girls.

Observation Definitions and Procedures

On-task and off-task disruptive behaviours. During story writing sessions observers recorded pupil behaviour using three observation categories.

On-task behaviours were defined as writing (pencil in hand, and not more than five centimetres above the paper being written on, or pencil actually making purposeful lines on the page); the child looking at the blackboard with pencil in hand; the child consulting a dictionary; and the child reading what s/he had written. Any occurrence of these behaviours in the 10-second interval meant that the interval was coded on-task unless off-task disruptive behaviour occurred. An interval was coded off-task if any off-task disruptive behaviour occurred during the 10-second observation internal.

Off-task disruptive behaviours were identified as behaviours incompatible with story writing and likely to interrupt the teacher and other children. These behaviours were defined as talking (voice clearly audible to the observer, facing another pupil and saying more than one word); laughing (audible to the observer); touching other pupils so that they respond in some way (e.g. looking up); and out of seat behaviour (the child completely out of the seat so that no part of his/her person touches the chair).

Where behaviours that were neither on-task nor off-task disruptive occurred throughout a 10-second observation interval then these were coded as neutral. This category included hand up, indicating that the pupil wished to see the teacher; rubbing out what had been written; sharpening pencil; opening and closing desk; turning pages of a book; teacher talking to pupil; fiddling with objects; and watching other children.

Observation procedures and reliability. Interval recording involving a 10-second observation interval followed by five seconds for recording was used. An electronic timer provided auditory signals to earphones and this allowed a second observer to operate concurrently but independently in every third session to provide reliability data. The first author was the main observer for the study, with three other trained observers who were unaware of the aims of the research acting in turns as reliability observers. Inter-observer agreement was calculated by comparing the two records interval by interval for each child and dividing the number of observer agreements by the total number of agreements plus disagreements. Agreement was scored when both observers recorded the same behaviour during the same 10-second observation interval. Disagreement was scored when one observer recorded a behaviour code that the other had not.

Evaluation of Children's Stories

During the baseline phase, at the end of sessions 3, 6, 9, 10 and 11 all of the children's stories were collected by the teacher and the number of words written by the target subjects and by children in the comparison group were counted and recorded. This was not done for every session because of the additional demand it placed on the teacher. The children were not aware that their stories were evaluated in any way.

During the experimental phases at the end of each session, all pupils in the class counted the number of words they had written and then entered this information on to a bar-graph which was pasted into a folder. While they were doing this, the observer/s and the teacher moved round the room, picking up stories and counting the number of words written. Target children's scores were always checked; the total number of words being checked against the number entered by the pupil. If the numbers differed, then the teacher/observer and the pupil recounted together. All words were counted, including titles, crossed out words and attempted words.

A qualitative evaluation of stories written by target subjects from the first three phases of the study was undertaken. Stories from one session occurring midway in each of these phases (chosen because all children started a new story) were typed with no identification of name or date and exactly as presented by the children. The stories were then given separately to two Teachers' College lecturers who specialised in children's writing. They were told that the stories were written by children in a standard 3–4 class and were asked to give qualitiative assessments of the stories on a 1 to 5 scale, with 1 indicating a low rating and 5 a high rating.

Experimental Conditions

General procedures. As an introduction to each session, the teacher described the topic for the day's writing. This usually involved a presentation of 5–15 minutes, showing relevant books, pictures or maps, and asking the children questions about the topic. Instructions were then given on what the children were to write about, such as, "Today I want you to pretend that you were a boy or girl living in Dunedin 100 years ago and I want you to write about what it was like at home. Describe your home and the jobs you had to do".

Before the pupils went to their desks, the teacher asked if there were any questions about the set task and then reminded students that this was a quiet writing time and that they were not to talk or leave their desks. They were told that they had 25 minutes to write their story and could seek assistance from the teacher if necessary by raising their hand. These procedures were followed through all phases of the study.

Phase 1: baseline phase. The general procedures operated and observers recorded the children's behaviour and counted the number of words in subjects' stories as earlier described.

Phase 2: self-recording. This procedure was applied to the whole class but data was collected only for the target subjects and the comparison group. General procedures continued, but an audio-tape was played during the lesson which emitted a series of auditory signals on a variable interval schedule. The intervals between signals varied between 1 and 5 minutes.

All children were given folders which contained self-recording charts. The children were told that when a signal tone sounded, they were to immediately write into their chart either 'W' for working, or '—' for not working. To enter 'W', they had to be either writing, reading what they had written, reading words from the blackboard or pausing to think what to write next with pencil in hand. If they were not doing any of these they were to record a minus sign to indicate not working at that time. At the end of the lesson the children counted the number of 'W's, entered this on to a graph and wrote a brief comment on their effort during the lesson, such as "very good". On a second graph they entered the number of words they had written.

Although the class teacher moved round informally, noting if children were accurately recording behaviour, no effort was made on the part of the experimenter to assess the degree to which pupils were being honest. However, checking on the number of words per story was carried out, as already described.

Phase 3: return to baseline conditions phase. Pupils' folders containing their charts were collected and held by the experimenter for a period of six days. No explanation was given. General procedures continued and observers recorded behaviours during the story writing periods.

Phase 4: reinstatement of self-recording phase. The same conditions operating in Phase 2 were reinstated.

Phase 5: correspondence training. The intervention involved in this phase was intended for those children who might benefit from assistance in addition to any provided by the self-monitoring.

In this phase correspondence training was undertaken in an unused staffroom adjacent to the classroom before each of the story writing sessions began. The participating child attended alone and sat opposite the experimenter at a table. Each session lasted approximately three minutes and conformed to the say-do training requirements identified by Risley (1977), except that the sessions commenced with children supplying their own feedback. They displayed their charts and described the results from the previous story writing lesson. Where appropriate, the experimenter praised the child's recording and/or working behaviour. Where recording or work was deemed inadequate, the experimenter asked the child to complete the recording task each day as directed.

Correspondence training commenced in the first training session with the experimenter holding up a chart on which were listed the four desired behaviours and then proceeding as follows:

> Here are some things you can do to make sure you will work really well during story writing time:
> 1. I will work on my story.
> 2. I will try to write a really good story.
> 3. I will not talk to others.
> 4. I will ignore people who try to interrupt me.
>
> Now, tell me what you are going to do during story time tomorrow... (child responds). That's very good. Now I will cover this chart and you tell me again what you are going to do during story time next day.

At all successive training sessions the child was asked: "Now tell me what you are going to do to make sure you will work really well during story writing time today". (If the child forgot what to say, the experimenter uncovered the chart, let the pupil read the statements. Then the chart was covered again and the above question was repeated.)

When the child had repeated the statements accurately, the experimenter commented on the previous story writing session, e.g. either "Yes, and I saw you do that" or, "Yes, but you didn't do that last time I was watching. I saw you turn round and talk to Paul when he called out to you".

The training session was completed with the experimenter saying, "All right, now we'll see how you go today".

Experimental Design and Data Analysis

Evaluation of the experimental effects of self-recording involved an ABAB withdrawal design. Evaluation of the effects of say-do training on five individual children involved a multiple baseline design across five subjects.

In a withdrawal design, experimental control is demonstrated if, after baseline measurement, the application of a treatment leads to improvement, and conversely a deterioration results after treatment is withdrawn (Hersen & Barlow, 1976). In a multiple baseline design, experimental control is shown when the experimenter applies a treatment procedure to one subject and demonstrates an improvement while no change occurs in other monitored subjects. The same treatment is then applied in sequence to each subject to demonstrate that behaviour changes only at the time an intervention occurs.

Results

Reliability of Observation Measures

Interobserver agreement data for the classroom observation sessions were obtained on 16 of the 50 sessions; that is for 32% of all sessions. Interobserver agreement ranged from 89% to 100% with a mean of 96%.

Results of Experimental Data

Fig. 1 presents the percent on-task behaviour, percent off-task disruptive behaviour and the number of words per story in each session for the target children over all phases of the study. From Fig. 1 it is evident that for the children S3, S4, S5, S6 and S7, self-recording was associated with an increase in on-task behaviour and number of words written, and with a decrease in off-task disruptive behaviour, compared to baseline levels. Target children S1 and S2 show more variable responding, with a marked increase in on-task behaviour and words written for S1 toward the end of the phase, while S2 shows improvements over baseline levels on occasion. The return to baseline phase shows no clear reversal to baseline patterns of on-task behaviour, although Fig. 1 shows that S6 was markedly high in off-task disruptive behaviour and therefore low in on-task behaviour in this phase, an apparent continuation of responding evident in the last session of the preceding phase. However, in the withdrawal phase all target children show number of words written closer to baseline than self-recording phase levels.

From Fig. 1 it can be seen that reinstatement of self-recording was associated with recovery of high levels of on-task and low off-task disruptive behaviours for S6, while S7 showed a continued high on-task and low off-task disruptive pattern, but with overall lower number of words per story than achieved for this subject in the self-recording phase.

For S1 to S5 variable responding was evident in the second self-recording phase and so these children were involved in say-do training. From Fig. 1 it can be seen that each of these children showed consistently high levels of on-task behaviours and low levels of off-task disruptive behaviours in comparison to the data for each child in all preceding phases. Fig. 1 shows that the number of words written by these children in the say-do training phase was generally above baseline levels and above the levels recorded in the second self-recording phase.

Table I summarises the data for the target children and presents the mean number of words per story for the comparison children in each phase. For target children, Table 1 shows that on-task behaviour and words written were higher and off-task disruptive behaviour lower in self-recording phases in contrast to the two baseline phases. It also shows the further improved responding achieved in the say-do training phase for five children. Table I also shows that for the comparison children self-recording alone was associated with a substantial increase in amount written and that this maintained during the withdrawal phase. Each individual, except for one, more than doubled their baseline output, the exception being a child already writing 109 words per session in baseline who, nevertheless, increased in subsequent phases.

Finally, subjective evaluation of stories written by target children from the first three phases of the study showed that 43% received the same grades from both judges, 52% differed by one grade and 5% by two grades. The judges' ratings were combined and gave a mean baseline rating of 2.7, self-recording 3.3 and withdrawal

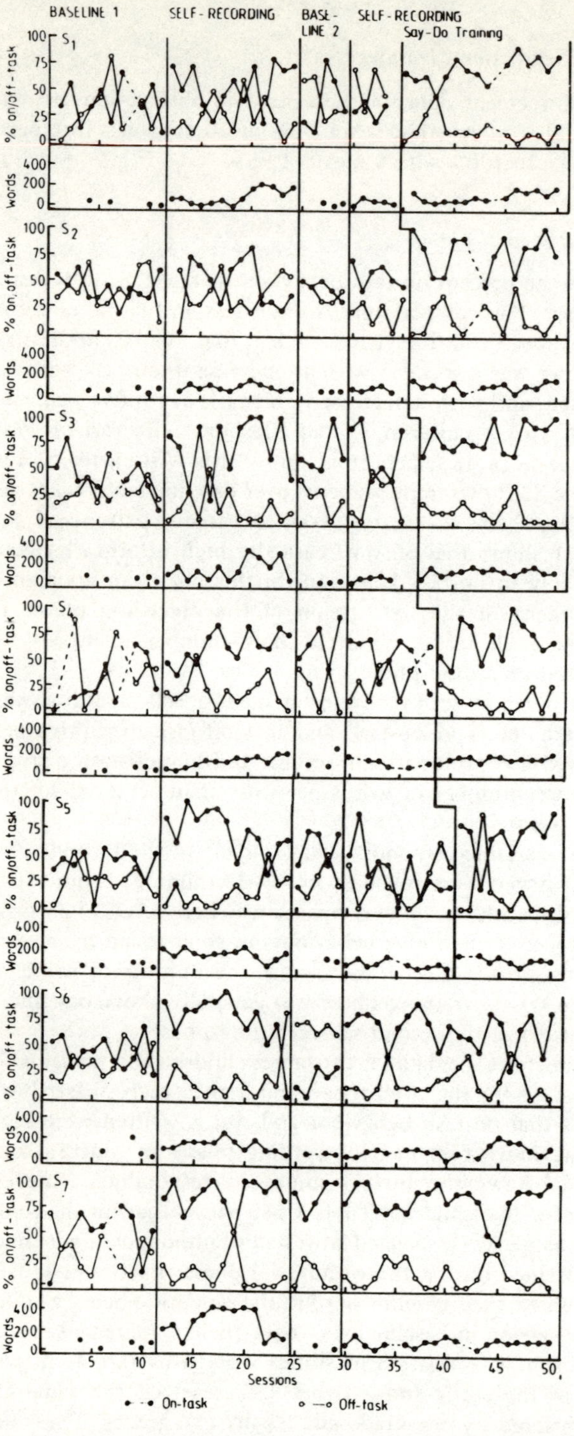

FIG. 1. Percent on-task behaviour, percent off-task disruptive behaviour and number of words per story, for target children across all phases of the study.

TABLE I. Mean percent on-task behaviour, mean percent off-task disruptive behaviour and mean number of words for target children and mean number of words for the six comparison children, across all phases of the study

	Phase 1 baseline	Phase 2 self-recording	Phase 3 withdraw self-recording	Phase 4 self-recording	Phase 5 say-do training (five children)
Target children					
On-task	38	66	54	56	74
Off-task disruptive	32	19	32	26	12
No. of words	48	140	60	71	116
Comparison children					
No. of words	57	130	129	111	

phase mean 2.9. In phase two, the children S2, S4, S5, S6 and S7 improved their subjective rating, S3 remained the same, while S1 showed a decrease in qualitative rating in comparison to baseline scores.

Discussion

In the present study self-recording alone was shown to be associated with an increase in on-task behaviour, a decrease in off-task disruptive behaviour and an increase in the number of words written during writing time by seven children who initially showed low levels of independent work and displayed behaviours that impeded both their own work and that of others in the classroom. For five of the seven children the subjectively evaluated quality of the stories also improved when the amount written increased. One child showed no change and one a decline in qualitative rating with increased output.

The self-recording procedures were applied to the whole class and data on six non-target children showed substantial increases over baseline levels in words written occurring with the introduction of self-recording. Removal of the self-recording folders had no obvious impact on the amount written by this group. This result is clearly a threat to causal attribution in the withdrawal design for this group. However, given that all comparison group children showed substantially increased responding in the intervention phase, it may also be argued that naturally occurring contingencies associated with story writing maintained responding for these children when formal self-recording was not present.

These results contribute to other findings that have shown self-recording alone to be an effective self-management strategy for some children (e.g. Broden, Hall & Mitts, 1971; Johnson & White, 1971; Lovitt, 1973). In the present case both children experiencing behaviour problems in the classroom and non-exceptional individuals in the same setting showed improved academic responding in story writing. The target children also increased their independent attention to assigned work and consequently reduced their interference with the work of other children.

In the present study the effects of the say-do intervention can only be seen in the context of the children's prior experience of the self-recording phases. Nevertheless, in this context, teaching children to state an intention to work independently, not interact with others and try to write a good story and subsequently having an informed adult comment on correspondence between statement and performance, were associated with high levels of on-task story writing behaviour and low levels of off-task disruptive behaviour for five children who initially showed behaviour difficulties in class work.

Few studies have used say-do training with school age children (Ballard, 1983). The present results therefore are significant in suggesting that this strategy warrants further evaluation as a device for helping children learn to manage their own behaviour. Each training session required only two to three minutes of adult and child time, suggesting, as Ballard & Jenner (1981) showed, that this intervention may be readily implemented by classroom teachers. Alternatively, as in the present study, a psychologist or some other resource person in a school could be involved in running the training sessions.

A limitation of the present study that future research should attend to is the lack of follow-up data showing child behaviour beyond the end of intervention. The present investigation ran over 23 weeks and resources were not available for further data collection. Nevertheless, the present data were collected during regular classroom sessions over 6 months and they represent an applied study of child self-management procedures in a natural setting.

Acknowledgements

Grateful acknowledgement is extended to the teacher and children who participated in the study, and to Hilary Hornbrook, Bill Harper and John Smith for their valued assistance with the research.

This paper is based on a study submitted by the first author in partial fulfilment of the requirements for the MEd degree, University of Otago.

REFERENCES

BALLARD, K.D. (1983) Teaching children to do what they say they will do: a review of research with suggested applications for exceptional children, *The Exceptional Child*, 30, pp. 119–125.

BALLARD, K.D. & JENNER, L. (1981) Establishing correspondence between saying and doing as a procedure for increasing the social behaviours of two elementary school children, *The Exceptional Child*, 28, pp. 55–62.

BRODEN, M., HALL, R.V. & MITTS, B. (1971) The effect of self-recording on the classroom behavior of two eighth-grade students, *Journal of Applied Behavior Analysis*, 4, pp. 191–199.

GALLOWAY, D., BOSWELL, K., PANCKHURST, F., BOSWELL, C. & GREEN, K. (1982) Satisfaction with teaching, *National Education*, 64, pp. 206–213.

HERSEN, N. & BARLOW, D.H. (1976) *Single Case Experimental Designs: strategies for studying behavior change* (New York, Pergamon).

ISRAEL, A.C. & BROWN, M.S. (1977) Correspondence training, prior verbal training, and control of non-verbal behavior via control of verbal behavior, *Journal of Applied Behavior Analysis*, 10, pp. 333–338.

JOHNSON, S.M. & WHITE, G. (1971) Self observation as agent of behavioral change, *Behavior Therapy*, 2, pp. 488–497.

KLEIN, R.D. (1979) Modifying academic performance in the grade school classroom, in: M. Hersen, R. M. Eisler & P. M. Miller (Eds) *Progress in Behavior Modification*, Vol. 4, pp. 293–321 (New York, Academic Press).

LOVITT, T.C. (1973) Self-management projects with children with behavioral disorders, *Journal of Learning Disabilities*, 6, pp. 138–150.

O'LEARY, S.G. & DUBEY, D.R. (1979) Applications of self-control procedures by children: a review, *Journal of Applied Behavior Analysis*, 12, pp. 449–465.

RISLEY, T.R. (1977) The social context of self-control, in: R. B. Stuart (Ed.) *Behavioral Self-management: strategies, techniques and outcomes*, pp. 77–81 (New York, Bruner-Mazel).

ROGERS-WARREN, A. & BAER, D.M. (1976) Correspondence between saying and doing: teaching children to share and praise, *Journal of Applied Behavior Analysis*, 9, pp. 335–354.

RUTTER, M. (1975) *Helping Troubled Children* (Harmondsworth, Penguin).

WHITMAN, T.L., SCIBAK, J.W., BUTLER, K.M., RICHTER, R. & JOHNSON, M.R. (1982) Improving class-room behavior in mentally retarded children through correspondence training, *Journal of Applied Behavior Analysis*, 15, pp. 545–564.

A Behavioural Approach to Teaching Subsidiary Physics to Engineering Students

BRIAN PICKTHORNE & KEVIN WHELDALL

ABSTRACT *A modified version of the Keller Plan or Personalised System of Instruction (PSI) was employed in a controlled experiment designed to evaluate the success of an innovatory behavioural teaching approach in Higher Education. Technology students studying subsidiary physics were randomly allocated to two groups. One group was taught under a traditional lecture format and the other under a modified PSI format. The PSI group were able to earn free time and bonus coursework marks for successfully completing fortnightly criterion tests. The results showed that fewer PSI students failed the course or passed with low marks and that overall their mean scores on the exam were significantly higher, by about 10%.*

Problems of unsatisfactory student motivation and consequent poor attainment constitute a continual challenge in many areas of higher education. This is often particularly serious in the case of Higher Education courses which are ancillary or subsidiary to the student's main course of study. Unfortunately, little has been done to resolve these problems effectively and little consideration has been given to the potential applications of applied behavioural analysis in this context, in spite of the fact that there are good grounds for believing that such measures might be both effective and efficient. In this paper a novel strategy, based on applied behavioural analysis, which was devised in an attempt to improve both the motivation and attainment of students undertaking a typical subsidiary Higher Education course, is described and analysed. The behavioural approach employed was based on Keller's Personalised System of Instruction.

The Personalised System of Instruction (PSI) or 'Keller Plan' was originally devised by F. S. Keller in 1964 for implementation in the newly founded Department of Psychology at the new University of Brasilia. PSI constitutes a radical innovation in higher education teaching being based primarily on the behavioural psychology of B. F. Skinner. It calls for a drastic reappraisal of current educational philosophy and practices and requires that we implement what we know about the processes of learning directly into the students' study programme. Its emphasis is on the student learning rather than on the tutor teaching since little overt teaching is employed. Keller's original paper on this was in fact entitled 'Goodbye teacher...' (Keller, 1968).

PSI has five defining characteristics: (1) mastery learning; (2) self-pacing; (3) emphasis on the written word; (4) student proctors; and (5) lectures as inspirational/motivational devices rather than as information giving devices.

In practice this means that courses are very carefully structured into a series of units of (primarily written) material. The student's task is to master the material in each unit and to be able to demonstrate his mastery before he is allowed to proceed to the next unit. Mastery of a unit is assessed by means of short (10–20 minute) criterion tests in which the student answers questions on the material he has learned. Typical questions often require one word answers or selection from multiple choices and are similar, in some respects, to the type of questions employed in teaching machines or programmed texts. The student is allowed to attempt the test as many times as is necessary to demonstrate mastery of the subject matter. (This is often operationally defined as 80 to 90% correct responses.) Success is rewarded by the student being allowed to proceed to the next unit whilst there are *no* penalties for failure. Thus the student can pace himself and progress at his own preferred speed.

Emphasis on the written word follows from the first two defining characteristics, since students will require different amounts of time to master the unit topic. The material, however, must be of higher quality than is usually the case, and must be more carefully structured with the objectives clearly laid out. It is the tutor's role to produce such materials and continually to adapt and modify them, contingent upon student feedback. In order to do this successfully (i.e. to allow sufficient time), it is urged that student proctors are employed. Student proctors act as teachers' aides by providing individual attention, when needed, and also by administering and marking criterion tests.

Finally, lectures (and films, demonstrations, etc.) are not used in their traditional manner (i.e. in an attempt to convey information), but are employed primarily to inspire and motivate students and are *contingent* upon the students having mastered sufficient units of material so as to appreciate them. Further specific details of PSI are given in 'The Keller Plan Handbook' by F. S. Keller and J. G. Sherman (1974). The system has met with considerable success in the United States, but has been relatively slow to catch on in the UK. When it has been tried in this country it has mainly been in the teaching of science and technology although on the social science side it has been employed by Mack in the Department of Social Psychology, University of Loughborough (Mack, 1977).

Kulik, Kulik & Cohen (1979) have recently presented a 'meta-analysis of outcome studies of Keller's Personalised System of Instruction'. Meta-analysis is a relatively new technique and is defined as "the application of statistical methods to results from a large collection of individual studies" with the aim of thereby being able to "draw reliable and general conclusions from a diverse and voluminious literature" (p. 307). Kulik *et al.* present their meta-analysis of 75 comparative studies employing PSI.

Of the 61 studies in which final examination performance was compared for PSI and lecture teaching, 48 studies (79%) reported statistically significant results, *all* of which favoured PSI. Of the 48 studies where class averages could be converted to percentages, PSI averaged 73.6% in the final examination, compared with 65.9% in 'conventional' classes ($p<0.0001$). Course grades and students' rating of courses were also shown to be significantly higher for PSI taught courses. Investigations of study time revealed that PSI required no more time investment by students than study time on conventional courses. Retention examinations, taken several weeks after the completion of the course (and which did not affect course grade), showed clearly that PSI course students retained more than conventionally taught students, after the effects of last minute exam cramming had begun to wear off. PSI superiority was also shown to be present in both essay type and objective, multiple choice methods of assessments; nor was there any evidence to suggest that PSI was less effective with 'high-aptitude' students since high and low aptitude students benefitted equally. On the other hand, there was evidence to show that the 'PSI effect' (superior performance on PSI taught courses) was stronger for certain courses than others. Mathematics, engineering and psychology yielded a stronger PSI effect than the "physical and life sciences and the social sciences". In summary, Kulik *et al.*'s meta-analysis confirms the more subjective reviews of the PSI literature (e.g. Boud, 1975).

The main aim of the present study was to investigate the employment of behavioural techniques, in the form of a modified personalised system of instruction, with the object of increasing levels of student motivation and consequent attainment. Our aim was to demonstrate that students taught by these methods would score significantly higher in mastery tests, and also in their final examination, than students taught by a traditional lecture method.

Method

Subjects

Thirty-one male first year British Higher Education (technology) students studying a subsidiary course in physics were randomly allocated to two groups. The two groups were taught by two different lecturers, both of whom had been teaching a similar course to similar groups for five years. During this time there had been no significant differences between the pass rates of their respective groups of students. Both lecturers were experienced and were of similar background and qualifications. The age range of the students taking this course was 18–23 years. Their qualifications were closely comparable as were their 'entry test' scores. In all respects these students had backgrounds which were comparable to those of students who had taken this course in the previous five years. Group 'A' ($N=16$) was subsequently designated the 'control' group and group 'B' ($N=15$) was designated the 'experimental' group. The latter, experimental, group was taught by the first author.

Course Details

The subsidiary course under investigation was of 20 weeks duration culminating in a 2 hour written examination. Each weekly session lasted for 2½ hours, and consisted of a 1 hour lecture with demonstrations, tutorial/assignment work and student experiments occupying the remainder of the time. The teaching environment, time allocation for the course and the course and general facilities were generally satisfactory. Both groups were given the same syllabus and course content as had been given to students in previous years.

The success rate for this course was particularly unsatisfactory in view of the fact that it was not considered to be academically demanding. In the previous year nine students out of a total of 27 had failed the course outright. Even though the pass mark was only 40% many of the remainder only just passed the course. There was a similar pattern in the previous 4 years and a number of attempts had been made to improve the overall pass rate. It was felt that the students considered that the course was not important (even though they had been repeatedly informed of the essential value of the course and the fact that they were required to pass it). In view of all these factors the course had acquired a poor reputation.

Procedure

Students in the 'experimental' group were told that the course would be divided into four main modules made up of two associated 'topics' and that they would be given tests of their understanding of these using a special electronic 'feedback testing' system (described later). These eight tests were each of 15 minutes duration and were presented on a two-week schedule. The students were informed that they were required to satisfy a 'target score' on each test and that this score would commence at 50% which would then increase in small steps to 80%.

Those students who satisfied the criterion were allowed a 15 minute break, during the session in which the test was presented and also during the following week's session. Students who failed to reach target were required to undertake remedial work during these 15 minute sessions and carry out corrections on the test. The feedback from these tests gave each student a clear picture of the progress which he was making and the tests also helped to reveal areas of difficulty at an early stage (when the problems could be more easily rectified). They were told that they all had the opportunity of being successful in the tests and would be given full facilities.

The students in the experimental group were given a specially devised 'personal learning package'. This consisted of a series of 'organic notes' on each topic and they could build up their own understanding on this basic structure using the factual information, data sheets, references, worked examples of problems, a special series of linked laboratory experiments and 'self-testing' questions with which they were also provided. This 'personalised' scheme and the small, precise learning objectives were all geared towards maximising motivation.

So that level of motivation was sustained the students were told that those who obtained the 'target scores' in tests 4–8 could leave the session 15 minutes early (and thus miss the rush-hour traffic). In order to provide additional incentive the students were subsequently informed that if they satisfied the criterion in the last three tests they would be awarded a bonus of 15% on their final course assessment grade.

Students in the 'control group' were given five of the eight tests on the same schedule as the students in the 'experimental group'. However, they were not given target scores to satisfy or the special 'learning package'.

The criterion tests consisted of a range of multiple choice objective questions, reasoning problems and mathematical problems. Several of the tests were supplemented by written questions and numerical problems. These were all designed for rapid marking so that they could be returned to the student by the end of each session. The final assessment for the course was an externally validated and double marked written examination.

Unlike the basic Keller Plan the mastery tests were given on a fixed 'group' rather than on an 'individual' basis. Nevertheless, aspects of both the individuality and tutorial elements of the Plan were retained by the use of a special electronic 'feedback testing' system. Each student had an individual response unit connected to the master console on which all the responses were monitored. If the student pressed the correct response button in answer to a test question he was *immediately* (but privately) reinforced by a small light illuminating on his response unit. In this way the student was able to learn as he progressed through the test items. By looking at the 'pattern' of both individual and 'group' responses on the master console the lecturer could undertake more appropriate remedial action than would otherwise be possible in a short space of time.

Results

Table I shows criterion test scores for the experimental and control groups. As can be seen the 'experimental group' increase their scores appreciably over time. It also shows that their scores became significantly higher than those of the 'control group'. Even though the criterion was steadily increased, 13 out of the 15 students in the experimental group satisfied the criterion of 80% in the final test.

Those students who failed to satisfy a particular criterion still achieved considerable progress over the sequence of tests. Care was taken to inform such students that they were making good progress. For example there was one student who failed to satisfy any of the target scores but he still progressed from scores of around 30% to scores of around 70%. These effects also generalised and were accompanied by an overall improvement across the experimental group in all their experimental and assignment work for the courses.

There were no complementary or significant improvements over time in experimental or assignment work identified for the 'control group'. As can be seen from Table I there was no marked improvement in the test scores of the 'control group' who had been taught by a traditional lecture method. Analysis of the relative means of the test scores for both groups was undertaken. The results show that for tests 1 and 2 the means were not significantly different, but for the final three tests all mean differences were highly significant ($p<0.001$).

TABLE I. Criterion test scores for the two groups over the eight tests

		Experimental group (B) ($N=15$)			Control group (A) ($N=16$)					
Test no.	Criterion (%)	No. passing criterion	Mean	(sd)	No. passing criterion	Mean	(sd)	t	DF	p
1	50	10/15	51.60	(13.71)	10/16	48.31	(9.72)	0.77	29	NS
2	55	11/15	57.00	(12.31)	5/16	49.63	(7.92)	2.00	29	NS
3	60	12/13	66.78	(9.37)		—	—	—	—	
4	65	10/13	67.62	(9.00)		—	—	—	—	
5	70	8/15	69.93	(8.66)		—	—	—	—	
6	70	12/14	76.14	(7.85)	0/16	50.31	(6.87)	9.61	28	<0.001
7	80	11/15	80.93	(7.16)	0/16	54.13	(7.61)	10.09	29	<0.001
8	80	13/15	84.00	(6.60)	0/16	51.00	(6.83)	13.66	29	<0.001

In the final examination three students in the control group failed outright and a further two students had very poor marks of 45% or less. No students in the experimental group failed and the lowest score was 45% (one student). The mean score for the experimental group in this examination was 66.33% (sd 13.29) whereas the mean for the control group was only 55.94% (sd 15.77). This 10% difference was significant at the 5% level ($t=1.98$, one tailed). In previous years the differences between the groups, taught by the same two lecturers, were not significant. This is clearly illustrated by the results for 1977, which is typical of previous years; group A mean 48.71%, group B mean 49.93% (sds 10.94 and 7.52 respectively).

The students' performance in other examinations such as mathematics, electro-technology, chemistry, electronics and mechanical technology was also analysed. No significant differences in overall performance were observed except that the mean for the control group was slightly higher in each case and was significantly *higher* in chemistry. A subject closely related to physics, electronics, was used in an analysis of covariance which was subsequently undertaken of physics examination marks. Electronics examination marks were co-varied in an attempt to reduce error variance and thereby increase the sensitivity of the significance test. This confirmed the significant result of our earlier, simple one-tailed *t*-test ($F=6.01$, $p<0.025$).

Discussion

The results of this study supported the hypotheses that students taught by the modified PSI strategy show significant improvements in mastery test scores over time, that students taught by this strategy subsequently score significantly higher on mastery tests than the control group and that they also score significantly higher on the post course examination. Hence the investigation has demonstrated that student motivation and subsequent attainment can be significantly improved by the use of behavioural techniques.

It is interesting to note that Lee & McLean (1980) report improvements in attitude and achievement for students taught under a modified mastery learning method. In our method the students were given more information, assistance and hints in solving problems and undertaking experimental work than in Keller's basic scheme. Moreover, not only were lectures used to aid motivation but also to help prevent pitfalls and confusion from having adverse effects on motivation (i.e. students were alerted to potential learning difficulties and any confusion which was identified was immediately rectified).

In devising student experiments and exercises particular care was taken to ensure that these helped to stimulate interest. It was found that the employment of criterion tests, free-time bonuses and bonus assignment marks were acceptable and effective reinforcers for the Higher Education students. A weekly 'log' of observations and comments was kept during the investigation and analysis of the student's views indicated that they all considered the approach was beneficial in terms of increasing and maintaining their motivation. Moreover, they reported that the provision of the personalised system of instruction helped them to study at their own pace. It was felt to be a particularly 'cost effective' strategy in terms of the returns obtained for their effort.

It could be argued that the enthusiasm/motivation of the lecturer might have influenced the performance of the experimental group, via some sort of Hawthorne or teacher expectancy effect. This is shown to be an unlikely major, additional, influential independant variable since the changing criterior design clearly demonstrates control by the experimental procedure. Such a design, involving a changing criterion, is not a usual feature of PSI research and it must be emphasised that the present procedure differed in many important ways from traditional PSI. Student proctors were not employed, failed criterion tests were not re-taken and led to extra remedial work, testing was carried out on a group basis and the element of self-pacing was reduced. Hence, this experiment cannot be considered as a demonstration study of classic PSI in operation but rather that overtly behavioural techniques (based loosely on PSI methods) can be effectively employed in higher education.

Another criticism centres on the fact that the control group did not take all of the mastery tests. It could be argued that continual mastery testing led to the experimental effect. The question is, of course, one of balance between appropriate control versus dilution of the experimental effect by the incorporation of features of the experimental procedure into the control condition. Mastery testing is an essential feature of the experimental procedure but not of traditional lecture methods. Five of the eight tests were given to the control group as a compromise so as to allow comparison between the two groups at the beginning and end of the programme. This study was not an attempt at an experimental demonstration of any one single element of the method but of the overall behavioural teaching package. Clearly there is ample scope for research in refining the approach further by determining systematically the critical elements in the package. It could be, for example that extra time off or bonus course marks were unnecessary to the success of the programme.

From the lecturer's point of view although the implementation of the scheme was demanding on both time and preparation, the resulting improvements in motivation and attainment made this a most worthwhile exercise. However, having set up this scheme, the time and effort required in future would be considerably reduced. It would be interesting to compare the effort required by this strategy, once it was established and working, with that required by the conventional teaching method. We feel that this study demonstrates the value of behavioural approaches in Higher Education.

REFERENCES

BOUD, D.J. (1975) P.S.I. now—a review of progress and problems, *British Journal of Educational Technology*, 2, pp. 15–34.

KELLER, F.S. (1968) Goodbye teacher . . ., *Journal of Applied Behaviour Analysis*, 1, pp. 79–80.

KELLER, F.S. & SHERMAN, J.G. (1974) *The Keller Plan Handbook* (California, Benjamin).

KULIK, J.A., KULIK, C.C. & COHEN, P.A. (1979) A meta analysis of outcome studies of Keller's Personalized System of Instruction, *American Psychologist*, 34, pp. 307–318.

LEE, M.M. & MCLEAN, J.E. (1980) A comparison of achievement and attitudes among three methods of teaching educational psychology, *Journal of Educational Research*, 72, pp. 86–90.

MACK, D. (1977) Personalising learning in the introductory psychology course, *Bulletin of the British Psychological Society*, 30, pp. 312–314.

Section E.

Training Teachers and Parents to Use Behavioural Methods

Training Parents and Teachers in Remedial Reading Procedures for Children with Learning Difficulties

JEANETTE M. SCOTT & KEITH D. BALLARD

ABSTRACT *The mothers and classroom teachers of four 11–12-year-old low progress readers were trained in tutoring procedures that involved delaying attention to child reading errors, providing cues to help correct errors and praising specific reading strategies and achievements. A multiple baseline design across subjects was used to evaluate the effects of tutor training in both home and school settings. Baseline measures showed that one class teacher delayed attention to child errors and two teachers provided appropriate prompts, while the parents showed no occurrence of the tutoring behaviours. Following training, both teachers and parents applied the specific tutoring behaviours and these behaviours were shown to persist across a three to five week maintenance period during which the experimenter reduced training and feedback to tutors and at three one-month follow-up assessments. Pre-tests showed the children to have reading age levels three to five years behind an expected level for their chronological age. Post-tests showed the children to have an average gain in reading level of 28 months (range 24–48 months).*

Children who experience difficulty in learning to read will have problems in coping with most academic tasks. While research and debate continue to promote various strategies for teaching reading, one to one interactions between a tutor and a child has been suggested as an optimal setting for learning reading skills, particularly when regular classroom instruction appears to have failed (Glynn & McNaughton, 1975; McNaughton & Delquadri, 1978). Where professional resources are limited, then training parents or other interested persons to act as reading tutors can ensure delivery of remedial services (Bergan, 1977; Nay, 1979).

The present study was designed to train teachers and parents in the contingent praise and error correction procedures for tutoring reading developed by McNaughton and his co-workers (Glynn & McNaughton, 1975; McNaughton & Delquadri, 1978; McNaughton & Glynn, 1981). The effectiveness of these procedures for training parents as reading tutors and concomitant gains in child reading skills has been reported in a number of studies (Glynn, 1980; Glynn *et al.*, 1980; McNaughton, Glynn & Robinson, 1980; Love, 1981 [1]). One investigation by Glynn (1980) showed reading gains achieved in the home generalising to the school setting. However, Glynn *et al.* (1980) found that although their trained parent tutors achieved a mean reading age improvement in their children of 6.5 months across nine weeks of tutoring, only two of the eight children in the study showed reading gains in school. These researchers suggested that in order to achieve gains at school, instructional and motivational support in the regular classroom is probably necessary. In training both teachers and parents in the tutoring procedures, the present study attempted to assess the value and acceptability of the procedures to teachers and to evaluate the effect on child reading in both home and school settings of such a cooperative home-school approach.

The present study was also designed to assess the persistence of tutoring behaviour beyond the training phase. Research on training others has been criticised for failure to show generalisation and maintenance of skills (Bergan & Duley, 1981; Berkowitz & Graziano, 1972; O'Dell, 1974) and Glynn and his co-workers have not reported data on their parent tutors beyond the training phase. O'Dell (1974) suggested that effective training of others requires three steps: the person must acquire the modification skills and thus change their own behaviour; these changes must be implemented with the child; and the changes must generalise and persist. The present study was designed to include all three of these steps. Following the training and implementation phases the experimenter faded her involvement with tutors, but continued to collect data to see if tutor behaviours would persist in her absence.

The tutoring procedures described by Glynn *et al.* (1979) train the instructor in behaviours shown to promote independent error correction strategies by child readers. McNaughton & Delquadri (1978) showed that child reading skills improved if tutors delayed attending to errors until the end of a sentence and suggested that attention to errors should minimise interference with the meaning of the story, while providing just enough information for the reader to identify appropriate cues. If after two simple prompts the child fails to correct the error then the tutor provides the correct word to get the child reading again (Glynn *et al.*, 1980). The tutoring procedures also specify that praise should be given contingent on correct performance of a sentence or page, for self-correction of errors and for error correction following a prompt.

Method

Participants

The child participants for the study were four children, three boys and one girl (S2), aged 11–12.4 years old (mean age 11 years 10 months), attending regular classes at an Intermediate school in Dunedin city. The subjects were selected from children referred by their teachers as requiring remedial reading. To be included in the study both the classroom teacher and one of the child's parents must have agreed to train in the tutoring procedures. Pre-testing confirmed that all the children were having significant difficulty with reading. S4 had a three year delay in reading progress, while S1, S2 and S3 each recorded more than five years' reading retardation when their chronological ages were compared with their reading ages on the reading tests used in this study. Children in regular classrooms who show reading performance more than two years below their age appropriate reading level are usually regarded as having marked learning difficulties (Reynolds, 1981).

The adult participants in the study were the children's teachers and parents. S1's teacher had 40 years of professional experience, S2 and S3 had the same teacher who had seven years of professional experience, while S4's teacher was in his first year of teaching. All teachers were male.

In the home setting the mothers acted as the reading tutors. Family size varied between one sibling and six siblings and there was one single parent family (S2). Three of the mothers held part-time jobs. Only one child (S1) had previously received any remedial assistance with reading. The procedures of the study were explained to the parents, teachers and the children. All who were contacted agreed to participate in the study.

Settings

Tutoring was conducted by the mothers in the home setting and by the teachers in the school setting. The place and time of day was decided during the initial interview to suit the tutors. While the home tuition was carried out in the same area of each home throughout the study, either in the living room or kitchen, tutoring was conducted within several settings within the school. These included the classroom (with or without the remainder of the class), the school library (with or without the remainder of the class) or in a small office.

While the physical conditions were different for each subject, the physical setting for each tutor and child was constant throughout so that the tutor and the child sat side by side where both could read the book.

Throughout the study children participated in the regular classroom reading programme as well as the research procedure.

Reading Texts Used in the Study

One graded series was principally used throughout the programme with other similar remedial material used to supplement the series. The graded series consisted or high interest novels designed for older children, Approach Trend and Trend (Bird & Falk, 1977).

Assessment and Observation Procedures

Assessment of Reading Age Levels. At pre-test in March (prior to baseline) and post-test in December (after the three month follow-up period) the children were assessed on the Dunedin Teachers' College Informal Prose Inventory [2] and the Analytical Reading Inventory (Woods & Moe, 1977). Both of these inventories provide graded reading passages. The Analytical Reading Inventory established its reading levels on American norms (Spache, 1974; Harris & Sipay, 1975). The Dunedin Teachers' College Inventory uses a series of passages taken from the New Zealand Department of Education School Journals and bases reading age levels on the Elley noun frequency method (Elley, 1975).

Evaluation on two tests meant that the children responded to more reading material than would be the case with a single assessment. Also, given uncertainties surrounding the concept and measurement of reading age (Hansen & Lovitt, 1976), a more reliable and valid assessment might be achieved using two assessments. The children's reading age level was identified as the age level of the highest passage read with 95% accuracy. The grade levels of the Woods & Moe assessment were converted to the equivalent age levels.

A further indication of the instructional reading level achievement of the children at the beginning and close of the study was provided by the age level assigned by the publishers to the graded books used in tutoring. The level of achievement was identified as the highest grade reader being read with 95% accuracy. It is possible that test performance and book reading performance could differ. This may reflect inaccuracies in the assessments or different norming procedures by test developers and publishers. It would seem important, however, to evaluate both test performance and reading accuracy on book material, book reading providing a stronger context for reading cues based on meaning.

Assessment of Tutor and Child Reading Behaviours. Reading sessions were recorded in the home and school using a portable audio cassette recorder. All recorded reading was with novel (encountered for the first time) material. Children read from different books of the same series at home and at school.

Tapes were collected from the school and home each week and analysed prior to the next reading session. The analysis provided data indicating when a child was ready to proceed to the next level of reading difficulty. Promotions were made only at the end of a book, the books being selected by the experimenter.

An initial reading level and subsequent promotion from one reading level to the next, was based on the child reading the material with 95% accuracy rate. Woods & Moe (1977), among others (e.g. Hansen & Lovitt, 1976), suggest 95% accuracy as indicating the appropriate level of instructional reading material. The calculation of reading accuracy included prompted corrections and self-corrections as reading errors (Glynn & McNaughton, 1975).

Measures of Tutor Behaviour. The three tutor behaviours that were trained were to *pause* (measured by delayed attention), to *prompt* and to *praise* (McNaughton *et al.*, 1981).

The measures of tutor behaviour derived from the audio tape data were as follows:

Total Error Attention. This was the percentage of child errors which received some form of attention from the tutor. All errors, except those self-corrected by the child, offered an opportunity to direct the child's attention to the error. Tutors were trained to give verbal attention as the use of non-verbal cues, such as finger pointing to attract the child's attention to an error, would not be indicated on an audio recording. Total error attention was calculated by the formula,

$$\frac{\text{Number of errors attended}}{\text{Number of errors}} \times \frac{100}{1}\%.$$

Total error attention was not graphed, but formed part of the calculation of subsequent tutor measures.

Delayed Attention. If a tutor response was made after an interval of five seconds, this was scored as delayed attention. If the tutor made any kind of response to the child's error within an interval of five seconds, this was scored as immediate attention. Delayed attention was calculated by the formula,

$$\frac{\text{Number of instances of delayed attention}}{\text{Total error attention}} \times \frac{100}{1}\%.$$

Percentage Prompts. A prompt was defined as a clue about the meaning of the word or a direction to look at the context of the story or at the graphophonic features of a word. More than one kind of prompt could be given for one error. The percentage of prompts was calculated by the formula,

$$\frac{\text{Number of instances of prompts}}{\text{Total error attention}} \times \frac{100}{1}\%.$$

Percentage Modelling. Modelling was defined as the tutor responding to a child's error by directly telling the child the correct word. This may occur immediately the error has been made or following one or two prompts by the tutor. The percentage of modelling was calculated by the formula,

$$\frac{\text{Number of instances of word supplied}}{\text{Total error attention}} \times \frac{100}{1}\%.$$

Praise for Self-correction. This involved a tally per session of praise statements which were contingent on the child correcting an error without any attention from the tutor. That is, praise statements made by the tutor that immediately followed a self-correction. Explicit statements were encouraged such as 'Good girl, you corrected that word by yourself. Good work'—but often the tutor indicated only 'Good', or 'Good work', to limit the interruption to the story. This did, however, depend upon the reading level the child had attained and the more explicit comments were encouraged with children on the lower levels of reading where more supportive informative praise was encouraged.

Praise for Prompted Corrections. This was a tally of the number per session of tutor praise statements which were contingent on the child responding correctly following a tutor prompt.

Praise for Other Responses. This was a tally of the number of other tutor praise statements per session. These included praise contingent on error free reading of a whole sentence, a paragraph, a page, general praise statements or praise referring to a whole session.

Participant Questionnaire

At the conclusion of the intervention phase, all participants in the study completed a questionnaire. The tutors (parents and teachers) completed a similar questionnaire, while the children completed a separate questionnaire. The questionnaires, adapted from Johnson (1979) were designed to gauge the participants' attitudes to the study, and allowed them to offer critical appraisal of the study (Wahler & Fox, 1981).

Reliability of Measures

All sessions were tape-recorded and analysed by the first author. A research assistant, who was naive about the experimental design, procedures and objectives of the study, independently scored a sample of the recorded reading sessions to provide reliability measures.

The reliability observer was trained by the first author, who gave a verbal explanation accompanied by written instructions. The experimenter and observer then proceeded to work through two audio tapes of reading sessions together, repeating observations until 100% agreement was achieved using the response definitions.

During reliability assessments the reliability observer scored all observations in the same way as the experimenter, observations being recorded on the Oral Reading Record sheet. Photocopied passages from the relevant books, or the books themselves if available, were supplied to the observer with each tape.

Reliability was calculated on each reading session by comparing the agreement and the disagreements of the two observers, using the formula,

$$\frac{\text{Agreements}}{\text{Agreements and disagreements}} \times \frac{100}{1}\%.$$

It was planned that reliability checks should be carried out on one third of all recorded sessions (i.e. one session out of each three), across subjects and settings.

Experimental Conditions

Throughout the study all aspects of the procedures were duplicated in the home and the school settings.

All measures for the study were taken from three random samples of reading sessions recorded in each home and school each week, thus providing six samples of each child's reading every week of the study.

Baseline. Baseline measures were recorded between parent and child and between teacher and child, to assess the level of tutor and child behaviours before intervention commenced. Tutors were requested to record three reading sessions with the child each week, interacting with the child as and when they considered it necessary. Between sessions 6 and 7 there was a ten week break when the experimenter was absent through illness.

Intervention: tutor training. Following the baseline phase, the training programme was introduced to both the parent and teacher of each child, at the same time.

Tutor training consisted of a screening of the film 'Helping you to help your child' (Glynn *et al.*, 1979), and each tutor was given a copy of the booklet *Remedial Reading at Home: helping you to help your child* (Glynn *et al.*, 1979)—the film and the booklet covering the same material. Tutors were also given a chart outlining the tutoring procedure. The chart summarised the tutoring procedures, telling the tutor to pause before attending to errors, to praise for sentences read correctly, self-correction of errors and prompted corrections and explaining how to prompt with contextual, graphic and phonic cues.

Intervention was planned on a multiple baseline schedule, the film to be shown and discussed individually with each tutor. However, the fact that they had the same classroom teacher meant that intervention commenced in the same week for the tutors of S2 and S3.

After viewing the film, tutors were given specific directions on how to carry out tutoring sessions. Tutors were instructed to allow the child to look through a new book and to give the child a brief introduction to the study, indicating the names of the characters, places, sequences of events, unfamiliar language and experiences. This was to enable the reader to make use of contextual cues during the oral reading session (Wong & McNaughton, 1980).

Instructions for the reading sessions were that sessions should be no longer than ten minutes, and should be scheduled three or four times a week, preferably at the same time each day. One session was to be held during a weekly visit by the experimenter.

At each visit to both home and school the experimenter provided feedback in the form of spoken explanation and graphical representation of results to both tutor and child. A reading session was then recorded providing an opportunity for the experimenter to praise and shape appropriate tutor responses, model or prompt where necessary and praise child reading behaviour. The period of tutor training varied between five and seven weeks.

Maintenance. When the data indicated that the tutors were appropriately using the trained tutoring procedures, experimenter visits were reduced from weekly to fortnightly. Weekly tapes were still collected and analysed, and new reading material provided if this was indicated by the data. Data feedback to tutors was still provided at the fortnightly visit, but reading sessions were not recorded in the experimenter's presence. Between sessions 35 and 40 there was a two week school vacation.

S3's parent tutor showed earlier mastery than did S2's parent tutor, so the maintenance phase began earlier for S3. No maintenance phase was included for S4. Here, subject illness and equipment failure had meant a delay in intervention.

Follow-up. Three follow-up visits were planned to each child and parent, and child and teacher. These occurred at monthly intervals, beginning one month after the end of the maintenance phase. During these visits a sample of the child's reading with their tutor was recorded. This was later analysed. Reading material was based on material the child was currently reading either at home or at school. S4 moved away from the district toward the end of the study and only one follow-up session was recorded in his home.

Experimental Design and Data Analysis

A multiple baseline design across subjects was used. Here a treatment variable is applied sequentially to the same behaviour, in this case tutor behaviours, and indirectly to child reading behaviours, across different subjects with similar environmental conditions (Hersen & Barlow, 1976). Experimental control is demonstrated when behaviour changes from stable baseline levels only at the time of intervention (Baer, Wolf & Risley, 1968). In the present study, given that intervention occurred at the same time for two subjects, intervention occurred at three different times. Unfortunately, data for S4 were reduced by both subject illness and equipment failure in both home and school settings. Data analysis involved visual evaluation of the graphed data.

Results

Reliability of Measures

Reliability was calculated for 74 reading sessions of a total 304 reading sessions —that is, for 24% of all sessions. Reliability was calculated on the total number of observations in any one session. The mean percentage agreement between experimenter and the reliability observer for all child and all tutor behaviours during recorded reading sessions was 94.83% with a range from 85 to 100%. Reliability was below 90% on four out of 74 occasions.

Multiple Baseline Analysis of Intervention Effects on Tutor Behaviours

Delayed Attention to Child Reading Errors. These results are presented for Home in Fig. 1, and for School in Fig. 2.

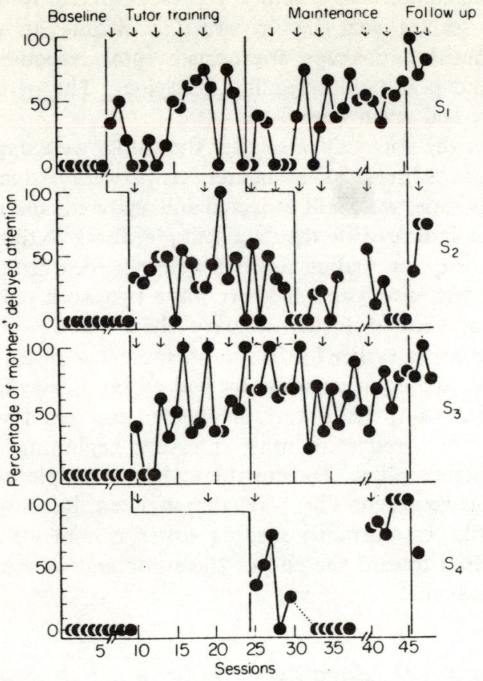

FIG. 1. The percentage of mother tutors' delayed attention to the child's errors recorded during reading sessions in the home. Arrows show when a new book with a higher reading level was introduced. Missing data for S4 were the result of illness and equipment failure.

From Fig. 1 it can be seen that none of the mother tutors delayed attention to errors during baseline. Then following tutor training, mother tutors started to delay attention (for five seconds or more) to the child's error. There is considerable variability in this response, through tutor training and maintenance, ranging from 0 to 100%. Data for S1 and S2 show a reduction in delayed attention in later training and early maintenance sessions, but substantially higher levels at follow-up.

Following a baseline of no delayed attention, the mother tutor of S3 showed a continued improvement through subsequent phases. The limited data for S4 show that this mother tutor did not delay attention during baseline, but paused for longer than five seconds after a child reading error during intervention and follow-up. Data loss was the result of child illness and equipment failure.

From Fig. 2 it can be seen that the teacher of S1 did not delay attention to errors during baseline. The teacher of S2 and S3 did show some delayed attention to errors during later baseline sessions. Following intervention it can be seen from Fig. 2 that the teacher tutors of S1, S2 and S3 gradually increased their delayed attention, with follow up measures remaining well above baseline levels of responding. Considerable variability is evident in this post-treatment data. The limited data available for S4's teacher tutor indicated that there was little change between baseline and tutor training.

Percentage Modelling and Prompting. These results are presented for Home in Fig. 3, and for School in Fig. 4.

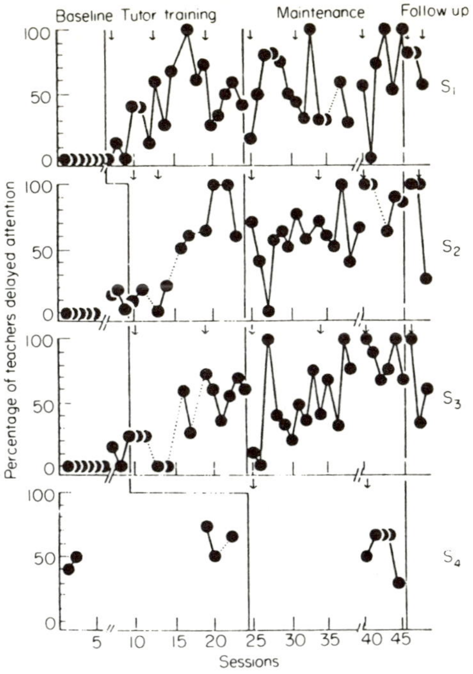

FIG. 2. The percentage of teacher tutors' delayed attention to the child's errors recorded during reading sessions at school. Arrows show when a new book with a higher reading level was introduced. Missing data for S4 were the result of illness and equipment failure.

From Fig. 3 it can be seen that baseline levels generally indicated a high percentage of modelling and a low percentage of prompting by mother tutors. The mother tutor for S3 showed modelling reducing to zero level in baseline but increased prompting in the last baseline session, where she gave prompts for each error the child made. While there was no modelling shown for S4 during sessions 4 and 5, this, together with no prompting, represented no attention to the child's errors by the mother tutor during these sessions.

Following intervention, the level of modelling was reduced, and the level of prompting increased by all tutors in the Home. During maintenance, there were instances of mother tutors increasing levels of modelling and reducing prompting, but the follow-up data indicated a clear reversal of the baseline data, with low levels of modelling and high levels of prompting.

From Fig. 4 it can be seen that the data for the teacher tutors of S2, S3 and S4 showed little change throughout the study. While there was variability, there were low levels of modelling and high levels of prompting during baseline which were not changed following intervention. The teacher tutor for S1 shows an ascending baseline for modelling and a descending baseline trend for prompts. Following intervention there was a general reduction in modelling and a marked increase in frequency of prompts (Fig. 4). Throughout the tutor training and maintenance phases, both these teacher behaviours show variability.

Follow-up data for all teacher tutors indicated low levels for modelling and high levels of prompting.

Praise. The frequency of the three categories of praise, praise for self-correction,

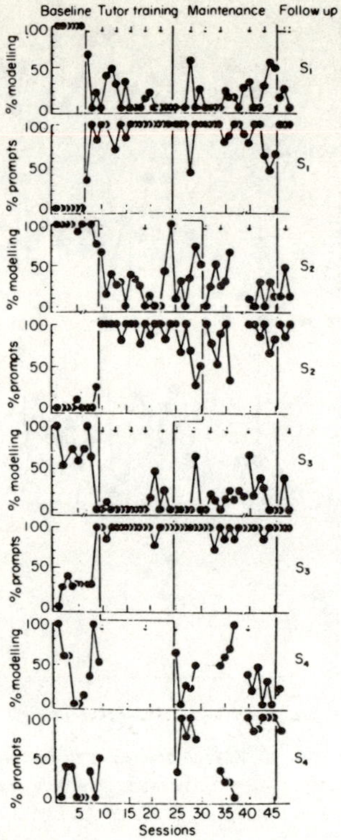

FIG. 3. The percentage of mother tutors' modelling and prompting the correct response recorded during reading sessions in the home. Arrows show when a new book at a higher reading level was introduced. Missing data for S4 were the result of illness and equipment failure.

praise for prompted correction and other praise comments are presented for Home in Fig. 5 and for School in Fig. 6.

It should be noted that any sample of reading contained a maximum of ten errors, and therefore the combined maximum frequency of specific praise for self-corrections and for prompted corrections for any one session is ten.

From Fig. 5 it can be seen that during baseline the mother tutors gave either no praise, or very low levels of praise. The mother tutors of S2 and S4 made one praise comment, while the mother tutor of S3 praised the child once during sessions 7 and 8 and made three praise statements during session 9. Following intervention all mother tutors praised their child's reading. The frequency of praise was increased or maintained by each mother tutor through the maintenance and follow-up phases (Fig. 5).

From Fig. 6 it can be seen that during baseline there was a low frequency of praise by the teacher tutors. Following intervention there was an increase in the frequency of praise, which was maintained throughout the maintenance and follow-up phases. The frequency of teacher tutors' praise was seldom lower during intervention and follow up, than the highest frequency recorded during baseline.

Children's Reading Progress. Table I presents the age levels achieved on the two reading tests at pre-test in March and post-test in December, and the reading age gain across the study.

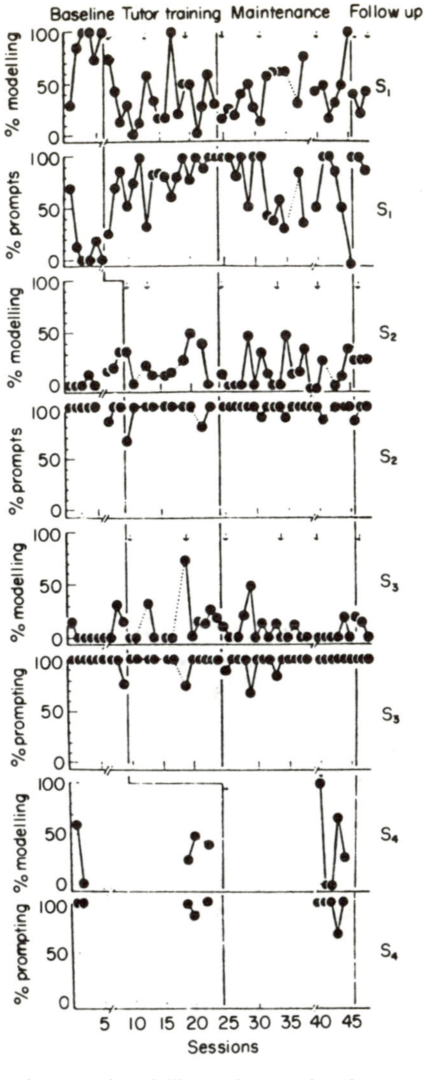

FIG. 4. The percentage of teacher tutors' modelling and prompting the correct response recorded during reading sessions at school. Arrows show when a new book with a higher reading level was introduced. Missing data for S4 were the result of illness and equipment failure.

It is evident that the two measures agreed on the achieved reading level in most cases, with disagreement being within one reading level. From Table I it can be seen that, assessed on these measures, the subjects made gains of from two to four years in reading age.

Table II presents the reading age level of the graded book material each child was reading with 95% accuracy at home and at school, at the end of each phase of the study, and the total gain in reading level on this measure over the study.

It is evident that the initial book reading levels in Table II differ from the reading test performance reported in Table I. This may reflect different procedures, or inaccuracies, in the publisher evaluation and grading of the book material. Nevertheless, on the graded book material, the children were shown to make reading gains

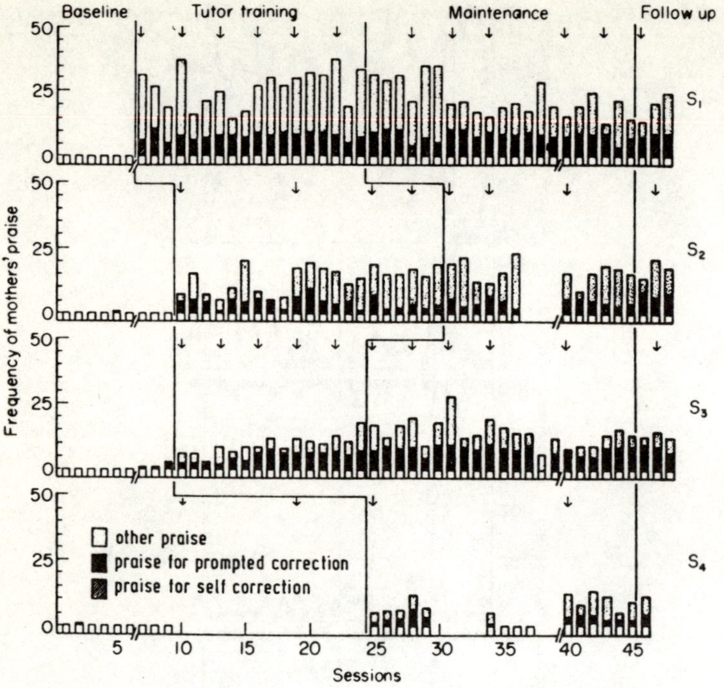

FIG. 5. The frequency of mother tutors' praise for self-corrections, prompted corrections and other praise recorded during reading sessions in the home. Arrows show when a new book with a higher reading level was introduced. Missing data for S4 were the result of illness and equipment failure.

TABLE I. The reading age level (in years) of the highest passage read with 95% accuracy from the Woods & Moe (W & M) and Dunedin Teachers' College Informal Prose Inventory (DTC) assessments, at pre-test and post-test, and the reading age gain (in years) across the study

	Pre-test (March) RA		Post-test (December) RA		
	W & M	DTC	W & M	DTC	Gain
S1	5	5	–	8	3
S2	5	5	7	8	2–3
S3	5	6	9	10	4
S4	8	8	10	10	2

of from 1 year 7 months to 4 years in the home setting, and from 1 year 7 months to 3 years 10 months in the school setting. From Table II it can be seen that gains were similar in both home and school settings for S2 and S3. S1 and S4 show greater gains at home that at school.

TABLE II. The reading age level of the graded book material each child was reading with 95% accuracy at the end of each phase of the study, together with the total gain achieved over baseline levels at the end of the follow-up phase, in both home and school settings

	Home					School				
	BLN	Int	Maint	FU	Total gain	BLN	Int	Maint	FU	Total gain
S1	6y 8m	7y 2m	8y 3m	9y 6m	2y 10m	6y 8m	7y 4m	7y 10m	8y 9m	2y 1m
S2	6y 8m	7y 4m	8y	8y 3m	1y 7m	6y 8m	7y 4m	7y 10m	8y 3m	1y 7m
S3	7y 4m	8y	9y 6m	11y	3y 8m	7y 2m	8y	9y	11y	3y 10m
S4	8y	11y	—	12y	4y	8y 3m	11y	—	—	2y 9m

The Results of the Participant Questionnaire

Completed at the end of the intervention phase, this questionnaire gave the subjective evaluations of the participants regarding the tutors experience of the programme and the children's reading progress.

All of the mothers, teachers and children considered that participation in the study had been of value to them, and that the time required for tutoring was reasonable. Two of the teachers, while agreeing that the time required was reasonable, also said that it was sometimes awkward to arrange their class programme to accommodate the tutoring procedure.

The tutors, both mothers and teachers, reported meaningful changes in both their own and the children's behaviours and said they would recommend the procedure to other tutors, and intended to continue to use their new tutoring skills with children requiring remedial help.

The social relevance of the study was further indicated by other tutor comments regarding the children which included 'increased confidence and positive attitude to reading'; 'willing to take greater part in class activities, especially blackboard work'; 'more confident and relaxed'; 'happier'. One tutor considered it important to comment about 'feeling that I as a mother helped in some small way'.

The children themselves stated that they were 'reading a lot better', and simply 'I read better'.

Discussion

Interpretation of the results of this study must involve some caution. Intervention at the same time for S2 and S3, and the limited data available for S4, threatens the level of experimental control demonstrated within the multiple baseline design. Also, the 10 week break during baseline must weaken the design. Nevertheless, data with a high level of interobserver reliability showed clear changes in both teacher behaviours and parent behaviours and these changes occurred following intervention. Also, following tutor training, the children showed marked increases in reading levels. Although absence of a control group demands caution in relating child reading gains to the intervention, the considerable gains observed were in contrast to the progress of the children over six years of regular classroom instruction.

The results of this study showed that the training procedures could have a marked impact on teacher as well as parent behaviour in delaying attention to errors and in increasing praise for appropriate child reading behaviours. While training also

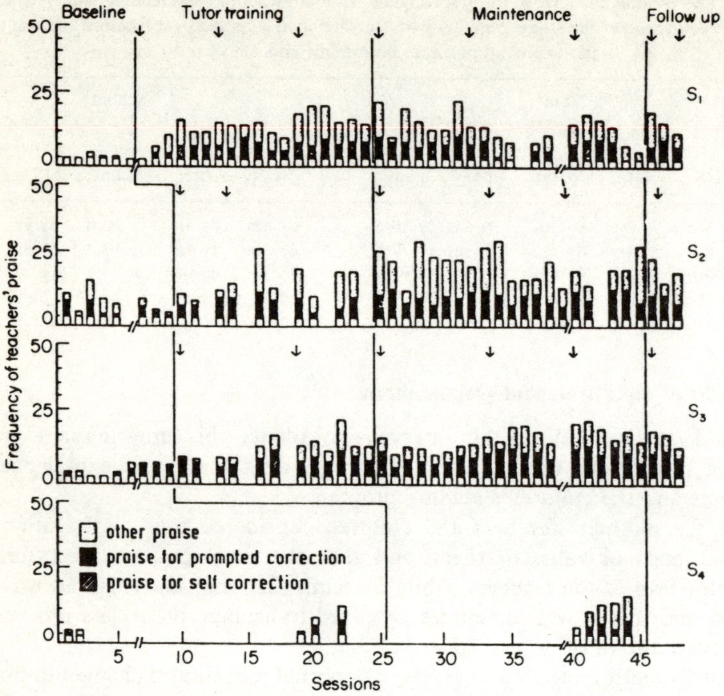

FIG. 6. The frequency of teacher tutors' praise for the child's self-corrections, prompted corrections and other praise recorded during reading sessions at school. Arrows show when a new book with a higher reading level was introduced. Missing data for S4 were the result of illness and equipment failure.

substantially changed parents' use of modelling and prompts, only the teacher for S1 showed a marked change in these tutor behaviours. The other teachers were already using these strategies appropriately prior to intervention.

The study also showed that tutors could maintain the newly acquired tutoring behaviours after the experimenter stopped providing training and reduced the amount of feedback. Reducing the frequency of experimenter visits to each tutor child unit, following the initial intervention phase, may have contributed to this maintenance effect. Follow-up data were recorded over a three month period, during which neither training nor feedback was provided. During follow-up it was shown that tutors maintained, and even further increased, intervention levels of tutoring behaviours. O'Dell's (1974) suggestion for effective training of others, as involving acquiring new skills and the implementation and persistence of skills, was therefore achieved in the present study.

The four children in this study had attended school for six years. When the study began, S4 recorded a three year reading deficit, while the other three subjects showed reading levels five years behind an expected level for their chronological age.

Following 7 to 13 weeks of trained tutoring and maintenance, the three months follow-up assessment on two formal reading tests showed a mean increase in reading level of 28 months (range 24–48 months). Reading gains were also estimated from the reading age levels of the graded books read at the start and completion of the study. On this measure, the mean reading age increase at home was 36 months (range 19–48 months) and at school 30 months (range 19–46 months). While the absence of a control group demands caution in attributing these gains to the tutoring procedures, this outcome is, nevertheless, encouraging and it seems possible that the trained tutors influenced the children's reading skills in both settings.

The improvement in the children's reading behaviours in this study, as measured by mean reading age level, is considerably higher than recorded in previous research. Glynn *et al.* (1980) recorded a mean increase in reading level of 6.5 months (range 3–15 months) during 10 weeks of parent trained tutoring. Glynn (1980) recorded a mean increase in reading level of 6.25 months (range 4–8 months) during 12 weeks of home tutoring. Love [1], using similar tutoring procedures with parents of mildly retarded children, recorded increases in reading level of between 6 and 12 months, with four to seven weeks of tutoring. It may well be that the gains made by the present children reflect the fact that they received more reading and more tutoring than would be achieved if only one tutor had worked with each child.

The use of the tutoring procedures in both the home and the school was supported by the subjective comments expressed in the questionnaire completed by all participants in the study. Teachers and parents were positive about the idea of working together to help the child. On the basis of the present study the tutoring procedures can be seen to be practical for use by teachers in the regular classroom, as well as being readily taught to and used by parents, as shown in earlier research (Glynn, 1980; Glynn *et al.*, 1980; Love [1]).

Acknowledgements

The authors express their appreciation to the parents, teachers and children who participated in this study, and acknowledge the valued assistance of Mr A. B. Galland, Principal of Dunedin North Intermediate School.

This paper is based in part on a research study submitted by the senior author in partial fulfillment of the MEd degree in the Department of Education, University of Otago.

NOTES

[1] Love, J.M. (1981) *Training parents of mildly retarded pupils as reading tutors.* A study presented in partial fulfilment for the requirements of the MEd degree, Department of Education, University of Otago (Dunedin).

[2] *An informal prose reading test* (Dunedin Teachers' Training College, 1972).

REFERENCES

BAER, D.M., WOLF, M.M. & RISLEY, T.R. (1968) Some current dimensions of applied behavior analysis, *Journal of Applied Behavior Analysis,* 1, pp. 91–97.

BERGAN, J.R. (1977) *Behavioral Consultation* (Columbus, Charles E. Merrill).

BERGAN, J.R. & DULEY, S.M. (1981) Behavioral consultation with families, in: HENDERSON, R.W. (Ed.) *Parent-Child Interaction: theory, research and prospects,* pp. 265–288 (New York, Academic Press).

BERKOWITZ, B.P. & GRAZIANO, A.M. (1972) Training parents as behaviour therapists: a review, *Behavior Research and Therapy,* 10, pp. 297–317.

BIRD, B.L. & FALK, I.H. (1977) *Trend Books* (Wellington, Reed Books).

ELLEY, W.B. (1975) *Assessing the Difficulty of Reading Materials: the noun frequency method* (Wellington, New Zealand Council for Educational Research).

GLYNN, E.L. (1980) Parent-child interaction in remedial reading at home, in: CLARK, M.M. & GLYNN, T. (Eds) *Reading and Writing for the Child with Difficulties*, University of Birmingham Educational Review, Occasional Publications, No. 8.

GLYNN, E.L. & MCNAUGHTON, S.S. (1975) Trust your own observation: criterion referenced assessment of reading progress, *Slow Learning Child*, 22, pp. 91–108.

GLYNN, T., MCNAUGHTON, S.S., ROBINSON, V. & QUINN, M. (1979) *Remedial Reading at Home: helping you to help your child* (Wellington, New Zealand Council for Educational Research).

GLYNN, T., MCNAUGHTON, S.S., ROBINSON, V. & QUINN, M. (1980) Training parents as remedial reading tutors, in: ATKINSON, J.K. (Ed.) *Too Late at Eight: prevention and intervention* (University of Queensland, Schonell Educational Research Centre).

HANSEN, C.L. & LOVITT, T.C. (1976) Reading: round one—matching the child to the book, in: BRIGHAM, T.A., HAWKINS, R., SCOTT, J.W. & MCLAUGHLIN, F. (Eds) *Behavior Analysis in Education: self control and reading* (Dubuque, Iowa, Kendall/Hunt).

HARRIS, A.J. & SIPAY, E.R. (1975) *How to Increase Reading Ability*, 6th edn (New York, David McKay).

HERSEN, M. & BARLOW, D.H. (1976) *Single Case Experimental Designs: strategies for studying behavior change* (New York, Pergamon Press).

JOHNSON, B. (1979) *Reading Appraisal Guide* (Melbourne, Australian Council for Educational Research).

MCNAUGHTON, S.S. & DELQUADRI, J. (1978) Error attention tutoring in oral reading, in: GLYNN, T. & MCNAUGHTON, S.S. (Eds) *Behaviour Analysis in New Zealand, 1978: Proceedings of the First New Zealand Conference for Research in Applied Behaviour Analysis* (University of Auckland).

MCNAUGHTON, S. & GLYNN, T. (1981) Delayed versus immediate attention to oral reading errors: Effects on accuracy and self correction, *Educational Psychology*, 33, pp. 57–65.

MCNAUGHTON, S., GLYNN, T. & ROBINSON, V. (1981) *Parents as Remedial Reading Tutors* (Wellington, New Zealand Council for Educational Research).

NAY, W.R. (1979) Parents as real life reinforcers: The enhancement of parent-training effects across conditions other than training, in: GOLDSTEIN, A.P. & KANFER, F.H. (Eds) *Maximising Treatment Gains: transfer enhancement in psychotherapy*, pp. 249–302 (New York, Academic Press).

O'DELL, S. (1974) Training parents in behavior modification: a review, *Psychological Bulletin*, 81, pp. 418–433.

REYNOLDS, C.R. (1981) The fallacy of "two years below grade level for age" as a diagnostic criterion for reading disorders, *Journal of School Psychology*, 19, pp. 350–358.

SPACHE, G.D. (1974) *Good Reading for Poor Readers* (Champaign, Illinois, Garrard Publishing).

WAHLER, R.G. & FOX, J.J. (1981) Setting events in applied behavior analysis: Towards a conceptual and methodological expansion, *Journal of Applied Behavior Analysis*, 14, pp. 327–338.

WOODS, M.L. & MOE, A.J. (1977) *Analytical Reading Inventory* (Columbus, Charles E. Merrill).

WONG, P. & MCNAUGHTON, S.S. (1980) The effects of prior provision of context on the oral reading proficiency of a low progress reader, *New Zealand Journal of Educational Studies*, 15, pp. 169–175.

Training Teachers to Use the Behavioural Approach to Classroom Management: a review

FRANK MERRETT & KEVIN WHELDALL

ABSTRACT *A review is presented of the various attempts to devise courses to train teachers in the behavioural approach to classroom management. The early American studies and later British Studies are reviewed separately. The final section considers criticisms of the previous courses and brings together suggestions for an improved training model.*

There is now a vast literature demonstrating the benefits to be enjoyed by teachers from adopting a behavioural approach to teaching. Demonstration studies of enhanced classroom management engineered by behavioural methods are legion (see Merrett, 1981a for a thorough review of British work in this area). This has prompted many educational psychologists, and others, to attempt to 'give psychology away' by mounting in-service courses for teachers on 'behaviour modification in the classroom' or, as we prefer to call it, the 'behavioural approach to teaching' (Wheldall & Merrett, 1984a, b). However, such courses have not always met with the same success, in terms of improved classroom performance, as have one to one interventions carried out by educational psychologists with a single teacher and his or her class. In this paper we will examine why this should be the case and the related questions of whether behavioural teaching methods can be taught effectively and efficiently to groups of teachers and what are the best ways for them to learn these methods.

First, we will present a review of the origins and development of training courses in the behavioural approach to classroom management for groups of teachers in mainstream education since, to our knowledge, no such review currently exists. Bernstein (1982) has provided a conceptual review on training behaviour change agents but this is primarily concerned with clinical practice. Kazdin & Moyer (1976) present a chapter on 'Training teachers to use behaviour modification' but this does not include a full review and is now, of course, rather dated. Most of the early work in this area is American (apart from a few antipodean studies which, for convenience, we have bracketed with the American work) and we will review this separately before considering more recent British work in the area. This review does not claim to be exhaustive and includes only major studies. There is little reference to studies in Special Education contexts or to studies involving only a few children except where they have special relevance to the main theme or are used to make general points. Finally, we will present a summary of detailed criticisms of behavioural training courses and of the lessons to be learned from them.

American Studies

There are two main elements in any training programme for teachers; the theoretical basis and the technology. Any programme which aims at the implementation of behavioural techniques in school must ideally be concerned to change the teacher's behaviour in the classroom. Where a study is carried out in the context of an experiment designed to evaluate a specific procedure, teachers can be instructed or persuaded to try to behave in certain ways just for the purpose of the exercise (e.g. Becker, *et al.*, 1967; Hall, Lund & Jackson, 1968). As many experimenters have found, however, once the research team leaves the school, the use of such techniques ceases.

Ulrich, Wolf & Bluhm (1970) were concerned,

> That teachers themselves should become more expert in handling children so that problems could be dealt with immediately in the classroom and would not have to be referred to specialists at a later time. (pp. 339–40)

Consequently, they were among the first to set up centres for in-service courses for teachers with two objectives:

(1) to introduce teachers to the best principles of behaviour management;

(2) to help teachers to adapt principles into techniques for classroom behaviour management which would have practical value for them. Most subsequent attempts at training teachers have aimed at both theoretical and practical aspects.

Hall *et al.* (1968) report another early attempt to train teachers in operant procedures to improve classroom control. They concentrated on three novice teachers, helping them to increase the study behaviours of their children through increasing teacher attention to on-task behaviour. They claim that their experiment demonstrates how a few simple techniques, which took only 15–30 minutes to explain, together with daily feedback (providing positive social reinforcement to the teacher), can prove very helpful.

> We are well aware that good teachers had been using these same techniques effectively long before B.F. Skinner formulated the principles of operant conditioning. Even these teachers, however, had not looked at behaviour closely enough and with enough understanding to be able to specify precisely what they had done and what the ineffective teacher needed to do to bring about the desired pupil behaviour. (p. 321)

Hall *et al.* were concerned at the fact that most young teachers found themselves facing classes on first appointment without having been taught even basic coping techniques for classroom management.

Gropper *et al.* (1968) also attempted a training programme with local teachers. They used programmed texts, films and workbooks, individual classroom assignments and discussion sessions. Although paper and pencil tests showed 100%

improvement in theoretical knowledge the classroom application of the technology was not so impressive. In other words few appreciable changes in teacher behaviour were in evidence. This emphasises the need for training to be skills-based.

Cooper, Thompson & Baer (1970) attempted to teach two teachers working in a pre-school Head Start programme to give positive attention to appropriate child behaviours. They had a good measure of success but only with the skills specifically taught. Generalisation of skills was not demonstrated and some of the later studies reported tell the same story.

Andrews (1970) reported a four week pilot study of in-service training arranged for 11 teachers in elementary schools who had had up to 10 years' experience. Four 90 minute sessions were held in which half of the time was in school time and the other half was in the teachers' free time. A programmed text, *Living with Children* by Patterson & Gullion (1968), was used. The teachers were all volunteers and were, as part of the course, encouraged to carry out a simple intervention on one specific behaviour with one child. As a result teachers were found to be capable of effecting changes using behavioural techniques and the effort was considered to be justified.

Wetzel (1970) reported a more thorough attempt to train teachers' aides in five groups each comprising a teacher and two or more aides. Prior observation had shown that the aides used threats and punishment a great deal with little positive reinforcement and little or no involvement in instruction.The programme stressed the importance of setting goals for behaviour, of contingency management, especially the shaping and positive reinforcement of good behaviours, and the evaluation of methods and procedures. The subjects observed trained staff involved in a process of 'behavioural engineering' for two weeks in the schools where they participated in the routines, received corrective feedback and had the opportunity for discussion. One thing that emerged was that although prior to training the subjects were able to talk about the importance of positive reinforcement they had to *learn* how to smile, hug and praise in the real life situation. Altman & Linton (1971) suggest that once a programme is under way, daily feedback from the recording of observations will help to maintain enthusiasm. They suggest that 10–20 hours of instruction will probably be needed.

In their discussion of problems in the teacher use of selected behaviour modification techniques, Thomas & Adams (1971) suggested that teachers found great difficulty in altering their rates of emission of appropriate and inappropriate remarks in response to children's behaviours. In particular, they found it difficult to ignore behaviours to which they had been responding previously. Most teachers will agree with positive reinforcement in principle (though they find it difficult to implement) but they usually say that they cannot ignore inappropriate behaviour because of the effect upon the other children of letting one child 'get away with it'. Thomas & Adams suggest that the best time for teachers to learn this sort of procedure would be in initial training but then problems concerned with attitudes of supervising tutors and of class teachers, whose cooperation is essential, are almost bound to occur.

Zimmerman *et al.* (1971), after their experiences in organising workshops in behaviour management suggest that,

> Objective behaviour measurement is the essence of behaviour modification. By measuring behaviour on a daily basis, both before and after the application of procedures, the teacher can clearly determine whether his

> procedure improves behaviour, has little or no effect, or perhaps, even makes things worse. (p. 329)

Hall (1971), however, suggests that whilst feedback from successful intervention should give sufficient reinforcement to teachers it does not always do so. He stresses the need for continuing support from the group who are taking in-service training in contingency management in a course which used mainly films, discussions and quizzes. School-based in-service training would appear to meet Hall's point.

Hall & Copeland (1972) subsequently developed the 'responsive teaching model' which they describe as a first step in shaping school personnel as behaviour modification specialists and which became very influential. They, too, point out that demonstrations carried out under the guidance of research teams have limited value because the teachers often give up after the departure of the team.

> Thus although experimental studies carried out by skilled researchers have played an important part in generating interest and demonstrating that behaviour modification works in the classroom they have not provided a good model for training teachers, nor have they necessarily provided procedures which teachers can adapt and use in their classrooms with the resources currently available to them. (p. 126)

The responsive teaching programme was designed (Hall, 1971) to:

(1) provide reinforcement through the earning of professional and/or academic credit;
(2) teach practical measurement and recording techniques which can be used in the classroom;
(3) present basic learning theories which are the basis of behaviour modification, after baselines have been obtained;
(4) present information on previous research and applications in school settings;
(5) have participants carry out studies in their own school situations;
(6) provide contact with other participants and with those already skilled.

They claimed that their system fitted in with the then current in-service pattern (in the United States); provided reinforcement for the participants; provided a background of learning theory; spurred on the participants to further learning and/or experimenting; gave further training for those who acted as sessional group leaders; provided teachers with measurement and research skills and a disposition to observe and measure behaviour and provided examples of practical issues and outcomes thus indicating teaching procedures. It was an important early step in shaping educational practice towards behaviour modification.

Borg (1972) found that a minicourse (a self-contained, self-instructional package designed to help teachers to master specific skills and strategies) was as effective as normal courses taken by teachers. In a follow-up study which looked at the effectiveness of such courses after a period of up to three years he concluded,

> We have learned . . . that it is extremely difficult to get a teacher regularly to emit specific behaviours that are not part of his teaching practice. Even though our model lessons are typically designed to provide examples of only two or three very simple skills, we find we must work with teachers many hours before these skills appear. (p. 578)

Other researchers have looked at specific techniques of teacher training in the behavioural approach. Saudargas (1972) using VTR and observer's ratings of teachers' praise behaviour found that the amount of praise given varied with the criterion set, say, two or five praising comments per minute. He suggests that some such aid as this is a necessary condition for changing teacher behaviour.

Rule (1972) compared three different types of feedback on teachers' performance. The experiment involved nine teachers between the ages of 19 and 29 two of whom were experienced and the remainder rather inexperienced. A multiple baseline design across subjects and across techniques was employed. The three procedures used were: (i) instruction and experimenter feedback, (ii) video feedback and scoring own behaviour, and (iii) direct intervention in which the subject was displaced by the experimenter when his/her behaviour fell below criterion. In the third procedure the subject observed and recorded the tutor's behaviour and this proved to be by far the most effective. Rule suggests that this is because the procedure is highly aversive and gives the opportunity for modelling. She says that the first procedure (instruction and feedback) was quite ineffective. Modelling has been shown to be an important element in a number of studies but why an aversive technique should prove so effective in a system which on the whole avoids punishing consequences is a paradox.

A systematic attempt to measure the effects of experimenters' instructions, feedback and social praising on the amount of praise given by teachers and the resultant response in the attending behaviour of their pupils was attempted by Cossairt, Hall & Hopkins (1973). They worked with three teachers in a down-town area of Kansas City, all of whom were competent but had no knowledge of operant methods. Using a multiple baseline design with three experimental conditions, they too, found that instructions and feedback were largely ineffective. Feedback with social praise and instructions with feedback and social praise were both very successful. They comment that,

> The increased rates of praise by all three teachers suggest that social praise is a necessary ingredient in changing teacher praise behaviour . . . A notable aspect of this study was that teacher praise was maintained and even increased when the teachers were placed on an intermittent schedule of social praise. This would seem to suggest that the excuse that Principals and supportive staff do not have the time for the social reinforcement of teacher behaviour is invalid. (pp. 99–100)

Ringer (1973) also used a modelling procedure to teach the use of a simple token system using a 'token helper' in the management of classroom behaviour problems. The experiment was carefully controlled and included a multiple baseline element and a reversal phase. After the 'token helper' was withdrawn the teacher maintained her changed behaviour. This sort of training is, however, very expensive in manpower as it operates on a one to one basis.

Greenwood *et al.* (1974) report a study employing the Program for Academic Survival Skills (PASS) developed at the Centre at Oregon for Research in the Behavioral Education of the Handicapped. Greenwood *et al.*, using 'personalised instructional units', taught three regular classroom teachers to use PASS in a multiple baseline design. They showed, as have several other studies, that 'rules' and 'rules and feedback' are not very effective on their own. PASS, however, which entails the use of social and other positive reinforcement contingencies being applied to successful rule-keeping, brought about great positive change. Follow-up measures showed that two of the teachers were able to maintain their high levels of correct positive reinforcement whilst all three maintained their low levels of incorrect responding.

Van Houten & Sullivan (1975) compared two conditions under which teachers were taught to praise their children for acceptable behaviour. In the first condition teachers recorded their praise statements, calculated the rates and drew graphs for comparison day by day. In the second they were cued to praise their pupils twice (and later three times) per minute through the public announcement system. The second procedure (cueing) was found to shape and maintain much higher rates of praising.

Horton (1975) taught two teachers, randomly selected from a number of volunteers, to use 'behaviour specific praise', i.e. positive statements in which the behaviour being praised is identified, e.g. 'You did that problem very well, John!' The teachers were taught to recognise appropriate behaviour to criterion using video recordings and were then given a target of one such 'behaviour specific praise' comment per minute. Audio-taped samples of their classroom performances showed that they responded very well. However, the skills were observed not to generalise into subject areas for which they had not been taught and practised.

> An implication of this study is that teacher trainers and consultants should not be surprised to find that training directed towards one set of teaching conditions does not guarantee that the behaviours trained will appear under another set of teaching conditions. (pp. 317–318)

Jones & Eimers (1975) used role playing to train teachers to use a classroom management skills package. This was the Classroom Management Teaching Project (CMTP) material which included specific skills for dealing with periods when free discussion between teacher and pupils was taking place and for occupied seat work. Role-play sessions used fellow teachers as 'players' and included modelling by the tutor and practice for the teachers who were then observed in their own classrooms. Jones & Eimers suggested that the course, which was of six 90-minute sessions would be suitable for in-service courses, especially in view of the proposed integration of special education units in the United States at that time. In this study, product measures were used and the results showed that children's academic output improved, the lowest third of each class making the most improvement.

McKeown, Adams & Forehand (1975) using four groups, each of five teachers, compared the effects of differently based courses. Two groups had a laboratory-based course of six weekly sessions each lasting ninety minutes which included lectures, discussions, workshops, case-studies, role-playing and so on. For one of the groups this was accompanied by a manual with instructions to read it section by section as the course progressed. The other group received the same manual after the laboratory course was completed. A third group had the manual to read as a preparation for the laboratory course to be taught at a later date whilst the control group had no instruction at all. All the teachers taking part in the experiment were observed in their own classrooms during the two weeks before and after the laboratory course. The teachers who had had the course, and the manual to read along with it, showed the most significant behaviour changes whilst generally the classes of those taking the laboratory course were shown to be relatively less disruptive than before.

On a more pessimistic note Harris *et al.* (1975) report that in a centre for teachers in which volunteers worked to model good procedures only bonus payments proved successful in bringing about good demonstrations. Instructions, feedback and praise alike proved insufficient to motivate these adults.

An experiment by Clark & McRae (1976) attempted to discover which elements in training packages are most acceptable to teachers. All teachers preferred packages in which there was an element of self-selection. However, it was not the elements which were open to choice but the means by which they were to be taught. These included modelling, verbal and graphic feedback and quiz contingencies. All packages were taught under a grade contingency. Teachers' choices included all alternatives except the quiz. Outcomes from the packages with modelling, feedback and so on were compared with those that used instructions alone. Instructions alone were effective with only one student but all students responded well when the other, chosen contingencies were added.

Bowles & Nelson (1976) report a study in which the 'bug in the ear' technique was employed to good effect with a group of teachers to increase their classroom behaviour of praise and contingency statements. Whilst this may be useful in experimental settings its practical application is severely limited in terms of its use for training large numbers of teachers.

Jones, Fremouw & Carples (1977) trained three regular elementary teachers to use the CMTP material used by Jones & Eimers (1975). Subsequently, these teachers each taught three more in a form of pyramid training. It was demonstrated that not only did the second tier of trainees do as well as the first but that the performance of the fist tier improved as a result of their acting as tutors to the second cohort. The relative time investment of the original trainers was only a quarter that of the first tier training. The British EDY programme (referred to in the next section) employs a similar pyramid training model.

Sanders (1978), in discussing self-recording and self-reinforcing, makes the point that since programmes concerned with behaviour change in children depend mainly upon behaviour change in adults, it is here that self-control techniques can best be applied. Motivation would clearly be positive and the tendency to cheat would, it is hoped, be less. Perhaps the first stage in observation of behaviour for teachers should be self-observation. This would lend itself to practical application from the outset in any course for serving teachers.

Greenwood *et al.* (1979) report a very thorough evaluation of PASS, referred to earlier, taught on a behavioural-consultancy model (pyramid teaching) in two states, Utah and Oregon. They concluded that teachers used their newly-learned skills differently (suggesting that even packages allow for individual variations according to style of teaching), that the results were generally favourable and that the enterprise was cost-effective.

Rosenfield (1979), surveying the field, points out that so often when reports are made of failed programmes the authors stress the fact that the mediators had not been trained in the systematic use of behavioural principles. She herself stresses the need for knowledge about behavioural principles together with guided practice, feedback and support and how teachers have to learn a new and more objective way of regarding behaviour. She concludes,

> Success requires the consultant to be sensitive to the concerns and questions that teachers have regarding behavioural interventions and to appreciate that the demands made upon the teacher in implementing a behavioural programme may be considerable. Resistance should be understood in this light if the techniques of behaviour modification are to become more widely used by the classroom teacher. (p. 339)

British work

Following the pioneering work in the United States, various attempts were made by British behaviourally orientated educational psychologists to run similar courses for British teachers. These early British pioneers were working in a very different educational climate from their American counterparts. Not only was *knowledge* of behavioural psychology far less widespread but, in addition, the educational 'zeitgeist' in Britain was far from sympathetic. Post-Plowden progressivism stressed the importance of discovery learning and freedom of expression whilst the student radicalism of the late 1960s and early 1970s had created a legacy of suspicion towards (apparently) manifestly authoritarian methods such as 'behaviour modification'. Among the early British workers who attempted to train teachers in behavioural methods were Critchley and Harrop; Ward; Presland; Yule, Berger and Wigley and the present authors.

Critchley & Harrop [1] (see also Harrop, 1974) set up an in-service course for teachers in Liverpool consisting of six two-hour evening sessions based upon the 'responsive teaching model' of Hall & Copeland (1972) reviewed earlier. They set out to achieve all but the first of the six objectives of this model (academic credits), which was not suited to the situation in the United Kingdom. Eight of the 16 teachers who attended the opening session completed all their studies. Six of the others completed the course without a practical study. The interventions all used the Madsen, Becker & Thomas (1968) 'rules, praise and ignoring' paradigm and the authors claimed that, "Taken as a whole the results were very encouraging" (p. 9). They argue that since behaviour frequently deteriorates before improving, when certain techniques are first applied, the value of group support and the opportunity for discussion are important considerations.

Ward (1976) attempted a comprehensive review of behavioural applications and gave a very useful model for programme implementation in which teacher training is prominent. He pointed to the necessity of success for both teacher and experimenter and how their criteria may not match. He stressed the importance of the workshop and especially of providing convincing evidence in the form of video tapes of good practice and the verbal evidence of successful practitioners and draws attention to the danger of trying to 'sell' behaviour modification as a panacea. He went on to suggest ways in which resistance to change may be overcome through voluntary involvement providing that not too much is promised and open-mindedness is maintained. Professional trust and confidence are important since a feature of behaviour modification is the remorseless identification of weak teaching, especially on the organisational side. Nevertheless, this summary ended on a note of optimism,

> Behaviour modification is compatible with significant trends in modern curriculum development and educational management; and there is ample evidence that teaching methods are moving towards more informed use of reward and away from negative reinforcement and punishment. (pp. 18–19)

In another paper, Ward (1975) states,

> In the writer's experience, approaches which involve regular, practically orientated seminars, fairly immediate try-out of the methods and feedback on progress, work best with primary contact personnel. (p. 80)

and again,

> The effective application of behaviour modification demands objective definition of a problem and agreement on the means by which it is to be attacked. However, it is paradoxical that where a programme appears to be most needed, in a behavioural sense, the conditions creating the behavioural situation may conspire against an efficient application of the method. Thus in the simplest case of difficulties over management, many teachers, parents and case-workers are temperamentally incapable of consistent reinforcement. (p. 92)

Presland (1974, 1975, 1978), apart from organising training courses for teachers in the West Midlands, has made a major contribution by keeping the issues and the potentialities of behavioural methods in the forefront. His work and ideas have been disseminated mainly through the Association of Educational Psychologists and their journal but he has also produced a pamphlet for the guidance of those who wish to help teachers to apply interventions in their own classrooms. His later efforts have been directed towards teachers in ordinary schools.

Cook (1975) also organised in-service courses in behavioural methods but these were for teachers from Special schools. She pointed hopefully to the applications of the methods of teachers in 'ordinary' schools.

In 1977 Wolff & Rennie reported a workshop course for teachers of children with special needs run by the Schools Psychological Service in Kirklees. This course lasted seven weeks and catered for 11 teachers from a wide range of schools (Secondary to Infant levels whilst one teacher came from a Special school). Sessions which lasted for two and a half hours used discussions, practical observation work based on the use of films, notes and handouts using Poteet (1973) as a class reader. Teachers carried out studies on individual children from their own classrooms and in most cases these were reported to be successful.

One of the longest running projects in this area is the Teacher-Child Interaction Project carried out by Yule, Berger & Wigley (1977) for the Inner London Education Authority. This project was set up in 1974 when Wigley was seconded from teaching for this work and was an attempt to adapt Hall's 'Responsive Teaching Model' for use in Britain. Its main focus appears to have been on teachers working with behaviourally troublesome individuals rather than on general classroom management. There is, as yet, little information on the effectiveness of this project.

Firman & Hastings (1984) organised a similar course for teachers in the Reading area. In this course teachers were given specific weekly assignment tasks and were required to use specifically designed 'bleepers', which emitted a regular signal, audible only to the teacher, in order to observe and record child behaviours. All teachers taking part were visited in their schools by the tutors who were able to follow up the attempted interventions and to give advice. They used Leach & Raybould (1977) as a course reader. A considerable amount of data was collected but the analyses have yet to be fully reported.

Raymond (1980) organised a workshop in Glamorgan "in an attempt to provide teachers with some of the skills of using behaviour modification techniques". The four days of the course, which were spaced out to allow for practical work and report-back sessions, took place in the summer term. Few details of the nature of the course are given and none about the number, sex and so on of the teachers attending but each was required to "work with one pupil whom they felt they had not succeeded with" and all were visited in their classrooms by the organiser. A considerable degree of success was claimed.

Moss (Moss & Childs, 1981) set up a course in behavioural psychology for teachers in Avon based on the American text 'Behavioral Psychology for Teachers' (Vargas, 1977). This was for six to eight teachers at a time and consisted of six sessions each of two and half hours held in the evenings. Each session included a theoretical element and a workshop where an attempt was made, for example, to teach observation skills using video recordings of classroom interactions. Workshops also included the consideration of set exercises and of case-studies. This course included among its aims a consideration of what to teach but a later definition of this showed it to be delimited and mainly concerned with task analysis and behavioural objectives in academic skill learning. Moss evaluated his course by measuring attitude change and theoretical knowledge gained.

Kolvin *et al.* (1981) worked on a large project in Newcastle using teachers in 'ordinary' schools with social workers and teacher-aides to assist them to apply operant methods in their classrooms. This study is one of the few to compare behavioural methods in classrooms with others. Neither the behavioural methods used nor the method of training the teachers was very complex. Nevertheless, behaviour modification, as they termed it, stood up very well when compared with other methods of helping teachers to cope. These were parent counselling, teacher consultation and group therapy. Behaviour modification was used at the Secondary level in this study and, considering the relatively low-key nature of the intervention, the most remarkable finding was of generalisation over time into different classrooms with different teachers and into the home situation.

Clayton (1983) has also reported on workshops in behaviour modification for teachers, parents and social workers in Wiltshire. This has included the development of a Behaviour Modification Wallet (BMW) which consists of lecture notes, examples of programmes, published articles, recording forms and a check-list summarising the main steps in programme construction.

Finally, the present authors have been involved in attempts to train teachers to use behavioural techniques since the mid-1970s in their academic courses for teachers and student-teachers and in in-service work. Merrett & Wheldall (1982) reported a study which attempted to demonstrate that teaching student teachers about behavioural approaches would improve their classroom practice. The ratings of tutors supervising education students' final teaching practice were used to compare those students who had followed a course in behavioural methods (mainly theoretical) with those who had not. It was hypothesised that for two categories, i.e. classroom control and use of praise, ratings would be higher for those students who had taken the course in behavioural methods, but this did not prove to be the case. They concluded that there was thus no evidence to suggest that teaching teachers *about* behavioural methods improves their teaching performance in the classroom. There was evidence, however, for improved attitudes towards the behavioural approach resulting from the course, in line with Wheldall & Congreve's (1980) earlier findings. These findings also confirm those of Gardner (1972) who showed that whilst lectures may teach behavioural principles quite well they are not so good at teaching performance skills. Wheldall & Merrett are currently developing a more appropriate and effective course in behavioural teaching methods at the pre-service level based on their introductory text 'Positive Teaching' (Wheldall & Merrett, 1984b).

Merrett has also reported a series of case-studies demonstrating successful behavioural interventions carried out by teachers in their own classrooms following attendance at his annual in-service course, 'Encouragement works better than punishment' (Merrett, 1981b, 1982, 1984).

This work, alongside their programme of experimental research (reviewed in Wheldall, 1981), has influenced their development of the Behavioural Approach to Teaching Package (BATPACK) (Wheldall & Merrett, 1984a) which is designed to teach classroom management skills for use by teachers in Primary and Middle schools. BATPACK is distinguished from other such courses by being skills- and school-based, by involving participants in a course contract and by being deliberately limited to simple techniques of classroom management. It has passed through several metamorphoses and at each stage an attempt was made to evaluate what had been achieved. This was done by traditional methods of eliciting evaluative comments from students, measuring student's attitudes before and after the course and by measuring their knowledge of behavioural techniques before and after the course. More importantly, however, BATPACK has also been evaluated by direct observation of teacher and class behaviour on a pre- and post-test basis. BATPACK has been successively modified in the light of the findings from these evaluations so as to achieve its main objectives of changing teacher behaviour and, as a result, thereby changing children's behaviour.

Criticisms and Conclusions

This review has shown clearly that teachers *can* be taught to use behavioural methods and to understand the accompanying theory. As a result, the responses of their classes may also change in a more positive direction. However, there is some disagreement among researchers about how easy it is to bring about such changes. Hall *et al.* (1968) and Andrews (1970), for example, suggest that it is a relatively simple process whilst others warn that it is quite difficult (e.g. Altman Linton, 1971, Thomas & Adams, 1971, Rosenfield, 1979, Kazdin, 1981 and also Berger, 1980).

Some of the earlier studies involved the training of teachers for specific intervention experiments. These are useful in relation to specific aspects of technique but we are chiefly concerned here with those studies aiming to train *groups* of teachers in order to improve their general knowledge about and their *use* of behavioural techniques in classroom management. Berger (1980) was among the first to articulate the difference between courses which teach *about* behavioural methods (i.e. the theory) and those that seek to teach *how* (i.e. skills training). He makes a strong plea for the inclusion of courses in initial teacher training, "Teaching about behavioural approaches can be presented at any time in the career of a teacher but should become an essential part of initial training" (p. 47).

It is not clear exactly what sort of courses Berger (1980) has in mind but it is extremely doubtful if, in the present climate of teacher education, anything more than a rudimentary theoretical course could be offered. Skills-based training can, then, only be provided by in-service courses. Berger shares our fear that delaying such courses brings extra difficulties which are embodied in the aphorism about teaching old dogs new tricks.

MacKrell (1983), like Berger, points out that whilst teaching specific management skills may be relatively easy, to teach the skills of applied behaviour analysis is another matter altogether. He refers to the fact that it is all too easy for the student with a little theoretical knowledge to confuse a strategy (shutting a child in a room for a short period) with a principle ('time-out') and to fail to understand that the point of the short period of isolation in a situation giving minimum situation is, in fact, time-out from positive reinforcement. "Therefore, it is important to provide nurse, teacher and parents with the skills necessary to analyse behaviour rather than to teach techniques with little or no reference to functional analysis" (p. 11). MacKrell has employed a personalised system of instruction (PSI, see Keller, 1968) in an attempt to achieve this training on in-service training courses for clinical workers with varying degrees of success. The present authors are also interested in the possibility of using PSI in the training of classroom teachers in the behavioural approach and are experimenting with PSI in a similar course for full-time education students.

In addition to the points raised above we feel that the following distinctions are also necessary. Courses may be designed:

(a) for teachers in Special *or* in 'ordinary' schools;
(b) for teachers in Secondary *or* in Primary schools;
(c) to help teachers to deal with individual problem children *or* to teach the basic skills of classroom management;
(d) for individuals coming to a course *or* for the whole staff of a school.

(a) Behavioural methods are already in general use in many Special schools. Because their problems are more obvious and more serious, teachers in this area have been forced to examine their methods and to adopt a more systematic and powerful model of instruction. Since the level and pace of learning is different and because some Special school teachers will already have had practical experience, the type of course suitable for teachers in Special education must be different from that for teachers in ordinary schools. The needs of teachers in Special schools have been largely satisfied already by such courses as the Education of the Developmentally Young (EDY) project materials, for example (Foxen & McBrien, 1981; McBrien & Foxen, 1981). There are very few well-designed courses for teachers in main-stream schools, however.

(b) One of the crucial issues in the use of behavioural methods in schools is that of consistency. Where children are taught in the same room by the same teacher for long periods every day it is possible to establish a rule structure within a particular milieu and for the teacher to apply this structure consistently. This is the pattern in most Primary schools but it is not so in Secondary schools, except for the small number of pupils who may find themselves in a remedial department. Generally, Secondary schools are organised to allow for teacher specialisation so that classes move from one subject specialist to another throughout the day. Where single periods are favoured a child could meet up to seven or eight teachers in a day each with different standards and methods for attempting to enforce them. Moreover, older children may be less sensitive to the use of positive social reinforcement of teacher approval and more influenced by peer group reinforcement. This does not mean to say that the behavioural approach has nothing to offer teachers of older children but simply that courses for teachers in Secondary and Primary schools will have to concentrate upon different strategies for behaviour management.

(c) Some of the courses under review have attempted to teach behavioural methods to teachers and have, at the same time, recommended teachers to carry out interventions with individual children with social or academic problems. This appears to be a sound idea because it is encouraging the teacher to apply the theory and to learn through carefully monitored practice (e.g. Hall & Copeland, 1972, Greenwood *et al.*, 1979 and Yule *et al.*, 1977). However, this calls for a lot of theoretical knowledge before the process can begin which means a rather lengthy course and involves the student in the complex business of applied behaviour analysis at an early stage. For this, expert guidance is needed which means that the number of students on the course has to be limited. Some courses which adopt this model arrange for course members to be visited in their schools so that their programmes can be overseen (e.g. Firman & Hastings, 1984; Raymond, 1980). This is an excellent practice but is very expensive in tutor time. There is another type of course, however, which concentrates upon class teaching as a series of techniques and seeks to impart a package of teaching skills to be applied to the class as a unit rather than to individual members. The Program of Academic Survival Skills (PASS), Classroom Management Teaching Project (CMTP) and BATPACK are all examples of such packages. Packages such as these give teachers the opportunity to learn a number of well-tried management techniques which they can then implement, together with a background of theory which may be relatively simple and rudimentary. Zimmerman *et al.* (1971), Hall & Copeland (1972) and Sanders (1978) suggest that it is very important for teachers to be able to monitor the results of the strategies they employ. If this is satisfactorily achieved then it should not only provide positive reinforcement and thus lead to programme maintenance but, in addition, provide a good basis for further courses in which the more complex skills of analysis and individual intervention programmes could be tackled. Greenwood *et al.* (1979) and Jones *et al.* (1977) showed that such courses can be taught on a pyramid model making for cost-effectiveness. The EDY programme (*op. cit.*) for teachers of severely mentally-handicapped children is a British example of a pyramid model course.

(d) Most of the courses reviewed have brought together groups of teachers, usually from schools at a similar level, who have volunteered for a course in behavioural methods applied to the classroom. Such a course may well enthuse individuals, perhaps because they feel a special need for help, but when they go back into school the climate of opinion and custom may well be against them. Georgiades & Phillimore (1975) have spelled out in some detail how difficult it is for the individual 'hero-innovator' to make headway against the 'system'. Some course organisers (e.g. Firman & Hastings, 1984; Merrett, 1981b, 1982, 1984) have tried to have two or more teachers from the same school attending courses so as to provide mutual support against the 'system' and have found it to be useful, especially if one of the pair holds a position of responsibility as head or deputy. School-based courses (like BATPACK, for example) would appear to enjoy many advantages. When all the staff, including the head and other management staff, agree to take a course and to apply behavioural management strategies, then many of the difficulties made manifest by Georgiades & Phillimore can be overcome.

Once decisions have been taken about the design and purpose of a course (based upon the above four distinctions), then further decisions have to be taken about course *content*. The consensus of experimenters in this field seems to suggest that it is necessary to teach theory as well as technology (cf. especially Berger, 1979; MacKrell, 1983). The questions are; how much and when? Most researchers have come to the conclusion that enough theory to allow teachers to know what they are doing is essential and that it should, as far as possible, accompany the practical work. This is usually done by using a class textbook or specially prepared handouts. For example, Firman & Hastings (1980) used Leach & Raybould (1977), Wolff & Rennie (1977) used Poteet (1973), Moss & Childs (1981) used Vargas (1977) and Wheldall & Merrett (1984a, b) used their own text. A further constraint upon an in-service course is how much extra effort can reasonably be expected from teachers who are already fully engaged by their regular employment. By using a skills package in which the techniques are introduced in sequence it is possible to underpin these with the minimum necessary theory both in the session notes and in take-home notes written specially for the purpose.

When a package of skills is being introduced it is necessary to ensure that the teachers involved do, in fact, make an effort to apply them. This is a point made by many experimenters as is the need for the teachers to be observed in this. Even when all the teachers are in the same school it is difficult to observe them all. Teaching teachers to monitor their own behaviour is one way out of this. This can be accomplished by arranging for the carrying out of some of the suggested strategies and the self-monitoring of teacher behaviour to be part of a contractual agreement between tutor and student, as in BATPACK (Wheldall & Merrett, 1984a). The contractual basis has the added advantage of showing in the structure of the course itself, an element from the behavioural approach. Moss (Moss & Childs, 1981) claims to do this also and McKeown *et al.* (1975) attempted to use shaping in a similar way.

Two other devices which have been found useful in training courses are cueing and modelling. Saudargas (1972) found cueing a valuable help. To some extent the monitoring of the teachers' own response rates contains an element of cueing. The use of a tally counter (as in BATPACK) or some other device for self-recording tends to become a conditioned stimulus or cue for the behaviour. Modelling has also been found to be effective (Ringer, 1973, Jones & Eimers, 1975 and McKeown *et al.*, 1975). The use of course members as surrogate pupils is one possibility but role play is not always popular with teachers. However, an alternative is to include short video sequences in which good practice is modelled for comment, discussion and for subsequent copying.

Hall & Copeland (1972), Harris *et al.* (1975) and Greenwood *et al.* (1979) suggest that apart from success in the course itself the members do best if they are provided with some bonus or back-up reinforcement. Hall & Copeland arranged for this in the form of academic credits whilst Wheldall & Merrett (1984a) offer a course completion certificate. Cossairt *et al.* (1973) and McKeown *et al.* (1975) found that teachers learned more effectively when their efforts were rewarded with social praise. This is manifestly in line with the precepts of the behavioural approach to teaching and, as Cossairt *et al.* (1973) found, contingent social praise was even more effective when delivered on an intermittent schedule. The inclusion of the management staff on a course might allow a special role for the headteacher and others who may be in a position to oversee their colleagues as they attempt to apply behavioural strategies. The fact that authority figures are aware of all that the teachers have learned and what they are attempting to do will make them very potent in guiding and reinforcing their colleagues. They would probably be more effective than outsiders (such as course tutors) offering an occasional visit. They would also have an important role to play in programme maintenance. The present authors are currently developing this idea.

We now turn to vital issue in the development of any training programme, that of *evaluation*. Some of the later American studies have attempted to pay proper attention to evaluation. However, few of the courses devised and run in Britain have attempted to evaluate outcomes systematically and those that have done so have used non-behavioural devices such as questionnaires. This is hardly to be wondered at when one reads in an article in an issue of the *Journal of Education for Teaching*, especially concerned with in-service training, that,

> If the course described in the case study is to be evaluated by reference to *the teachers' perception, which is the normal way of evaluating INSET*, then it

> seems to have been well thought of as a useful and interesting course . . . If, on the other hand, it is to be evaluated by reference to its ability to promote curriculum change in schools, the course components would be evaluated quite differently. (Campbell, 1982, p. 219, our emphases).

The author goes on to differentiate two levels of evaluation but is not very hopeful about success in relation to measuring the second, the degree of change brought about by INSET.

Some teachers of behavioural training have evaluated outcomes in terms of knowledge gained, e.g. Moss & Childs (1981). But for a course which aims at changing children's behaviour through bringing about change in teacher behaviour, and which is behavioural to boot, nothing short of the demonstration of behaviour change, using some objective method of observation, can be considered sufficient. Milne (1984) notes that, "Dissemination of the behavioural approach to a variety of client groups and problem areas has proceeded rapidly in recent years" but comments that there "has not been any comparable growth in the evaluation of the training of such groups". He continues, "somewhat paradoxically, evaluations of *behaviour* in behaviour therapy are outnumbered by assessments of knowledge and attitudes, with very few controlled examinations of the most relevant parameter of all, skill". He goes on to describe five measures of behavioural skill, presenting reliability and validity data for each, but none of these, however, is based on systematic observation of trainees' actual behaviour in *in vivo* situations.

Topping & Brindle (1979), writing generally about in-service training courses, put it this way,

> Few studies have demonstrated relevant post-course behaviour changes by a substantial proportion of the course members, and even when these did occur, they proved mostly short-lived at longer term follow up. (pp. 49–50)

Thus, there are two problems. First, we have to demonstrate behaviour change in teachers and their children as a result of the training course. Secondly, we have to be able to demonstrate generalisation across types of problems and situations and, above all, over time. The second is basically a problem of programme maintenance. Most of the British reports have contented themselves with reporting case studies of successful inteventions by some of the students attending courses (e.g. Merrett, 1981b, 1982, 1984). Some have obtained data from the completion of anonymous questionnaires (e.g. Clayton, 1983) but none has attempted to measure behaviour change *per se*, except Wheldall & Merrett (1984a). Even where tutors have been able to go into the classrooms of course members (e.g. Firman & Hastings, 1984; Raymond, 1980) it has been for the purpose of monitoring the progress of interventions and not to gain objective observational data on behaviour change of teachers or children. Farrell & Sugden (1984), who report an evaluation of some of the outcomes of the EDY programme, have made an attempt to show behaviour change, by observing video-tapes made during the course.

The generalisation of behavioural teacher training was examined by Robinson & Swanton (1980). They identified six reports of behavioural teacher training courses, all of which were published in the *Journal of Applied Behavior Analysis.* In their summary and conclusions section they state,

> There are very few studies available that have attempted to establish that behavioural training of teachers results in generalised change. Of those that have attempted this demonstration (approximately six studies) only half

> provides convincing evidence. On this criterion, the efficacy of behavioural training has not yet been established ... The design and methodology of teacher training studies suggests that researchers do not consider a clear demonstration of generalisation to be a necessity. Only a small proportion of the resources invested in any one study is devoted to collecting data in a monitoring condition and to establishing the reliability of that data. (p. 496)

If hard-nosed American behaviourists have generally failed to demonstrate generalisation we should hardly expect to find it in British contexts. Woods & Cullen (1983) have been concerned with this problem in the context of long-term hospitalised mentally handicapped patients. They suggest that the rate of client behaviour change and the permanency of client behaviour change are of prime importance. They make the point that measures of how much the students enjoy a course or how much they think they have gained from it, or even measures of their improved knowledge, have little relationship to their changed behaviour in the wards. They suggest that the business of programme maintenance is a highly complex one and difficult to demonstrate, which probably accounts for the fact that not many researchers have attempted to do so. Few courses, and none in this country apart from the EDY programme and BATPACK (Farrell & Sugden, 1984; Wheldall & Merrett, 1984a) have attempted to measure outcomes objectively but those that have usually report a failure to generalise skills and/or failure to maintain teacher behaviours at the high rates which tend to operate just after course completion.

In this paper we have attempted to review some of the relevant literature concerning the topic of how best to train teachers in the behavioural approach. We have also tried to provide an analysis of this research yielding a series of critical features which a successful model of training for teachers should embody. Some progress has been made towards designing an appropriate model but, equally, many of Kazdin & Moyer's points made in 1976 are still true,

> effective teacher training techniques exist ... unfortunately, effective techniques have not been implemented on a large scale to train teachers to utilize the available technology ... dissemination of information is often a substitute for actually training teachers to implement the procedures effectively. Even when specific procedures are used to train teachers, they are rarely evaluated in terms of their effect on teacher or student classroom behaviour.

Their concluding paragraph is worth quoting in its entirety since it still sums up admirably the state of the art in 1984. It also reflects the views of the present authors on the need for continued attention to be devoted to the problems of generalisation and 'programme maintenance' and for change in the educational system *per se*.

> Preliminary evidence suggests that various approaches alter teacher behaviour in the classroom. Certainly additional work needs to be conducted to determine the most effective and efficient training 'package'. Hopefully, such a package can be incorporated into the curriculum of student teachers when their actual classroom behaviour is supervised. Whatever training procedures are implemented, schools need to foster continued use of skills after training has been terminated. Presently, there is no empirical justification for the notion that desirable teacher behaviours will be reinforced (by change in the students) while undesirable or ineffective teacher behaviours will extinguish. Specific procedures need to be implemented to sustain

teacher performance. Perhaps, one means to ensure the long term maintenance of teacher behaviour is to restructure the contingencies of reinforcement in which teachers operate. Teachers represent only one position or level in the educational structure. It is unrealistic to expect performance of certain teacher behaviours unless those behaviours are actively supported by the environment. Perhaps, changes in educational systems will be required to ensure effective and accountable teacher classroom practices.

NOTES

[1] Critchley, C. & Harrop, L.A. (1974) A behavioural workshop for the management of classroom problems, *paper presented to the Annual Conference of Education Section of the British Psychological Society,* Edinburgh.

REFERENCES

Altman, K.I. & Linton, T.E. (1971) Operant conditioning in the classroom setting—a review of research, *Journal of Educational Research,* 64, pp. 277–286.

Andrews, J.K. (1970) The results of a pilot program to train teachers in the classroom application of behavior modification techniques, *Journal of School Psychology,* 8, pp. 37–42.

Becker, W.C., Madsen, C., Arnold, C.R. & Thomas, D. (1967) The contingent use of teacher attention and praise in reducing classroom behavior problems, *Journal of Special Education,* 1, pp. 287–307.

Berger, M. (1979) Behaviour modification in education and professional practice: The dangers of a mindless technology, *Bulletin of the British Psychological Society,* 32, pp. 418–419.

Berger, M. (1980) Behaviour modification and teacher education, *Psychology Teaching,* 8, pp. 43–48.

Bernstein, G.E.S. (1982) Training behaviour change agents: a conceptual review, *Behaviour Therapy,* 13, pp. 1–23.

Borg, W.R. (1972) The mini-course as a vehicle for changing teacher behavior, *Journal of Educational Psychology,* 63, pp. 572–579.

Bowles, P.E. & Nelson, R.O. (1976) Training teachers as mediators: efficacy of a workshop versus the 'bug in the ear' technique, *Journal of School Psychology,* 14, pp. 15–26.

Campbell, R.J. (1982) Some aspects of INSET and subsequent curriculum change: a case study and discussion, *Journal of Education for Teaching,* 8, pp. 203–222.

Clark, H.B. & McCrae, J.W. (1976) The use of imposed and self-selected training packages to establish classroom teaching skills, *Journal of Applied Behavior Analysis,* 9, p. 105.

Clayton, T. (1983) The behaviour modification workshop: an antidote to mindless technology, *Behaviour Analysis,* 4, pp. 18–21.

Cook, J. (1975) Easing behaviour problems, *Special Education—Forward Trends,* 2, pp. 15–17.

Cooper, M.L., Thomson, C.L. & Baer, D.M. (1970) The experimental modification of teacher attending behavior, *Journal of Applied Behavior Analysis,* 3, pp. 153–157.

Cossairt, A., Hall, R.V. & Hopkins, B.L. (1973) The effects of experimenters' instructions, feedback and praise on teacher praise and student attending behavior, *Journal of Applied Behavior Analysis,* 6, pp. 89–100.

Farrell, P.T. & Sugden, M. (1984) An evaluation of an EDY course in behavioural techniques for classroom assistants in a school for children with severe language difficulties, *Educational Psychology,* in press.

Firman, N. & Hastings, N. (1984) A teaching approach to managing classroom behaviour, *Behavioural Approaches with Children,* forthcoming.

Foxen, T. & McBrien, J. (1981) *Training Staff in Behavioural Methods: the EDY in-service course for mental handicap practitioners (Trainee Workbook)* (Manchester University Press).

Gardner, J.M. (1972) Teaching behaviour modification to non-professionals, *Journal of Applied Behavior Analysis,* 5, pp. 517–521.

GEORGIADES, N.J. & PHILLIMORE, L. (1975) The myth of the hero-innovator and alternative strategies for organisational change, in: KIERNAN, C.C. & WOODFORD, F.P. (Eds) *Behaviour Modification with the Severely Retarded* (Amsterdam, Associated Scientific Publishers).

GREENWOOD, C.R., HOPS, H., DELQUADRI, J. & GUILD, J. (1974) Group contingencies for group consequences in class management: a further analysis *Journal of Applied Behavior Analysis*, 7, pp. 413–425.

GREENWOOD, C.R., HOPS, H., WALKER, H.M., GUILD, J.J., STOKES, J., YOUNG, R., KELEMAN, K.S. & WILLARDSON, M. (1979) Standardised classroom management program: social validation and replication studies in Utah and Oregon, *Journal of Applied Behavior Analysis*, 12, pp. 235–253.

GROPPER, G.L., KRESS, G.C., HUGHES, R. & PECKICH, J. (1968) Training teachers to recognise and manage social and emotional problems in the classroom, *Journal of Teacher Education*, 19, pp. 477–485.

HALL, R.V. (1971) Training teachers in the classroom use of contingency management, *Educational Technology*, 11, pp. 33–38.

HALL, R.V. & COPELAND, R.E. (1972) The responsive teaching model: a first step in shaping school personnel as behavior modification specialists, in: CLARK, F.W., EVANS, D.R. & HAMERLYNCK, L.A. (Eds) *Implementing Behavior Programs for Schools and Clinics* (Champaign, Illinois, Research Press).

HALL, R.V., LUND, D. & JACKSON, D. (1968) Effects of teacher attention on study behaviour, *Journal of Applied Behavior Anlaysis*, 1, pp. 1–12.

HALL, R.V., PANYAN, M., RABON, D. & BRODEN, M. (1968) Instructing beginning teachers in reinforcement procedures which improve classroom control, *Journal of Applied Behavior Analysis*, 1, pp. 315–322.

HARRIS, V.W., BUSHELL, D., SHERMAN, J.A. & KANE, J.F. (1975) Instructions, feedback, praise, bonus payments and teacher behavior, *Journal of Applied Behavior Analysis*, 8, pp. 462.

HARROP, L.A. (1974) A behavioural workshop for the management of classroom problems, *British Journal of In-Service Education*, 1, pp. 47–50.

HORTON, G.O. (1975) Generalisation of teacher behavior as a function of subject matter specific discrimination training, *Journal of Applied Behavior Analysis*, 8, pp. 311–319.

JONES, F.H. & EIMERS, R.C. (1975) Role playing to train elementary teachers to use a classroom management skill package, *Journal of Applied Behavior Analysis*, 8, pp. 421–433.

JONES, F.H., FREMOUW, W. & CARPLES, S. (1977) Pyramid training of elementary school teachers to use a classroom management skill package, *Journal of Applied Behavior Analysis*, 10, pp. 239–253.

KAZDIN, A.E. (1981) Behaviour modification in education: contributions and limitations, *Developmental Review*, 1, pp. 34–57.

KAZDIN, A.E. & MOYER, W. (1976) Training teachers to use behavior modification, in: YEN, S. & MCINTIRE, R.W. (Eds) *Teaching Behavior Modification* (Kalamazoo, Behaviordelia).

KELLER, F.S. (1968) Goodbye teacher, *Journal of Applied Behavior Analysis*, 1, pp. 79–89.

KOLVIN, I., GARSIDE, R.F., NICOL, A.R., MACMILLAN, A., WOLSTENHOLME, F. & LEITCH, I.M. (1981) *Help Starts Here: the maladjusted child in the ordinary school* (London, Tavistock Press).

LEACH, D.J. & RAYBOULD, E.C. (1977) *Learning and Behaviour Difficulties in School* (London, Open Books).

MCBRIEN, J. & FOXEN, T. (1981) *Training Staff in Behavioural Methods: the EDY in-service course for mental handicap practitioners (Instructor's Handbook)* (Manchester University Press).

MCKEOWN, D., ADAMS, H.E. & FOREHAND, R. (1975) Generalisation to the classroom of the principles of behavior modification taught to teachers, *Behavior Research and Therapy*, 13, pp. 85–92.

MACKRELL, K. (1983) Teaching behaviour modification and behaviour analysis skills, *Behaviour Analysis*, 4, pp. 2–17.

MADSEN, C.H., BECKER, W.C. & THOMAS, D.R. (1968) Rules, praise and ignoring—elements of elementary classroom control, *Journal of Applied Behavior Analysis*, 1, pp. 139–150.

MERRETT, F.E. (1981a) Studies in behaviour modification in British educational settings, *Educational Psychology*, 1, pp. 13–38.

MERRETT, F.E. (1981b) Encouragement works better than punishment, *Behavioural Approaches with Children*, 5(3), pp. 31–34 and 5(4), pp. 17–26.

MERRETT, F.E. (1982) Encouragement works better than punishment, *Behavioural Approaches with Children*, 6(2), pp. 27–33.

MERRETT, F.E. (1984) Encouragement works better than punishment: a progress report of further studies, *Behavioural Approaches with Children*, 8(2), pp. 66–75.

MERRETT, F.E. & WHELDALL, K. (1982) Does teaching teachers about behaviour modification techniques improve their teaching performance in the classroom?, *Journal of Education for Teaching*, 8, pp. 67–75.

MILNE, D. (1984) Skill evaluations of nurse-training in behaviour therapy, *Behavioural Psychotherapy*, 12, pp. 142–150.

MOSS, G. & CHILDS, J. (1981) In-service training for teachers in behavioural psychology: problems of implementation, in: WHELDALL, K. (Ed.) *The Behaviourist in the Classroom: aspects of applied behavioural analysis in British educational contexts* (Birmingham, Educational Review Publications).

PATTERSON, G.R. & GULLION, E.C. (1968) *Living with Children* (Champaign, Illinois, Research Press).

POTEET, J.A. (1973) *Behaviour Modification—a practical guide for teachers* (University of London Press).

PRESLAND, J.L. (1974) Modifying behaviour now, *Special Education—Forward Trends,* 1, pp. 20–22.

PRESLAND, J.L. (1975) Advising on school behaviour modification, *Journal of Association of Educational Psychologists,* 3, pp. 5–9.

PRESLAND, J.L. (1978) Modifying behaviour in ordinary schools, *Newsletter of the Association for Behaviour Modification with Children,* 2(4), pp. 15–19.

RAYMOND, J. (1980) Workshop on behaviour modification, *Links,* 6, (1) pp. 13–17.

RINGER, V.M.J. (1973) The use of a "token helper" in the management of classroom behavior problems in teacher training, *Journal of Applied Behavior Analysis,* 6, pp. 671–677.

ROBINSON, V. & SWANTON, C. (1980) The generalisation of behavioural teacher training, *Review of Educational Research,* 50, pp. 486–498.

ROSENFIELD, S. (1970) Introducing behaviour modification techniques to teachers, *Exceptional Children,* 45, pp. 334–339.

RULE, S. (1972) A comparison of three different types of feed-back on teachers' performance, in: SEMB, G. (Ed.) *Behavior Analysis and Education* (Lawrence, Kansas, University of Kansas Press).

SANDERS, M.R. (1978) Behavioural self-control with children and adolescents: a review and critical analysis of educational applications, *The Exceptional Child,* 25, pp. 83–103.

SAUDARGAS, R.A. (1972) Setting criterion rates of teacher praise: the effects of video-tape feedback, in: SEMB, G. (Ed.) *Behavior Analysis and Education* (Lawrence, Kansas, University of Kansas Press).

THOMAS, J.D. & ADAMS, M.A. (1971) Problems in teacher use of selected behaviour modification techniques in the classroom, *New Zealand Journal of Educational Studies,* 6, pp. 151–165.

TOPPING, K. & BRINDLE, P. (1979) Evaluation of in-service courses, *British Journal of In-Service Education,* 5, pp. 49–51.

ULRICH, R., WOLF, M. & BLUHM, M. (1970) Operant conditioning in the public schools, in: ULRICH, R., STACHNIK, T. & MABRY, J. (Eds) *Control of Human Behaviour II—from cure to prevention* (Glenview, Illinois, Scott-Foresman).

VAN HOUTEN, R. & SULLIVAN, K. (1975) The effects of an audio-cueing system on the rates of teacher praise, *Journal of Applied Behavior Analysis,* 8, pp. 198–201.

VARGAS, J.S. (1977) *Behavioral Psychology for Teachers* (New York, Harper & Row).

WARD, J. (1975) Behaviour modification in special education, in: WEDELL, K. (Ed.) *Orientations in Special Education* (New York, Wiley).

WARD, J. (1976) Behaviour modification in education—overview and model for programme implementation, *Bulletin of the British Psychological Society,* 29, pp. 257–268.

WETZEL, R.J. (1970) Behavior modification techniques and the training of teacher aides, *Psychology in the Schools,* 7, pp. 325–330.

WHELDALL, K. (1981) Applied behavioural analysis in British educational contexts (with particular reference to the Birmingham Group), in: HORNE, D.J. DE L. & MCMURRAY, N.E. (Eds) *Behaviour Therapy in Australia: Proceedings of the Third Australian Conference on Behaviour Modification,* 1980, Melbourne, Australian Behaviour Modification Association. Also in *British Psychological Society Education Section Review,* 5, pp. 17–25, 1982.

WHELDALL, K. & CONGREVE, S. (1980) Attitudes of British teachers towards behaviour modification, *Educational Review,* 32, pp. 53–65.

WHELDALL, K. & MERRETT, F.E. (1984a) Training teachers to be more positive: the behavioural approach, in: BENNETT, S.N. & DESFORGES, C.W. (Eds) *Recent Advances in Classroom Research,* monograph of the *British Journal of Educational Psychology* (Edinburgh, Scottish Academic Press).

WHELDALL, K. & MERRETT, F.E. (1984b) *Positive Teaching: the behavioural approach* (London, Allen & Unwin).

WOLFF, D. & RENNIE, E. (1977) *Children with Special Needs: a workshop on teacher-child interaction,* course report and evaluation to the Directorate of Educational Services, Kirklees Metropolitan Council.

WOODS, P.A. & CULLEN, C. (1983) Determinants of staff behaviour in long-term care, *Behavioural Psychotherapy,* 11, pp. 4–17.

YULE, W., BERGER, M. & WIGLEY, V. (1977) The teacher-child interaction project, *Bulletin of the British Association for Behavioural Psychotherapy,* 5, pp. 42–47.

ZIMMERMAN, J., ZIMMERMAN, E., RIDER, S.L., SMITH, A.L. & DINN, R. (1971) Doing your own thing with precision: the essence of behavior management in the classroom, *Educational Technology,* 11, p. 26–32.